# Microcompu in biology

# a practical approach

## Edited by
## C R Ireland

Department of Biology, University of Essex,
Colchester, Essex, England

## S P Long

Department of Biology, University of Essex,
Colchester, Essex, England

1686000

IRL PRESS
Oxford · Washingto

IRL Press Limited
P.O. Box 1,
Eynsham,
Oxford OX8 1JJ,
England

First published January 1985
First reprinting January 1986
Second reprinting March 1987

British Library Cataloguing in Publication Data

Microcomputers in biology : a practical approach.
—(Practical approach series)
 1. Biology—Data processing
 I. Ireland,C.R.   II. Long,S.P.   III. Series
 574′.028′5404    QH313


ISBN 0-904147-57-6

ISBN 0-904147-98-3

(book plus software)

Printed in England by Information Printing, Oxford.

# Preface

Computers have, since their introduction into universities and research establishments in the early 1960s, been widely employed by biologists. However, the mainframe computer was always an entity isolated from the laboratory and its use was commonly restricted to post-experimental analysis of data and computer modelling of biological systems. Users of these systems had to master not only unhelpful high-level languages, but also often complex control and operating systems. The advent of the inexpensive microcomputer, providing interactive conversational languages, has completely altered this concept and has allowed the transfer of instant computer power directly into the laboratory. The danger inherent in this is of course that it is very simple to leap upon the bandwagon without first examining exactly what the microcomputer may or may not be able to achieve for the user, and without establishing whether any real advantage is to be conferred by becoming 'computerised'.

The major objective of this book is to introduce the concept of the microcomputer as a piece of laboratory equipment and to demonstrate not only what advantages may be acquired, but also what pitfalls may be met. The first pitfall is always likely to be the jargon. As is stated in the introductory chapter, overcoming the jargon is half the battle and an attempt is made to explain, in a clear and concise way, the most common terminology that the user is likely to meet. The subsequent three chapters describe the problems and provide some of the solutions to communicating between laboratory equipment and the microcomputer, the graphical display of biological data and the use of microcomputers as data-loggers. These will be common requirements of nearly all users who are research biologists. The rest of the book deals with more specialist topics. The use of microcomputers in the analysis of enzyme-catalysed reactions and of nucleic acid sequences are described in two following chapters. The next three chapters describe the employment of microcomputers in chromatography, spectrophotometry and centrifugation and the final chapter outlines the use of the microcomputer in the control of the biological environment. In each case the chapter authors, who have been carefully selected for their expertise, provide a practical guide to the use of the microcomputer in their field.

The appendices to eight of the ten chapters contain a number of complete program listings. These are programs constructed by the chapter authors and which are explained in the text. The programs are written, with few exceptions, in BASIC language, this being the almost universal language for microcomputers. However, a large number of forms of BASIC exist and to avoid the dependence of the book on any one brand of microcomputer the programs are listed as written by the author for their particular machines. Fortunately, the various forms of BASIC are not vastly different and are readily intertranslatable so readers with some programming experience should be able to modify any of the programs for their own use without great difficulty. The programs have, however, been translated into software packages on floppy disc for four common microcomputer systems and further translations may follow. Initially discs are available for the Apple, IBM (Personal Computer), BBC and Commodore PET to enable immediate use of the programs with these brands of machine. While the editors have done their utmost to ensure that the program listings appearing in this book and upon the accompanying floppy discs are without fault they can take no responsibility if a few minor 'bugs' are still retained.

Possibly the major use of the microcomputer within biology will remain as a powerful calculator in the quantitative and statistical analysis of biological data. There are on the market a vast number of publications describing the employment of the microcomputer in this role and the authors have no desire to add to this particular glut, however a package of statistical programs in BASIC is included on the accompanying floppy disc. This book is thus meant essentially as a practical guide to the use of the microcomputer as a piece of laboratory equipment, a concept which is rapidly becoming commonplace.

C.R. Ireland and S.P. Long

# Contributors

R.J.Beynon
*Department of Biochemistry, University of Liverpool, P.O.Box 147, Liverpool L69 3BX, UK*

S.W.Burrage
*Department of Horticulture, Wye College (University of London), Wye, Ashford, Kent TN25 5AH, UK*

M.J.C.Crabbe
*Nuffield Laboratory of Ophthalmology, University of Oxford, Walton Street, Oxford OX2 6AW, UK*

C.R.Ireland
*Department of Biology, University of Essex, Wivenhoe Park, Colchester, Essex CO4 3SQ, UK*

A.Lodola
*Biological Laboratory, The University of Kent, Canterbury, Kent CT2 7NJ, UK*

S.P.Long
*Department of Biology, University of Essex, Wivenhoe Park, Colchester, Essex CO4 3SQ, UK*

K.C.Persaud
*Istituto Industrie Agrarie, Università degli Studi, 56100 Pisa, Italy*

G.A.Place
*Department of Biochemistry, University of Liverpool, P.O.Box 147, Liverpool L69 3BX, UK*

D.Rickwood
*Department of Biology, University of Essex, Wivenhoe Park, Colchester, Essex CO4 3SQ, UK*

R.J.Smith
*Department of Biological Sciences, The University of Lancaster, Lancashire LA1 4YQ, UK*

J.Steensgaard
*Institute of Medical Biochemistry, University of Aarhus, DK-8000 Aarhus C, Denmark*

M.J.Varley
*Department of Horticulture, Wye College (University of London), Wye, Ashford, Kent TN25 5AH, UK*

R. Virden
*Department of Biochemistry, Ridley Building, University of Newcastle-upon-Tyne, Newcastle-upon-Tyne, NE1 7RU, UK*

# Contents

CHAPTER 1

# An Introduction to Microcomputers

S.P. LONG and C.R. IRELAND

## 1. OBJECTIVES

It may seem that no field of study is more prone to the use of jargon than Microcomputer Technology. Yet understanding this jargon is basic to any understanding of microcomputers. This chapter examines the basic structure of microcomputers and in so doing will explain some of the key terminology, in so far as this is important to those interested in computers as a means rather than an end; a more extensive explanation of microcomputer terms may be found in reference (1).

## 2. FUNDAMENTALS OF MICROCOMPUTERS

The **microcomputer** has come to be regarded as a small stand-alone desk-top computer. The word is derived from **microprocessor**, the term commonly used to describe a digital electronic processor of **CPU** (central processor unit) contained on a single **IC** (integrated circuit) chip (2). Strictly, a microcomputer is a computer system built around a microprocessor. The centre of the microcomputer consists of three basic parts (*Figure 1*).

(i)     The **CPU**, including the Control Logic — which co-ordinates the whole system and manipulates data according to a pre-programmed set of instructions.

(ii)    The memory — which is both the working space or volatile memory termed **Random Access Memory (RAM)** and the permanent memory termed **Read Only Memory (ROM)**.

(iii)   The **buses** and **I/O** (input and output interfaces) — which connect the CPU to the other parts of the microcomputer and to the outside world.

In modern microcomputers these parts are reduced to microscopic circuits on one or a few individual chips. Thus, the basic part of the computer may be housed in a small box which will fit comfortably onto a desk or bench. Three other pieces of **hardware** (the physical parts of the system) will complete a basic microcomputer system.

(i)     The keyboard — normally **QWERTY** (i.e., typewriter style board), but more rarely a calculator or finger ball keypad.

(ii)    The screen — a **CRT** (Cathode Ray Tube) monitor or, built-in to some of the more recent portables, an 80 column x 8 or 16 line **LCD** (liquid crystal display).

(iii)   The back-up store — tape cassette and/or discs.

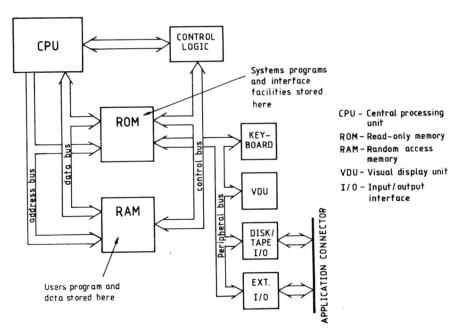

**Figure 1.** Block diagram illustrating the essential architecture of a typical microcomputer. Note that the control logic circuitry will often be included with the CPU. The address, data and control buses may also feed to an expansion port allowing the user to add further RAM chips.

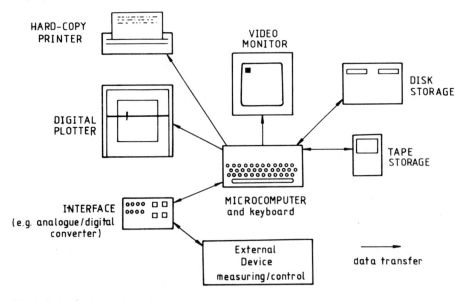

**Figure 2.** A microcomputer system.

Microcomputer systems in biological research laboratories will commonly include other peripherals – typically a printer, an x/y plotter and possibly a graphics tablet. A typical microcomputer system is diagramatically illustrated in

*Figure 2*. Items of laboratory equipment with a compatible digital interface may be connected directly to the system (Chapter 2) or *via* an interposed data-logger (Chapter 3). Alternatively, equipment with an analogue output may be connected *via* an analogue to digital converter (discussed in Chapter 2), such as those described in Chapters 3 and 10, to allow data acquisition and the control of a wide range of laboratory equipment.

To understand how the basic components of the microcomputer system, i.e., the CPU, Memory and I/O interfaces, function it will be first necessary to consider the digital data fundamental to their operation.

## 2.1 Digital Data

The CPU, like the CPU of a mainframe computer, can only handle **binary logic**, i.e., the two numbers 0, for off or false, and 1, for on or true. Within the computer these correspond to particular voltage levels. For example, in **TTL** (Transistor-Transistor-Logic) circuits, binary 0 and 1 correspond in theory to 0 V and 3.5 V, respectively. In practice most manufacturers allow some flexibility in these values such that any voltage of less than or equal to 0.7 V will be interpreted as binary 0 and any voltage of 2.4 V or more will be interpreted as binary 1. Other types of IC will use different voltage levels. Digital electronics concerns the manipulation of this 0/1 logic system according to the set of rules known as **Boolean algebra**, which is closely related to normal arithmetic using a binary number system (2,3). Thus, the alphabet, numbers and symbols of the keyboard must all be represented by permutations of just two numbers, i.e., 0 and 1 and all data, programs and internal manipulations are translated into and back from binary.

Each binary digit is stored at a single on/off or 0/1 position known as a **bit**. These bits are arranged in sets of eight, termed **bytes**. Most microcomputers manufactured in the 1970s and most of the cheaper (< £1000) microcomputers today are 8-bit, that is, they can only handle one byte at a time. Increasingly, new microcomputers are **16-bit**, i.e., they handle two bytes simultaneously, these two bytes being known as a **word**. The IBM Personal Computer and Olivetti M20 are examples of 16-bit microcomputers, while even 32-bit, i.e., 4-byte word, microcomputers have become established in the mass-market, for example, the Apple Macintosh and the Sinclair QL. However, determining the bit size of processors is not as simple as it may seem from manufacturers' descriptions. Not all operations will use the same bit size. For example, the processor used in current versions of the IBM-PC (the Intel 8088) may manipulate 16-bits simultaneously in calculations, but has only an 8-bit interface (4). A useful definition is that a processor may be described as *n*-bit if the largest operand handled by the majority of data operations is *n*-bit (5). Regretably, some manufacturers have shown a tendency in their advertisements to interpret 'majority' as 'any one'.

The organisation of bits into bytes is relevant to the internal representation of the keyboard characters. The most common code for the conversion of keyboard characters and commands into binary is **ASCII** (American Standard Code for Information Interchange). Representation of a single character or decimal number requires a whole byte, or strictly the last seven bits out of the byte. For

3

**Table 1.**

| Binary (base 2) | Hexadecimal (base 16) | Decimal (base 10) | Binary (base 2) | Hexadecimal (base 16) | Decimal (base 10) |
|---|---|---|---|---|---|
| 0000 | 0 | 0 | 1000 | 8 | 8 |
| 0001 | 1 | 1 | 1001 | 9 | 9 |
| 0010 | 2 | 2 | 1010 | A | 10 |
| 0011 | 3 | 3 | 1011 | B | 11 |
| 0100 | 4 | 4 | 1100 | C | 12 |
| 0101 | 5 | 5 | 1101 | D | 13 |
| 0110 | 6 | 6 | 1110 | E | 14 |
| 0111 | 7 | 7 | 1111 | F | 15 |

Thus the eight digit binary number of a byte, e.g.

$$7\ 6\ 5\ 4\ 3\ 2\ 1\ 0 \quad \text{(bit number)}$$
$$\text{Byte:} \quad \mathbf{1\ 0\ 0\ 0\ 1\ 1\ 0\ 0}$$

Would be represented in hexadecimal as: **&8C**

Where: '&' is used to indicate that the number is hexadecimal; C represents the values of bits $0-3$; 8 represents the value of bits $4-7$.

example the English letter 'H' is represented in a byte as '1001000', whilst the lower case 'h' is slightly different '1101000' (2). Despite the implication in the name that this is a standard, there are in fact many forms of ASCII, whilst some computers may use a completely different code.

Programming at the level of bits is only required for Machine Code operations. Although the computer can only operate with Machine Code, programs may and are usually written in higher level languages, i.e., languages which use a limited English vocabulary. These are translated into Machine Code by a compiler or interpreter (discussed further in Section 8.2). Representation of Machine Code in strings of eight binary digits is cumbersome and more conveniently represented in the **hexadecimal** system (base 16) where each byte may be represented by exactly two digits. The hexadecimal system needs 16 single characters to specify the decimal numbers $0-15$. The characters $0-9$ are naturally used to specify decimal $0-9$, and the letters $A-F$ are used to specify decimal $10-15$ (*Table 1*).

Both the memory and CPU bytes are contained on miniaturised ICs or chips. There are several types of these chips, according to the way in which they are constructed and operate (2,3). One common group of chips are the **MOS** (metal oxide semiconductors). Most frequently these are NMOS (MOS using currents of negative charge); these circuits being faster in operation than their PMOS (MOS using currents of positive charge) counterparts. Recently CMOS (complementary MOS), which is a hybrid using both negative and positive charges on the same silicon substrate, has started to be employed. The major advantage of CMOS is its far lower power consumption, roughly 1/20th of NMOS. CMOS also has better tolerance of supply voltage fluctuations and better noise immunity, whilst its lower power consumption and heat dissipation means that a more compact arrangement of electronic components is possible (6). This development has important implications for environmental biology since it allows the development of truly portable, battery operated systems as powerful as many of today's common microcomputers, which could be used in the field or at remote field stations.

## 2.2 The Central Processing Unit (CPU)

This is essentially the unit around which the computer is built. The CPU of a mainframe computer system may occupy the space of several large filing cabinets and require precise air-conditioning. In contrast, the CPU of a microcomputer is contained on a single chip and may operate under most ambient conditions. Two components with distinct functions in a computer system have traditionally been combined into the CPU. First, the **ALU** (Arithmetic Logic Unit) which, using the rules of Boolean algebra, will change the data presented at its inputs according to a specified plan of action. Secondly, the **Control Logic** under the aegies of which all other components act. This part of the CPU decodes instructions to determine which byte transfers are to be performed, in which order and to where. The methods used vary considerably between processor types and have been described in detail elsewhere (2,3,5). Associated with the CPU is the **clock,** a device with no inputs but an output which changes at a fixed frequency between logic levels. During the execution of a program, events within the microprocessor (e.g., fetching and sending of data, accumulation and examination of a given byte) occur at discrete intervals which are synchronised by the clock. The clock speed therefore determines the rate of execution of instructions by the processor. Clock speeds are measured in **Hz** (Hertz) i.e., the number of cycles per second. Microprocessor clock speeds vary from 500 kHz to 10 MHz. For example, the Acorn BBC model B operates its 6502 processor at 4 MHz, i.e., 4 million events per second.

The tremendous diversity of microcomputer models is in fact based on a relatively narrow range of CPUs or microprocessor chips. The most commonly used microprocessor chips have been the **6502**, Zilog **Z80** and Intel **8080**. The 6502 was one of the first cheap CPU chips to be produced in volume and has been used in the Commodore PET, the APPLE II, and the Acorn BBC model B. The development of a CMOS version of this processor, the Rockwell R65C02, may revive interest in the 6502 (6). The Z80 has been used in many business machines, e.g., the Cromenco Sys. 0, Radio Shack TRS-80 Model 16 and DEC Rainbow 100, but may also be found in some microcomputers manufactured for the home-computer market, most notably the Timex/Sinclair SPECTRUM and ZX81. A particular advantage of Z80 processors is that they may use the operating system **CP/M** (Control Program for Microprocessors). **Operating systems** supervise and control the running of user programs and input to or output from peripherals, such as disc drives and printers. Many manufacturers have incorporated CP/M into their design and thus a large body of software for use under CP/M has been written and is interchangeable between different models and brands. Many other operating systems have been developed in competition with CP/M, most notably **MS-DOS** (MicroSoft Disc Operating System).

The processors considered above are all 8-bit. Increasingly, 16-bit or 32-bit microprocessor chips are being incorporated into microcomputers. Most notably the Motorola **68 000** series, Zilog **Z8000** and Intel **8086**. These processors are not only faster but can also handle considerably more RAM, and where 32k or 64k has become standard on 8-bit machines, 124k or 256k is standard for current 16-bit machines. A temporary disadvantage of these machines is a lack of software. To bridge this gap, **CP/M-86** has been produced as an operating system to follow on from CP/M and this allows much of the software written for use with CP/M to be adapted for use on 16-bit machines. Some microcomputers may use more than one operating system, for example the IBM-PC will take both **PC-DOS** (Personal Computer Disc Operating System), which is very similar to MS-DOS, and CP/M-86. However, the greater capacity and speed of the newer 16-bit and 32-bit machines may mean that software originally written for medium size computers can be adapted for these microcomputers. Indeed, **UNIX**, an operating system originally developed by Bell Laboratories for large mini-computers, is now available for some 16-bit microcomputers, e.g., the Hitachi CIES 680/10, thus making software developed for larger computer systems potentially available to these microcomputers (4).

Another development has been the use of dual processors, i.e., two CPU chips in one microcomputer. Dual processors allow greater speed, since one processor can look after disc control, the monitor, etc., while the other deals with the user program. It may also facilitate access to a wider library of software. It is of note that some 16-bit microcomputers, such as the DEC Rainbow 100 and Radio Shack TRS-80 Model 16, include the Z80 as a second processor, so allowing their use with existing CP/M software.

### 2.3 Communications

The CPU is connected to the memory and both of them to the outside world through input and output (I/O) ports (*Figure 1*). The connection is achieved through a **data bus** which is a common connection to CPU, memory and I/O ports. In an 8-bit computer the bus will commonly be 8-bit, i.e., it will consist of eight parallel conductors, which allow all 8 bits of a byte to be transmitted simultaneously. Since all devices are connected to the same bus the computer must be able to define exactly where the data transmission should go. The destination is commonly assigned through a second common bus, the **address bus** (*Figure 1*). In microcomputers using the 6502 CPU, the address bus will consist of 16 parallel conductors which will transmit simultaneously the address to which the transmission in the data bus is to be sent or from which address data is to be read. The Motorola 68000 CPU currently uses a 16-bit data bus and 24-bit address bus. A commonly used standard for bus wiring is the **S100** bus establish-ed by the Institute of Electrical and Electronic Engineers (**IEEE**) (4). Thus, even equipment built by different manufacturers may be combined within one system if they use the IEEE S100 bus standard.

Communication with the outside world, e.g., with printers, graph plotters and research equipment, may be achieved through an external bus which connects to all **peripherals** (e.g., printers, monitors, plotters and interfaced laboratory equipment) or achieved through I/O ports connected to single peripherals. The most common external bus is the **IEEE 488**, as used, for example, on the Com-modore PET microcomputers. Two types of I/O connection may be identified.

(i)     **Parallel I/O** which consists of a number of parallel wires (at least eight) so that devices may transmit/receive one byte (8 bits) at a time.

(ii)     **Serial I/O**, in contrast, uses a single wire to transmit/receive a series of bits, one at a time, with extra bits to mark the beginning and end of each byte. A detailed consideration of external communications is presented in Chapter 2.

## 2.4 **Memory**

The **memory** is a store for digital data. This data is of three types:

(i)      The microprocessor's operating system; at the minimum this will include instructions on what to do when the power is switched on and how to interpret keyboard entries.

(ii)     The user's program.

(iii)    Data generated by program execution and data input to the computer.

Two basic forms of solid-state electronic memory, as opposed to mechanically driven magnetic memory (i.e., discs and tapes) are used. **RAM** (Random Access Memory) is normally used for (iii) above and often also for (ii). The processor may both write to an read from RAM which is usually volatile, i.e., its memory is lost when the machine is switched off, or when the power fails! **ROM** (Read Only Memory) is non-volatile, but can only be read and not written to by the processor. It is used for data and instructions which never need altering, e.g., the operating system and the final versions of regularly used programs. In many microcomputers a BASIC interpreter is supplied as a built-in ROM as is the operating system. Indeed the games cartridges available for some 'home-computers' are simply plug-in ROMs. More correctly, RAM should be termed read and write memory (RWM), since access to ROM is also random (3). However, the terms RAM and ROM, despite their illogicality, have become so firmly embedded in manufacturers descriptions that it would be confusing to try to use the term RWM here. A **PROM** (Programmable ROM) is a ROM into which the user can place a program, using special equipment, but once in, the program is permanent. An **EPROM** (Eraseable PROM) contains a program(s) that may be erased by ultra-violet light treatment and then be reprogrammed,while in an **EAROM** (Electrically Alterable ROM) the program may be electrically altered (3). These types of ROM are normally limited to equipment under development.

Both RAM and ROM are contained on specific chips. Commonly RAM is contained in **16k** memory chips. In computer jargon a **k** is an abbreviation for kilobyte which is in fact 1024 bytes, but for our purposes it may be considered to approximate to the correct usage of kilo, i.e., 1000. Thus a 16k memory chip contains approximately 16 000 bytes (or 128 000 bits) and therefore has the capacity to store 16 000 ASCII characters at any one time. An important trend in microcomputer development has been the development of higher capacity memory chips at an ever-decreasing price. Increasingly, new systems incorporate **64k** chips and soon **256k** chips may become commonplace (4). The amount of RAM is always emphasised in sales descriptions of Microcomputers and obviously a program requiring 60k RAM cannot be run on a 32k machine. However, equally important in this respect is the amount of RAM used by the operating systems. It is not uncommon to find that the operating system and the interpreter, if that must also be loaded into RAM, will claim more than half of the available RAM. The key information is thus the amount of RAM actually available for user programs and data.

Each byte of memory has a **memory address** or location which is also specified in hexadecimal. For example, in the Acorn BBC model B four hexadecimal numbers specify the address, e.g., &FFDD is the address of instructions for the loading and saving of files, thus each time there is an instruction to load or save a file the machine code generated will call upon address &FFDD to provide instructions to the CPU on how to proceed. (Note that the prefix & simply denotes that the number following is in hexadecimal.) The first two digits of an address are known as the **page**, where each page of memory contains 256 bytes. Memory address &FFDD therefore signifies byte DD on page FF.

On most systems, RAM is seen as a temporary data-store, since it is erased when the power is lost. Discs and tapes provide a permanent, but slower and less convenient store. The advent of CMOS RAM with its far lower power consumption means that the information in RAM may be maintained by a low power rechargeable battery over days, or even weeks. This development is likely to lead to a decreasing dependence on tape and disc, particularly if the cost of CMOS RAM continues to fall, and this will allow the development of more truly portable microcomputer systems which dispense with any motor-driven parts.

## 2.5 Storage Media

Magnetic discs and tapes are also a form of memory, providing a medium on which data or programs produced while the microcomputer is switched on may be kept after the machine has been switched off and the contents of its RAM lost. They also provide one means by which data produced by one stand-alone microcomputer may be transferred to another. Unlike RAM and ROM, this memory is not rapidly accessible, retrieving even small segments of data from cassette tape can take several minutes whilst from a disc a few seconds may be needed, compared with fractions of a second for RAM and ROM. However, disc does provide a useful medium on which large bodies of data required by or generated by a program may be stored, either temporarily or permanently, so freeing the RAM for more immediate needs.

Two types of disc are used on microcomputer systems **floppy discs** and **hard discs**. Floppy discs are magnetic discs, superficially similar in appearance to gramophone records, but contained in a permanent sleeve with one read/write slot. They are in fact thin or floppy plates with a magnetic coating on which data is stored in concentric circles or tracks. Whilst they fulfil the same function as cassette tape (i.e., a cheap removable storage medium) their great advantage is that, whilst to access data at the far end of a cassette it would be necessary to wind the whole cassette past the read/write head, to reach information on the inside of a disc the read head simply needs to locate the track to be read (or written to). Of course this mechanism is obviously more complex, requires a **DOS** (disc operating system) and is more expensive (approximately 10−20 times) than a

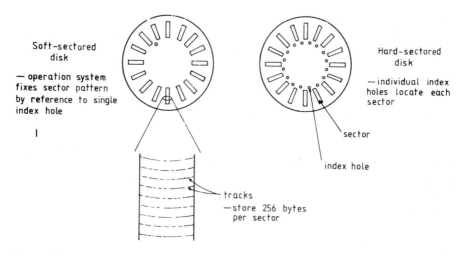

**Figure 3.** Surface format of both hard- and soft-sectored floppy discs.

cassette tape recorder. Floppy discs may be either **3 inch, 3.5 inch, 5.25 inch** or **8 inch**, and **single-sided** or **double-sided** (i.e., data may be recorded on one or both surfaces). Discs are divided into sectors and tracks as shown in *Figure 3*. The portion of each track within any one sector represents a block. Discs of 5.25 inch diameter may contain either 40 or 80 tracks, and bits may be packed onto the tracks either at **single density, double density,** or **quadruple density**, i.e., 32, 64 or 128 bytes per block, respectively.

There are two types of sectoring, **hard** and **soft**. On a hard-sectored disc sectors are defined and marked by a series of corresponding holes. While on a soft-sectored disc one or two holes mark the origin and the sectors are then magnetically marked onto the disc during formatting (*Figure 3*). Drives are normally suitable only for one type of disc, either hard-sectored or soft-sectored, and because of their physical differences the two types of floppy disc may not be used interchangeably. Once single density drives were the standard, but now double density have become commonplace and recently quadruple density drives have appeared. This ability to pack more information onto smaller discs has meant that smaller discs have become more practical. A few years ago the 8 inch disc was regarded as the standard, today it is the 5.25 inch disc, while this in turn is beginning to be superseded by the 3.5 inch floppy disc and the 3 inch compact disc. The major advantage of these smaller discs, is that drives may be incorporated into truly portable microcomputers since they are both physically smaller and lighter, whilst the compact 3 inch disc is small enough to place in a jacket pocket.

All discs require formatting. A formatting program will be provided with a disc drive, this may be in ROM or provided on a 'Systems' floppy disc. When this program is executed the positions of sectors and tracks are marked onto the blank disc, together with a directory space for the disc. Even though two discs may be physically identical this does not mean they may be used interchangeably, unless they have been identically formatted. Thus, even though the Apple II disc drive and the Commodore 8080 both use soft-sectored 5.25 inch floppy discs, information written with one cannot be read by the other. Some manufacturers have recognised this problem and have provided software to allow their drives to read and write in a number of formats, e.g., the Kaypro microcomputers.

**Hard discs** are basically similar to floppies, excepting that they are precision rigid discs permanently installed into a drive. These were called **Winchester Discs** by their IBM inventors and the two terms are often used synonymously. A typical hard disc holds 5000k (compared with 500k for a double-density and double-sided floppy). Newer versions have a capacity of 10 000k, 15 000k or 20 000k ( = 20 **Megabytes**). A hard disc greatly extends the rapidly accessible store of the computer, but it is considerably more expensive than a floppy disc drive (typically more than five times). A disadvantage has been that the hard disc could not be removed and its information would need to be backed up onto removable floppy discs. However, some of the newer drives for microcomputers have overcome this problem by allowing the use of exchangeable hard discs.

## 3. PROGRAMMING

So far only the hardware of the microcomputer system has been considered. Much of this book concerns the programming of that hardware. A **program** is a logical set of instructions on which the computer can act. The general term for computer programs is **software**.

While few biologists could, or would wish to, build their own hardware, many do construct their own software. As a result, interest often focuses on the capabilities of the hardware when a system is being selected for a laboratory, since it is considered, perhaps mistakenly, that software deficiencies may be overcome. It is however, all too easy to underestimate just how much time and effort is needed to construct appropriate software. Since software will rarely be available for specific tasks, it will often be necessary to construct this as a one-off. However, few tasks will be totally unique, many for example, may require averaging of input data (Chapters 2 or 3), two-dimensional graphics (Chapter 4) or statistical analyses, for which many pre-written programs are available (7 – 9). For these tasks, much time will be saved by incorporation of existing tried and tested routines, rather than duplicating effort. When it does become necessary to write your own software it is salutory to consider the allocation of time recommended for professional programmers (*Table 2*).

Three important points may be made with respect to *Table 2*. First, considerable thought and planning is necessary before any attempt is made to code a

**Table 2.** Allocation of Time in Software Development.

| | |
|---|---|
| Requirements and specification | 20% |
| Design | 15% |
| Coding | 20% |
| Module test | 25% |
| Integration test | 20% |

After Ref. (10).

program. Secondly, the program should be structured or modular, i.e., each task should be written into a self-contained subroutine that may be tested separately and preferably could be easily used in other programs. Finally, modules and the complete program must have a complete set of test data which will allow checking at all stages of development.

## 3.1 Machine and Assembly Code

Programs must be written in a form which the computer can understand; this is achieved by writing the instructions in a code known as a **computer language**. The CPU itself can only understand one language, that is **Machine Code** written entirely in hexadecimal. Machine Code is specific to a CPU and thus 6502 Machine Code will be meaningless to a Z80. Machine Code programming does have one important advantage, that is, its speed. Since addresses are specified in Machine Code programming, the computer wastes no time during program execution looking-up addresses as it has to when high level languages are used. Machine Code programming is extremely difficult and appears to the novice to be a jumble of random numbers (*Table 3*). Remembering which number corresponds to which action in the CPU is also difficult. **Assembly language** or **assembler** is a mnemonic code for different processes in the CPU which can be quickly converted into Machine Code and which aids Machine Code programming.

Machine Code programming was often necessary to obtain a satisfactory performance from the early microcomputers, today however, it should be discouraged (10) except when it is absolutely essential, i.e., the program is too slow to be of use when written in a high-level language or requires more memory than is otherwise available. With respect to the speed of execution, examination will often show that the computer spends more than 90% of the execution time working with less than 10% of the program, usually these will be routines contained within loops. It will often be sufficient to write only these segments or routines in Machine Code; many forms of BASIC will allow segments of Machine Code to be inserted within the body of the program. Another use of Machine Code, illustrated in Chapter 6, is where there are limited alternatives e.g., nucleic acid bases. Here it is possible to make more effective use of the memory by employing

**Table 3.** Comparison of 6502 Machine Code, Assembler and BASIC for Adding Two Variables.

| Machine code | Assembler | BASIC (approx. equivalent) |
|---|---|---|
| &0210 D8 | CLD | 10 LET S = N1 + N2 |
| &0211 A5 | LDA NUM 1 | |
| &0212 01 | | |
| &0213 18 | CLC | |
| &0214 65 | ADC NUM 2 | |
| &0215 02 | | |
| &0216 85 | STA SUM | |
| &0217 00 | | |
| &0218 00 | BRK | |

Machine Code, each base being descibed by two bits, rather than the seven used to store ASCII characters.

## 3.2 High-level Languages

Machine Code and assembler are known as **low-level languages** because they are close to that understood by the processor itself. **High-level languages** are symbolic languages operating at a level more easily understood, i.e., they use a limited 'English' vocabulary. The near ubiquitous language of current microcomputers is **BASIC**; an anacronym for **B**eginners **A**ll-purpose **S**ymbolic **I**nstruction **C**ode. Originally produced as a simple introductory language for teaching, the vast majority of microcomputer programs are still written in BASIC. Its wide use has meant that the language has evolved rapidly through a variety of extended versions to overcome, at least in part, its early limitations, i.e., difficulty of use in structured programming, formatting control and limited variable names. Examples of modified forms of BASIC which include capacity for modular program development and have an unlimited range of variable names are Acorn BBC BASIC and Sinclair QL BASIC, while the language **COMAL**, is essentially a development of BASIC which has been adapted for structured programming.

Other languages used with microcomputers include **FORTH, FORTRAN, C, LOGO** and **PASCAL**, the last being of growing importance. PASCAL was developed as a teaching tool and is now the major language taught in academic departments of computer science (11). PASCAL has been promoted in academic computer science departments (11) as a language developed to meet programming ideals and a language which encourages 'good programming habits'. In contrast to BASIC, PASCAL is rarely standard in microcomputer systems, and must therefore be purchased as an add-on ROM or must be loaded from disc, so consuming valuable RAM space. The apparent contest between the 'divinely created' PASCAL, and the 'naturally selected' BASIC holds a certain fascination for biologists due to its parallels with 19th century arguments between church and science over evolution. FORTH, supposedly a language for the fourth generation of computers, has been recommended as an ideal language for control applications (Chapter 10). By comparison with BASIC and PASCAL it is considerably faster in operation. This is because it is designed for the programming of machine level functions, programs in FORTH being constructed by combining a limited series of pre-written routines into more complex user defined routines. An example of a FORTH program is presented in Chapter 5, while further discussion of program languages suitable to microcomputer control systems is included in Chapter 10.

High-level languages are largely machine independent, e.g., a BASIC program written for the Apple II (CPU 6502) should, with only slight modification, execute on the Vector 3 (CPU Z80) even though the resulting Machine Codes are totally different. This is because most microcomputer systems include **compilers** or **interpreters** which are system programs that translate the high-level language into Machine Code. A compiler translates a whole program permanently into Machine Code, i.e., it takes a program (the **source code**) and converts it into

Machine Code which may then be executed. Compiled programs are faster to run, but difficult to edit, normally, the source code will be edited and re-compiled. An interpreter converts a program line-by-line into Machine Code leaving the program in its original high-level form. This makes it slower to run than a compiled program, but easier to edit. However, the Machine Code created is not retained as it would be had a compiler been used. Interpreters are therefore more convenient during program development; however, once a final form has been reached, considerable execution time can be saved by using a compiled version of the program.

## 4. CHOOSING A MICROCOMPUTER SYSTEM

It is disconcerting that any two microcomputer specialists are rarely able to agree on a choice of system for any given application. This is perhaps not surprising in a rapidly changing market, where even specialists appear to have difficulty in keeping abreast of developments. Choice has to be dependent on both the immediate applications and any potential future applications. The first stage in making a choice should be that of drawing up a specification, i.e., ascertaining the essential features required for the applications. The following is a list of some of the major points to be considered when selecting a microcomputer system.

(i) *Is the machine compatible with the pre-existing software written for the application?* There must be an operating system that will allow the use of the existing software. (N.B. beware of manufacturers' promises of what will be available in the future, concentrate solely on what is available now.) If software has to be written for your application then the following points must also be considered in the specification. There must be good editing and file handling facilities, i.e., a screen editor which will accept full-length programs, provide numbering, allow searching, block movements and multiple changes. There must also be program debugging aids, such as the facility to trace execution steps prior to an error and a compiler or interpreter which provides informative error messages. Attention to these points when choosing a system will save many hours and much frustration later.

(ii) *What interfaces must the system possess to communicate with the laboratory equipment?* (see also Chapter 2.) It is not sufficient to establish that the system and equipment both have a compatible interface. Two further questions will need to be addressed relating to interfaces; does the system include the software for controlling the transmission and receipt of data in the form used by the equipment to be interfaced, and what speeds of transmission and receipt can the system accept? Data will be transmitted at specific speeds, this is normally specified as the **baud rate** (bits per second). For example, suppose that the equipment to be interfaced has an RS232C serial interface which transmits at 1200 baud, it could not then communicate with a microcomputer with an RS232C capable of receiving only at 300 baud. Where a microcomputer system is being purchased for one application, but it is expected that it will later be used in further applications which cannot, as yet, be fully defined, then interface provision must be carefully considered since it will affect the extent to which the system may be expanded. Here it will be important to ensure that the system allows for as wide a range of the more common interfaces as possible. A serial RS232C, or compatible interface, capable of receiving and transmitting at a range of baud rates and a Centronics parallel interface should be considered as the bare minimum. An IEEE 488 external bus would greatly extend the expansion capabilities. Further, external sockets providing for the addition of further RAM and a bus for the addition of a further processor, such as the 1 MHz 'Tube' on the Acorn BBC model B, would allow great flexibility if it becomes necessary to upgrade the system for new applications.

(iii) *What speed of program execution will be necessary?* An indication of the speed with which different microcomputers perform specific operations is given in the benchmark tests reported in the independent microcomputer user magazines. If the most frequently executed steps of the program are known then some estimate of execution time may be made using the benchmark times. However, other factors may be equally important, in particular the time taken to transfer data. In most biological applications speed will not be important. Exceptions will be where iterative calculations are used, where large data sets are searched (e.g., DNA sequences) or where data has to be received at short time intervals, i.e., milliseconds. In the latter case the speed of sampling may be limited by the speed with which the microcomputer may transform and store the received data.

(iv) *What solid-state memory will be needed?* Will the 64k RAM maximum supportable by most 8-bit microcomputers be adequate, or will the larger quantities of RAM supportable by 16- or 32-bit microcomputers be necessary? When considering RAM requirements, it is most important to know what will actually be available for user programs and data. An examination of the small print will show that the available RAM on different microcomputers, advertised as 64k, will vary considerably. This is because differing amounts of this 64k will be claimed by operating systems, graphics and interpreters; some may allow the user almost the full 64k others leave less than 10k! Ensure also that there is space for the addition of further ROM chips and, where appropriate, further RAM. Normally these will take the form of empty IC sockets connected to the CPU data and address buses.

(v) *What back-up storage will be required, will floppy discs provide adequate and sufficiently rapid storage, or is a hard disc necessary?* It is important not to underestimate the amount of back-up store required. As use of the system progresses, programs and the data generated are likely to become more sophisticated and more detailed. As a general rule the maximum storage capacity available for the disc size chosen should be sought, in the case of 5.25 inch floppy discs, 80 track, double-sided, and double or quadruple density should be selected. However, to ensure an ability to read software written to other formats, a 40/80 and single/double-sided switchable disc system should be preferred.

(vi) *What peripherals will be required?* Other parts of the microcomputer system, in particular the keyboard, monitor and printer must be considered at this stage. If the microcomputer keyboard is only to be used to activate or stop the system then a keypad or low-quality QWERTY keyboard will be more than adequate. If, on the other hand, the keyboard is to be used for program development or perhaps word-processing then a high quality QWERTY keyboard, similar to that found on a good quality electric typewriter, will be essential. At the minimum it should include a repeat facility on all keys, a Capitals lock as well as a Shift lock, and arrows for cursor movement. The keys should have a positive feel and should never stick. If a microcomputer is being purchased with a view to later expansion, a good quality keyboard will be a worthwhile initial investment. There will be little point in having a dual processor 256k RAM system, if the 'R' or ' + ' on the keyboard is inoperative! Similarly, care must be taken over the purchase of the monitor. Again if the system is to be used for program development or regular output inspection, then care must be taken that the size and resolution of characters will not lead to eye-strain. For many applications, an 80- rather than a 40-column display will be necessary, this being the standard text width. However, at this width a high-resolution monitor will be necessary; N.B., a good television set is unlikely to provide adequate resolution. High-resolution colour monitors will be expensive, typically $4-5$ times the cost of an equivalent black and white; careful thought should therefore be given to the question of whether colour is really essential.

The majority of printers now used with laboratory microcomputer systems, are of the dot-matrix type. These are commonly faster and more versatile than daisy-wheel printers which would only be appropriate if the system was required primarily for word-processing. As well as printing text they may also be used for low resolution graphics, by reproducing graphs displayed on the monitor through a screen-dump program (Chapter 4). The speed of the printer should also be considered, 20 c.p.s. (characters per second) might sound fast on paper, but will seem painfully slow in practice when it is realised that $2-3$ min are required to print a full page of text. For most applications requiring a dot-matrix printer 80 c.p.s. should be regarded as a minimum, especially if it is to be used for screen-dumps of graphs. Whilst a tractor feed will be useful, if the printer is to be left printing unattended, the option to use friction feed will ensure that the printer is never rendered out of action due to a failure in supplies of the appropriately punched tractor feed paper.

Once a specification has been obtained then an examination of manufacturers leaflets and trade magazines should suggest some of the alternatives. At this stage discussions with other microcomputer users on the reliability and service support should be undertaken. If there is some uncertainty as to the suitability of a system for a specific application, and even if there is not, it will always be invaluable to arrange a demonstration or trial before making any decision. More detailed guides and brand analyses for choosing microcomputers are provided in references 4 and 12.

## 5. REFERENCES

1. Chandor,A. (1981) *Dictionary of Microprocessors,* published by Penguin, Harmondsworth, 183 pp.

2. Ogdin,C.A. (1978) *Microcomputer Design,* published by Prentice-Hall, Egelwoold Cliffs, 190 pp.
3. Williamson,I. (1983) *Microprocessors and Microelectronics,* published by Cambridge Learning, Cambridge, 171 pp.
4. Lieff,J.A. (1982) *How to Buy a Personal Computer Without Anxiety,* published by Ballinger, Cambridge, MA, 113 pp.
5. Wakerley,J.F. (1981) *Microcomputer Architecture and Programming,* published by Wiley, New York, 692 pp.
6. Taylor,S. and Watford,R. (1984) *6502 revival. Personal Computer World,* 7, 174.
7. Lee,J.D. and Lee,T.D. (1982) *Statistics and Numerical Methods in BASIC for Biologists,* published by Van Nostrand Reinhold, New York, 267 pp.
8. Poole,L., Borchers,M. and Donahue,C. (1980) *Some Common BASIC Programs,* published by Osborne/McGraw Hill, Berkeley, 200 pp.
9. Barlow,A.B. (1983) *Biodata Handling with Microcomputers,* published by Elsevier-Biosoft, Cambridge, 261 pp.
10. Pinches,C. (1984) The effective use of microprocessors in a scientific environment, in *Instrumentation for Environmental Physiology,* Marshall,B. and Woodward,F.I. (eds.), Cambridge University Press, Cambridge, in press.
11. Horowitz,E. (1983) *Fundamentals of Programming Languages*, published by Springer-Verlag, Berlin, 450 pp.
12. Personal Computer World (1984) *Microcomputer Benchtest Special,* published by Computing Publication, London.

CHAPTER 2

# Communicating with Microcomputers

R.J. BEYNON

## 1. INTRODUCTION

In common with all computers the microcomputer is capable of automatic and rapid manipulation of data. Although currently limited in speed and in the relative magnitude of the data that can be processed, the level of computational power provided by microprocessor based systems is demonstrably adequate for many applications within the biological laboratory. In particular, the potential for linking the microcomputer to analytical equipment introduces the possibility of dedicated data collection and analysis. In removing the tedium and hence, tendency to make errors in repetitive procedures the microcomputer can make possible more extensive and accurate analyses of the collected data (1).

The laboratory microcomputer system is obtained as a collection of discrete components such as VDU or monitor, printer and plotter often purchased from different manufacturers. Consequently, the task of establishing correctly functioning electrical connections between the individual components can be onerous. Further, the problem of communicating with the microcomputer is exacerbated when analytical laboratory equipment is included among the devices to be linked, especially when a considerable proportion of existing analytical equipment provide no facilities for interfacing to a computer system. Increasingly, laboratory equipment includes a computer interface to enable communication with computer systems. The installation of a laboratory microcomputer system inevitably demands at least a cursory familiarity with the methods and protocols of computer communication. Where possible, expert help should be sought but if it is not available the user must face the problems presented by a plethora of interface types, communication protocols and even electrical connectors. At best, the information contained in this chapter will enable the microcomputer user to resolve his particular interfacing requirements. At the least, the intention is to provide an explanation of some of the jargon that prevails in microprocessing and so help to overcome the communication barrier that exists between biologists and microcomputer specialists. Several interfaces that are available commercially have been listed in Chapter 10 together with circuit designs and software for the construction of a versatile microcomputer interface.

Computer communication as used in biological research falls into two distinct classes (2) (*Table 1*). The first, where the microcomputer is linked to other digital devices, enters the realm of digital communication. Data are packaged into discrete 'quanta' representing binary 0 or binary 1 and are then transmitted either

**Table 1.** Classes of Microcomputer Communications.

| |
| --- |
| *Digital Communication* |

*Serial communication*

RS232(C) protocols
RS423 protocols
20 mA current loop

*Parallel communication*

Centronics interface
Binary Coded Decimal Interface
IEEE 488 interface

*Single bit communication*

*Analogue communication*

*Digital to analogue (D/A) conversion*

*Analogue to digital (A/D) conversion*

one bit at a time along a single conductor (serially) or as several bits using a number of conductors simultaneously (in parallel). Clearly, serial and parallel interfaces are incompatible, additionally, both describe a variety of standards that are in turn incompatible.

The second class of computer communications is where it is desired to interface the microcomputer (that handles data in discrete digital format) to devices that yield or employ data in a continuously variable form (analogue devices), such as spectrophotometers or x/y recorders. The total incompatibility of the form of data in digital and analogue devices demands that one type of data be translated into the other and thus analogue to digital and digital to analogue communication is required.

## 2. INTERFACING TO DIGITAL DEVICES

### 2.1 Parallel Communication

The major part of the processing time of a microcomputer is dedicated to the transfer of bytes (8-bit words) of data from one location to another or to external devices such as video displays or printers. Within the microcomputer the need for rapid data movement is indicated by the provision of an 8-bit wide data 'bus' that conducts all 8 bits of a word simultaneously. Parallel transmission of data is rapid and very effective over short distances but the cost of cabling and the need to prevent interference between parallel conductors means that serial transmission is usually employed over distances longer than 2 or 3 m (1).

Parallel interfaces cannot, however, be implemented with only eight data lines and signal ground. In the simplest case, if the microcomputer was to place an ASCII code upon the 8-bit data line and output that code to a printer there would be no means for the microcomputer to establish that the printer:

(i)   was able to accept the data;

(ii)  had captured the data and was awaiting the next code.

It is essential that the computer and printer transmit this information to each other by means of 'handshaking' sequences. Provided that handshaking protocols are established, the data transfer can take place at the highest speed permitted by the slower of the two devices. Parallel data paths within the microcomputer system are in general not controllable by the user and the remainder of this section will be concerned with the transmission or reception of 8-bit parallel, byte serial data *via* interfaces inbuilt into the computer system for the purpose of communication with external devices.

### 2.1.1 *Centronics Printer Interface*

The Centronics interface has been adopted as a standard by many manufacturers of printers and microcomputers. It is a straightforward interface to implement and usually requires that the printer be connected *via* a 36-pin Amphenol plug (*Figure 1*). The type of connector used to link the microcomputer will vary and generalisations cannot be made here. Of the 36 connectors, 10 are used to carry data or handshake signals, the remainder are all connected together and to signal ground (*Figure 2*). Handshaking is accomplished by means of two signals; 'strobe' and 'acknowledge'. The former is generated by the computer system to indicate that there is valid data on the eight lines while the latter is generated by the printer to indicate successful capture of the data. The sequence of changes in

**Figure 1.** Amphenol plug used in Centronics standard parallel printer interface. Note the ribbon cable clamped and connected to the plug using insulation displacement techniques. This precludes the need for soldering of closely spaced connectors.

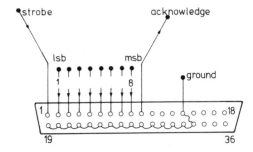

**Figure 2.** Pin assignments used in Amphenol plug to implement Centronics standard interface. Pins 2 – 9 are wired to the parallel data path lsb (least significant bit), msb (most significant bit). All other pins should if possible be wired to signal ground but if they serve other purposes, such as 'out of paper' indicators this may not be possible.

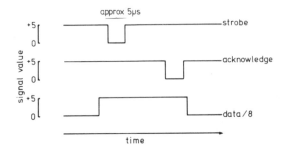

**Figure 3.** Handshake sequence during data transfer according to Centronics standard. Only one of the eight data lines is shown. The strobe pulse (active low) is generated by the transmitter, the acknowledge pulse is generated by the receiver.

these lines is shown in *Figure 3*. Additionally, some printers or interfaces implement a 'busy' line that inhibits the computer transmitting further data, for example after receipt of a carriage return character (ASCII 13) to allow time for the printhead to return to the beginning of a new line. Wiring of the 'busy' line to the interface connector marked 'acknowledge' (or ACK) will establish similar handshaking.

The voltages that signify 'high' or 'low' states, on these control lines as well as the data lines, are TTL (transistor/transistor logic) levels. This means that 0 V represents binary '0' and +5 V represents binary '1'. A negative going signal is normally at logic '1' and drops to logic '0' to indicate a change of status, while a positive going signal changes in the opposite direction from logic '0' to logic '1'. Even a simple interface such as the Centronics standard has been complicated by the use of negative going or positive going control signals. Some interfaces may be able to operate under either protocol and it is therefore important to establish which option has been implemented by the printer manufacturer. The Centronics standard requires that both 'strobe' and 'acknowledge' lines be active low or negative going. *Figure 3* shows the handshaking sequence for negative going signals.

### 2.1.2 *IEEE 488 Interface*

Less commonly found in low cost microcomputer systems, the IEEE 488 (synonymous with the HP-GPIB: General Purpose Interface Bus) bus is a versatile and sophisticated interface that is supported by some microcomputer systems and by many types of measuring equipment and computer peripherals (3). Unlike the Centronics interface, which connects a single computer to a single peripheral, the IEEE 488 bus permits many devices to be linked on a common bus and to be switched independently from an inactive to an active state whereupon they can generate/receive data to/from other devices. Unsurprisingly, such a complex interface requires greater complexity both in controlling software and in the number of conductors required to implement the bus. In fact 16 lines are needed: eight data lines, three handshaking lines and five bus control lines (*Figure 4*). Each device connected to the bus (up to a maximum of 15) can be one of four types:

(i)   controllers;
(ii)  listeners;
(iii) talkers;
(iv) listener/talkers.

The controller assumes primary responsibility for bus management and may activate or de-activate other devices on the bus in order to control data flow. Inherent in this concept is the capability for communication between a talker and a listener without the necessity for data flow through the controller, but this level of complexity is unlikely to be met in an average biological laboratory. The IEEE 488 bus appears to be most suitable for interfacing to specialised instruments that implement bus protocols and as such, further coverage is not warranted here. The reader interested in this parallel interface is referred to the excellent book (4) that describes its use and implementation on one popular microcomputer system.

### 2.1.3 *Binary Coded Decimal Interfaces*

In normal binary representation there is no grouping of bits into different decimal digits, for example decimal 16 (0001 0000) requires 5 bits while decimal 15 (0000 1111) requires 4 bits. To overcome this difficulty in coding decimal values, binary coded decimal (BCD) format has been adopted. BCD format employs groups of 4 bits (2/word) to code for a single decimal digit from 0 (0000)

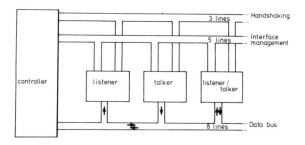

**Figure 4.** Generalised bus structure for IEEE 488 interface.

**Table 2.** Binary Coded Decimal Representation of Numbers.

| Decimal | Binary coded decimal | Binary |
|---|:---:|:---:|
| 0 | 0000 0000 | 0000 0000 |
| 2 | 0000 0010 | 0000 0010 |
| 5 | 0000 0101 | 0000 0101 |
| 10 | 0001 0000 | 0000 1010 |
| 19 | 0001 1001 | 0001 0011 |
| 99 | 1001 1001 | 0110 0011 |
| 121 | overflow | 0111 1001 |

Note: 4-bit numbers >1001 (9) are illegal in binary coded decimal.

to 9 (1001). Thus, a single byte is restricted from its normal range of $0 - 255$ (0000 0000 $-$ 1111 1111) to the more limited range of $0 - 99$ (0000 0000 $-$ 1001 1001) (*Table 2*).

BCD output is commonly provided as an output option on instruments that utilise digital displays. Such instruments incorporate A/D converters and express the digitised value as a true decimal number (e.g., absorbance from 0.000 to 1.999) rather than as a simple result of the A/D conversion. The scaling of this code value into a decimal value is readily achieved using BCD representation which incidentally provides a convenient output for external devices such as printers. A typical example is the output of absorbance by simple spectro-photometers ranging from 0.000 to 1.999. In this case, a '3½ digit' BCD output would be provided; one BCD digit for each digit after the decimal point and a '½' digit output to indicate whether or not the absorbance value equals or exceeds 1.0. Additionally, an 'overrange' signal and the sign (+ or −) must be transmitted; this requires an additional two lines. Fifteen lines must therefore be connected to the microcomputer (3 x 4 + 1 + 1). Further, the data available at the BCD interface will be unreliable during the updating of the display − an additional control line 'data ready' must be implemented to prevent the microcomputer interface from reading the value at that time. The BCD interface is complex and the user is advised either to look for a ready made BCD interface or to consider using an A/D converter (see Section 3.2) to digitise the data anew. BCD interfaces have been constructed but they produce a minimum of 16 bits of data as two bytes on input ports; the software required to read and manipulate these ports can become complex. Finally, the resolution afforded by the BCD interface on many items of equipment is inferior to the quality of the signal. For example, a spectrophotometer that displays absorbance values to a resolution of 0.001 will invariably generate a signal at a higher resolution, as indicated by the analogue signal to a chart recorder. The truncation of the data by the BCD output may in some cases be problematical.

## 2.2 Serial Communication

Data transfers using parallel communication protocols are 'byte serial, bit parallel' in nature. Although each bit of the data word is transmitted in parallel, multiple bytes must be sent in succession. Serial communication between devices is markedly different in that the data is transferred in a 'byte serial, bit serial' fashion, which is economical because uni-directional data transfers can be accomplished using just two signal lines (signal and ground). This economy must be countered, however by lower rates of data transfer as each byte must now be transmitted as eight serial bits. Nonetheless, the applicability of serial communication to long distance data transfer, in particular over existing telecommunication channels has resulted in the development of several standards that have been implemented on microcomputer systems (1,5,6).

### 2.2.1 *Synchronous/Asynchronous Transmission*

In the simplest concept of serial transmission, the transmitting device places each bit of data onto the signal line for a fixed length of time, during which the receiving device must pick up that bit and store it in a register until a whole byte of data has been received. It follows then that the transmitter and receiver must operate at identical rates if the two are not to fall out of step and generate errors in data transfer. As an extreme case, consider the situation where the receiver operates at twice the frequency of the transmitter; a situation that will result in the capture of two identical bits for each one sent. In practice, the devices would operate at closely similar rates, but any discrepancy, however slight, would eventually result in a transmission error.

One solution to this timing requirement is to generate a 'clock' signal that provides the timing for data transmission and is transmitted to the receiver. In this case the receiver uses the clock signal to establish when a new bit has been set up on the signal line and it is therefore maintained in synchrony with the transmitter. Obviously, this requires an additional conductor to transmit the clock signal. Communication protocol of this type is referred to as synchronous transmission.

The despatch of data over telephone lines restricts the number of conductors to two and therefore alternatives to synchronous transmission are required. Asynchronous serial data transmission refers to the situation where the transmitter and receiver use isolated clocks for data generation or capture. The clocks run at approximately the same rate but are not synchronised. It is assumed that the clocks are sufficiently close in frequency that a byte of data will be received correctly by examining the mid-point of each bit; the clocks are then resynchronised by the use of start and stop bits.

### 2.2.2 *Start/Stop Bits*

In the majority of serial transmission protocols the data word is prefixed and suffixed by 'start' and 'stop' bits. These are of different logic state; start bits are usually 'low' and stop bits are 'high' so that the beginning of a new data word is always marked by a high to low transition. The start bit permits synchronisation of the receiver clock so that the remaining bits will be captured correctly while the stop bits allow time for the receiver to prepare for the next word and guarantee a high to low transition. The number of start bits is normally fixed at one, but there may be either one or two stop bits, depending on the rate of data transmission. Two stop bits are normally employed at the low data rates associated with mechanical devices such as teleprinters. A single stop bit is normally associated with high speed electronic devices such as VDUs. Some mechanical devices such as printers although operating at low data rates employ semiconductor 'buffers' to store incoming data that is subsequently acted upon. In these instances the data transfer rate may be far higher than expected and a single stop bit may be specified. In this case, handshaking protocols are needed to prevent the transmitter from sending data when the receiver buffer is full (see Section 2.2.5). Typical changes in the signal line during data transmission are shown in *Figure 5*.

### 2.2.3 *Baud Rate*

For the relatively simple serial transmission protocols that are described here the term 'baud rate' is synonymous with the term 'bit rate' and refers to the speed of transmission. To establish correct communication protocols the baud rate must be the same in the transmitter and the receiver or at least sufficiently close for the start bit to enable resynchronisation at each word of data. In practice, the selection of baud rate is limited to eight discrete values from 50 baud (bits/sec) to 9600 or 19 200 baud. Most devices and interfaces will allow selection of baud rate by means of software control, by the setting of switches or by jumper wires. Low data rates will be needed for directly responsive electromechanical devices but VDUs can be connected at the highest rate that is available. Long signal paths or electrically noisy environments may enforce the selection of a lower rate, as the high values are more susceptible to error.

### 2.2.4 *Parity*

Error detection schemes have been incorporated into specifications for serial data communication protocols; the most common of these is a parity check which introduces an additional bit per word into the data stream. The extra parity bit is given a value by the transmitting device that ensures that the number of bits equal to 1 in the word is odd (odd parity) or even (even parity). Provided that the receiving device performs the same type of parity check (odd or even) a single bit error, in which one bit of the word changes state, can be readily detected by comparison of the actual state of the parity bit with the expected value. Odd parity is most

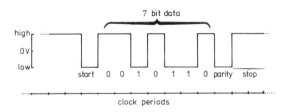

**Figure 5.** Changes in signal line during the transmission of a single byte of data using a serial interface. The sequence of status changes is 1 start bit, 7 data bits (001 0110), 1 parity bit and 2 stop bits. The parity check is even; the parity bit is set to '1' to maintain an even number of '1's in the word. The magnitude of the voltages corresponding to 'high' and 'low' is dependent upon the type of interface.

commonly used because no word then consists solely of zeros. Many devices, especially those intended to be connected over short data paths, do not implement parity checking. They are often designed to read in the parity bit, although its value is subsequently ignored.

### 2.2.5 *RS232C Serial Interface*

Serial communication using the protocol specified in Electronic Industries Association (EIA) RS232 (revision C) is widely distributed. The specifications in RS232C are virtually identical to the CCITT (Comité Consultatif International Téléphonique et Télégraphique) V.24/V.28 standard; equipment claiming either standard should be compatible (5).

RS232C devices are normally linked *via* a standardised 25 pin connector (DB25; *Figure 6*). In the complete RS232C specification, 21 lines of the 25 are defined but the majority of these are concerned with telecommunication protocols and microcomputer peripheral equipment will invariably require that only a limited number of these lines be connected, providing for data transfer and handshaking signals. The most common signal lines, together with their pin numbers and a description of their function are given in *Table 3*.

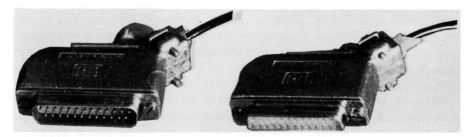

**Figure 6.** Standardised DB25 connector (left:male right:female), specified in RS232C.

**Table 3.** Pin Assignments in Part of RS232C.

| Pin | Name | Input/output | Function |
|-----|------|--------------|----------|
| 1 | Protective ground | – | Maintains chassis of both devices at same potential |
| 2 | Transmitted data | Output | Signal line |
| 3 | Received data | Input | Signal line |
| 4 | Request to send | Output | Handshake line |
| 5 | Clear to send | Input | Handshake line |
| 6 | Data set ready | Input | Handshake line |
| 7 | Signal ground | – | Reference for signal voltages |
| 20 | Data terminal ready | Output | Handshake line |

The RS232C lines shown above are those that are most commonly employed in microcomputer applications. The names of the signals correspond to those in the RS232C standard but the description of their functions refers to their likely application in DTE (data terminal equipment) to DTE communications such as computer to printer.

Unlike TTL logic levels, in which 'high' is represented by $+5$ V and 'low' by 0 V, RS232C uses a combination of positive and negative voltages to discriminate between two binary digits, such that high = '0' = $+3$ V to $+15$ V and low = '1' = $-3$ V to $-15$ V; typically, voltages of $+5$ V and $-5$ V or $+12$ V and $-12$ V are found. The minimum magnitude for these voltages is $+3$ V and $-3$ V which marks the transition region between binary 0 and binary 1. Because of the large voltage changes that are generated, RS232C interfaces require a power supply capable of providing at least 12 V; the voltage change produced by TTL logic is insufficient to span the transition region. The RS232C standard was designed to connect data terminal equipment (DTE) such as computers, VDUs or printers to a telecommunication device known as a modem (modulator/demodulator). A modem converts a serial bit stream into a series of audio tones suitable for telephone communication, and the signal specification is such that the DTE to modem connection is a straightforward pin for pin equivalence. Problems arise however when the RS232C protocol is 'misused' in the connection of one DTE to a second DTE. Thus, both devices would transmit data on pin 2 and receive data on pin 3 — an unworkable conflict that is removed by the simple act of cross-wiring pins 2 and 3. Connection of pins 1 and 7 (protective and signal ground) completes the minimal bi-directional communication that can be used where data is processed more rapidly than it is received. However, if the data rate exceeds processing speed there is a danger of an 'overrun' error which occurs when data is transmitted but is not received correctly because the receiver cannot keep up with data flow. Handshaking between the two DTE devices can eliminate overrun errors. Again, RS232C signals can be 'misused' to implement a hardwired handshake using an electrical connection between the devices. In its simplest form, that of uni-directional transfer of data from a computer to, for example, a serial printer, a signal is required to indicate whether or not the printer buffer can receive further data. The two lines used commonly for this purpose are pin 4 (Request to send) or pin 20 (Data terminal ready), both of which will be 'high' if sufficient room remains in the buffer but which will drop to a 'low' state when the buffer is full. Either of these lines may be connected to either pin 5 (Clear to send) or pin 6 (Data set ready) in order to establish communication, but no general rules can be given. It is necessary to establish which handshaking lines individual manufacturers have employed. Bi-directional handshaking may require that both sets of lines are connected (4/5 and 6/20) but other signals may be included — the possibilities extend beyond the general discussion given here. A typical application in the author's laboratory is given in *Table 4* to illustrate a simple RS232C link.

RS232C specifies a maximum data rate of 19 200 bits/sec and a maximum transmission distance of 50 ft; neither should prove prohibitive in typical laboratory applications. Two stop bits are specified at data rates below 200 bits/sec; in practice this refers only to rates lower than 110 bits/sec (1 start bit, 7 data bits, 1 parity bit and 2 stop bits = 11 bits/word; yield a rate of 10 characters/sec). Another option likely to be encountered is that of 7 or 8 data bits, 7 bits are sufficient to encode the complete alphabet, numerals, punctuation

**Table 4.** Typical RS232C Communication Link.

| Microcomputer interface pin number | Function | Digital plotter interface pin number |
|:---:|:---:|:---:|
| 1 | Protective ground | 1 |
| 2 | Data from computer to plotter | 3 |
| 3 | Data from plotter to computer | 2 |
| 7 | Signal ground | 7 |
| 5 | Handshake line from plotter to computer | 20 |

The handshaking line is restricted to the plotter to microcomputer direction as it is likely that the slow mechanical device will be unable to process data faster than the transmission rate (4800 baud in this instance). In contrast, it has been assumed that the microcomputer will be able to process data rapidly, such that overrun errors will not occur.

and control codes (ASCII coding), 8 bits are more efficient for non-alphanumeric data transfer.

To conclude, RS232C is the most common protocol used for serial data transmission. The available options including baud rate, parity, stop bits, data bits and handshaking protocols combine to make this interface one of the most tedious to implement successfully in microcomputer applications. A high impedance voltmeter can be used to assess the presence of a high or low state signal line; alternatively a simple diagnostic tool that uses a green or a red light-emitting diode to indicate line status such as the one found in reference (7) may be worth constructing.

More complex diagnoses require the use of a communications analyser that monitors all lines, interprets and prints the characters corresponding to the data and permits rapid selection of baud rate and parity options. Such instruments are expensive but should be found in central microcomputer systems laboratories. Before making any attempt to establish RS232C communications between a microcomputer and peripheral device, all aspects of the interfaces should be considered; the checklist in *Table 5* may prove of value. It is worth noting that a significant proportion of laboratory equipment now supports RS232 protocols and that this interface may become more widely used in the foreseeable future.

### 2.2.6 *RS423A Serial Interface*

The RS232C standard has been recognised as containing several difficulties; particularly with respect to the electrical transmission properties. Firstly, the protective ground connections are often unmade which introduces the possibility that the signal ground may be at different potentials at transmitter and receiver. If this potential difference is large enough, transmission errors ensue. Secondly, the transition region of 6 V between signal high and signal low required power supplies that generated voltages other than the $\pm 5$ V normally found in modern digital equipment. To circumvent these problems a new electrical standard,

**Table 5.** Checklist for RS232C Communications.

| Parameter | Options |
|---|---|
| Baud rate | 50 − 19 200 baud must be set to the same rate at both transmitter and receiver |
| Data bits | Normally 7 or 8 (can be less in special circumstances) |
| Stop bits | Normally 2 (rate <200 baud) or 1 (>200 baud) but can be up to 127 to allow recovery time for slowly responding devices |
| Parity | Enabled or disabled. If disabled, is parity bit set permanently high or low and expected by receiver |
| Parity option | Odd or even parity selected |
| Pin assignments | Computer to peripheral (pin 2 − 3)<br>Peripheral to computer (pin 3 − 2)<br>Handshaking options (see text) |

RS422A, (CCITT V11, X.27) was published (5). RS422A specifies that each signal be transmitted over a pair of wires (balanced transmission) such that the status of the signal be assessed by measuring the voltage on one wire relative to the second. Signal ground is no longer used as a common reference and problems with ground potential are largely eliminated. Secondly, and consequential to the elimination of a common signal ground, the transition region was reduced from 6 V to 400 mV, such that a signal of $+200$ mV or more would be interpreted as 'high' and a signal of $-200$ mV or less would be interpreted as 'low'. The narrow transition region meant that the serial data could be generated using the normal $\pm 5$ V power supply.

RS422A represented a major development but suffered from the disadvantages that:

(i)   RS422 transmitters could not drive RS232 receivers.

(ii)  extra cabling was needed to provide pairs of conductors for each data line.

This incompatibility resulted in the introduction of an intermediate specification; RS423A (CCITT V24/V.10, X.26) (5). This standard specifies that a single signal ground be connected only at the transmitter. Ground potential problems cannot therefore arise. RS423A receivers must be sensitive to the 400 mV transition region but RS423A transmitters must generate signals of $\pm 4$ V (a transition region of 8 V). Power supply requirements have not therefore been resolved with this standard. It should be clear that RS423A transmitters can drive RS232C and RS422 receivers and that RS423A receivers will react to signal levels according to RS232C or RS422A. RS423A can thus be seen either as an improved serial interface or as a step in the upgrade from RS232C to RS422A. Few applications require RS422A but some microcomputer systems are now offering RS423A for serial communication, and it is relevant to this discussion to appreciate that it can be considered as fully compatible with RS232C.

### 2.2.7 *20 mA Current Loop Serial Interface*

Common among microcomputer systems and inherited from teletypes in earlier systems, the 20 mA current loop interface is not an accepted standard, and rarely includes signals other than transmit or receive data. Briefly, the presence of a 'high' or 'low' status on the data line is established by the magnitude of the current flowing through it to ground; such that 'high' = 20 mA and 'low' = less than 2 mA. Serial data is generated by switching the current on and off. Voltages of the order of $12-25$ V are commonly used to produce the required current flow.

Current loop interfacing is capable of data transmission over reasonably long distances (1500 ft) and has the advantage of relative immunity to noise on the signal line. It offers little more than minimal connections and where RS232C protocols are offered as a switchable or jumpered option the user is well advised to choose the latter.

## 2.3 Single Bit Interfaces

A need often arises for the control of binary devices by a microcomputer such as the detection of the 'full/not full' status of a level sensor and the open/closed status of a valve produced as a response. Such switches may be either detected or elicited using single bit output from the microcomputer. For example, an 8-bit output port can be employed to control eight valves, each bit regulating the state of one valve (e.g., 'high' = 'open'; 'low' = 'closed'). The choice of 'high' and 'low' depends primarily upon the 'fail safe' operation of the system. Should the port fail the values must switch to their relatively safe positions. Because any 8-bit number may be written to this output port, from 0000 0000 to 1111 1111 any combination of valve status can be achieved. Similar arguments apply to sensors of continuously variable quantities such as optical density, which can be converted to binary sensors by the use of threshold devices that change state at a fixed value. The simplest sensor can consist of a switch that connects a signal line to ground and changes its status from 'high' to 'low'; many more complex sensors can also be connected to TTL inputs.

Unsurprisingly, the user may well have some reservations about connecting a microcomputer to external voltage sources that could prove damaging. Effective electrical isolation can be attained using optoisolators, which are solid-state devices comprising a light-emitting diode and a photosensitive semiconductor such as photodiode or phototransistor. Application of a voltage to the input causes light activation of the phototransistor with the consequence that it switches state thus transmitting the signal line status, at safe TTL logic voltages and currents, to the microcomputer. Similar devices may be employed in output stages. The switching of mains a.c. currents either by relay or semiconductor switch should not be attempted unless the user is fully aware of the possibilities for insulation breakdown and the hazards of such an application (8).

The wide variety of applications that could use single bit inputs/outputs mean that a complete survey cannot be given here. However, a simple circuit such as the

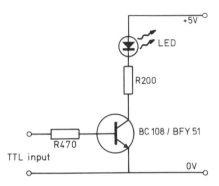

**Figure 7.** Simple circuit used to drive a light-emitting diode from a TTL output.

one shown in *Figure 7* will illustrate the use of a single bit output in the control of a light-emitting diode. Eight of these small circuits, connected to the eight lines of an output port will permit a safe investigation of the use of single bits in the control of a number of outputs.

## 3. INTERFACING TO ANALOGUE DEVICES

### 3.1 Digital to Analogue Conversion

Digital to analogue (D/A) conversion techniques are not widely used in biological laboratories. The simplest case of D/A conversion likely to be encountered is in the presentation of a voltage that is recorded on an x/t or x/y recorder, in for example, archival recording of data or output of the result of a simulation. Knowledge of the principles of D/A conversion is essential to an understanding of its counterpart, A/D conversion and it is therefore covered here (9–12).

The basic principle of D/A conversion is the generation of an output voltage that is proportional to the value of a binary word, n bits long. D/A converters are multiplying devices in that they output a proportion (between 0 and 1) of a reference voltage ($V_{ref}$); the term 'multiplying' is often reserved for those D/A converters that require an external $V_{ref}$ (9).

Both $V_{ref}$ and n influence the magnitude of the output voltage, although n is the determinant of the accuracy with which an output voltage can be generated in response to a binary word. All D/A converters employ a ladder network of resistors that act as a potential divider of $V_{ref}$ (*Figure 8*) and the maximum value obtainable, when all n bits are high ('1') is given by $V_{ref} (2^n - 1)/2^n$. Thus, the analogue voltage increases in discrete voltages of value $V_{ref}/2^n$ for every increment of 1 bit in the digital word. This represents the maximum accuracy with which the analogue output may be generated; clearly, therefore the larger the value of n, the greater the accuracy of the output voltage. Further discussion of word length is deferred until Section 3.2. Commercial D/A converters are available for most common microcomputers; in general they operate at sufficiently high speeds that this need not be a significant consideration for the sort of applications described above. Of greater importance is the need to establish that the A/D converter shows an acceptable linearity between the digital word and the

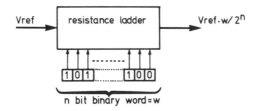

**Figure 8.** Block diagram of a digital to analogue converter. The binary input to the D/A converter is used to switch in a network of resistors that attenuate an applied reference voltage ($V_{ref}$). Other elements of a D/A converter, such as latches to hold the binary input at a fixed value during the conversion process, are not shown.

output voltage (13). A straightforward check of this linearity may be obtained by sending several repetitions of each word to the D/A converter and then incrementing the value of the word before repeating the whole procedure. If a chart recorder is connected to the output of the D/A converter the 'staircase' produced should be linear across the whole width of the paper (assuming that the recorder shows a linear response; this can be evaluated using a precision voltage source). The fundamentals of a BASIC routine to conduct this simple test are given below.

```
REM N = NUMBER OF BITS IN WORD
MAX = 2∧N − 1               (maximum value 2ⁿ − 1
FOR WORD = 0 TO MAX         (loop through all of word
                            (values
FOR SAME = 0 TO 200         (send repeatedly the same
                            (value
SEND WORD TO A/D CONVERTER  (send word; e.g. POKE to
                            (output
NEXT SAME                   (end repeat loop
NEXT WORD                   (end word loop
```

## 3.2 Analogue to Digital Conversion

### 3.2.1 *Resolution*

Analogue to digital (A/D) converters take an analogue input (a current or voltage) and convert it into an equivalent n-bit binary word. Because the analogue signal is digitised by this process each value of the n-bit binary word represents a subrange of the total range of values that are possible. It follows therefore that the larger the value of n, the greater the accuracy of the A/D conversion. The effect of n on the resolution of an analogue signal is shown in *Table 6*. As the number of bits in the digital value increases, the accuracy of the digitised result increases dramatically. Most microcomputers utilise 8-bit microprocessors and therefore handle data most readily in 8-bit words (see Chapter 1); a word length of 8 bits means that the accuracy of the digitised signal can never be greater than approximately 0.4%. By comparison, a good quality

**Table 6.** The Effect of Word Length on the Resolution of D/A and A/D Conversion.

| Word length (bits) | Range | Resolution (%) |
|---|---|---|
| 4 | 0 – 15 | 6.2500 |
| 6 | 0 – 63 | 1.5625 |
| 8 | 0 – 255 | 0.3906 |
| 10 | 0 – 1023 | 0.0977 |
| 12 | 0 – 4095 | 0.0244 |
| 14 | 0 – 16 383 | 0.0061 |
| 16 | 0 – 65 535 | 0.0015 |

The range of discrete values that are available for the digital signal are given for word lengths of between 4 and 16 bits, and the resolution is expressed as a percentage of the full scale signal.

chart recorder will reproduce data to a determinable accuracy of better than $0.1 - 0.2\%$. Thus in most cases an 8-bit A/D converter will result in some degradation of the analogue signal when compared with a mechanical recording device.

The A/D conversion cannot however, be used to provide an additional 'gloss' of accuracy on otherwise unreliable data. To illustrate, 12-bit resolution permits the decomposition of the signal into $2^{12}$ (4096) discrete values. Each of these values may only be considered as distinct if the analogue signal can be determined to an accuracy of better than $0.024\%$ (for example, an absorbance of $0.00024$ with a full scale value of $1.0$). Few analogue signals are in fact determined this accurately and the surplus digitising capacity of a 12-bit converter would therefore be responsible for the assimilation of the 'noise' component of the signal. Depending on the application and the data acquisition software this sensitivity to noise is not without value, and can permit refinement and smoothing of the analogue signal. Averaging of the repeatedly sampled signal can eventually eliminate much of the noise, which is generally considered to be randomly dispersed around the true signal value. In this case the higher resolution of the A/D conversion process has an additional function in processing the signal.

The effect of word length can be seen in the hypothetical example in *Table 7*. With a full scale deflection of $1.0$ V the digitisation of a signal of magnitude $0.79$ V is expressed at $6 - 16$ bits resolution. The error between the true and digitised value decreases rapidly with increasing word length; as a 'rule of thumb' 10- or 12-bit resolution would appear to represent a reasonable degree of accuracy of the digital value.

It does not follow that the A/D converter with the longest word length available should be automatically chosen; this choice is compromised by other considerations. Unsurprisingly, high resolution A/D converters are more costly than their lower resolution counterparts. Further, the speed of the A/D conversion is strongly influenced by the method employed in the integrated circuit; this in turn is modulated by the word length of the converter (see Section 3.2.3). Lastly, the current generation of laboratory microcomputers process data most readily in 8-bit words (bytes). An increase in resolution above 8 bits dictates that the

**Table 7.** Effect of Resolution on Accuracy of A/D Conversion.

| Word length (bits) | Digital value corresponding to 0.79 V | | | | (Decimal) | Error (mV) |
|---|---|---|---|---|---|---|
| | (Binary) | | | | | |
| 4 | | | | 0110 | 12 | 40.0000 |
| 6 | | | 11 | 0010 | 50 | 8.7500 |
| 8 | | | 1100 | 1010 | 202 | 0.9375 |
| 10 | | 11 | 0010 | 1000 | 808 | 0.9375 |
| 12 | | 1100 | 1010 | 0011 | 3235 | 0.2051 |
| 14 | 11 | 0010 | 1000 | 1111 | 12943 | 0.0219 |
| 16 | 1100 | 1010 | 0011 | 1101 | 51773 | 0.0067 |

The effect of word length is shown in the digitisation of a signal of 0.79 V, where the full scale value (all n bits high) is adjusted to 1.0 V. The binary and decimal values of the result of the A/D conversion are given, together with the error between the true voltage and the voltage equivalent to the digitised value.

digitised value is stored in two bytes of memory, incurring an additional software overhead to store, retrieve and reconstruct the digitised value. Additionally, the extra RAM required for the storage of data points in two bytes may represent an unacceptable incursion into available memory.

### 3.2.2 Conversion Speed

Factors that influence the selection of an appropriate rate for an A/D converter include the time scale of the event of interest, the number of samples required to capture the event and the storage capacity available for samples.

It is instructive to consider rather different applications in a discussion of these factors (*Table 8*). First, a transient kinetic event measured by stopped-flow spectrophotometry can be complete in 100 msec whereas separations in low pressure liquid chromatography may require data sampling for 24 h, a range of 0.86 million to one! Clearly, the magnitude of the difference in time scale of the processes suggests that A/D converters with different performances in terms of conversion rate are needed. One solution to the problem of such widely disparate time scales demands the acquisition of data at the highest possible rate, commensurate with the fastest process under investigation. Slower processes can be sampled at equivalent, high rates and the surfeit of data can then be discarded or used to improve the quality of the signal (see Section 3.2.4).

It is obvious that if the sampling rate is too slow then the information inherent in the analogue signal will be degraded by the A/D converter (*Figure 9*). The consequence of this observation, that the A/D converter should operate at the highest possible rate, is compromised by the high cost of rapid A/D converters and by the need to process the 'surplus' information that is captured. It is possible to specify the lowest feasible rate by reference to the Nyquist theorem which states that the minimal sample rate should be equal to one half of the highest frequency component of the signal. With periodic signals lower sampling rates yield superficially acceptable but erroneous data − a phenomenon known as aliasing

**Table 8.** Influence of Sample Rate on the Acquisition of Data.

| Process | Duration | Number of samples acquired at | | | Sampling rate needed for 500 samples/ process |
| --- | --- | --- | --- | --- | --- |
| | | 1 Sample/ 50 µsec | 1 Sample/ sec | 1 Sample/ 50 sec | |
| Stopped flow kinetics | 100 msec | $2 \times 10^3$ | 0 | 0 | 5 kHz |
| Enzyme kinetics | 10 sec | $2 \times 10^5$ | 10 | 0 | 50 Hz |
| Chromatographic analysis | 10 ksec | $2 \times 10^8$ | $1 \times 10^4$ | $2 \times 10^2$ | 0.05 Hz |

The effect of sampling rate is calculated from three different examples of processes likely to be found in biological laboratories, and is expressed as the number of samples acquired over the duration of the process. The last column gives the sample rate required to capture 500 values during each process.

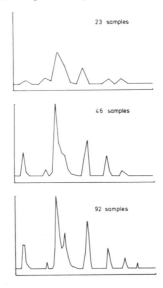

**Figure 9.** The effect of sampling frequency on the quality of a digitised signal. The figure shows a simulated chromatographic trace that was sampled with an accuracy of better than 0.5%, but at different frequencies. The digitised values have been joined to give the overall shape of the profile. At the lowest sampling rate whole peaks are missed and the heights of the peaks are misrepresented.

(*Figure 10*). Most biological data do not present a complex fluctuating signal and many signals tend to be uni-directional, thus, sampling at audio frequencies (10 kHz) is rarely required. Chromatographic data, particularly from high pressure liquid systems can generate data from the detector that contain information on a large number of peaks; in this instance it is essential that the sampling rate be sufficiently rapid to capture the data specifying both the height and width of each peak (see Chapter 8). In practice, this might mean obtaining at least 10 data points per peak, imposing a requirement for a large number of samples to be collected, many of which might represent background values from the detector (14). Simpler signals, such as the linear absorbance/time curve due to the action

34

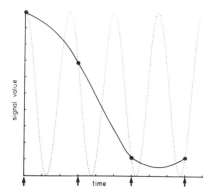

**Figure 10.** The phenomenon of aliasing. Aliasing occurs when a rapidly changing signal is sampled at insufficient rates. The example shows how a true signal (dotted line) is misrepresented by slow sampling rates. The solid lines show the signal produced by reconstruction of the digitised value.

of an enzyme on a chromogenic substrate would require fewer samples, although if linearity was a property of the data to be tested, more samples would be required. With data as variable in nature as found in the biological sciences it is difficult to provide specific rules for sampling rate; there is much to be said for repeatedly sampling 'worst case' data at various frequencies and assessing the degradation of the signal that ensues.

A factor often overlooked in the specification of a data capture system is the subsequent fate of the digitised data. Microcomputers with an 8-bit data and a 16-bit address bus (see Chapter 1) are designed to service a maximum of 64k of RAM. Given that a significant proportion of the memory is required for operating system functions, interpreter and user program, it would seem reasonable to apportion no more than 25% of this RAM to store incoming data in a buffer (16k 16 384 bytes). This memory restriction limits the sampling rate or number of samples, in that an 8-bit A/D converter running at 1 kHz would fill this buffer in under 16.5 sec; a 12-bit converter would, at the same rate, take just 8 sec. For transient kinetics this rate of data assimilation might be acceptable; for chromatographic analysis it is quite unsuitable. Similarly, if an application requires the storage in RAM of 10 chromatographic separations a maximum of 800 12-bit samples could be deployed for each. Such memory limitations may be overcome by transfer of the data in RAM to backing store (floppy disc or hard disc) for subsequent analysis.

### 3.2.3 *Methods of A/D Conversion*

The goals of A/D conversion; namely extended resolution, high conversion rates, cost and immunity from signal noise constitute a set of specifications that are often self contradictory. In an endeavour to emphasise some properties at the expense of others, many types of A/D converters have been designed that employ widely differing techniques. In the sense that the biologist will often purchase a ready built data acquisition system there would seem to be little need to understand the fundamentals of the functioning of the various types of converters.

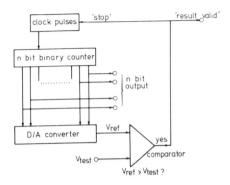

**Figure 11.** Block diagram of a binary ramp analogue to digital conversion. At a rate determined by the clock frequency the binary counter applies an increasing word to the D/A converter. When the reference voltage ($V_{ref}$) equals or exceeds the sample voltage ($V_{test}$) the comparator triggers a 'stop' signal to the clock and asserts 'data ready' on the appropriate pin of the device, to indicate that the current value of the n-bit binary word represents a valid result.

There is however some value in a background knowledge of the various techniques that becomes essential if a new analogue interface is being specified or constructed.

It is possible to identify three primary classes of A/D converters. The first are 'feedback' devices in that they employ a D/A converter (see Section 3.1) to generate a reference voltage ($V_{ref}$) that is compared with the unknown voltage ($V_{test}$). When $V_{ref}$ assumes its value closest to $V_{test}$ the binary word applied to the D/A converter is taken to be the digital value closest to $V_{test}$. The second class integrate the applied signal and relate the accumulated value to the time taken to integrate the sample. This category includes single, dual and multiple slope integration D/A converters. Finally, 'flash' converters operate extremely rapidly but are relatively costly; they are most commonly found in techniques involving video signals and other than in the highly specialised area of image processing, have little application in biological sciences. These 'flash' converters will not be considered further here, see reference (6) for further information.

The simplest of the feedback A/D converters is the 'binary ramp' or 'servo' type and is shown diagrammatically in *Figure 11*; the events during conversion are given in the flowchart in *Figure 12*. After initialisation, the binary word n-bits long is set to zero and the output of the D/A converter is compared with $V_{test}$. If $V_{test} > V_{ref}$ the word is incremented by 1 and the process is repeated until the $V_{ref} > V_{test}$, at which time the computer stops the clock pulses that increment the word and flags the conversion to be complete. Additional signals are required for 'start of conversion' and 'overflow' (where $V_{test} > V_{ref}$, even when the binary word is at its highest value). The simplicity of the binary ramp A/D converter is compromised by the fact that it takes a variable time to complete a digitisation. A high value of $V_{test}$ will require many more clock pulses than a small value, up to the maximum of $2^n$ pulses.

A different type of feedback technique that overcomes this difficulty is provided by the successive approximation A/D converter (15,16). This device utilises a

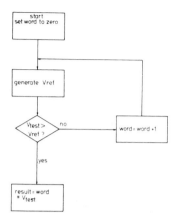

**Figure 12.** Flow chart of the steps involved in a binary ramp A/D conversion. (Reproduced from ref. 1 with the permission of Elsevier-North Holland Biomedical Press.)

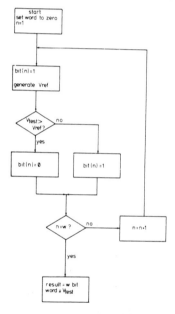

**Figure 13.** Flow chart of the steps involved in a successive approximation A/D conversion. (Reproduced from ref. 1 with the permission of Elsevier-North Holland Biomedical Press.)

logical trial and error method to digitise $V_{test}$, illustrated in the flow chart of *Figure 13*. Upon initialisation, the binary word is set to zero and at the next trial the most significant bit of the binary word (msb) is set to 1. $V_{test}$ is then compared with $V_{ref}$ and if it is greater than or equal to $V_{ref}$, the msb remains at 1 but is otherwise set to 0. Next msb $-1$ is set to 1 and the same comparison is made. When this process has been repeated for all n bits of the word, the value of the word is the digitised value of the applied signal. The sequence of values assumed by $V_{ref}$ is given in *Table 9* and *Figure 14*, which illustrate the operation of an 8-bit

**Table 9.** Digitisation of an Analogue Voltage by Successive Approximation Techniques.

| Test | Word before | $V_{ref}$ | $V_{test} > V_{ref}$ ? | Word after |
|------|-------------|-----------|------------------------|------------|
| 1 | 1000 0000 | 0.5 | No | 0000 0000 |
| 2 | 0100 0000 | 0.25 | Yes | 0100 0000 |
| 3 | 0110 0000 | 0.375 | Yes | 0110 0000 |
| 4 | 0111 0000 | 0.4375 | No | 0110 0000 |
| 5 | 0110 1000 | 0.40625 | Yes | 0110 1000 |
| 6 | 0110 1100 | 0.421875 | Yes | 0110 1100 |
| 7 | 0110 1110 | 0.4296875 | Yes | 0110 1110 |
| 8 | 0110 1111 | 0.4335737 | No | 0110 1110 |

At each step, one bit in the test word is altered and word is applied to a D/A converter. The reference voltage so produced is compared to the test voltage and the status of the bit is altered or retained depending upon the result of the test. The changes are shown diagrammatically in *Figure 14*. (Reproduced from ref. 1 with the permission of Elsevier-North Holland Biomedical Press.)

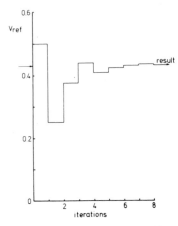

**Figure 14.** Sequence of values of $V_{ref}$ assumed during an A/D conversion using a successive approximation A/D converter. See text and *Table 9* for explanation. (Reproduced from ref. 1 with the permission of Elsevier-North Holland Biomedical Press.)

resolution, successive approximation A/D converter.

It will be readily appreciated that the successive approximation A/D converter requires constant n + 1 comparisons of $V_{test}$ with $V_{ref}$ which contrasts markedly with the $2^n$ comparisons required by the binary ramp technique. The superiority of the successive approximation technique in terms of mean conversion time is more notable as the number of bits (n) in the digital value becomes larger; 8, 10 or 12 bit. Successive approximation converters tend to be considerably faster than binary ramp devices that operate at the same resolution.

Single, dual and multiple slope integrator A/D converters do not use D/A converters but operate on an entirely different principle. The most common type, the dual slope A/D converter, functions as follows. First, the unknown voltage is applied to the input and the signal is integrated (summed) by storage in a capacitor for a fixed period of time that is monitored by a digital counter ($t_1 - t_0$, *Figure 15*).

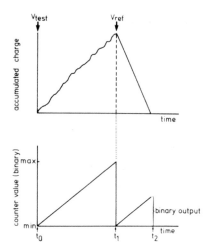

**Figure 15.** Dual slope integration method of analogue to digital conversion. The test voltage ($V_{test}$) is applied to the input and is accumulated in a capacitor as the counter increments to its maximum value. After this phase, the input is disconnected from the test voltage and a fixed reference voltage ($V_{ref}$) of opposite polarity is applied. The counter is re-set and the time required to 'bleed' off the accumulated charge is proportional to the magnitude of the applied $V_{test}$.

At the end of the integration period the stored charge is allowed to discharge and the time taken for complete discharge to occur is measured, once again by means of the counter ($t_2 - t_1$, *Figure 15*). The time taken to discharge the summed signal is proportional to the input voltage, because the discharge phase is effected by application of a fixed reference voltage of opposite polarity. Thus, the reference voltage is also integrated, and errors or non-linearities in the integrative step of the A/D conversion process affect signal and reference equally and are consequently eliminated (17).

At a simpler level, single slope integrator A/D converters measure the time required to integrate the signal ($t_1 - t_0$, *Figure 15*). Multiple slope integrator A/D converters function in the same way as dual slope devices in the first phase of the process. However, the discharge phase employs two reference voltages, one providing a coarse discharge ramp that allows approximation to the final value and the second a finer ramp that permits higher resolution. Such devices provide faster conversion times at equivalent resolution to successive approximation devices.

### 3.2.4 *Signal Noise*

The voltage that is supplied to the input of an A/D converter will not be absolutely steady but will contain a greater or lesser degree of random fluctuations of voltage at various frequencies and amplitudes. This signal noise can compromise the quality of the data that is obtained by the A/D converter and make an accurate determination of the true signal value impossible.

Signal noise can be periodic, as in the case of the superimposition of a 50 Hz modulation due to the a.c. mains supply, or it may be random in nature, as exemplified by the erratic vibration of a chart recorder pen at high scale expansion. Several factors influence the degree to which this noise component of the signal interferes with data acquisition.

First, the rate of sampling can have considerable consequences. Consider a signal that contains a noise component when it is sampled at either 50 Hz or 500 Hz. In the former case the noise will be eliminated, in the latter the data acquisition system will obtain an accurate record of the signal together with its noise component; this admits the possibility of software-based signal smoothing at a later stage.

Related to the sampling rate is the second factor; that of sample aperture time. Aperture time is a measure of the period that an A/D converter is obtaining the sample, as distinct from the time required for the subsequent A/D conversion. Some A/D converters, notably the successive approximation devices, employ a 'sample and hold' amplifier that samples the signal very rapidly and subsequently maintains that value for the duration of the conversion, providing a constant signal for the A/D converter. This is useful because noise or monotonic variation in the signal may result in the signal voltage changing between the start and end of an A/D conversion.

Because of the narrow aperture time of the sample and hold circuitry there is a stronger likelihood of capture of a transient noise spike. Dual slope integration A/D converters are open to the signal for much longer time intervals (their aperture time is large) and because they are summation devices, the effect of transient noise spikes is attenuated. They are therefore much less susceptible to signal noise although that advantage is associated with relatively slow conversion rates (10 – 100 msec).

Finally, software may be used to identify and eliminate the noise component of the signal. One of the simplest ways to achieve this is to calculate a mean signal value of a number of samples. For example, a simple data refinement loop might store in RAM the mean value of every 20 samples. Alternatively, a moving average could be calculated; this retains the same number of data points but each data point is now the mean of a surrounding number of samples (S). It is not necessary to retain the S values in RAM, a simple way to calculate a moving average of S samples is given by the formula:

$$\bar{V} = \bar{V}' \cdot \left(1 - \frac{1}{S}\right) + \frac{V}{S}$$

where $\bar{V}$ is current moving average; $\bar{V}'$ is previous moving average; V is current signal value; and S is number of samples to be averaged.

This is the digital equivalent of an R.C. filtering network with a time constant of approximately S sampling intervals. Readers may be familiar with such a filter in the 'time constant' control used to dampen noise in analogue signals from spectrophotometers or fluorimeters. To illustrate such a digital filter, *Figure 16* shows the effect of S on the randomly varying noise component. In this example, a simulated randomly noisy signal, of discrete values of 99 ± (a random integer between 1 and 11) had a sample mean of 105.18 and a standard deviation (s.d.) of ± 3.099 at S = 1 (i.e., unfiltered data). When filtered, the mean value remained

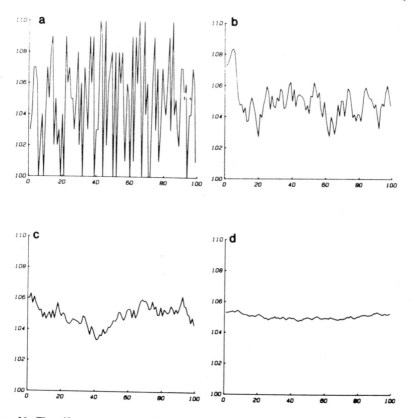

**Figure 16.** The effect of digital filtering on signal noise. A simulated sample (**a**) consisting of 100 values of 100 ± a random digit between 0 and 10 was subject to digital filtering in the form of calculation of a moving average of every (**b**) 5, (**c**) 10 and (**d**) 50 values.

unchanged ($p > 0.5$) but the standard deviation was reduced such that at $S = 2$, s.d. $= \pm 1.85$; $S = 5$, s.d. $= 1.02$; $S = 10$, s.d. $= 0.75$; $S = 50$, s.d. $= 0.198$; $S = 100$, s.d. $= 0.14$. This trend, shown diagrammatically in *Figure 16* illustrates the value of calculating a moving average in this fashion.

This smoothing of the data is not achieved without cost. Genuine fluctuations of the signal that occur within the 'time constant' or S samples will be averaged out of the data such that in chromatographic analysis, for example, small sharp peaks may be eliminated. It is essential that the user is aware of the consequence and limitations of any data refinement techniques that are employed (18).

## 4. ACKNOWLEDGEMENTS

I should like to thank Ms. G. Mahon for typing the manuscript and Miss E. Aspinall for preparation of the figures.

## 5. REFERENCES

1. Beynon,R.J. (1983) in *Computing in Biological Science*, Geisow,M.J. and Barrett,A.N. (eds.), published by Elsevier North Holland Biomedical Press, Amsterdam, p. 395.

2. Witten,I.H. (1980) *Communicating with Microcomputers*, published by Academic Press, London.
3. Hewlett-Packard (1975) *Condensed Description of the Hewlett-Packard Interface Bus*, HP Part No. 59401 90030.
4. Fisher,E. and Jensen,C.W. (1980) *Pet and the IEEE 488 BUS (GPIB)*, published by Osborne-McGraw Hill, Berkeley.
5. Witten,I.H. (1983) *Byte*, **8(2)**, 146.
6. Artwick,B.A. (1980) *Microcomputer Interfacing*, published by Prentice Hall Inc., Englewood Cliffs.
7. Ciarcia,S. (1983) *Byte*, **8(4)**, 28.
8. Cosgrove,D. (1981) *Byte*, **6(11)**, 84.
9. Carr,J.J. (1980) *Microcomputer Interfacing Handbook, A/D and D/A*, published by TAB Books Inc., Blue Ridge Summit.
10. Garrett,P.H. (1981) *Analog I/D Design-Acquisition, Conversion, Recovery*, published by Reston Publishing Co., Reston.
11. Garrett,P.H. (1978) *Analog Systems for Microprocessors and Minicomputers*, published by Reston Publishing Co., Reston.
12. Lesea,A. and Zaks,R. (1978) *Microprocessor Interfacing Techniques*, published by Sybex Inc., Berkeley.
13. Lenz,J.E. and Kelly,E.F. (1980) *IEEE Trans. Biomed. Eng.*, **27**, 668.
14. Reese,C.E. (1980) *J. Chromatogr. Sci.*, **18**, 201.
15. Hallgren,R.C. (1980) *IEEE Trans. Biomed. Eng.*, 27, 161.
16. Seeds,M.A. and Levision,H.F. (1981) *Byte*, **6(10)**, 458.
17. Daggitt,R. (1981) *Byte*, **6(6)**, 378.
18. Reese,C.E. (1980) *J. Chromatogr. Sci.*, **18**, 249.

CHAPTER 3

# Data-logging with Microcomputers

K.C. PERSAUD and R. VIRDEN

## 1. INTRODUCTION

Automation of data collection by attaching an experiment directly to a micro-computer suffers from the limited ability of the microcomputer to time-share between different tasks. In many cases, a microcomputer is fully occupied either in acquiring and storing data or in processing previously stored data. This leads to the bad practice of collecting results from a succession of experiments and not assessing them until later. This may be too late to salvage the original experimental material and the whole series is then flawed. In other cases instrument manufacturers provide interfaces and software that guarantee the inefficient use of microcomputers. A striking example is the sad spectacle of a scintillation counter infrequently sending data through a serial output port to a slave microcomputer. The computing power of the microcomputer is wasted for most of the working day.

A solution to both of these problems is to interpose a data-logger between the experiment and the microcomputer. Although magnetic tape still has its place for large capacity storage, dramatic decreases in the price and increase in the capacity of memory integrated circuits have led to memory-based data-loggers with capacities comparable with those of many microcomputers. We shall consider examples of such data-loggers applied to situations where data are stored and later transferred to a microcomputer on demand. In this way an experiment can be analysed and saved on disc, if required, while another experiment is being logged.

Data to be collected may be discrete (integer numbers) or continuous (analogue). The first are readily transformed into binary voltages which, with suitable buffering, may be attached directly to the lines of standard interface adaptors. The second, represented as samples of a continuously variable voltage, require an analogue-to-digital (A/D) converter (perhaps preceded by a scaling operational amplifier) to provide binary approximations of the sampled voltage.

We shall discuss a selection of methods for use during the collection, transformation and storage of data (Section 2) and examples of data-loggers (Section 3).

## 2. METHODS USED IN DATA-LOGGING

### 2.1 Collection and Storage of Data

The primary objective in using a data-logger is to obtain a faithful representation of the information being sampled. It is important to ensure that the sampling rate is sufficiently high to meet this need. However, because the capacity of memory-based devices is finite, it is often desirable to use the minimum sampling rate compatible with the required fidelity. Other economies in the use of memory also need to be considered.

### 2.1.1 *Sampling Rates*

The incoming signal must be sampled at a rate high enough to be represented in stored form within acceptable error limits. A signal that varies regularly in intensity may be considered to be composed of one or more superimposed sinusoidal wave forms. Under ideal conditions, the original signal can be recovered without distortion if it is sampled at twice the highest frequency ($f$) present in the signal (1). However, ideal conditions are rarely attained in practice because of random noise superimposed on the signal. Sampling data at a frequency as low as $2f$ when higher frequency noise is present will distort the representation of the data. This can be alleviated by sampling at higher frequencies and by filtering out the unwanted components of the input signal using analogue, hardwired digital or software methods (2,3) as discussed in Section 2.2.1.

The rate of data collection required depends upon the application and may vary from MHz for temperature-jump experiments or kHz for stopped-flow experiments to as little as $10^{-3}$Hz for some types of column chromatography. This influences the type of program to be used. A maximum number of measurements is often desirable but the recording of numerous data points from slowly changing inputs does not lead to improved precision or sensitivity once the rate is sufficient to deal with any high frequency noise components in the signal.

With a microprocessor-based data-logger an external digital pulse or internal timer is typically used to interrupt the microprocessor at the time a sample is to be taken. During an interrupt the current task is stopped and a data collection routine is carried out. This done, the microprocessor returns to its original task. The data collection routine must be sufficiently fast that the processor will not receive an interrupt request again before it has serviced the previous one. High level languages such as BASIC are often too slow for use in interrupt routines and assembler programs are then used to write machine code instructions which are specific to each type of microprocessor. The execution times of machine code instructions vary from 2 to 6 $\mu$sec for the MOSTEK 6502 and ZILOG Z80 processors to $10-20$ $\mu$sec per instruction for the older MOTOROLA 6800 and INTEL 8080 processors. A typical data collection routine contains at least 30 instructions and the time needed to carry them out limits the rate at which data can be collected. When sampling analogue data the conversion time of the A/D converter imposes an additional limitation. For example, the AD574 12-bit converter requires 25 $\mu$sec. If data are to be collected at rates greater than $4-5$ kHz it is advisable to use electronic methods, which bypass the microprocessor, to write data directly into memory which can later be accessed by the microprocessor. This is a complex operation but single chip direct memory access controllers are now widely available which allow data collection at rates greater than 100 kHz. Lieber *et al.* (4) describe a method of high speed data acquisition, using direct memory access techniques, suitable for measuring changes in sarcomere length during contraction of isolated skeletal and cardiac muscle cells.

If data are collected at relatively slow rates then the microprocessor is free to carry out many operations between interrupts. These may include manipulation of data points as they are collected, graphical display or an unconnected task. On the other hand, high data collection rates mean the microprocessor must be totally dedicated to that task. In the former case the main program may be written in a high level language such as BASIC with an interrupt routine written in machine code. In the latter case it may be necessary to write the entire program in machine code. Machine code routines are not difficult to write but they require detailed knowledge of the microprocessor used. Even quite simple routines require a surprisingly large number of programming steps. Programming errors may take appreciably more time to find than with a high level language mainly because of the large size.

### 2.1.2 *Data Accuracy and Format*

The accuracy with which data should be recorded depends on the application. For analogue data in a normal laboratory environment a recording accuracy of at least 12 bits (1 part in 4096 or 0.025%) is a minimum if a large dynamic range of inputs is to be recorded. In other applications, an accuracy of 8 bits (1 part in 256 or 0.4%) is satisfactory. If the data consist of digital pulses which are accumulated with time it may be convenient to scale these if the numbers become very large.

Microprocessors are not, as yet, very efficient at storing and retrieving floating point numbers, therefore for speed of access from memory, magnetic tape or disc storage it is desirabe to store primary data as integers. This technique also increases the memory available for data storage since an integer in the range $0 - 65\,535$ occupies only two bytes as opposed to seven bytes for the corresponding floating point number. Normally this is easily achieved since A/D converters or pulse counters provide data in integer format. However, if calculations have to be done before data are stored in memory, some form of scaling may be necessary for the results to be stored in integer form without loss of precision. Truncation of real numbers must be avoided when scaling is carried out and a rounding algorithm used (5).

## 2.2 **Data Reduction**

### 2.2.1 *Filtering and Smoothing*

In analysing signals from various sources, separation of background noise from the signal is often necessary. Filters are devices which attenuate unwanted frequencies. The mathematical background and the principles of some filters are described by Lynn (6). A detailed discussion of filter design is provided by Lam (2). Three filter types are shown in *Figure 1*. The lowpass type has the familiar application of suppression of high frequency random noise. Highpass filters, which suppress unwanted low frequencies, and bandpass filters, which suppress both low and high frequencies, also have uses in biology.

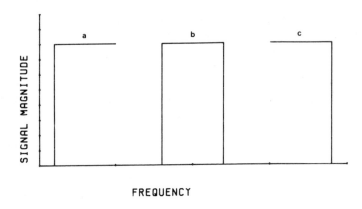

**Figure 1.** Filter types **(a)** Highpass; **(b)** Bandpass; **(c)** Lowpass.

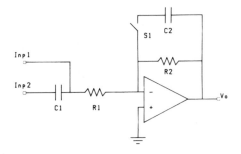

**Figure 2.** Circuit diagram for an operational amplifier-based filter.
Lowpass:     Input 1, S1 closed.
Highpass:    Input 2, S1 open.
Bandpass:    Input 2, S1 closed.

Many biological instruments are fitted with a simple analogue filter, often a capacitor and a resistor, to damp unwanted noise of frequency higher than the underlying signal. Such a lowpass filter cannot provide the ideal sharp cut-off shown in *Figure 1*. Successful filtering is therefore limited to noise of several times the frequency of the signal. Using only passive components, greater complexity and signal attenuation are the results of improving the cut-off. Active filters, which incorporate one or more active devices such as amplifiers, are a practical means of achieving nearly ideal analogue filters. This owes much to advances in the design of operational amplifiers (7). A simple example of an operational amplifier used as a filter is illustrated in *Figure 2*. The output voltage Vo is determined by the difference in voltage between the inputs ( + , − ) and the feedback components (C2 and R2).

Although it may be desirable to use analogue filters either within experimental instrumentation or within a data-logger, the alternative of digital filtering offers a flexible way of enhancing the desired frequencies. An advantage of the digital filter is that it is not prone to drift with age and temperature as are analogue components. This is of particular value when monitoring low frequency signals.

Digital filters may be made up from hardwired components but the advent of the programmable data-logger allows a variety of filters to be selected without the expense of additional electronics.

Digital filters may involve transformation of the signal into its spectrum, typically by a Fourier transform algorithm, but this approach requires considerable computing power. We shall therefore deal only with filters operating in a time domain. The most economical filter algorithms calculate a new output in response to every input value. If this calculation is completed before a new sample is taken, it will not be necessary to store the whole of the sampled data to compute the filtered data.

*Listing 1* illustrates a moving average lowpass filter that yields a representation (Y) of each new data point (X) as the sum of the K most recent data points. The transfer magnitude (output/input) of a constant value of X is equal to K. It is evident that the output divided by K is equal to the mean of K values. In a datalogger the time and memory may not be available to implement the division before collection of a new sample and it is then convenient to store the output sum and scale the data later after transfer to a microcomputer. The program also demonstrates the general 'start-up' property of filters, namely that given a constant input value or waveform, the filtered output is delayed in proportion to the value of K. An allowance for the delay imposed by a filter usually has to be made in subsequent treatment of the data. By altering the value of K it may also be shown that the cut-off frequency decreases as K increases.

Other moving average filters assign different weights to different input values. *Listing 2* implements a filter described by Hamming (3). In *Listing 2*, Y and X are the current output and input values respectively; X1 and X2 are the two previous input values. Multiplication and division by 2 and 4 are readily implemented in machine code and the filter can operate rapidly. The program gives a transfer magnitude of unity for a steady input and gives zero at half the sampling frequency. All frequencies in the data are delayed to an equal extent.

The principle of *Listing 2* may be extended to yield an estimate of a point on a polynomial curve, that best describes a segment of the input data by minimising the sum of the squared errors. Given an odd number of data points the least-squares estimate of the mid-point value is obtained by use of appropriate convolution integers as coefficients (8,9). For example, a cubic/quadratic equation is fitted to a swathe of five points by *Listing 3*.

In this form, where $X(N + 1)$ and $X(N + 2)$ represent points collected later than $X(N)$ the algorithm is suitable for smoothing a complete stored data set, but in some cases it may be fast enough to be amended for use during data collection. This produces a filter with a cut-off frequency of 0.5 times the data sampling frequency $(f_s)$ while an 11-point fit has a cut-off point at about $0.2 f_s$. It may also be used to reduce the total number of data points to be recorded by sliding the polynomial along the data set five points at a time and recording only the resultant fitted point at the centre of the polynomial.

When data points are separated by unequal intervals, curvilinear regression methods are required for smoothing. A curvilinear regression for the dependence of data $y$ on the successive powers of $x, x^2, ....x^p$ is fitted as if it were a multiple regression of $p$-independent variables $x_1$, $x_2$, ....$x_p$ and each power of $x$ is treated as if it were a separate independent variable (10).

Filters of the above kind become progressively less efficient as the swathe width increases. Recursive filters, which include one or more previous outputs in the calculation applied to each input, are much more economical than the corresponding non-recursive filters. *Listings 4* and *5* illustrate simple recursive lowpass and highpass filters. In *Listing 4* the transfer magnitude is a maximum $[1/(1-A/B)]$ at a frequency of zero and a minimum $[1/(1+A/B)]$ at half the sampling frequency. In *Listing 5* the transfer magnitude is zero at a frequency of zero and a maximum $[2/(1-A/B)]$ at half the sampling frequency.

*Listing 6* illustrates a bandpass filter which gives a maximum transfer factor of $K/2$ at a frequency of a quarter of the sampling frequency and rejects higher and lower frequencies to a greater extent as K increases. Multiplication and division, which make *Listings 4* and *5* expensive to execute in a data-logger, are avoided here at the cost of storage of a greater part of the input stream. Other filters of this type are discussed by Lynn (6).

### 2.2.2 Peak Detection

In many data-logging applications only the main features of the incoming data need be recorded, such as peaks in a chromatogram or electric spikes from a neural discharge. No general algorithm exists for this purpose since random error and other instabilities in the input data complicate the criteria needed to define a significant feature in the data. Any program must be carefully tailored to suit the shape of the signal. Changes in a pattern of data may be detected by differentiation. The successive values of the derivative of an unchanging baseline are zero so that an appropriate sequence of positive and negative values can be interpreted as peaks, subject to a threshold value which depends on the type of data being collected. It is often appropriate to filter the data using one of the algorithms given above before differentiation or else to take many successive points to calculate the differential.

Differentiation may be carried out using analogue methods with the same limitations discussed in Section 2.2.1. Among methods for differentiating an input signal digitally, the simplest algorithm subtracts from the newest data point the one before it. This algorithm is fast and easy to implement but it is often fatally misled by high frequency noise. A better method is to fit a polynomial to the data and to calculate the slope at the centre point. For example, the slope at the mid-point of a quadratic with a swathe-width of five points is given by *Listing 7*. Second and higher derivatives may be obtained by similar methods (8). The degree of smoothing associated with the derivative increases with the number of data points in the polynomial but more computing time is required. Where fast data sampling rates are required, analogue differentiation of the input signal may be necessary.

Van der Molen and de Kramer (11) have described a peak discriminator which gives very fast data sampling times. A block diagram of their device is shown in *Figure 3*. On the occurrence of a peak in the input signal, the device generates a

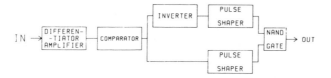

**Figure 3.** Outline circuit plan for a peak discriminator.

shaped pulse that functions as a sample command for an A/D converter. Peaks are denoted where the first derivative of the input crosses zero, the derivative being generated by an operational amplifier.

### 2.2.3 *Signal Averaging*

Many signals recorded from biological systems have small amplitudes and large noise components so that noise removal is essential before analysis. Conventional filtering techniques may be used if the noise has frequency components which are higher or lower than the signal of interest. However, when signal frequency components and noise frequency components overlap with each other, different methods have to be used to improve the signal-to-noise ratio.

A common method is signal averaging. Consider a single data point $p$ which consists of the sum of the signal (S) and noise (N). The signal and noise are repetitively recorded. After $n$ repetitions the value accumulated is:

$$\sum_{i=1}^{n} p = \sum_{i=1}^{n} S + \sum_{i=1}^{n} N \qquad \text{Equation 1}$$

Whereas the accumulated signal intensity increases by a factor of $n$ the standard deviation of the noise increases as $n^{1/2}$ (12). Signal averaging can be considered to be a digital filter which preferentially allows non-random signals through, the selectivity of the filter increasing with the number of repetitive scans recorded.

In practice, signal averaging methods can only be used if the required signal can be accurately synchronised to the $x$-axis to allow repetitive scans. This can easily be done with spectrophotometers, or with repetitive waveforms such as electrocardiograms. If the noise distribution is strictly periodic (e.g., mains frequency) misleading results may be obtained. Errors may also occur if the noise is of sufficiently low frequency that the levels in adjacent samples along the $x$-axis are correlated with each other (13).

## 2.3 **Error Sensing and Control**

In many applications it is necessary to collect data and to respond immediately to control a process. For example, the incoming data are compared with a set of reference data and electronic switching is used to operate equipment that acts to minimise the difference between the input and reference data. Instrument control

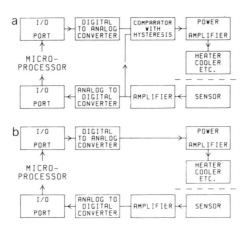

**Figure 4.** Outline circuit plan for a simple environmental control unit. (**a**) Open loop. (**b**) Closed loop.

can be divided into two main categories:

(i)   the control of environmental factors such as temperature or humidity;
(ii)  the control of data collection.

Two applications of microprocessors to environmental control are shown in *Figure 4*. The important components are a sensor, a comparison device, and a servo to drive a heater, cooler, motor or other device for control of the monitored parameter. *Figure 4a* illustrates control without direct intervention of the micro-processor (i.e., open loop control). The controller is self-contained and responds to a parameter-setting word entered from the microprocessor, with provision for data-logging. Closed loop control is illustrated in *Figure 4b*. In this case the comparison of the measured parameter with its required value takes place within the microprocessor, which then actively controls the external servo system to bring about the required response. Open loop control is desirable when the micro-processor is under a heavy load, but closed loop control offers more flexibility with regard to the dynamic response of the control system.

## 2.4 **Pattern Recognition**

In an extension of the operations described in Section 2.3 it may be necessary to collect data for later analysis, and to do some real-time checking and analysis. A typical application in the medical field is cardiac monitoring, where the aim is for abnormal electrocardiograms to be recognised and signalled immediately and automatically.

Two main pattern processing problems may be identified, namely detection and recognition. Pattern detection methods usually involve fitting a reference pattern to the data set with some criterion for accepting or rejecting the data. Recognition of the pattern involves statistical classification tests to determine which of a finite number of labels should be attached to the data. Many algorithms have been devised for pattern detection and recognition (14). Among these, we consider only classical statistical classification models. In the first stage the input data are subjected to a battery of tests, each of which generates a number. This part of the system is called the 'receptor'. The output of the 'receptor' may be represented by a $p$-dimensional column vector

$$X = \begin{bmatrix} X_1 \\ X_2 \\ \vdots \\ X_i \\ \vdots \\ X_p \end{bmatrix}$$

where $p$ is the number of tests, and $X_i$ is the output of the ith test. Thus, each input is mapped into a point of a $p$-dimensional space. Corresponding to each input category there exists a set of points in the $p$-dimensional space. Points from any category may fall anywhere in the space, each category generating a certain density of points at each location in the space (i.e., there is a probability density function corresponding to each category). Any pattern recognition algorithm has to be able to determine whether the points generated in $p$-dimensional space fall within the probability density of any stored set of patterns.

A detailed design example of a microprocessor-based pattern recognition system is that of Abenstein (15). A portable device is described which monitors heart signals and recognises and responds to abnormal situations which include 12 classes of arrhythmia and conduction disturbances. It detects and stores such patterns, transmits them to a central computer for display and analysis, and generates alarms in real-time.

## 2.5 Intelligent Data-loggers

The techniques described above coalesce into a machine which can collect data, reject artefacts, recognise patterns and adapt to the surrounding environment. Learning from previous experience to adapt and react to new types of input data is the next step. A simple example, described by Furno and Tompkins (16), is a learning filter for removing noise interference in data-logging. A microprocessor-based filter removes mains-induced electrical interference from biopotential signals by learning one period of the noise waveform and subtracting it from the signal. A noise template is created so that the filter can remove noise waveforms containing several harmonics of the mains frequency. This filter is limited in that it must learn the noise waveform during a quite period of the input signal and does not tolerate amplitude variations in the noise waveform. However, there are many possibilities for development.

Other applications of artifical intelligence are in error sensing and control, as discussed in Section 2.3, to compensate for mechanical, electrical and human failures. With increasing computing power, more interpretation of the data will be taken over by the data-logger so that the user will not see raw data but will be presented with conclusions and inferences.

# 3. EXAMPLES OF DATA-LOGGERS

## 3.1 **Hardwired versus Programmable Data-loggers**

Use of a microprocessor allows the operation of any desired program during data collection, compared with, at most, a few switchable options in a data-logger containing only hardwired logic. There are several potential benefits.

(i)   There is usually a decrease in the number of electronic components needed. This increases reliability and may also reduce the cost of production.

(ii)  The investment of effort in a single electronic development covers a wide range of applications. Development of software is often more cost-effective than development of new hardware to do the same job.

(iii) There is an increase in the range and variety of performance available from microprocessor-based products which has been illustrated in the sections above.

(iv)  The device can interact with the user in a unified way. The switches and knobs of conventional electronic devices are replaced by a display and keyboard which is usually easier to operate.

However, using a microprocessor may create new problems. Some of these problems are summarised below.

(i)   The system may generate radio-frequency interference which would be deleterious in certain applications.

(ii)  Electrical spikes in power supplies, and static interference from nearby equipment may interfere with the operation of the microprocessor, leading to the corruption of data stored in memory.

(iii) The labour cost of writing assembly language software is high.

(iv)  Microprocessors are limited by the speed at which they carry out instructions.

Electrical problems may be largely eliminated by careful design and electrical screening. The cost of software development will remain high for some time to come but the advent of mass-produced pre-programmed single-chip microprocessors for many applications will ease the burden of programming for individual requirements. However, given better tools, users usually have higher aspirations and it would be unwise to predict a decrease in software development costs.

The problem of speed of operation is being alleviated by the development of new types of microprocessors and memories with faster operating speeds. New 8-bit processors are at least 10 times faster than their predecessors of the 1970s. The development of 16-bit and 32-bit microprocessors offers great computing power and speed, but at the cost of increased complexity of both hardware and software. Because of the high cost of developing software these microprocessors are unlikely to be used for dedicated data-logging unless there is the prospect of a large commercial gain. However, as a consequence of increased microprocessor power, interface programming in high level languages is becoming more practicable, avoiding the need for machine code programming. This will ultimately lower the software development costs for many data-logging applications.

Pre-programmed microprocessors on single integrated circuits are now available for applications ranging from process control and timing to complex signal processing (17). However, logging of many biological experiments may be met by simple means. Hardwired electronics suited for simple types of data collection and storage are often easily built provided that the electronic components are not too numerous. Our view is that when a design calls for more than about 40 integrated circuits it is better to use a microprocessor and reap the benefits of use of standard electronic hardware. This saving is, of course, to some extent offset because the microprocessor must be programmed for each new application.

The following section describes a hardwired approach to data-logging. A hardwired data-logger suitable for accumulating digital pulses with time has been constructed and interfaced to a standard microcomputer. This has been used for collecting pH stat kinetic data. An alternative approach would be a programmable data-logger with its own microprocessor which may be interfaced to an external microcomputer.

## 3.2 Specification of a Hardwired Data-logger

### 3.2.1 *An Example of a Data-logging Problem*

A pH stat may be used to measure the kinetics of reactions which generate or remove protons and to control pH during fermentation and other processes. *Figure 5* shows the principal features of a typical pH stat. It consists of:

(i)   pH electrodes;
(ii)  an amplifier and comparator which compares the electrode voltage with a reference voltage and outputs a voltage proportional to the difference;
(iii) a means of converting this voltage into a series of digital pulses (a voltage to frequency converter);
(iv)  a stepper motor which operates a burette filled with titrant solution.

Initially, the reference voltage is set to define the pH end-point. Thereafter, any difference of appropriate sign between the measured pH and the reference pH leads to the generation of digital pulses which trigger the addition of titrant from the burette so that the pH approaches the end-point. The kinetics of a reaction may be recorded in terms of the amount of titrant added to the reaction mixture as a function of time, for example as a chart recorder trace. A recent electronic design for such a system is given by Warner *et al.* (18).

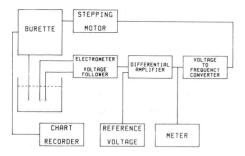

**Figure 5.** Typical pH stat system.

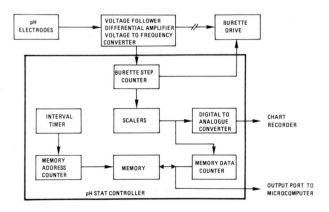

**Figure 6.** Outline circuit plan for a pH stat data logger/controller.

When zero-order kinetics are involved the resulting data are easily analysed unless they are numerous. However, analysis of higher order and mixed order kinetics requires that many data points be fitted to an appropriate kinetic model, for example, in the substrate-induced inactivation and reactivation kinetics of penicillinase (19). It is then convenient to transfer data into a computer for manipulation and statistical analysis. The method selected was to record the number of digital pulses sent to the burette during successive time intervals; these numbers being directly proportional to the amounts of titrant added. For this a data-logging system may be interposed in place of the previous connection between the stepper motor and the burette (*Figure 5*).

Before it is decided whether the data-logger should be constructed solely from conventional electronic components or whether a microprocessor should be included, a detailed plan is needed. Digital pulses have to be counted and, after a given time interval, the count must be stored in memory. It is desirable to have a visual record of a run, by an analogue output to a chart recorder. It is necessary to be able to scale the sensitivity of recording to cope with different reaction rates as discussed in Section 3.2.3. The resulting design is shown in *Figure 6*. It can be built simply, without a separate microprocessor. For cheapness and simplicity 8-bit counting and memory are used, but it is easy (Section 3.2.3) to reconstruct data to greater precision by a simple routine used in the microcomputer. This type of design could be used in other data-logging applications where digital pulses are to be counted and stored.

### 3.2.2 *Circuit Description*

The controller includes 19 integrated circuits. Nine are used for the burette step counter, scalers and D/A converter (*Figure 7*) and the rest are for timing and memory (*Figure 8*). A pulse from the voltage-to-frequency converter of the pH stat is taken to IC1c which, when enabled, outputs a pulse to the burette stepper motor. To avoid interference with other functions, a delay imposed by mono-stable IC2a inhibits acceptance of any new signal at IC1c and so limits the burette

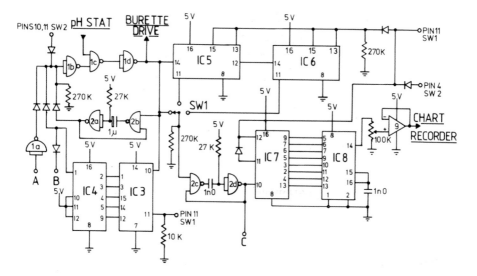

**Figure 7.** Circuit for pH stat controller. Integrated circuits (IC) are as follows: 1 = CD4011, 2 = CD4001, 3 = CD4020, 4 = CD4068, 5 and 6 = CD4017, 7 = CD4040, 8 = ZN425 and 9 = CA3140. Other components: Diodes = IN4148, Resistors are 0.25 W 5%, Electrolytic capacitors are Tantalum 35 V, other capacitors are Ceramic disc and the power supply is 5 V stabilised 0.5 A.

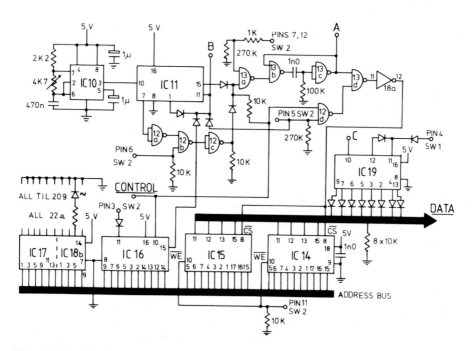

**Figure 8.** Circuit for pH stat data logger section. Integrated circuits (IC) are as follows: 10 = LM555, 11 = CD4040, 12 and 13 = CD4011, 14 and 15 = 2114, 16 = CD4040, 17 and 18 = 74LS04, 19 = CD4040. Other components are as for Figure 7.

motor frequency (to 200 Hz in this case). To suit other stepper motors this delay should be longer than the step pulse. The frequency could be at least a factor of 10 faster than that used here. The output from IC1 also fulfills two other functions. Firstly, the 14-bit binary counter IC3 is set by means of AND logic with IC4 to disable IC1 and IC11 when the burette is empty. This occurs after 12 000 pulses in the present case, but any value less than 16 384 ($2^{14}$) pulses could be substituted or a 16-bit counter could readily be used if a greater value was required. Secondly, the output from IC1 is taken to the decade counters IC5 and IC6 which provide scaling by division (1, 10, 100). The scaled signals pass *via* the monostable IC2b,c to two 8-bit binary counters in parallel. One of these, IC7, provides data for an 8-bit D/A converter (IC8) the output of which is buffered by the operational amplifier IC9 to provide a calibrated voltage output (1V/255 pulses) for a chart recorder.

The second 8-bit counter IC19 is the memory data counter (*Figure 8*). The interval timer (IC10, IC11) is adjusted by a variable resistor to give a 5 sec interval. Accuracy and stability are achieved by running IC10 at a frequency close to 20 kHz and dividing the output by a factor of $2^{12}$ with the binary counter IC11. This gives good reproducibility (0.04% at $20-25°C$) at very low cost. The rising edge of each signal from the timer enables the writing of data into memory by triggering the monostable IC13. The memory can then receive data from the data counter IC19. The subsequent negative edge of each signal from the timer increments the memory address counter IC16. After the final memory address has been used the clock is inhibited so that no overwriting of memory can occur. The status of the address bus is displayed on 10 LEDs *via* the drivers IC17 and IC18. The connections of the two switches used are shown in *Table 1*. The five-position switch SW1:

(i)   inhibits IC1 and thereby stops operation of the pH stat;

(ii)  re-sets the counters for the chart recorder output and memory;

(iii) sets the scale factor at IC5.

Memory is cleared in sequence through all addresses when SW1 is in position 5 and SW2 is in position 6 by taking clock pulses at 10 kHz from pin 7 of IC11 *via* the gate IC12a to the same point as normal data on IC13. When SW2 is in this position the controller may be used simply to provide a chart recorder trace of a pH stat experiment under the control of SW1.

To initiate transfer of data into memory SW2 is moved to position 1. Normally this will be done after moving SW2 through positions 4 and 3 to re-set the address counter and the memory data counter. Position 2 allows data transfer to memory to be delayed when desired. Transfer of data from memory to the output port is enabled when SW1 is in position 5 and SW2 is in position 5. The external control line is disabled through the gate IC12b when SW2 is in any other position. When the control line is held logically high (+5 V) by an external microprocessor, a byte from the first memory address appears on the eight data lines of the output port. When the line is sent low (0 V) the address counter is incremented. Repetition of the sequence of high/low permits all 1024 bytes to be read.

**Table 1.** Switch Functions and Connections. Each switch is a 6 way 2-pole rotary type. SW1 controls statting functions (pole 1 to IC2c, pole 2 to 5 V). SW2 controls timing and memory functions (both poles to 5 V).

| Switch | Position | Function | Pin used |
|--------|----------|----------|----------|
| SW1 | 1 | Scale 1 | 1 |
| | 2 | Scale 10 | 2 |
| | 3 | Scale 100 | 3 |
| | 4 | Stop | 4 |
| | 5 | Re-set step and scaler counters | 11 |
| | 6 | Not used | – |
| SW2 | 1 | Write | 7 |
| | 2 | Inhibit memory | 2 |
| | 3 | Re-set memory data counter | 3 |
| | 4 | Re-set address counter | 4 |
| | 5 | Read | 5 |
| | 6 | Clear (SW1 position 5) | 12 |

### 3.2.3 *BASIC Program*

*Listing 8* has three functions:

(i)  to load scaled data from the memory of the pH stat controller;
(ii)  to convert each point to a 16-bit number which includes the number of completed spans of the data counter;
(iii)  to facilitate selection of unwanted points, optionally averaging several adjacent points, and to put the results into arrays which are then available for use in curve-fitting and other routines.

The complete 16-bit record or the final arrays may be listed either at the control port or at a second port such as a line printer. Because of the interactive nature of the program, attention has been given to protecting the user against entering out of range values.

The program was written for a Southwest Technical M6800 microcomputer with 12k of user RAM. Apart from small differences in syntax between different versions of BASIC the few changes necessary to implement the program with another microcomputer include the routines to control the parallel interface port (at address A1) and the details of defining a block of 2048 bytes of RAM (starting at address A2) to receive the data from the pH stat data-logger. The relevant lines (185 – 260) may readily be modified by users of other systems.

*Conversion of data to 16-bit form.* The 1024 8-bit words received from the pH stat controller, including zeros after the last datum, are stored at alternate addresses. Then, each preceding address receives the count of the number of completed spans of the data counter (lines 290 – 395). The appropriate value is obtained by exploiting the fact that the burette reading cannot decrease with time, implying that any observed decrease between successive data points must indicate completion of a span of the counter. To provide immunity against a variety of possible errors it is required that a minimum of five points shall occur within any span and that any implied completion shall only be counted if the resulting increase in volume is not more than one fifth of a span. Any exception generates an error message and a count is kept of the total number of errors.

*Data reduction.* The user may select a block of data points from within the full data set (lines 405 – 545). Because points collected during the period of interest may be too numerous for convenient analysis or display, provision is made to skip any number of points within a block of data, so that points are taken at a fixed multiple of the sampling interval. When a block does not include a sharp inflection it may be appropriate to average several adjacent points, thereby smoothing short-term irregularities in the progress curve. The polynomial smoothing method described in Section 2.2 is applied here to give an estimate of the mid-point of five adjacent points. The appropriate coefficients (Section 2.2.2) are used to give the first derivative of the fitted five point curve as an estimate of the reaction velocity at that point. On exit from this routine the arrays X and Y contain the selected time and quantity of titrant, respectively.

*Entry points to further routines.* The arrays X and Y are available for use in routines such as curve-fitting or display. In each case the choice of a suitable routine depends on the microcomputer system. For example, the non-linear least-squares regression program of Duggleby (20) may be combined with the present program with minor modification.

Other entry points are given for saving data and for loading previously saved data. The user must provide a routine for each of these functions.

### 3.3 Programmable Data-loggers

Programmable data-loggers have great potential with respect to the format of data which they may receive and the way in which raw data may be processed. For example, in the measurement of chlorophyll fluorescence a programmable data-logger can be used to receive and reduce the initial fast transients freeing the microcomputer for other tasks. Programmable data-loggers have been used widely in spectrophotometry. Such data-loggers are commercially available but may require machine code programming. Such loggers may also be built using the microprocessors found in the common microcomputers.

#### 3.3.1 *Choice of a Microprocessor*

There are now several hundred types of processors available. In a commercial environment where large numbers of identical devices are to be manufactured it is probably reasonable to use the most compact and lowest power version available. For the user developing a device it is probably better to choose an older and better documented processor. If a laboratory microcomputer is to be used to develop the program for the data-logging task it is sensible to use a microcomputer of the same family as that in the microcomputer to reap the advantages of compatibility, both electrically and in the instruction set. The MOSTEK 6500 series has much to commend it for data-logging. It is the microprocessor in several widely used microcomputers including Apple 2 series, Commodore, PET, and Acorn BBC models. It has a small instruction set, simplifying programming in machine code, and it has a memory-mapped input/output system allowing easy interfacing. Faster, lower powered versions for portable equipment are almost constantly being produced. Other types such as members of the MOTOROLA 6800 series may be equally suitable; versions such as the 6805 combine processor, memory, input/output ports and A/D conversion on a single chip. the ZILOG Z-80 family includes such a processor which allows programming to be carried out in BASIC and is suitable for many control and logging applications. The Z-80 and related family have extremely large instruction sets which make then more flexible, but more difficult to program in machine code.

### 3.4 Results

#### 3.4.1 *Data Collected with a Hardwired Data-logger*

*Figure 9* illustrates typical kinetic data collected from a pH stat. Curve (a) shows the kinetics of hydrolysis of the substrate benzylpenicillin catalysed by staphylococcal $\beta$-lactamase. Curve (b) shows the non-linear reactivation kinetics observed when the enzyme is inactivated by the synthetic penicillin quinacillin and then diluted into an excess of benzylpenicillin. A model (21) has been fitted to the data (continuous lines). Curve (c) shows a non-linear baseline presumably caused by spontaneous hydrolysis of substrate in the absence of enzyme, uptake of carbon dioxide from the air and electrode disequilibration. This baseline is subtracted from curves (a) and (b) before calculations of initial and final velocities are made. These calculations are readily carried out by a computer once the problem of collecting the many data samples has been solved.

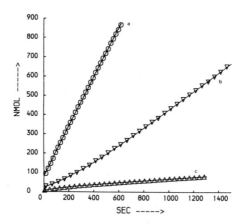

**Figure 9.** Kinetic data collected with the pH stat for benzylpenicillin hydrolysis catalysed by $\beta$-lactamase.(**a**) Normal enzyme. (**b**) Inactivated enzyme. (**c**) Control, no enzyme.

## 4. DISCUSSION

The advantages of being able to manipulate data within the memory of a micro-computer have led to the development of a variety of data-logging methods. The electronic and software designs discussed in Section 3 introduce the reader to some of the complexities and rewards of data-logging. The technology of digital electronics and software design is one of the most rapidly expanding fields. This means that detailed electronic design such as the hardwired data-logger discussed previously, are rapidly outmoded and superseded by more compact designs with more powerful features. This fact has to be accepted by the user who has to solve a particular problem without waiting to see what the next generation of electronic devices will bring.

Many types of laboratory equipment now incorporate data-logging systems as standard items and it is becoming commonplace for new models of electronic equipment to include an output port for data transfer to an external computer. However, many users will have non-standard requirements or may wish to collect data from outdated but functional instruments with conventional analogue outputs.

We have shown that once the basic data-logging problem has been defined, it is not difficult to design a solution to it. The solution may be of several levels of complexity, depending on the expertise of the designer. It is hoped that the algorithms and designs presented will be of use to readers with these requirements. On a cautionary note however, often a long period elapses between defining a problem and putting the solution into routine use. This is usually because a new design must be rigorously tested at every stage of development. This requires many man-hours and may often lead to the re-design of particular portions of the project.

## 5. ACKNOWLEDGEMENTS

This work was supported by a grant from the Science and Engineering Research Council. We are grateful to Mr. G.J. Flannagan, Department of Medical Physics, University of Newcastle-upon-Tyne, for advice on electronics.

## 6. REFERENCES

1   Gardenhire,L.W. (1964) *ISA J.,* **11(4)**, 59.
2.  Lam,H.Y.-F. (1979) *Analog and Digital Filters: Design and Realisation*, published by Prentice Hall, Englewood Clifts, NJ, USA.
3.  Hamming,R.W. (1977) *Digital Filters,* published by Prentice Hall, Englewood Clifts, NJ, USA.
4.  Lieber,R.L., Roos,K.P., Lubell,B.A., Cline,J.W. and Baskin,R.J. (1983) *IEEE Trans. Biomed. Eng.,* Vol. BME-30, No. 1, p. 50.
5.  Cooke,D., Craven,A.H. and Clarke,G.M. 61982) *Basic Statistical Computing,* published by Macmillan Press, London.
6.  Lynn,P.A. (1973) *An Introduction to the Analysis and Processing of Signals*, published by Macmillan Press, London.
7.  Carr,J. (1976) *OP-Amp Circuit Design and Applications*, published by Foulsham-Tab Ltd., Slough.
8.  Savitzky,A. and Golay,M.J.E. (1964) *Anal. Chem.,* **36**, 1628.
9.  Pearson,E.S. and Hartley,H.O. (1964) *Biometrika Tables for Statisticians,* Vol. **1**, published by Cambridge University Press, Cambridge, UK.
10. Davies,O.L. and Goldsmith,P.L. (1980) *Statistical Methods in Research and Production*, published by Longman Group Ltd., London.

11. Van der Molen,J.N. and de Kramer,J.J. (1978) *Med. Biol. Eng. Comput.*, **16**, 564.
12. Spragg,S.P. (1967) *Anal. Chim. Acta*, **38**, 137.
13. Cox,J.R.,Jr. (1965) in *Computers in Biomedical Research*, Vol. **2**, Stacy,R.W. and Waxman, B.D. (eds.), Academic Press, New York, p. 67.
14. Winston,P.H. (1979) *Artificial Intelligence*, published by Addison-Wesley Publ. Co., Reading, MA, USA.
15. Abenstein,J.P. (1981) in *Design of Microcomputer-Based Medical Instrumentation*, Tompkins, W.J. and Webster,J.G. (eds.), Prentice Hall, Englewood Clifts, NJ, USA, p. 345.
16. Furno,G.S. and Tompkins,W.J. (1983) *IEEE Trans. Biomed. Eng.,* Vol. BME-30(4), 234.
17. Motorola M6805 HMOS M146805 CMOS (1983) *Family Computer/Microprocessor Users' Manual*, published by Prentice Hall, Englewood Clifts, NJ, USA.
18. Warner,B.D., Boehme,G., Urdea,M.S., Pool,K.H. and Legg,J.I. (1980) *Anal. Biochem.,* **106**, 175.
19. Pain,R.H. and Virden,R. (1979) in *Beta-Lactamases*, Smith,J.T. and Hamilton-Miller,J.M.T. (eds.), Academic Press, London, p. 141
20. Duggleby,R.G. (1981) *Anal. Biochem.,* **110**, 9.
21. Ainslie,G.R., Shill,J.P. and Neet,K.E. (1972) *J. Biol. Chem.,* **247**, 7088.

# APPENDIX

## Program listings

**Listing 1.** Moving average lowpass filter.

```
10   REM . PROGRAM 1
20   REM . MOVING AVERAGE LOWPASS FILTER
30   DIM XS(100)
40   K = 5
50   INPUT X
60   Y = X
70   FOR I = 1 TO K - 1
80   XS(I) = XS(I + 1)
90   Y = Y + XS(I)
100  NEXT I
110  XS(K) = X
120  PRINT Y
130  GOTO 50
```

**Listing 2.** Weighted moving average lowpass filter.

```
10   REM . PROGRAM 2
20   REM . WEIGHTED MOVING AVERAGE LOWPASS FILTER
30   X1 = 0:X2 = 0
40   INPUT X
50   Y = (X + 2 * X1 + X2) / 4
60   PRINT Y
70   X2 = X1:X1 = X
80   GOTO 40
```

**Listing 3.** Quadratic/cubic least-squares smoothing.

```
10   REM . PROGRAM 3
20   REM . QUADRATIC/CUBIC LEAST SQUARES SMOOTHING
30   DIM X(1000),Y(1000)
40   INPUT "NUMBER OF SAMPLES ";M
50   FOR N = 1 TO M
60   INPUT X(N)
70   NEXT N
80   REM . UNSMOOTHED FIRST POINTS
```

```
90 Y(1) = X(1):Y(2) = X(2)
100 REM . SMOOTHED POINTS
110 FOR N = 3 TO M - 2
120 Y(N) = ( - 3 * X(N - 2) + 12 * X(N - 1) + 17 * X(N) + 12 * X(
    N + 1) - 3 * X(N + 2)) / 35
130 NEXT N
140 REM  UNSMOOTHED LAST POINTS
150 Y(M - 1) = X(M - 1):Y(M) = X(M)
160 FOR N = 1 TO M
170 PRINT Y(N)
180 NEXT N
```

**Listing 4.** Recursive lowpass filter.

```
10 REM . PROGRAM 4
20 REM . RECURSIVE LOWPASS FILTER
30 A = 9: REM . ANY POSITIVE INTEGER
40 B = A + 1
50 Y0 = 0:X0 = 0
60 INPUT X
70 Y = A / B * Y0 + X0
80 Y0 = Y:X0 = X
90 PRINT Y
100 GOTO 60
```

**Listing 5.** Recursive highpass filter.

```
10 REM . PROGRAM 5
20 REM . RECURSIVE HIGHPASS FILTER
30 A = 9: REM . ANY POSITIVE INTEGER
40 B = A + 1
50 Y0 = 0:X0 = 0
60 INPUT X
70 Y = - A / B * Y0 + X - X0
80 Y0 = Y:X0 = X
90 PRINT Y
100 GOTO 60
```

**Listing 6.** Recursive bandpass filter.

```
10 REM . PROGRAM 6
20 REM . RECURSIVE BANDPASS FILTER
30 DIM XS(100)
40 K = 12: REM  ANY POSITIVE INTEGER WITHIN DIM XS
50 INPUT X
60 FOR I = 0 TO K - 1
70 XS(I) = XS(I + 1)
80 NEXT I
90 XS(K) = X
100 Y0 = Y1
110 Y1 = Y2
120 Y2 = - Y0 + X - XS(0)
130 PRINT Y2
140 GOTO 50
```

**Listing 7.** Quadratic least-squares first derivative.

```
10   REM . PROGRAM 7
20   REM . QUADRATIC LEAST SQUARES FIRST DERIVATIVE
30   DIM X(1000),Y(1000)
40   INPUT "INTERVAL BETWEEN SUCCESSIVE SAMPLES ";T
50   INPUT "NUMBER OF SAMPLES ";M
60   FOR N = 1 TO M
70   INPUT X(N)
80   NEXT N
90   REM . ASSIGN ZERO TO FIRST POINTS
100  Y(1) = 0:Y(2) = 0
110   REM . CALCULATE FIRST DERIVATIVE
120   FOR N = 3 TO M - 2
130  Y(N) = ( - 2 * X(N - 2) - X(N - 1) + X(N + 1) + 2 * X(N + 2))
     / 10 / T
140   NEXT N
150   REM . ASSIGN ZERO TO LAST POINTS
160  Y(M - 1) = 0:Y(M) = 0
170   FOR N = 1 TO M
180   PRINT Y(N)
190   NEXT N
```

**Listing 8.** pH stat.

```
0005 REM ..............................................
0010 REM ....PHSTAT. LOAD AND REDUCE DATA
0015 REM ..............................................
0020 REM ....ARRAYS
0025 REM .    D       DATA FOR SMOOTHING
0030 REM .    Y       REDUCED DATA (TITRANT, NMOL)
0035 REM .    X       REDUCED DATA (TIME, S)
0040 REM ....SIMPLE VARIABLES (CURRENT VALUES SHOWN BY [ ])
0045 REM ....PHSTAT CONSTANTS
0050 REM .    N       MEMORY SIZE [1024]
0055 REM .    T0      TIME INTERVAL IN S [5]
0060 REM .    C0      BURETTE SCALE IN PULSE/ML [24000]
0065 REM .    A1      PIA DATA REGISTER ADDRESS [32798=$801E]
0070 REM ....EXPERIMENTAL VALUES
0075 REM .    T$      TITLE
0080 REM .    C1      TITRANT CONCN., MOLAR
0085 REM .    S0      SCALE FACTOR
0090 REM ....FOR CHECKING AND REDUCING DATA
0095 REM .    A2      START ADDRESS FOR STORAGE OF 2-BYTE WORDS
0100 REM .    C2      FACTOR FOR REACTION RATE
0105 REM .    D1-D2   DATA VALUES OR FIRST DERIVATIVE
0110 REM .    I2      ADDRESS OFFSET USED IN SMOOTHING
0115 REM .    J1      STEP BETWEEN REDUCED DATA
0120 REM .    N1      NUMBER OF REDUCED DATA
0125 REM .    N2-N4   DATA ADDRESS INDICES
0130 REM .    Z1      ZERO-CROSS COUNT
0135 REM ....MISCELLANEOUS VARIABLES
0140 REM .    I,J,K   LOOP INDICES
0145 REM .    Q1-Q2   OPTION SWITCHES
0150 REM .    O       CURRENT OUTPUT PORT
0155 REM .    O1      CONTROL PORT [1]
0160 REM .    O2      ALTERNATIVE OUTPUT PORT [7]
0165 REM ..............................................
0170 REM ....SET CONSTANTS
0175 REM ..............................................
0180 DIM D(5),X(100),Y(100)
0185 LET A1=32798:A2=24576:N=1024:T0=5:C1=24000:O1=1:O2=7
0190 LET A2=A2-1:GO TO 555
0195 REM ..............................................
0200 REM ....LOAD DATA FROM PHSTAT
0205 REM ..............................................
0210 PRINT "*LOAD FROM PHSTAT"
0215 REM .    INITIALIZE PORT
0220 POKE( A1+1,0): POKE(A1,0): POKE(A1+1,4)
0225 REM .    LOAD DATA
0230 FOR I=1 TO N
0235 POKE( A1+1,62): REM....CNTRL LINE HIGH
0240 LET D1=PEEK(A1): REM....DATUM FROM PORT
0245 POKE( A2+2*I,D1): REM....STORE DATUM
0250 POKE( A1+1,54): REM....CNTRL LINE LOW
0255 NEXT I
0260 POKE( A1+1,4): REM....CNTRL LINE TO HIGH IMPEDANCE
0265 REM ....INPUT EXPERIMENTAL VARIABLES
0270 PRINT "TITRANT (MOLAR) ";: INPUT C0
```

```
0275 PRINT "SCALE FACTOR     ";: INPUT S0
0280 PRINT "TITLE            ";: INPUT T$
0285 REM ....................................................
0290 REM ....CHECK RAW DATA
0295 REM ....................................................
0300 PRINT "*ERROR TEST"
0305 GOSUB 635
0310 LET D2=0: Z1=0: N1=0: N2=0: N3=1: E1=0
0315 FOR I=N TO 1 STEP -1
0320 IF PEEK (A2+2*I)=0 THEN 330
0325 LET N2=I: GO TO 340
0330 NEXT I
0335 STOP : REM....NO DATA
0340 FOR I=1 TO N2
0345 LET D1=PEEK(A2+2*I)
0350 IF Q1=1 THEN PRINT D1;
0355 IF D1<D2 THEN 370
0360 IF D1<=D2+63 THEN 385
0365 PRINT "*ERROR AT ";I;"*": E1=E1+1: N3=I: GO TO 385
0370 IF D1+256>D2+63 THEN 365
0375 IF I<N3+5 THEN 365
0380 LET Z1=Z1+1
0385 LET D2=D1: POKE(A2+2*I-1,Z1)
0390 NEXT I
0395 GOSUB 695
0400 REM ....................................................
0405 REM ....DATA REDUCTION AND OPTIONAL SMOOTHING
0410 REM ....................................................
0415 PRINT "*REDUCE DATA"
0420 PRINT "SMOOTH OFF (0): ON (1): ";: INPUT Q2
0425 IF Q2=1 THEN 435
0430 IF Q2<>0 THEN 420
0435 PRINT "FROM ";: INPUT N3: PRINT "TO ";: INPUT N4
0440 PRINT "STEP ";: INPUT J1: IF J1<1 THEN 560
0445 LET N1=INT((N4-N3)/J1)+1: IF N1<1 THEN 560
0450 LET N4=N3+(N1-1)*J1
0455 IF N3<1+2*Q2 THEN N3=1+2*Q2: GO TO 445
0460 IF N4>N2-2*Q2 THEN N1=N1-1: GO TO 450
0465 IF N3>N4 THEN 555
0470 LET N1=0
0475 GOSUB 635
0480 IF Q1=1 THEN PRINT "POINT NO.","TIME (S)","NMOL","NMOL/S"
0485 LET C2=S0*C0/C1*1E6
0490 FOR I=N3 TO N4 STEP J1: I2=A2+2*(I-3): D2=0
0495 FOR K=1 TO 5
0500 LET D(K)=PEEK(I2+2*K)+256*PEEK(I2+2*K-1)
0505 NEXT K
0510 IF I<3 THEN 520
0515 IF I<N2-1 THEN D2=(-2*D(1)-D(2)+D(4)+2*D(5))/10*C2/T0
0520 IF Q2=0 THEN D1=D(3)*C2: GO TO 530
0525 LET D1=(-3*D(1)+12*D(2)+17*D(3)+12*D(4)-3*D(5))/35*C2
0530 LET N1=N1+1: Y(N1)=D1: X(N1)=T0*I
0535 IF Q1=1 THEN PRINT I,X(N1),Y(N1),D2
0540 NEXT I
0545 GOTO 570
0550 REM ....................................................
0555 REM ....SELECT OPTION
0560 REM ....................................................
0565 LET N1=0: REM....ENTRY POINT TO SUPPRESS REDUCED DATA
0570 GOSUB 695: REM.... ENTRY POINT TO RETAIN REDUCED DATA
0575 PRINT "*SELECT OPTION"
0580 PRINT "   1.   DATA REDUCTION"
0585 PRINT "   2.   CURVE FIT"
0590 PRINT "   3.   DISPLAY"
0595 PRINT "   4.   SAVE (TAPE/DISK)"
0600 PRINT "   5.   LOAD (TAPE/DISK)"
0605 PRINT "   6.   LOAD (PHSTAT)"
0610 INPUT Q1
0615 IF Q1<1 THEN 575
0620 IF Q1>6 THEN 575
0625 ON Q1 GO TO 405,1000,3000,4000,5000,200
0630 REM ....................................................
0635 REM ....OUTPUT OPTION SUBROUTINE
0640 REM ....................................................
0645 PRINT "SUMMARY (0): FULL (1):";: INPUT Q1
0650 IF Q1=1 THEN 660
0655 IF Q1<>0 THEN 645
0660 PRINT "OUTPUT PORT ";O1;" OR ";O2;: INPUT O
0665 IF O=O1 THEN 675
0670 IF O<>O2 THEN 660
0675 PORT= O
0680 RETURN
0685 REM
0690 REM ....................................................
0695 REM ....DATA SUMMARY SUBROUTINE
0700 REM ....................................................
0705 PORT= 0: PRINT
0710 PRINT T$: PRINT "TITRANT ";C0;" M"
0715 PRINT "SCALE FACTOR = ";S0
0720 PRINT "DATA END AT ";N2
0725 PRINT "ZERO CROSSES = ";Z1
```

```
0730 PRINT "ERRORS = ";E1
0735 IF N1=0 THEN 755
0740 PRINT N1;"DATA IN ARRAYS X,Y ";
0745 IF Q2=1 THEN PRINT "SMOOTHED ";
0750 PRINT "FROM POINT ";N3;"TO ";N4;"STEP ";J1
0755 PRINT : PRINT: PRINT: PORT=01
0760 RETURN
0765 REM ...................................................
0770 REM ....ENTRY POINTS FOR OTHER ROUTINES
0775 REM ...................................................
1000 REM ....CURVE FIT PROGRAM
2990 GOTO 570
2995 REM ...................................................
3000 REM ....DISPLAY PROGRAM
3390 GOTO 570
3395 REM ...................................................
4000 REM ....SAVE T$, CO, SO, 8-BIT DATA VALUES
4490 GOTO 570
4495 REM ...................................................
5000 REM ....LOAD T$, CO, SO, 8-BIT DATA VALUES
5990 LET N1=0: GO TO 290
5995 END
```

# CHAPTER 4

# Graphical Techniques with Microcomputers

## G.A. PLACE and R.J. BEYNON

## 1. INTRODUCTION

The graphical facilities of microcomputers have contributed immensely to their growing popularity in scientific, educational, business and home environments. Initial encounters with computer graphics often involve rescue of the world from marauding invaders but this aspect of computing has more serious applications. One such application is the subject of this chapter. The presentation of data in a pictorial rather than a tabulated manner permits more rapid assimilation of information and assessment of trends in data. In this respect the processing power of the microcomputer, complemented by its graphics capability, permits rapid and error-free preparation and display of data in a graphical fashion. The aim of this chapter is to provide a series of routines that enable numerical data to be represented in several commonly used graphical formats.

## 2. OVERVIEW OF MICROCOMPUTER GRAPHICS

### 2.1 Resolution

Two of the most common methods of displaying a graphical image on a VDU are:

(i)   vector refreshed displays;
(ii)  raster scan displays.

In the vector refreshed display the electron beam moves directly from one point on the phosphor-coated screen to the next, tracing a continuous line in the process. The sequence of points that are to be joined are stored in a display file and are interpreted by a display processor that translates the commands into deflections of the electron beam. The display processor assumes much of the computational overhead which permits real time graphics and animation (animation requires a refresh rate, or rate of re-drawing of the image, of at least 30 Hz to give the appearance of continuous movement). The vector refreshed display is costly and requires sophisticated programming techniques. Consequently, it is not offered by single-user microcomputer systems.

Raster scan display systems are standard on all microcomputer systems presently available; mainly because the video image is designed to be displayed on a domestic television which uses raster scan techniques to generate a picture. Briefly, the picture is generated and refreshed continually by scanning the electron beam at a fixed rate through a pattern of horizontal lines over the whole of the picture area, irrespective of the information that is being displayed. Thus, the same raster scan is employed if the screen is completely dark or completely bright; the fluctuation of the beam intensity signal is the only determinant of this property of the display.

Because of the need to refresh the screen image during each complete cycle (at speeds of 25 – 30 Hz), it is preferable to maintain a complete copy of the image that can be used to generate the video display. This is achieved most readily by the use of semiconductor memory which retains or 'maps' the video image, hence the term 'memory mapped graphics'. Obviously, the user must be able to alter the image, and therefore the map, which means that the memory must be RAM.

The major advantage of memory mapped video displays is the ease with which the binary RAM image, and thus the picture can be altered. For example, to clear the screen to black it may be necessary to set every bit to 0 requiring a simple loop to write decimal 0 to every byte in the video RAM. The requirements for such a memory mapped technique differ, depending upon the need for display of text and/or graphics.

Textual displays typically comprise 24 lines consisting of 40 or 80 characters per line. In pure text displays, each character position is mapped by a single byte in RAM, the contents of this byte dictating the character that is displayed in that position. The video display circuitry first scans through the map and then, depending on the code (normally ASCII) of the character to be displayed, triggers an integrated circuit called a character generator to produce the appropriate video signals corresponding to that code. Each character is displayed on the screen in a 'cell' consisting of 5 x 7, 5 x 9 or 8 x 8 individual points but only one byte of memory is needed to specify each character. Thus text displays of 24 x 40 characters or 24 x 80 characters require 960 or 1920 bytes respectively to map the entire screen.

Text displays are economical in the amount of memory needed to map the screen image because each byte is only capable of specifying a maximum of 256 ($2^8$) possible characters; notably upper and lower case alphanumeric, punctuation and block and symbol characters. This maximum of 256 characters represents a very small subset of the total number of characters that can be displayed in an 8 x 8 matrix (even though most of them will be unrecognisable as characters). The economy of memory usage is therefore achieved by restriction of the dot patterns that are theoretically available. Thus, text displays cannot produce readily superscripted or subscripted characters; each character must be restricted to the vertical and horizontal position dictated by the limited memory map.

Clearly, if the information content of the graphic display is to surpass that of the text display there must be programmable control of dot patterns in a far less restricted manner. The type of display that is required demands greater control over individual picture elements (pixels) and at a higher resolution than the 24 x 40 or 80 points that can be offered by an alphanumeric VDU.

Microcomputer graphical displays are usually offered with a resolution of between $2^7$ (128) and $2^9$ (512) pixels square. Each pixel requires a minimum of 1 bit to specify its status (e.g., 1 = bright, 0 = dark). A minimal total of $x.y$ bits are therefore needed to map a simple graphical output which is $x$ pixels wide and $y$

pixels high. For example, a display of 256 x 256 pixels demands a memory map of size 65 536 bits (i.e., 8192 bytes or 8k).

Further incursions into RAM are needed for more complex displays. In the example above, each pixel possessed the single attribute of status (on or off). A more complex display containing colour or grey scale information causes the memory overheads to rise dramatically. A pixel that can assume four different properties such as colour or grey scale must be mapped at the minimal rate of 2 bits/pixel; the four values of the two bits (00, 01, 10, 11) yielding one of the four colours or grey levels. As a consequence of the need to display this additional information, the memory map has increased from $x.y$ bits to $2x.y$ bits.

The cost of semiconductor memory is now sufficiently low that it is no longer a significant factor in determining the graphics facilities that are incorporated into a microcomputer system. Addressing range is however a major consideration. The currently popular 8-bit microprocessors possess a 16-bit address range from 0000 0000 0000 0000 (decimal 0) to 1111 1111 1111 1111 (decimal 65 536) and can therefore utilise a maximum of 64k of RAM. An eight colour graphical display at a resolution of 256 pixels square must be mapped into 256 x 256 x 3 bits (24k) of RAM. This represents a significant portion of the total 64k and partitions RAM away from system software (e.g., operating systems, language interpreters, input/output control) and user programs. Because of this restriction the majority of 8-bit microcomputer systems offer medium resolution graphics ($\sim$ 256 x 256) with limited colour facilities as a compromise to the antagonistic demands on addressable memory. *Figure 1* indicates the effect of resolution on the quality of the image that is produced.

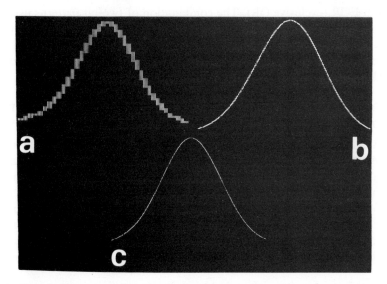

**Figure 1**. VDU displays of identical curves plotted at three different resolutions of **(a)** 40 x 40, **(b)** 160 x 256 and **(c)** 280 x 192 pixels to illustrate the effect of this parameter on the quality of the image produced.

## 2.2 **Graphics Software**

Software support for graphics facilities ranges from highly developed plotting to primitive functions. Any system that allows for graphical displays will provide a number of 'primitives' that include point plotting and vector generation. The first, of the form "PLOT x,y", may also permit repositioning of the graphics cursor (the position where the next point PLOT command would draw a pixel) so that "PLOT x,y to x',y'" and "PLOT to x,y" are both valid forms of line drawing commands. Some systems implement these 'primitives' using "MOVE x,y" and "DRAW x,y" commands; MOVE repositions the graphics cursor to *x,y*; DRAW draws a line from the current graphics cursor to *x,y*. Any graphics facility can be implemented in monochrome using these two 'primitives' (strictly, just using a point plotting routine) and can be written in a high level language. More frequently, and consequential upon software development for microprocessors, the BASIC interpreter includes additional commands that aid the production of graphical displays to varying extents. Most commonly found are the commands that permit the generation of regular structures, such as circles, and include facilities for filling or shading shapes which may be either regular in outline (e.g., triangle) or irregular. For example, to draw a circle in a high level language such as BASIC requires computation of trigonometric values at a resolution (9 digit) that is far in excess of the resolution of the screen. Floating point evaluation of trigonometric functions is a time-consuming process (typically 24 msec to calculate a sine or cosine) and although circle drawing can be performed without frequent reference to such functions (see Section 3.6), low level machine code calculations can offer dramatic increases in the speed of such computations.

A facility that is occasionally provided in bit-mapped graphics displays allows the overwriting of one image by a second, using logical operations such as OR, AND and EOR (exclusive OR). The combination of two bit patterns using these operators can produce effects which allow one pattern to appear to pass over a second or which allow an image to appear as the inverse of the background, ensuring for example that white text on a black background switches to black text when the background changes to white.

## 3. SUBROUTINES FOR GRAPHICAL DISPLAY ON THE APPLE II MICROCOMPUTER

It is virtually impossible to write programs generating graphical display that will run directly on every type of machine. However, since point plotting and line drawing form the basis of all graphical routines, and they are features provided by all microcomputers offering high resolution graphics, the translation of code from one dialect to another should not present too onerous a task. The programs described here are written in Applesoft BASIC to run on an Apple II Plus microcomputer. We have attempted to write the main routines in as general a fashion as possible enabling them to be used with other machines after only minor alterations.

All graphical subroutines are listed in Appendix A. Provided with each listing is a short description of its function and the variables used. The line numbering convention adopted permits some or all of the routines to be used in the same application program without any conflict of line numbers. The main aim was to develop a series of general subroutines that perform simple control operations, such as setting background colours, in addition to more sophisticated tasks like scaling and graphing. This approach limits the duplication of effort that occurs when similar but not identical routines are required for different application programs. In order to illustrate operation of the graphics routines Appendix B contains a number of short example programs that were used to produce many of the figures in this chapter.

## 3.1 Apple Graphics Facilities

### 3.1.1 *Memory Map*

The Apple has two areas of memory that can be used for high resolution graphics, they are Pages 1 and 2. These reside in the middle of free RAM ($\sim$36k) on a 48k system incorporating disc drives (*Figure 2*). In operation each graphics page requires 8k of memory and selection of either clears the contents of the corresponding area of RAM and erases the corresponding image. Between LOMEM and the bottom of Page 1, approximately 6k of memory are available for programs and variable storage. Programs may run into the area of RAM that doubles as the display area for Page 1 but if this graphics page is used at any time then erasure of part of the program will occur. The obvious solution to this problem is to use Page 2 for graphics display, releasing 14k of user memory between LOMEM and the bottom of the page. Further problems occur with longer pro-

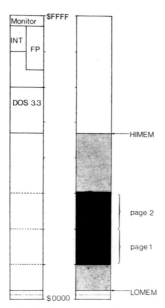

**Figure 2.** The Apple memory map indicating the two 8k areas of RAM utilised to map the high resolution graphics pages. Normally approximately 36k of contiguous user RAM is available on a 48k system which is further reduced to 20k if both graphics pages are in operation.

grams. Loading an 18k program from LOMEM upwards means it will extend right across Page 1 and 4k into Page 2. Now, invoking either of the graphics pages obliterates large sections of the program. One way round this is to relocate LOMEM, usually just above Page 1 providing 22k of RAM available between LOMEM and HIMEM and in addition a graphics page (Page 1) for display purposes.

Relocation of LOMEM is most easily achieved by execution of a series of POKEs using direct commands before the graphics program is loaded. *Listing 1* is a short routine that will move LOMEM above graphics Page 1 and also provides the necessary addresses for relocation above Page 2 if both graphics pages are required. This method makes the 6k of memory from the default for LOMEM to Page 1 unavailable for programs or variables, although this area can still be used for machine code routines or data storage using direct memory access instructions (PEEK and POKE). In fact it is possible to split long BASIC programs to load partly below and above specific areas in memory but the techniques for doing this are beyond the scope of this chapter.

### 3.1.2 *Resolution and Colour*

Both graphics pages yield a maximum resolution of 280 x 192 pixels. Each of the 192 horizontal lines of the screen is mapped in memory by 40 bytes. The first seven bits of each byte correspond to seven consecutive pixels on the screen, hence there are only 280 columns of dots rather than 320. The eighth bit dictates which colour group (see below) is selected for that byte and is not displayed. When drawing using just black and white the pixels whose corresponding bits are 'on' (or set equal to 1) appear white and conversely bits which are 'off' (equal to 0) display black pixels. With colour graphics the situation is more complex.

The discussion of memory mapping in Section 2.1 indicated that a system supporting an eight colour graphical display at a resolution similar to the Apple would require 24k of RAM for graphics purposes. However, the Apple offers such a specification and yet uses only 8k of memory. This is only achieved by making several compromises which severely restrict the flexibility of Apple colour graphics. In practice only six different colours are available and these are divided into two groups:

| *Group 1* | *Group 2* |
|-----------|-----------|
| Black 1 | Black 2 |
| White 1 | White 2 |
| Violet | Blue |
| Green | Orange |

As mentioned above, the colour group to be used within each byte mapping seven pixels of the graphics screen is selected by the eighth most significant bit (msb). If it is 'off' (equal to 0) group 1 colours are utilised whereas setting this bit equal to 1 allows the use of the group 2 complement. When plotting, any bit that is 'off' will result in its corresponding pixel being displayed as black, irrespective of which colour group is in operation. If a bit is 'on' the displayed colour of the pixel depends on its position on the screen. For example, assume that the msb of

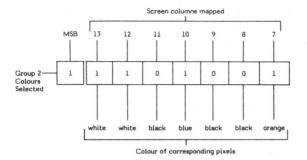

**Figure 3.** Illustration of the effects on pixel colour of switching mapping bits 'on' or 'off'.

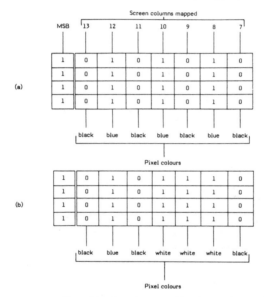

**Figure 4.** One of the many anomalies of Apple colour graphics. Part of a graphics screen cleared to blue is illustrated in the bit pattern shown in **(a)**. Attempting to draw an orange vertical line through column nine results in the display of a white line three pixels wide. This is because consecutive bits turned 'on' will always make corresponding pixels appear white. More exotic effects such as zebra stripes and colour flips can be generated when drawing non-horizontal coloured lines across coloured fields.

a particular byte is set equal to 1, thus selecting group 2 colours. If the pixel is in any even-numbered column (including 0) it will appear blue and if it is in any odd-numbered column it will appear orange. Furthermore, switching 'on' two consecutive display bits (even from different bytes) results in the two corresponding pixels appearing white (*Figure 3*). If the undisplayed bit was switched 'off' then blue and orange would be replaced by violet and green respectively. This arrangement means that within one byte it is impossible to have colours from group 1 and group 2 present.

This method of colour generation is economical in its use of memory but can produce some unusual and often unwanted effects. For instance, a screen cleared to blue will in fact consist of alternate blue and black columns. The situation is exacerbated when lines are drawn across coloured fields (*Figure 4*). Because of these unwanted effects, black and white are available in group 2 as well as in group 1. Group 1 black and white cause fewer problems when used with green and violet than do black and white from the second group; the converse is true when using orange and blue. The anomalous behaviour of Apple colour graphics means that certain applications are not well-suited to use of this facility. This is the case with the graphical displays described here and consequently all drawing routines utilise black and white exclusively. Many microcomputers do not impose the same limitations on colour as the Apple and the reader is encouraged to make full use of this facility whenever possible.

### 3.1.3 *Graphics Commands*

Applesoft commands controlling high resolution graphics are very limited and comprise a small section of the language. For convenience a list of all the Applesoft graphics instructions used in the routines described here is shown in *Table 1*. Many of these commands will have analogous counterparts (see Section 2.2) in other languages or dialects of BASIC which should aid translation for use on other machines. Note that Applesoft does not permit plotting out of bounds (e.g., $x<0$) and any attempt to do so results in program error. Hence graph drawing routines must test for points out of range and act on them accordingly. Although this is not the case for all microcomputers, testing for off-screen points is good practice.

A peculiarity of Apple graphics is the incorporation of a non-standard $y$-axis. This axis is inverted with $y=0$ located at the top of the screen and $y=191$ at the bottom. Obviously this could lead to confusion when plotting graphs since we expect the origin to be positioned at the bottom-left rather than top-left. Hence, an inversion statement must be included in graph drawing routines to correct $y$-values for plotting in standard orientation (see Section 3.3).

### 3.2 **Graphics Initialisation**

The high resolution graphics pages possessed by the Apple can assume several configurations. The default on selection of Page 1 is to display a partial

**Table 1.** Apple Graphics Commands.

| Applesoft instruction | Function |
| --- | --- |
| HGR | Selects high resolution graphics Page 1. Default condition is partial graphics/text. |
| HGR2 | Selects high resolution graphics Page 2. |
| HPLOT x,y | Plots a point with Cartesian co-ordinates $x,y$. |
| HPLOT x,y TO x',y' | Draws a straight line between points specified by co-ordinates $x,y$ and $x',y'$. |
| HCOLOR = a | Sets colour to be used for plotting (a = 0 – 7). |
| POKE-16302,0 | Sets full screen graphics display. |
| POKE-16301,0 | Sets screen to partial graphics/text display. |
| CALL 62454 | Clears graphics screen to colour last used for plotting. |

graphics/text screen which permits four lines of text to be displayed at the bottom of the screen. Switching Page 1 to full screen graphics or Page 2 to partial screen is possible by referencing specific memory locations (soft switches). Soft switches can also function to clear the graphics screens to white or black (or any high resolution colour). Since the correct addresses are often difficult to remember a routine covering all options has obvious advantages. *Listing 2* is a graphics initialisation subroutine that will act on a command string G$. The string must be six characters long and of the format:

$$G\$ = \text{``P2/P/B''}$$
$$G\$ = \text{``P1/F/W''}$$

The first example specifies graphics Page 2, partial graphics/text and clears the screen to black, while the second example displays Page 1, full screen, cleared to white. If a screen is cleared to white, plotting occurs in black and *vice versa*. The subroutine checks for errors in the syntax of the command string and will indicate any by sounding a diagnostic 'bell'. Clearly this routine will only run on the Apple but many other types of microcomputers offer several modes of graphics display and this example should provide a few hints on how to set up an initialisation program. It is important to note that once this routine is written, specific memory locations do not need to be recalled.

### 3.3 Scaling

A primary consideration of all graphical routines is the scaling of the limits of the numerical values of the data set to screen limits. The problem is how to convert real co-ordinates (variables XX, YY) into screen co-ordinates (variables PX, PY) and plot the transformed data points within a specified area on the screen. Before describing the method of transformation, eight variables must be defined:

*Screen area:* BX − bottom *x* co-ordinate
*Screen area:* BY − bottom *y* co-ordinate
*Screen area:* TX − top *x* co-ordinate
*Screen area:* TY − top *y* co-ordinate
*User area:* LX − lower *x* co-ordinate
*User area:* LY − lower *y* co-ordinate
*User area:* UX − upper *x* co-ordinate
*User area:* UY − upper *y* co-ordinate

The conversion of XX into a valid PX is given by:

$$PX = \frac{(XX - LX)}{(UX - LX)} \cdot (TX - BX) + BX$$

The fraction $(XX - LX)/(UX - LX)$ is the position along the user axis of the point which is then translated into the screen equivalent by multiplying the fraction by $(TX - BX)$ and finally offset by the bottom screen co-ordinate BX. This equation works for both positive and negative numbers.

Calculation of PY values is slightly different because of the inverted y-axis (Section 3.1.3). The problem is overcome by setting the upper and lower screen limits to their Apple values, making TY less than BY. In the routines given here an inversion statement is used that allows visualisation of the y-axis on the Apple screen as having y = 0 in the lower position and y = 191 in the upper position. Of course with other types of microcomputer employing a conventional position at the bottom of the screen for y = 0 the calculation of PY values is straightforward. The conversion of YY into PY is accomplished by:

$$PY = \frac{(YY - LY)}{(UY - LY)} \cdot (TY - BY) + BY$$

Throughout the graph plotting routines given here the user must specify eight variables BX, BY, TX, TY, LX, LY, UX, UY in order to convert a real point XX, YY correctly into a screen point PX,PY.

### 3.4 Cartesian Graph Plotting

This type of presentation, utilising the simple Cartesian co-ordinate system, is probably the most common method of displaying data in graphical format. A set of general graph drawing routines for such displays should fulfill a number of criteria including the ability to draw a graph anywhere on the screen, using any set of boundaries, and the possibility of using multiple graphs on a single screen with simple switching between individual areas. In addition, the physical (real or user) limits of the active graph area should impose no constraints and thus should include negative or positive values.

*Listings 3 – 7* provide the necessary routines to set up a graph plotting area(s), calculate and plot points at appropriate positions and erase selected areas of the screen. When plotting several sets of data on the same graph each group can be assigned a different symbol to aid identification. A total of five symbol types are catered for; point (*Listing 4*), square, circle, triangle and cross (*Listing 5*). When using the latter subroutine, the symbol that is required is selected by setting the variable SY to the appropriate value. Each symbol can extend beyond the screen area by up to two pixels so it is advisable to leave a small margin around any plotting area. Because these subroutines require specification of eight boundary values (Section 3.3) a display consisting of two or more areas that are being plotted, alternately or in sequence, can involve considerable setting and resetting of the limit variables. The multiple area initialisation routine (*Listing 6*) overcomes this problem by allowing the user to set up any number of different graphs on the screen. The required area for plotting is selected by setting the variable AR before calling the subroutine. The drawing routines perform out-of-range checking and a diagnostic 'bell' is sounded on error detection. Finally, when plotting data with values less than 0 the area drawing routine (*Listing 3*) will indicate the origin by drawing a line at the appropriate position.

### 3.4.1 *Plotting Data*

Essentially the protocol consists of setting up the screen and user limits, deciding on a symbol to represent plotted points, obtaining each data point in a loop and finally plotting data by calling the appropriate subroutine. As an example, *Figure 5* was generated by the program documented in *Listing 16*.

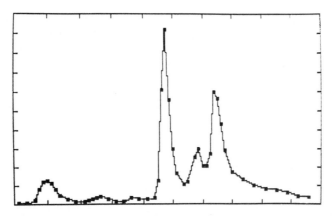

**Figure 5.** Example of the type of display possible when using the graph plotting routines (*Listings 3 – 7*) to exhibit experimental data. This graph of an elution profile was generated using program *Listing 16*.

### 3.4.2 *Plotting a Function*

To draw a function, co-ordinates are calculated over the plotting area rather than being obtained from data supplied by the user. The function has to be plotted between two limits, thus to fill the current screen area plotting from LX to UX would be necessary. The smoothness of the line drawn is dependent on the step size or the number of increments used between the plotting limits. A large step size will produce a dotted line whereas a small step will draw as continuous a curve as is possible on the microcomputer used. However when drawing a continuous line a very shallow or steep section of the curve may appear jagged due to the limited resolution of the graphics screen. Sometimes the display of a curve as a fine dotted line may yield a better quality presentation (*Figure 6*), but this is obviously a matter of personal taste. To plot a function, it is necessary to set up the screen limits, decide on or calculate a step size for the function, obtain a y-value for the current x-value, assign them to YY and XX respectively and then call the point plotting subroutine. This is repeated for each x,y pair. It is feasible to plot other symbols instead of points but this slows down the function drawing considerably. Finally, it is a straightforward process to superimpose experimental data on any line drawn using a function. Normally the function would be fitted to the data using, for example, non-linear curve fitting procedures, to obtain best fit parameters prior to display. *Figure 7*, which was created by program *Listing 17*, illustrates the type of display possible using these routines.

### 3.5 **Histograms**

Although in many instances Cartesian graphs will suffice for the display of data, certain types of information do not lend themselves well to presentation in this manner − for example when displaying an attribute of a group of samples. Histograms or bar charts are much more suitable for grouped data of this nature. As for line graphs several requirements should be met when using microcomputers for drawing histograms. Bars should be able to lie adjacent to each

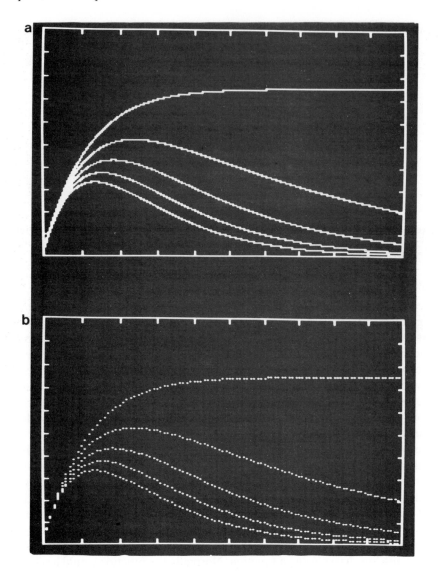

**Figure 6.** The limited resolution of a microcomputer graphics screen prevents plotting of perfectly smooth curves and very shallow or steep sections appear jagged (**a**). The display can sometimes be improved by representing the curve as a fine dotted line (**b**) but detail may be lost (lower left) if the step size on the abscissa is too large.

other or be separated by an interval. It should be possible to group the bars into sets and differentiate individual bars by colour or shading. Finally, calculation of the width of each bar should be performed automatically dependent on the number of groups, bars in each group and whether or not the bars lie adjacent to or separated from their neighbours. All of these specifications are catered for by the two subroutines shown in *Listings 8* and *9*. These subroutines cannot be used

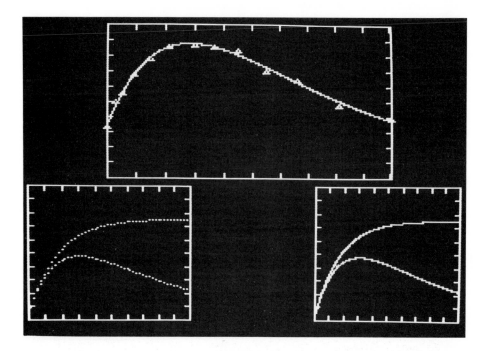

**Figure 7.** This display illustrates the versatility of the graph plotting routines and was generated using program *Listing 17*. Similar functions have been plotted in all three graph areas with experimental data superimposed on the top curve. Switching between individual areas is facilitated by assigning appropriate values to all the necessary limit variables in the multiple area initialisation routine (*Listing 6*).

in isolation but must be used in conjunction with several of the routines described previously. In particular, the graphics initialisation (*Listing 2*) and the area initialisation (*Listing 6*) routines must be resident in memory when using the histogram plotting procedures.

*Listing 8* is the histogram initialisation routine which sets up the plotting area, by drawing an appropriate boundary on the screen, and calculates the width of bar needed for each particular histogram. Plotting area limits are obtained from the multiple area routine (*Listing 6*) and it therefore follows that this subroutine must first be called to supply the parameters (screen and user limits) that are needed to draw the histogram border. With histograms the $x$-axis is divided into an equal number of intervals for bars or the space between bars therefore the value of the LX and UX user limits have no meaning. However, the same plotting area can be used for graphs as well as histograms if these values are retained in the initialisation routine (*Figure 8*).

Bar widths are calculated from the values of the two variables NG and BG. NG specifies the number of groups of bars and BG the number of bars per group. The bars will be drawn adjacent to each other if NG is set to zero.

Subsequent to histogram initialisation the bar plotting subroutine (*Listing 9*) is

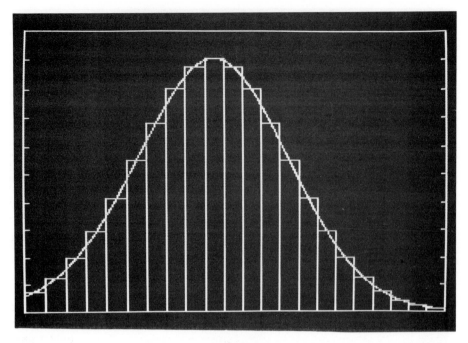

**Figure 8.** A Gaussian distribution represented in histogram format and as a function plotted between the same limits. This display was generated using program *Listing 18* and demonstrates the usefulness of retaining the LX and UX user limits in the multiple area initialisation routine (*Listing 6*) enabling the same plotting area to be used for both graphs and histograms.

called. Several parameters must be provided each time this routine is used:

GN – the group number of the current bar
BN – the bar number within the group
BH – the value of the data corresponding to this bar (bar height)
BC – the colour of the current bar.

Checks are made on the values of GN and BN to make sure that they do not exceed the range specified during initialisation. In addition, the data (BH) is checked to ensure that the bar does not exceed the currently specified limits for the histogram. Identification of individual bars on monochrome monitors can be achieved by filling-in or shading and the bar plotting subroutine caters for four types of shading. Obviously, users with colour monitors have greater scope in this area.

Probably the only limitation imposed on plotting histograms is the number of bars that can be displayed on one chart. Attempting to plot say 10 groups of bars, each containing 15 components will provide a correct histogram but it will appear compressed and will be confusing to interpret. *Figures 8* and *9* were generated using program *Listings 18* and *19* respectively and demonstrate several aspects of the routines.

These subroutines are by no means exhaustive and only allow display of basic histograms but should fulfil requirements in many cases. However, it should be

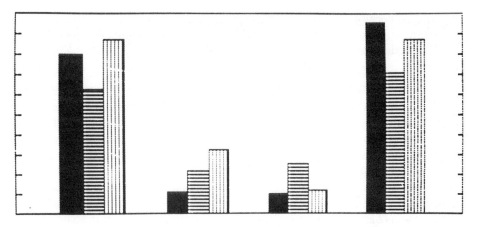

**Figure 9.** A histogram display created by program *Listing 19* illustrating the facilities of bar grouping and differential shading provided for in the histogram drawing routines (*Listings 8* and *9*).

noted that minor modifications would permit horizontal instead of vertical bars to be drawn. A little more thought would allow the user to enhance displays further by incorporating error bars on each column. Finally, the area of a bar can convey information in addition to that given by its height. Obviously this requires display of bars of unequal width which is a facility not catered for in the routines given here although it is certainly not beyond the capabilities of the microcomputer.

## 3.6 Pie Charts

Pie charts fulfil a different role to line graphs and histograms in that data is presented as a fraction of the total of a single variable rather than as a relationship between two different variables. For example, a pie chart would provide a suitable graphical illustration of the contribution of various metabolic pathways to total ATP generation within a cell. Microcomputer routines for displaying pie charts should, as a minimal specification, permit division of the pie into any number of sectors and incorporate a facility for highlighting information of particular interest.

A major computational task involved in the construction of pie charts is plotting the circular perimeter. There are several methods which can be employed to draw circles but only two will be considered here. The first, utilises the equations:

$$x = R.\cos(\theta) \qquad \text{Equation 1}$$
$$y = R.\sin(\theta) \qquad \text{Equation 2}$$

where R is the radius. These equations are used to generate co-ordinates of points on the circumference as $\theta$ is varied between 0 and 360°. The number of points required to plot a smooth curve is dependent on both the resolution of the graphics screen and the radius of the circle. Connecting only 36 equidistant points on the circumference produces surprisingly good, full screen diameter circles on the Apple.

Repeated calculation of sine and cosine values is an inefficient method of draw-

81

ing circles because of the relatively long time taken by microprocessors in evaluating trigonometric functions. This problem can be eliminated by using the trigonometric identities:

$$\cos(a + 1)\theta = \cos(a\theta)\cos(\theta) - \sin(a\theta)\sin(\theta) \qquad \text{Equation 3}$$
$$\sin(a + 1)\theta = \cos(a\theta)\cos(\theta) + \sin(a\theta)\sin(\theta) \qquad \text{Equation 4}$$

for a = 1 to n, where n is the number of points used. Circles can thus be drawn using a simple loop, requiring evaluation of only one sine and cosine before the loop is entered (see *Listing 10*). By this method an increase in plotting speed of up to 3-fold can be achieved over the first method described and therefore it is the technique employed here.

The pie chart drawing routines are documented in *Listings 10 – 14*. They have to be used in conjunction with just one other subroutine, the ubiquitous graphics initialisation (*Listing 2*). Construction of the perimeter of a chart is accomplished by *Listing 10* utilising the relationships described by Equations 3 and 4. The subroutine must be supplied with the screen co-ordinates for the centre of the circle, specified by the variables CX and CY, and a value for the radius, R. Note that no checking for off-screen co-ordinates is performed, since this would reduce the plotting rate significantly, therefore it is essential to choose reasonable values for these three parameters. The resolution (number of points) must also be set external to the subroutine. Also important here is the retention of the co-ordinates of each point on the circumference in two integer arrays, X%(I), Y%(I). This permits subsequent operations, such as sector extraction, to be performed rapidly by accessing the relevant co-ordinates from the array table. The alternative of repeated execution of the circle plotting loop to locate specific sections of the circumference is, by comparison, an operation the microcomputer performs more slowly. Inspection of *Listing 10* indicates that the values of the first elements [X%(0), Y%(0)] of the arrays should be equivalent to the last [X%(N), Y%(N)], but these usually differ slightly due to the approximate value of PI utilised. Any discrepancies are however rarely manifest in the drawing process due to the limited resolution of the screen. It is also apparent that the circle is drawn using N + 1 points which must be taken into consideration when sectoring and manipulating the chart. A possible disadvantage of saving co-ordinates in this manner is the amount of memory required for storage (usually reserved by means of DIM statements early in the program). Each element of an integer array occupies 2 bytes of RAM hence a circle drawn with 100 points would need 400 bytes of memory to store all the co-ordinates. Memory requirements increase accordingly for circles of higher resolution. Allocation of substantial sections of RAM for data storage may not always be tolerable and such circumstances dictate the use of repetitive methods (see above) for the preparation of pie charts. When drawing several charts in succession it is necessary to execute the circle plotting routine (*Listing 10*) only once, since subsequent circles can be generated by utilising the co-ordinate arrays. The required code has not been included in Appendix A but is relatively simple and involves the use of a loop to step through the arrays. The reduction in computational overheads afforded by this technique means that perimeters may be plotted even faster (up to 6-fold) and is thus worth considering when displaying large amounts of data.

Division of the circle into sectors is performed by the subroutine given in *Listing 11*. The number of sectors required is specified by the variable NS, and information for the fraction of the pie each sector represents is maintained in the array SF (I). While there is no limit to the number of sectors which may be drawn, the clarity and hence usefulness of any pie chart is always diminished by overcrowding. The routine initially ensures that the sum of the values of the array elements equals units (SF(1) + SF(2) + ....SF(NS) = 1) otherwise the error 'bell' is sounded and a return from the subroutine is executed. Sectoring occurs in a clockwise direction and commences at the same start point as that of the circle. It should be noted that on microcomputers locating y = 0 at the bottom of the graphics screen the situation is reversed with circle plotting and division occurring in the opposite direction. The subroutine utilises the co-ordinate table and treats the circle as being composed of N + 1 points. Although this is technically correct it is apparent that the routine will, as a final step, require values from array elements X%(N + 1), Y%(N + 1), which were not used by the circle plotting subroutine. In order to avoid a program error, the normal consequence of this action, the offending elements are given values by over-dimensioning the arrays. When a DIM statement is executed all the array elements are set to zero, hence in this case the 'extra' co-ordinate would be 0,0 which results in the sectoring routine plotting a point at the centre of the circle but with no other effect on the pie chart.

Finally, these routines provide a facility for emphasising important data. This is achieved in two ways:

(i)    by extracting the sector from the pie;
(ii)   by shading the sector.

The former is accomplished by the subroutine documented in *Listing 13*. The sector to be displaced is specified by the value of the variable SN, remembering that the circle is divided in a clockwise manner when setting this variable. The routine initially locates and then erases the relevant section of the circumference. To redraw the erased sector slightly removed from the rest of the pie it is necessary to calculate new co-ordinates for the centre of the circle and this is performed using the relationships described by Equations 1 and 2. The offset of the new centre and consequently the sector is specified by the variable OS (offset) which in the example given here is 20% of the radius.

Shading a sector is a simpler process as no erasing or re-drawing operations need to be performed. The sector shading routine (*Listing 14*) locates the relevant sector, again specified by the value of SN, and fills it with a series of radial lines. In the absence of ROM based machine code 'fill' routines this is the most straightforward method of shading. However unless sufficient radial lines are drawn the shading will be incomplete and, since the routine utilises the co-ordinate table, it follows that a perfectly filled sector will only be achieved if a large number of points are used to construct the circle. A full-screen diameter circle on the Apple must be drawn using approximately 600 points if shading is to be used for emphasis. It should be pointed out that a circle of this resolution requires

**Figure 10.** An example of the type of output possible using the pie chart drawing routines (*Listings 10–14*). In this display, generated by program *Listing 20*, both sector extraction and shading have been used for emphasis of data.

2.4k of memory to maintain the co-ordinates of the points. The sector extraction routine, however, does not possess an intrinsic requirement for the circle to be plotted to such a high resolution. One hundred points permits an accurate chart to be produced and allows sectors to be extracted cleanly. Therefore this technique is useful if memory is at a premium.

*Listing 20* illustrates the pie chart drawing routines in operation and was used to generate the display shown in *Figure 10*.

### 3.7 Text and Graphics

A deficiency of the Apple is an inability to combine directly text and high resolution graphics, mainly because the relevant 'pages' are mapped in distinct areas of RAM (although four lines of text may be added to the bottom of a high resolution graphics screen this is due to combination of text and graphics pages and does not represent true mixing). Consequently numbering and labelling of axes or sectors has been omitted from all of the screen displays presented in this chapter. Graphical displays of data are of course, incomplete without such labelling. Several methods have been employed to circumvent this difficulty. Most straightforward, if somewhat tortuous, is to use a shape table which consists of user-defined graphics; in this case alphanumeric characters. Each graphic, or shape, of the table is encoded as a series of plotting vectors that specify movement and whether or not plotting should accompany a move. In memory, 'bit-pairs' are used for movement (00 – up; 01 – right; 10 – down; 11 – left) and a single bit immediately following each pair denotes the plotting status. In this manner, the vectors for a particular shape are stored in sequential bytes in memory. The user must define each shape as a logical sequence of plotting vectors before entering the information (as hexadecimal coded bytes) into RAM at a convenient start address. It can be seen that defining by hand a minimal character set consisting of 37 shapes (alphabet, decimal point and the digits), would require considerable effort. Not surprisingly, several commercial programs have been developed to aid creation of shape tables by allowing the user to draw each shape on the screen using the keyboard or games paddles, automatically generating the correct bit-codes for that shape. Applesoft BASIC provides commands which allow manipulation of shapes in high resolution graphics. A shape may be drawn at any of the 280 x 192 available positions on the graphics screen meaning that, for example, scales and tic marks on graphs may be aligned easily. In addition, scaling and/or rotation of shapes is possible which is useful for the labelling of vertical axes.

Other methods for the superimposition of text on graphics have included the use of routines to 'read' the text page and then re-create the character on the graphics screen. The major drawback of this method is that the characters are usually limited to the normal 24 x 40 positions available, as on the text screen. This can be problematical especially when scaling axes of graphs as it will often be difficult to line up labels with the correct divisions.

A detailed discussion of these techniques and the provision of subroutines is inappropriate here since they would be largely specific to the Apple and are mentioned to illustrate the feasibility of enhancing graphics displays with text on this particular microcomputer. We should also emphasise that the Apple II Plus is a first-generation machine and many of the newer microcomputers incorporate text/graphics facilities as standard.

## 3.8 Saving Subroutines as Text Files

Emphasis has been placed on the general nature of the graphical subroutines and the reader should now be aware of the possibility of using the same routines for a large number of applications. Installing code into computer memory *via* the keyboard is however a time-consuming process and repetitious typing of the same routine is especially wasteful. Fortunately the Apple disc operating system (DOS) provides a facility for saving programs or subroutines on disc as text files which can subsequently be retrieved and loaded into memory without deleting an existing program. This permits a large program to be rapidly assembled in RAM by consecutively accessing a series of smaller routines captured as text files on disc.

*Listing 15* provides an example of the type of program used to create text files. Since a useful routine such as this will be required many times it should also be saved as a text file; this operation will serve as an example to illustrate functioning of the program. The file to be created is assigned a name, stored in the string variable P$. The required part of code to be captured is specified in line 10 where M and N are substituted for relevant line numbers. In this case the complete routine is to be saved hence line 10 should be altered to LIST 1, 12 or simply LIST. The program initially opens a text file on disc, identified according to P$, and then immediately deletes it, to ensure that any existing file of the same name is erased. Failure to do so may result in the information in the original file becoming part of the new file. Apple DOS always commences data storage at the start of a disc file, admitting the possibility that, unless the new file is larger than the original, some original data will remain intact. While it is possible to delete a text file without actually opening it, attempting to remove a disc file that does not exist will result in a DOS error. Such occurrences can be avoided by always opening a file before deleting it thus providing a type of fail-safe mechanism. After deletion of the file, it is re-created and re-opened to receive information. This is supplied by means of the LIST command. As each line of the program is listed the characters comprising the line are stored sequentially on disc as strings of ASCII codes which are converted back to a readable form when the file is read. Unless specifically requested the listing is not displayed on screen during this process. Finally, the end of data input is signified by closing the file.

A text file created in this manner can subsequently be loaded into memory using the DOS 'EXEC' command (it follows that such files are often termed EXEC files). This instruction stores a program in RAM as if it were being typed in at the keyboard, though at rates far superior to expert typing speeds! In addition, EXEC does not delete a program already resident in memory (unlike RUN and LOAD) enabling utility routines captured as text files on disc to be rapidly appended to application programs. However it is important to afford careful consideration to the line numbering of routines. EXEC of code with line numbers that are identical to a program in memory will over-write the existing lines of the latter resulting in a corrupted program. A reasonable strategy may be to use high line numbers for EXEC files, reserving lower values for application programs.

Most disc operating systems offer some form of EXEC file facilities but these are less common on cassette based systems. Each system possesses a unique complement of commands; the above discussion pertains to the Apple DOS only, nevertheless, the value of this technique may be perceived. Unfortunately, little advice can be provided to those users restricted to a cassette operating system that does not incorporate an EXEC file facility. With the graphics routines given here it may be advantageous to save all the routines together as one program file which can then be utilised as the basis for application programs, deleting those routines that are not required.

## 4. OBTAINING A PERMANENT RECORD OF GRAPHICAL OUTPUT

The graphics image presented on the video screen is transient and used to generate a short-term image of the relationship between items of data. The need for long-term images leads naturally into the domain of hard copy; the permanent record of the graphical representation of data. It is possible to differentiate between two approaches to hard copy production; one yields an exact copy of the screen image at an identical resolution, the other yields a newly created image that can be of higher or occasionally lower resolution than the original image.

### 4.1 Copying a Graphics Video Screen

#### 4.1.1 *Screen Photography*

Photographic reproduction of a video display as seen in several of the figures in this chapter (e.g., *Figures 5* and *8*) provides an accurate reproduction of the original image. Because of the raster scan nature of the video display, high shutter speeds cannot be used, and speeds of 1/30th to 1/8th sec are appropriate, using a 35 mm single lens reflex camera with standard (50 or 55 mm) lens. Such slow speeds necessitate the use of a tripod to eliminate camera shake; a cable shutter release can further improve sharpness of the negative. Because of the slow shutter speed there is little value in using a fast film; we have found that black and white film rated at 100 ASA (21°DIN) gives acceptable negatives at lens apertures of f 5.6 or f 8. Difficulties that might be encountered include incorrect exposure (resolved by the preparation of a trial film and bracketing of exposures by ±1 stop around the typical exposure value) and blurring of the image, eliminated by use of a tripod. Further, it is important that the plane of the video screen and the film are parallel if converging or diverging vertical lines are to be prevented. Finally, stray light may be reflected from the screen and impair the quality of the image. Such reflections may be eliminated by conducting the photography in a darkened room or photographic dark room. Alternatively, a light-proof pyramid shaped screen can be employed to provide a light-tight surround. This can be constructed to place the camera at the correct distance for a full negative image of the screen. The support provided by such a device might preclude the need for a tripod. Such masks have been used for many years with Polaroid cameras used to photograph oscilloscope screens.

Finally, the use of Polaroid cameras precludes the need for subsequent processing and printing of the negative, although the cost is higher, particularly if multiple copies are required. Specialised Polaroid films have been designed specifically for photography of video screens.

### 4.1.2 *Video Screen "Dumps" using Graphics Printers*

The majority of printers employed in microcomputer systems are dot matrix printers in which each letter or character is formed by a group of dots on paper, analogous to the arrangement of pixels on the video monitor. Again, the inbuilt character set of a dot matrix printer represents a minute proportion of the total patterns that are available.

The line of text produced by a dot matrix printer is formed by the print head, consisting of a vertical row of 7 – 11 solenoid activated needles that are impacted against the paper through an ink ribbon while the row of needles is traversed across the width of the paper. Theoretically, it is possible to conceive of two extremes, the first in which no needles are activated during the whole of the traverse, the second in which every needle is impacted at every vertical position across the paper, this allows for the full range of graphics patterns that are possible. Printer design has advanced to the stage where graphics capability is provided as standard and permits the control of individual print needles at each position on the paper thereby giving true graphics capability. Maximum resolution is limited but typical horizontal resolutions of 480 points are readily attainable equivalent to 80 characters printing at 5 dots width/character + 1 dot spacing (6 x 80). Some printers offer dual density modes and increase the number of

MSB

| 1 | 2 | 3 | 4 | 5 | 6 | 7 | 8 | Video RAM byte |
|---|---|---|---|---|---|---|---|---|
| MSB ● | | | | | | | | 128 1000 0000 |
| ● | | | | | | | | 128 1000 0000 |
| ● | | | | | | | | 128 1000 0000 |
| ● | ● | ● | ● | | | | | 240 1111 0000 |
| ● | | | | | ● | ● | ● | 135 1000 0111 |
| ● | | | | | ● | ● | ● | 135 1000 0111 |
| ● | | | | | ● | ● | ● | 135 1000 0111 |
| ● | | | | | | | | 128 1000 0000 |

| 255 | 16 | 16 | 16 | 0 | 14 | 14 | 14 | Printer byte |
|---|---|---|---|---|---|---|---|---|
| 1 | 0 | 0 | 0 | 0 | 0 | 0 | 0 | |
| 1 | 0 | 0 | 0 | 0 | 0 | 0 | 0 | |
| 1 | 0 | 0 | 0 | 0 | 0 | 0 | 0 | |
| 1 | 1 | 1 | 1 | 0 | 0 | 0 | 0 | |
| 1 | 0 | 0 | 0 | 0 | 1 | 1 | 1 | |
| 1 | 0 | 0 | 0 | 0 | 1 | 1 | 1 | |
| 1 | 0 | 0 | 0 | 0 | 1 | 1 | 1 | |
| 1 | 0 | 0 | 0 | 0 | 0 | 0 | 0 | |

**Figure 11.** Relationship between bytes in video RAM and corresponding bytes in a graphics dump routine.

points by a factor of two. This is usually achieved by reduction of the speed of the print head, so that it traverses the paper at one half of the original rate.

Software for graphics dumps is not particularly straightforward and involves more than simply transmitting each byte of the memory mapped display to the printer. The greatest obstacle lies in the fact that memory mapped displays employ each byte to specify the status of a group of horizontal pixels (*Figure 11*). The needles of the dot matrix head are arranged vertically however, and thus each byte sent to the printer must be a composite of several bytes in the memory map. For example, a typical printer may employ eight parallel lines to specify the status of each of eight (out of nine) print needles. Thus, the appropriate bits of the video RAM must be supplied sequentially to the printer in order to regenerate the image (*Figure 11*).

Software to perform this conversion is logical but if written in a high level language is slow. In contrast, machine code routines are efficient and considerably faster and should be employed if possible. The microcomputer literature is replete with subroutines for graphics dumps to suit almost any combination of microcomputer and printer. In addition, many printer interfaces provide graphics dump routines permanently encoded in ROM (*Figure 12*). These commercial routines are often sophisticated and provide additional facilities, for example to invert or rotate the image. We cannot recommend that routines be rewritten in the light of the availability of such sophisticated commercial products. A microcomputer user interested in graphics dump routines is well advised to consult the specialist periodicals as a source of such subroutines; a potential purchaser should ensure that such software is available for the system under consideration and that it is included in the package offered by the dealer.

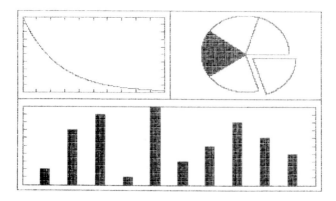

**Figure 12.** A dot matrix printer graphics dump of a screen display created using the routines discussed in this chapter. A ROM based machine code routine, which may be activated in direct mode or called from within an application program was provided with the printer interface and was used to perform the dump. Normally an exact copy of the screen image is produced but in this particular case an error in the dump routine alters the axial ratio resulting in the hard copy assuming a slightly squashed appearance.

## 4.2 Redrawing a Graphics Image

### 4.2.1 *Using a Dot Matrix Printer*

While the rapid machine code screen dump represents the most straightforward way of generating a graphical image there may be occasions when it is not possible to utilise this approach; for example, with microcomputer systems that do not possess a medium resolution graphical facility or when the use of a graphical display would represent an untenable incursion into available RAM. Under such circumstances, it would be possible to create a graphics image slowly by building up a section at a time and transmitting that section to the printer in graphics mode. This cannot be seen as anything other than a complex and tedious task and cannot be recommended as an approach worth consideration. It is conceivable that the memory required to program an algorithm for image generation in this way would require larger areas of memory than the original graphics display area! More simply, the use of the standard character set can yield crude, low resolution graphics images that provide a quick resumé of experimental data (*Figure 13*). Such algorithms are found in the literature (1) and will not be repeated here; this approach is being superseded rapidly by the availability of true graphical output facilities.

### 4.2.2 *Digital Plotters*

A digital plotter differs from a dot matrix printer in many respects. It provides accurate control of the movements of a pen over a sheet (or part of a roll) of paper. Because pen movement is controlled by accurate stepper motors the resolution of the plotter (the distance moved by the pen in response to a single pulse to the motor) is considerably superior to that obtained by dot matrix printers. The number of distinct pen positions can range from a limited

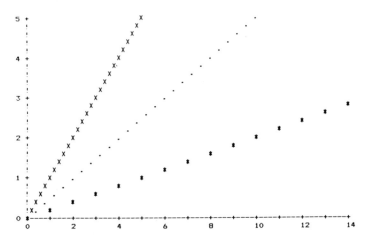

**Figure 13.** Printer hard copy of low resolution images such as this can be achieved using the standard character set by encoding the graph as a series of strings of identical length, containing the required characters at appropriate positions. The image is compiled by sequentially transmitting each string to the printer. An advantage of this method is that text can easily be incorporated into displays which is a much more difficult task with Apple high resolution graphics.

2000 x 1400 to a high quality 11 000 x 8000 over the area of an A4 sheet of paper. This precision of pen placement is far more accurate than the width of a typical drawing pen!

Clearly then, digital plotters are capable of generating graphics images of the highest quality, and to use a plotter simply to reproduce a copy of a graphics screen (*via* a 'dump' subroutine) represents a considerable sacrifice in quality. However, the ease of use of any plotter is governed by two classes of software, that which is intrinsic to the plotter (low level control, usually in ROM) and extrinsic software that provides higher level control of graphical output — normally maintained in the RAM of the host microcomputer.

Intrinsic plotter commands comprise at least a minimal set of functions for moving the pen across the paper $+X, -X, +Y, -Y$ and for raising $(+Z)$ and lowering $(-Z)$ the pen. It is possible to use such primitive functions to generate a graphics image, provided that a subroutine is written that permits the command "MOVE to X,Y, DRAW to X',Y'" which can then cover all eventualities. Nonetheless, simple procedures such as axis drawing and symbol generation (circles, triangles, etc.) involve extensive computational overheads that slow down the program and utilise large proportions of the available RAM. Accordingly, there has been a trend towards the provision of higher level commands in ROM as a part of the 'intelligence' of the plotter. Among the specifications of a currently available, state of the art digital plotter, designed for use with microcomputer systems (*via* RS232(C) or IEEE 488 interfaces) the following are found.

(i)   Specification of windows to which plotting commands will be restricted. Absolute or relative plotting permitted.

(ii)  Scaling of the plotting area into user units, obviating scaling routines such as those found in the early part of this chapter.

(iii) Selection of multiple character sets to be used for labelling in any direction, in any size and possessing an italic slant if required.

(iv)  Two colour plotting with automatic pen change commands.

(v)   Programmable line types (solid, dashed, dotted, mixed, etc.).

Sophisticated commands such as these are selected by means of simple

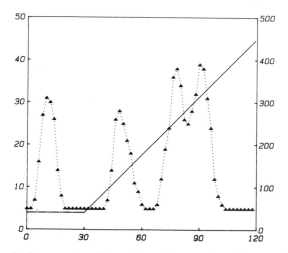

**Figure 14.** High quality images such as this are beyond the graphics display capabilities of a microcomputer. This graph was generated using a digital plotter offering a resolution of approximately 11 000 x 8000 points (see text for further details). An amount of RAM in excess of 1000k would be required to map a (practically unattainable) video display at the same resolution!

**Table 2.** Specifications of a General Graph Plotting Program.

| Function | Options |
| --- | --- |
| Plotting area | A4,A5, User selected. |
| Axes | *x*-axis, left hand *y*-axis, right hand *y*-axis linear: selectable limits and tic interval logarithmic: selectable starting value and number of cycles. |
| X,Y Data | Enter data, edit data, file data. |
| Graph type | Data joined/unjoined with option of function plotted over any range. |
| Symbol | Point, cross, square, circle, triangle. |
| Line type | Solid, dotted, dashed, mixed. |
| Pen colour | Either pen selectable for any discrete portion of the graph; axis, data, function. |

The need for flexibility in a package such as this is compromised by the demands of user friendliness. As a solution, the program assumes default values of most of the options that represent most commonly used selections (A5 area, data joined, cross, solid line, one pen plotting etc.). This ensures that interaction with the program may be as limited as possible, requiring at the simplest level entry (or file recovery) of data, setting up of axes and graph plotting.

91

character strings, transmitted to the plotter. Thus "SP2" selects pen 2, "PD 45.2 36.6" causes the pen to plot in absolute terms to the indicated co-ordinates, "LB Time(s)" draws the label Time (sec) at the current pen position and so forth. With facilities such as these it is a straightforward matter to produce sophisticated software that yields high resolution graphics images with a minimum of programming effort (*Figure 14*). These constitute the extrinsic commands that form part of the driver program written in a high level language and resident in the host computer. It is impossible to generalise here or to provide a set of listings that could avoid being highly system specific. To illustrate the type of software that is attainable *Table 2* gives some of the specifications of a general purpose graph plotting program used in our laboratory. This program occupies approximately 20k of memory and has been written to be as user friendly as possible within the constraints of the language and the limitations on available RAM. The reader who is interested in writing such a piece of software is strongly advised to scrutinise the microcomputer literature before doing so — such software is not produced without considerable endeavour; this is wasted if a package already exists!

## 5. CONCLUSIONS

In common with all tasks that can be assigned to computer processing, the generation of graphical displays offers advantages of speed of preparation and ease of amendment. Good quality software will obviously aid exploitation of microcomputer graphics facilities and the benefits of general purpose routines should be perceived from this chapter. Although current microcomputer graphics cannot rival the superior capabilities of mini and mainframe computers [now used in many scientific applications such as the display of complex molecules (2)] they are clearly adequate for exhibiting graphed data. Production of publication quality images is possible but requires the services of a digital plotter, the cost of which may be prohibitive; in many instances plotters are considerably more expensive than the microcomputer systems used to drive them. With appropriate software they undoubtedly provide the user with an extremely powerful hard copy device.

Selection of a system to include graphical display demands close scrutiny of facilities offered by individual microcomputers, in particular the versatility and range of pertinent graphics commands. For instance, mixed text and graphics and extensive control over colour may be essential in some applications. In addition, the partition of user RAM for graphics pages is very relevant in the planning of large programs. Most of the current generation of microcomputers incorporate high resolution graphics but not all offer useful machine code routines for plotting, for example, circles. Although for hard copy purposes a plotter may not be feasible, a printer is essential for serious program development. The availability of graphics dump routines for the particular microcomputer system under consideration is therefore of relevance. Judicious combination of hardware and software must obviously balance all requirements but the advantages in communication given by graphics facilities suggests that they should be a high priority in any general purpose system.

## 6. ACKNOWLEDGEMENTS

Reproduction of many of the graphics subroutines is by kind permission of Windfall (the Apple computer users magazine, available from Database Publications, Stockport). Thanks are also due to Miss E. Aspinall for preparing the plates and to Ms G. Mahon for typing the manuscript.

## 7. REFERENCES

### References in Text

1. Beech,G. (1976) *BASIC in Chemistry*, published bySigma Technical Press, Albrighton, UK, p. 40.
2. Langridge,R., Ferrin,T.E., Kuntz,I.D. and Connolly,M.L. (1981) *Science (Wash.)*, **211**, 661.

### General References

Korites,B.J. (1981) *Graphic Software for Microcomputers,* published by Kern Publications, MA, USA.
Rogers,D.F. and Adams,J.A. (1977) *An Introduction to Computer Graphics,* published by McGraw-Hill Inc.
Ryan,D.L. (1979) *Computer Aided Graphics and Design,* published by Marcel-Dekker Inc., New York, USA.

## APPENDIX A
### Graphics subroutine listings

**Listing 1.**          LOMEM mover
*Function:*          Relocates LOMEM above graphics Page 1 and then runs required program.
*Variables needed:*  None
*Variables used:*    P$,D$

```
100 :::: REM     LOAD PROGRAM P$ ABOVE GRAPHICS PAGE 1
110 :::: REM     BY RESETTING LOMEM
120 D$ = CHR$ (4):::: REM     DOS COMMAND
130 P$ = "PROGRAM NAME"
140 :
150  POKE 103,1
160  POKE 104,64
170  POKE 16384,0
180  PRINT D$;"RUN";P$
190 :
200 :
210 :::: REM     TO MOVE ABOVE PAGE 2
220 :::: REM     POKE 103,1
230 :::: REM     POKE 104,96
240 :::: REM     POKE 24576,0
```

**Listing 2.**          Graphics initialisation routine
*Function:*          Selects required graphics page and background colour (black or white). In addition the routine sets the display to full or partial graphics screen.
*Variables needed:*  G$
*Variables used:*    PC$

```
50000 :::: REM   GRAPHICS INIT ROUTINE
50010 :::: REM   REQUIRES G$
50020 :
50030 IF  LEN (G$) < > 6 THEN 50160
50040 PC$ = LEFT$ (G$,2)
```

```
50050 IF  LEFT$ (PC$,1) < > "P" THEN 50160
50060 IF  RIGHT$ (PC$,1) = "1" THEN  HGR : GOTO 50090
50070 IF  RIGHT$ (PC$,1) = "2" THEN  HGR2 : GOTO 50090
50080 GOTO 50160
50090 PC$ = MID$ (G$,4,1)
50100 IF PC$ = "F" THEN  POKE  - 16302,0: GOTO 50130
50110 IF PC$ = "P" THEN  POKE  - 16301,0: GOTO 50130
50120 GOTO 50160
50130 PC$ = RIGHT$ (G$,1)
50140 IF PC$ = "W" THEN  HCOLOR= 7: HPLOT 0,0: CALL 62454: HCOLOR= 4: GOTO 50180
50150 IF PC$ = "B" THEN  HCOLOR= 4: HPLOT 0,0: CALL 62454: HCOLOR= 7: GOTO 50180
50160 FOR L = 1 TO 5: PRINT CHR$ (7);: NEXT L::::: REM      ERROR BELL
50170 :
50180 RETURN
```

**Listing 3.**        Draws plotting area

*Function*:        Draws a box around the current plotting area defined by BX,TX,BY and TY.
The routine inserts tic marks every 10% along each axis and draws a line at x = 0
or y = 0 if necessary.

*Variables needed*:    BX,TX,BY,TY,LX,UX,LY,UY
*Variables used*:      TI,ZX,ZY

```
50200 :::: REM      DRAW PLOTTING AREA(S)
50210 :::: REM      NEED BX,TX,BY,TY - SCREEN LIMITS
50220 :::: REM           LX,UX,LY,UY - USER LIMITS
50230 :
50240 :::: REM      AXES
50250 HPLOT BX,TY TO BX,BY TO TX,BY TO TX,TY TO BX,TY
50260 :
50270 :::: REM      TIC MARKS ON X-AXES
50280 FOR TI = BX TO TX STEP (TX - BX) / 10
50290 HPLOT TI,BY TO TI,BY - 3: HPLOT TI,TY TO TI,TY + 3
50300 NEXT TI
50310 :
50320 :::: REM      TIC MARKS ON Y-AXES
50330 FOR TI = BY TO TY STEP (TY - BY) / 10
50340 HPLOT BX,TI TO BX + 3,TI: HPLOT TX,TI TO TX - 3,TI
50350 NEXT TI
50360 :
50370 :::: REM      DRAW ZERO LINES IF NEEDED
50380 :
50390 IF  NOT (LX < 0 AND UX > 0) THEN 50430
50400 ZX = (0 - LX) / (UX - LX) * (TX - BX) + BX
50410 HPLOT ZX,BY TO ZX,TY
50420 :
50430 IF  NOT (LY < 0 AND UY > 0) THEN 50470
50440 ZY = (0 - LY) / (UY - LY) * (TY - BY) + BY
50450 HPLOT BX,ZY TO TX,ZY
50460 :
50470 RETURN
```

**Listing 4.**          Point plotting
*Function*:         Plots a point in current active area. Testing for an out-of-bounds point is performed and signified by sounding of the 'bell'; the point is not plotted. Note, this routine is provided separate from the symbol plotting routine (*Listing 5*) in order to facilitate rapid function plotting.
*Variables needed*:   BX,TX,BY,TY,LX,UX,LY,UY,XX,YY
*Variables used*:     PX,PY

```
50500 :::: REM    PLOT A POINT
50510 :::: REM    NEED XX,YY (DATA IN USER UNITS)
50520 :::: REM    AND USER AND SCREEN PLOTTING LIMITS
50530 :
50540 :::: REM    CALCULATE SCREEN COORDINATES OF POINT
50550 PX = (XX - LX) / (UX - LX) * (TX - BX) + BX
50560 PY = (YY - LY) / (UY - LY) * (TY - BY) + BY
50570 :
50580 :::: REM    TEST FOR OUT OF BOUNDS
50590 IF PX > = BX AND PX < = TX THEN 50610
50600 PRINT CHR$ (7);: GOTO 50660
50610 IF PY = < BY AND PY > = TY THEN 50640
50620 PRINT CHR$ (7);: GOTO 50660
50630 :
50640 HPLOT PX,PY
50650 :
50660 RETURN
```

**Listing 5.**          Symbol plotter
*Function*:         Plots symbol in current active area. Again tests for out-of-bounds points and acts on them accordingly. Value of SY determines symbol type.
*Variables needed*:   BX,TX,BY,TY,LX,UX,LY,UY,XX,YY,SY
*Variables used*:     PX,PY

```
50700 :::: REM    PLOT SYMBOL AT XX,YY
50710 :::: REM    SYMBOL TYPE  1:SQUARE
50720 :::: REM                 2:CIRCLE
50730 :::: REM                 3:TRIANGLE
50740 :::: REM                 4:CROSS
50750 :
50760 PX = (XX - LX) / (UX - LX) * (TX - BX) + BX
50770 PY = (YY - LY) / (UY - LY) * (TY - BY) + BY
50780 :
50790 IF PX > = BX AND PX < = TX THEN 50810
50800 PRINT CHR$ (7);: GOTO 50860
50810 IF PY = < BY AND PY > = TY THEN 50840
50820 PRINT CHR$ (7);: GOTO 50860
50830 :
50840 ON SY GOSUB 50880,50940,51000,51060
50850 :
50860 RETURN
50870 :
50880 :::: REM    SY=1 SQUARE
50890 HPLOT PX - 1,PY - 1 TO PX + 1,PY - 1
50900 HPLOT PX - 1,PY: HPLOT PX + 1,PY
50910 HPLOT PX - 1,PY + 1 TO PX + 1,PY + 1
50920 RETURN
50930 :
50940 :::: REM    SY=2 CIRCLE
50950 HPLOT PX - 2,PY TO PX,PY + 2
50960 HPLOT PX - 1,PY - 1: HPLOT PX + 1,PY + 1
50970 HPLOT PX,PY - 2 TO PX + 2,PY
```

```
50980  RETURN
50990 :
51000 :::: REM      SY=3 TRIANGLE
51010  HPLOT PX - 2,PY + 1 TO PX + 2,PY + 1
51020  HPLOT PX - 1,PY: HPLOT PX + 1,PY
51030  HPLOT PX,PY - 1
51040  RETURN
51050 :
51060 :::: REM      SY=4 CROSS
51070  HPLOT PX - 2,PY TO PX + 2,PY
51080  HPLOT PX,PY - 2 TO PX,PY + 2
51090  RETURN
```

**Listing 6.**      Multiple area initialisation

*Function*:      Sets the boundary variables to values specified in the subroutine. This routine is useful when plotting to several different graph areas on the screen. Selection of individual areas is achieved by setting the variable AR to the appropriate value.

*Variables needed*:      AR

*Variables used*:      BX,TX,BY,TY,LX,UX,LY,UY

```
51100 :::: REM      MULTIPLE AREA INIT ROUTINE
51110 :::: REM      USER MUST SET AR TO CURRENT AREA
51120 :::: REM      IN THIS SUBROUTINE FIRST
51130 :
51140 :::: REM      SCREEN LIMITS BX TO TX, BY TO TY
51150 :::: REM      USER LIMITS LX TO UX, LY TO UY
51160 :
51170  ON AR GOSUB 51210,51250,51290,51330
51180  BY = 191 - BY:TY = 191 - TY:::: REM     INVERSION STATEMENT
51190  RETURN
51200 :
51210  BX = 50:TX = 229:BY = 95:TY = 186:::: REM      AR=1
51220  LX = 0:UX = 400:LY = 0:UY = 300
51230  RETURN
51240 :
51250  BX = 5:TX = 100:BY = 5:TY = 90:::: REM      AR=2
51260  LX = 0:UX = 300:LY = 0:UY = 400
51270  RETURN
51280 :
51290  BX = 180:TX = 275:BY = 5:TY = 90:::: REM      AR=3
51300  LX = 0:UX = 300:LY = 0:UY = 400
51310  RETURN
51320 :
51330  BX = 15:TX = 260:BY = 20:TY = 170:::: REM      AR=4
51340  LX = 0:UX = 300:LY = 0:UY = 400
51350  RETURN
```

**Listing 7.**          Area erase
*Function*:          Erases the current graph area. Useful for up-dating or re-plotting selected areas of the screen and avoids the need to clear the screen completely. The routine initially fills in the appropriate area with the background colour and then re-establishes the axes at the same position by calling the area plotting routine (*Listing 3*). Can be used to erase either Cartesian graphs or histograms, with alteration of line 52170 to GOSUB 53000 in the latter case.
*Variables needed*:          BX,TX,BY,TY,G$
*Variables used*:          HC

```
52000 :::: REM      ERASE AREA
52010 :
52020 :::: REM       SET COLOUR TO BACKGROUND
52030 IF RIGHT$ (G$,1) = "B" THEN HC = 4: GOTO 52050
52040 HC = 7
52050 HCOLOR= HC
52060 :
52070 :::: REM       FILL IN AREA
52080 FOR L = BX TO TX STEP 1
52090 HPLOT L,BY TO L,TY
52100 NEXT L
52110 :
52120 :::: REM       RESET COLOUR
52130 IF HC = 4 THEN  HCOLOR= 7: GOTO 52160
52140 HCOLOR= 4
52150 :
52160 :::: REM       RE-DRAW AXES
52170 GOSUB 50200
52180 :
52190 RETURN
```

**Listing 8.**          Histogram initialisation
*Function*:          Draws histogram plotting area and calculates the width of bar to be used subsequently. The routine inserts tic marks every 10% along the y-axes.
*Variables needed*:          BX,TX,BY,TY,LY,UY,NG,BG
*Variables used*:          ZY,TI,BI

```
53000 :::: REM      DRAW HISTOGRAM AREA
53010 :::: REM      NEED BX,TX,BY,TY - SCREEN LIMITS
53020 :::: REM      LY,UY - USER LIMITS
53030 :::: REM      NG (NUMBER OF GROUPS)
53040 :::: REM      BG (BARS/GROUP)
53050 :
53060 IF BG = 0 THEN  PRINT CHR$ (7);: GOTO 53260
53070 :
53080 :::: REM      AXES
53090 HPLOT BX,TY TO BX,BY TO TX,BY TO TX,TY TO BX,TY
53100 :
53110 :::: REM      TIC MARKS ON Y-AXES
53120 FOR TI = BY TO TY STEP (TY - BY) / 10
53130 HPLOT BX,TI TO BX + 3,TI: HPLOT TX,TI TO TX - 3,TI
53140 NEXT TI
53150 :
53160 :::: REM      ESTABLISH HISTOGRAM BASELINE
53170 ZY = (0 - LY) / (UY - LY) $ (TY - BY) + BY
53180 HPLOT BX,ZY TO TX,ZY
53190 :
53200 :::: REM      CALCULATE INTERVALS
```

```
53210  IF NG < > 0 THEN 53240
53220  BI = (TX - BX) / BG
53230  GOTO 53260
53240  BI = (TX - BX) / ((NG .# BG) + (NG # 2) + 2)
53250  :
53260  RETURN
```

**Listing 9.**        Bar plotter
*Function*:        Draws a single bar on the display. The subroutine must be supplied with information specifying the bar height, colour (or shade) required and the number of the bar within the group currently being plotted.
*Variables needed*:    BX,BY,TY,LY,UY,BH,BC,GN,BN,BI,ZY
*Variables used*:      OS,BF,BU,BL,HB,BB,SS

```
53500  :::: REM      DRAW BAR
53510  :::: REM      BH=BAR HEIGHT (USER UNITS)
53520  :::: REM      BC=BAR COLOUR
53530  :::: REM      GN=GROUP NUMBER
53540  :::: REM      BN=BAR NUMBER
53550  :
53560  IF BN < 1 OR BN > BG THEN  PRINT  CHR$ (7);: GOTO 53740
53570  IF NG = 0 THEN 53590
53580  IF GN < 1 OR GN > NG THEN  PRINT  CHR$ (7);: GOTO 53740
53590  OS = 2:BF = 0
53600  IF NG = 0 THEN OS = 0:GN = 1
53610  :
53620  :::: REM      CALCULATE BAR POSITION
53630  BU = (BN + ((GN - 1) # BG) + (GN - 1) # 2 + OS) # BI
53640  BU = BU + BX
53650  BL = BU - BI
53660  :
53670  :::: REM   CALCULATE BAR HEIGHT (SCREEN UNITS)
53680  HB = (BH - LY) / (UY - LY) # (TY - BY) + BY
53690  :
53700  :::: REM      BC SELECTS BAR TYPE
53710  GOSUB 53760
53720  IF BF = 1 THEN BF = 0: PRINT  CHR$ (7);: GOTO 53740
53730  ON BC GOSUB 53760,53810,53870,53950
53740  GOTO 54010
53750  :
53760  :::: REM      BC=1:OPEN BAR
53770  IF HB > BY OR HB < TY THEN BF = 1: GOTO 53790
53780  HPLOT BL,ZY TO BL,HB TO BU,HB TO BU,ZY
53790  RETURN
53800  :
53810  :::: REM      BC=2:FILLED BAR
53820  FOR BB = BL TO BU
53830  HPLOT BB,ZY TO BB,HB
53840  NEXT BB
53850  RETURN
53860  :
53870  :::: REM      BC=3:SHADED BAR (HORIZ.)
53880  SS = 2
53890  IF HB < ZY THEN SS = - 2
53900  FOR BB = ZY TO HB STEP SS
53910  HPLOT BL,BB TO BU,BB
53920  NEXT BB
53930  RETURN
53940  :
```

```
53950 :::: REM     BC=4:SHADED BAR (VERT.)
53960 FOR BB = BL TO BU STEP 2
53970 HPLOT BB,ZY TO BB,HB
53980 NEXT BB
53990 RETURN
54000 :
54010 RETURN
```

**Listing 10.**      Circle plotter

*Function:*      Draws a circle of radius R, with centre specified by screen co-ordinates CX,CY. The resolution of the circle is determined by the variable N. Note that in order to draw the circle as rapidly as possible no checks for off-screen points are performed. The subroutine also provides values for the arrays X%(I) and Y%(I).

*Variables needed:*      CX,CY,R,N

*Variables used:*      T,X,Y,PI,S,C,SX,SY,TH,X%( ),Y%( )

```
56000 :::: REM   DRAW CIRCLE
56010 :::: REM   NEED CX,CY,R,N
56020 :::: REM   RADIUS;R,CENTRE;CX,CY
56030 :::: REM   NO CHECKS FOR OFF-SCREEN!
56040 :
56050 PI = 3.1416
56060 T = 2 * PI / N
56070 S = SIN (T):C = COS (T)
56080 XZ(0) = R:YZ(0) = 0
56090 X = R:Y = 0
56100 HPLOT CX + XZ(0),CY + YZ(0):::: REM    START POINT
56110 :
56120 FOR TH = 1 TO N
56130 SX = X * C - Y * S
56140 SY = X * S + Y * C
56150 HPLOT TO CX + SX,CY + SY
56160 X = SX:Y = SY
56170 XZ(TH) = SX:YZ(TH) = SY
56180 NEXT TH
56190 :
56200 RETURN
```

**Listing 11.**      Constructs pie chart

*Function:*      Divides a circle into sectors. The number of sectors is specified by the variable NS and the size of each one is determined by the values contained in the array SF(I).

*Variables needed:*      CX,CY,X%(I),Y%(I),NS,SF(I)

*Variables used:*      FT,L,TH

```
56300 :::: REM   DRAW PIE CHART
56310 :::: REM   NEED CX,CY,NS,SF()
56320 :::: REM   NS=NUMBER OF SECTORS
56330 :::: REM   SF(1)....SF(NS)=FRACTION
56340 :::: REM   ASSOCIATED WITH EACH SECTOR
56350 :
56360 FT = 0
56370 :
56380 :::: REM   CHECK SUM OF FRACTIONS=1
56390 FOR L = 1 TO NS
56400 FT = FT + SF(L)
56410 NEXT L
56420 IF  INT (FT * 100) / 100 < > 1 THEN  PRINT CHR$ (7);: GOTO 56530
56430 :
56440 HPLOT CX,CY TO CX + XZ(0),CY + YZ(0)
```

```
56450 :
56460 :::: REM      DRAW SECTORS
56470 FT = 0
56480 FOR L = 0 TO NS
56490 FT = FT + SF(L):TH =  INT (FT * (N + 1))
56500 HPLOT CX,CY TO CX + X%(TH),CY + Y%(TH)
56510 NEXT L
56520 :
56530 RETURN
```

| | |
|---|---|
| **Listing 12.** | Erases pie chart |
| *Function:* | Analogous to *Listing 7* in that it permits a selected area of the screen to be erased, which is useful for complex displays. The subroutine calls two other pie chart routines (*Listings 10* and *11*). |
| *Variables needed:* | G$ |
| *Variables used:* | HC |

```
56600 :::: REM      ERASE PIE CHART
56610 :::: REM      NEED G$
56620 :
56630 :::: REM      SET COLOUR TO BACKGROUND
56640 IF  RIGHT$ (G$,1) = "B" THEN HC = 4: GOTO 56660
56650 HC = 3
56660  HCOLOR= HC
56670 :
56680  GOSUB 56000:::: REM      DELETE FOR SECTORS ONLY
56690  GOSUB 56300
56700 :
56710 :::: REM      RESET COLOUR
56720  IF HC = 4 THEN HC = 3: GOTO 56740
56730 HC = 4
56740  HCOLOR= HC
56750 :
56760  RETURN
```

| | |
|---|---|
| **Listing 13.** | Extracts a sector |
| *Function:* | Displaces a sector from the main body of the pie. The required sector is specified by the variable SN. |
| *Variables needed:* | CX,CY,R,NS,SN,SF( ),X%( ),Y%( ),G$ |
| *Variables used:* | FT,FS,TH,HC,L,OS,OX,OY |

```
56800 :::: REM      EXTRACT SECTOR
56810 :::: REM      NEED CX,CY,R,NS,SN,SF()
56820 :::: REM      SN=SECTOR NUMBER
56830 :
56840 FT = 0
56850 :
56860 :::: REM      SET COLOUR TO BACKGROUND
56870  IF  RIGHT$ (G$,1) = "B" THEN HC = 4: GOTO 56890
56880 HC = 3
56890  HCOLOR= HC
56900 :
56910  IF SN < 1 OR SN > NS THEN  PRINT  CHR$ (7);: GOTO 57140
56920 :
56930 :::: REM      ESTABLISH START AND END POINTS
56940 FOR L = 0 TO SN
56950 FT = FT + SF(L)
56960 NEXT L
56970 FS = FT - SF(SN)
```

```
56980 TH =  INT (FS # (N + 1))
56990 HPLOT CX + XX(TH),CY + YX(TH):::: REM        START POINT
57000 :
57010 :::: REM       ERASE SPECIFIED SECTION OF CIRCUMFERENCE
57020 FOR L = FS # (N + 1) TO FT # (N + 1)
57030 TH =  INT (L)
57040 HPLOT  TO CX + XX(TH),CY + YX(TH)
57050 NEXT L
57060 :
57070 :::: REM       RESET COLOUR
57080  IF HC = 4 THEN HC = 3: GOTO 57100
57090 HC = 4
57100 HCOLOR= HC
57110 :
57120 :::: REM       SECTOR POSITION
57130 TH = (FS + (FT - FS) / 2) # 2 # PI:::: REM        CENTRE OF ARC OF SECTOR
57140 OS = R / 5
57150 OX = CX + OS # COS (TH)
57160 OY = CY + OS # SIN (TH)
57170 :
57180 :::: REM       RE-DRAW SECTOR
57190 TH =  INT (FS # (N + 1))
57200 HPLOT OX,OY TO OX + XX(TH),OY + YX(TH)
57210 :
57220 FOR L = FS # (N + 1) TO FT # (N + 1)
57230 TH =  INT (L)
57240 HPLOT  TO OX + XX(TH),OY + YX(TH)
57250 NEXT L
57260 HPLOT  TO OX,OY
57270 :
57280 RETURN
```

**Listing 14.**         Shades a sector
*Function*:         Fills in a sector which is specified by the variable SN.
*Variables needed*:   CX,CY,NS,SN,SF( ),X%( ),Y%( )
*Variables used*:     FT,FS,L,TH

```
57300 :::: REM       SHADE SECTOR
57310 :::: REM       NEED CX,CY,NS,SN,SF()
57320 :::: REM       SN=SECTOR NUMBER
57330 :
57340  IF SN < 1 OR SN > NS THEN  PRINT CHR$ (7);: GOTO 57500
57350 :
57360 FT = 0
57370 :
57380 :::: REM       ESTABLISH START AND END POINTS
57390 FOR L = 1 TO SN
57400 FT = FT + SF(L)
57410 NEXT L
57420 FS = FT - SF(SN)
57430 :
57440 :::: REM       SHADE
57450 FOR L = FS # (N + 1) TO FT # (N + 1)
57460 TH =  INT (L)
57470 HPLOT CX,CY TO CX + XX(TH),CY + YX(TH)
57480 NEXT L
57490 :
57500 RETURN
```

**Listing 15.**       Subroutine saver
*Function*:           Used to capture utility routines as text files on disc enabling them to be subse-
                      quently EXECed into application programs
*Variables needed*:   None
*Variables used*:     P$,D$

```
1 :::: REM   SUBROUTINE SAVER
2 :
3 P$ = "NAME OF TEXT FILE"
4 D$ = CHR$ (4):::: REM   DOS COMMAND
5 :
6  PRINT D$;"OPEN";P$
7  PRINT D$;"DELETE";P$
8  PRINT D$;"OPEN";P$
9  PRINT D$;"WRITE";P$
10 LIST M,N:::: REM   M&N PROGRAM LINE NUMBERS
11 PRINT D$;"CLOSE";P$
12 :
13 END
```

# APPENDIX B
## Application programs

For maximal flexibility the graphics subroutines should be complemented with a data input routine.
Such a routine has been used in the first two application programs listed. A suitable code for numeric
input should perform rigorous checks to ensure that only numbers, +, −, E and the decimal point
may be entered and should include editing facilities for error correction. For convenience DATA
statements have been used in *Listings 19* and *20* to provide information for the graphics routines.

**Listing 16.** This driving program was used to generate the display shown in *Figure 5*.

```
10 :::: REM   GRAPH DISPLAY DEMONSTRATION
20 :
30 :::: REM   INITIALISATION
40 G$ = "P2/F/W": GOSUB 50000
50 :
60 :::: REM   SET PLOTTING LIMITS
70 :::: REM     BX=15;TX=260;BY=20;TY=170
80 :::: REM     LX=0; UX=300;LY=0; UY=400
90 AR = 4: GOSUB 51100
100 :
110 :::: REM   DRAW GRAPH AREA
120  GOSUB 50200
130 :
140 :::: REM   SELECT SYMBOL TYPE
150 SY = 1
160 :
170 :::: REM   PLOT DATA
180  FOR L = 1 TO DT:::: REM   DT=NUMBER OF DATA POINTS
190 XX = XD(L):YY = YD(L):::: REM    DATA PREVIOUSLY STORED IN ARRAYS XD() & YD()
200  GOSUB 50700
210  IF L = 1 THEN 230:::: REM   TEST FOR FIRST DATA POINT
220  HPLOT XOLD,YOLD TO PX,PY:::: REM   CONNECT DATA POINTS
230 XOLD = PX:YOLD = PY
240  NEXT L
250 :
260  END
```

**Listing 17.** *Figure 7* driver program.

```
10 :::: REM       GRAPH DISPLAY DEMONSTRATION
20 :
30 :::: REM       INITIALISATION
40 G$ = "P2/F/B": GOSUB 50000
50 :
60 :::: REM       GRAPH 1
70 :::: REM       BX=50;TX=229;BY=95;TY=186
80 :::: REM       LX=0; UX=400;LY=0; UY=300
90 AR = 1: GOSUB 51100: GOSUB 50200
100 :::: REM       PLOT DATA POINTS
110 SY = 3
120 FOR L = 1 TO DT
130 XX = XD(L):YY = YD(L)
140 GOSUB 50700
150 NEXT L
160 :
170 :::: REM       PLOT FUNCTION
180 P1 = 0.0116:P2 = 0.0044:P3 = 4.31:::: REM       FUNCTION PARAMETERS
190 SS = (UX - LX) / 500:::: REM       STEP SIZE
200 FOR XX = LX TO UX STEP SS
210 YY = 100 * EXP ( - P1 * XX) + (P3 * (P1 / (P2 - P1)) * 100 * ( EXP ( - P1 * XX) - EXP ( - P2 * XX)))
220 GOSUB 50500
230 NEXT XX
240 :
250 :::: REM       GRAPH 2
260 :::: REM       BX=5;TX=100;BY=5;TY=90
270 :::: REM       LX=0;UX=300;LY=0;UY=400
280 AR = 2: GOSUB 51100: GOSUB 50200
290 :
300 F = 0
310 :
320 P1 = 0.02:P3 = 3
330 SS = (UX - LX) / 50
340 FOR P2 = 0 TO 0.005 STEP 0.005
350 FOR XX = LX TO UX STEP SS
360 YY = EXP ( - P1 * XX) + (P3 * (P1 / (P2 - P1)) * 100 * ( EXP ( - P1 * XX) - EXP ( - P2 * XX)))
370 GOSUB 50500
380 NEXT XX
390 NEXT P2
400 :
410 IF F = 0 THEN 450
420 :
430 END
440 :
450 :::: REM       GRAPH 3
460 :::: REM       BX=180;TX=275;BY=5;TY=90
470 :::: REM       LX=0 ; UX=300;LY=0;UY=400
480 AR = 3: GOSUB 51100: GOSUB 50200
490 SS = (UX - LX) / 500
500 F = 1
510 GOTO 340
```

**Listing 18.** *Figure 8* driver program.

```
10 :::: REM        HISTOGRAM DISPLAY DEMONSTRATION
20 :
30 :::: REM        INITIALISATION
40 G$ = "P1/F/B": GOSUB 50000
50 :
60 :::: REM        SET PLOTTING LIMITS
70 :::: REM        BX=5;TX=274;BY=5;TY=180
80 :::: REM        LX=0;UX=22; LY=0;UY=0.11
90 AR = 4: GOSUB 51100
100 :
110 :::: REM        DRAW HISTOGRAM AREA
120 NG = 0:BG = 22
130  GOSUB 53000
140 :
150 :::: REM        DRAW BARS
160 P1 = 10:P2 = 4:::: REM        FUNCTION PARAMETERS
170 BC = 1:::: REM        OPEN BARS
180  FOR J = 1 TO BG
190 BN = J:GN = 0
200 BH = ( EXP ( - ((J - P1) $ (J - P1) / (2 $ P2 $ P2)))) $ (1 / (P2 $ SQR (2 $ 3.142)))
210  GOSUB 53500
220  NEXT J
230 :
240 :::: REM        PLOT FUNCTION
250  FOR XX = 0 TO 22 STEP 0.1
260 YY = ( EXP ( - ((XX - P1) $ (XX - P1) / (2 $ P2 $ P2)))) $ (1 / (P2 $ SQR (2 $ 3.142)))
270  GOSUB 50500
280  NEXT XX
290 :
300  END
```

**Listing 19.** *Figure 9* driver program.

```
10 :::: REM        HISTOGRAM DISPLAY DEMONSTRATION
20 :
30  HOME
40 :
50 :::: REM        INITIALISATION
60 G$ = "P1/P/W": GOSUB 50000
70 :
80 :::: REM        SET PLOTTING LIMITS
90 :::: REM        BX=5;TX=255;BY=50;TY=160
100 :::: REM        LY=0;UY=1000
110 AR = 1: GOSUB 51100
120 :
130 :::: REM        DRAW HISTOGRAM AREA
140 NG = 4:BG = 3
150  GOSUB 53000
160 :
170 :::: REM        DATA FOR HISTOGRAM
180  DIM X(12)
190  FOR L = 1 TO 12: READ X(L): NEXT L
200 :
210 :::: REM        DRAW BARS
220 F = 1
230  FOR A = 1 TO NG
240  FOR B = 1 TO BG
250 BC = B + 1
260 BH = X(F)
```

```
270 BN = B
280 GN = A
290  GOSUB 53500
300 F = F + 1
310  NEXT B
320  NEXT A
330 :
340  END
350 :
360  DATA     800,623,866,106,213,322,97,250,116,950,705,870
```

**Listing 20.** *Figure 10* driver program.

```
10 :::: REM       PIE CHART DEMONSTRATION
20 :
30 :::: REM       INITIALISATION
40 G$ = "P2/F/B": GOSUB 50000
50 :
60 :::: REM       PIE CHART NO.1
70 N = 500
80  DIM SF(10),XZ(N + 1),YZ(N + 1)
90 :
100 :::: REM       DRAW PERIMETER
110 CX = 70:CY = 95:R = 60
120  GOSUB 56000
130 :
140 :::: REM       DATA FOR CHART
150 SN = 0:NS = 7
160  GOSUB 410
170 :
180 :::: REM       SECTOR PIE
190  GOSUB 56300
200 :
210 :::: REM       EXTRACT SECTOR
220 SN = 2: GOSUB 56800
230 :
240 :::: REM     . PIE CHART NO.2
250 CX = 210:CY = 95:R = 60
260  GOSUB 56000
270 :
280 SN = 0:NS = 5
290  GOSUB 410
300 :
310  GOSUB 56300
320 :
330 :::: REM       SHADE SECTOR
340 SN = 4: GOSUB 57300
350 :
360  END
370 :
380  DATA       0.05,0.15,0.15,0.3,0.1,0.14,0.11
390  DATA       0.2,0.4,0.1,0.2,0.1
400 :
410  FOR L = 1 TO NS
420  READ SF(L)
430  NEXT L
440  RETURN
```

# CHAPTER 5

# The Analysis of Enzyme Reactions

## M.J.C. CRABBE

## 1. INTRODUCTION

This chapter introduces some uses for microcomputers in the study of ligand binding and biological catalysis. All the programs have been written on common, readily available machines. Where instructions specific to a particular machine have been used, this is pointed out in the text.

With one exception, programs are in BASIC. The exception is a program in FORTH (a word derived from fourth-generation computer language), a language which combines flexible 'user-friendliness' with high speed of execution.

Two types of computer program are detailed. The first contains programs to display features of ligand binding and catalysis. These have been of use in illustrating lectures and in class teaching. The second contains quantitative programs for analysing parameters in binding and catalysis. These are designed primarily for the research laboratory.

Microcomputers are an excellent tool in the everyday study of enzyme reactions. Their small size allows portability, and positioning near appropriate equipment, such as spectrophotometers, to which they can be interfaced. They can be transported easily to the lecture theatre, and used by students in practical classes. Today, most microcomputers have at least 32k of RAM. This allows considerable calculating power for kinetic and statistical transformations, and enough space to store alpha-carbon atom co-ordinates for about 300 amino acids. However, microcomputers are slower than mainframe machines when performing complex calculations. Their graphical display resolution is often limited and confined to raster rather than vector graphics. Despite their limitations, their wide availability and low cost make them a valuable tool for the biological scientist interested in the quantitative aspects of biological catalysis.

## 2. DISPLAYING ENZYME REACTION KINETICS AND MECHANISMS

One of the most important features of microcomputers to the enzymologist is their degree of graphical resolution. Early microcomputers, and small personal computers, had graphical resolutions in the order of 64 x 48 points or pixels. Now, resolutions of 300 x 200 pixels are common, and some microcomputers have resolutions up to 800 x 240 pixels, in colour. Clearly, the higher the resolution, the more graphical information can be imparted onto the screen. High resolution dot-matrix printers can provide hard copy of the screen output. The kinetic display and molecular modelling programs were written for higher resolution computers, 320 x 200 and 256 x 176 pixels.

These programs also illustrate the power of the small transportable computer. The molecular modelling program runs on a Sinclair ZX Spectrum with 48k RAM.

## 2.1 Displaying Basic Enzyme Kinetic Equations

A simple mathematical treatment of a one substrate enzyme catalysed reaction was made by Michaelis and Menten in 1913. If one assumes that the concentration of enzyme is much less than that of the substrate, the product concentration is effectively zero, and the product release step is much slower than the release of substrate from the enzyme-substrate complex. The reaction:

$$E + S \underset{k_2}{\overset{k_1}{\rightleftharpoons}} ES \xrightarrow{k_3} E + P \qquad \text{Equation 1}$$

is then considered to be at equilibrium, and the following relationship holds:

$$v = \frac{V_{max} [S]}{k_2/k_1 + [S]} \qquad \text{Equation 2}$$

where $V_{max}$ is maximum velocity and $k_2/k_1 = K_S$.

In this equilibrium assumption, $K_s$ is the dissociation constant of the enzyme-substrate complex. In 1925, Briggs and Haldane showed that a similar equation could be derived by utilising a less constraining steady-state assumption, whereby the concentrations of enzyme and enzyme-substrate complex remained effectively constant over the period of measurement. The rate equation now becomes:

$$v = \frac{V_{max} [S]}{K_m + [S]} \qquad \text{Equation 3}$$

The constant $K_m$ no longer represents a dissociation constant, but a concatenation of individual rate constants. Operationally, $K_m$ is the substrate concentration giving half maximal velocity. For multi-substrate reactions, the basic form of the rate equation is similar to Equation 3. However, in many cases enzymes can show non-hyperbolic kinetics because of random substrate addition, multiple binding sites, enzyme isomerisation, or co-operative interactions. In cases where a plot of initial velocity ($v$) *versus* total enzyme concentration ($E_0$) is linear and there is no significant enzyme polymerisation, the steady-state rate equation in the absence of products and when only one substrate (A) is varied is of the form:

$$\frac{v}{[E_o]} = \frac{\alpha_1[A] + \alpha_2[A]^2 + \dots \alpha_n[A]^n}{\beta_0 + \beta_1[A] + \beta_2[A]^2 + \dots \beta_{n+r}[A]^{n+r}} \qquad \text{Equation 4}$$

$\alpha$ and $\beta$ represent the kinetic constants. In most cases $r = 0$ except where dead-end complexes are formed. Where $n = 1$ and $r = 0$ the equation simplifies to the Michaelis-Menten equation. Squared terms in substrate concentration ($n = 2$) occur in the steady-state rate equation of a random order two-substrate reaction. The equation then becomes:

$$\frac{v}{[E_o]} = \frac{\alpha_1[A] + \alpha_2[A]^2}{\beta_0 + \beta_1[A] + \beta_2[A]^2} \qquad \text{Equation 5}$$

Botts showed that there are only four possible curve shapes that can be given by this equation, two with a sigmoid inflexion, and two with maxima, in *v versus s* space.

This program demonstrates the effects of changing the kinetic parameters on curve shape for both the Michaelis-Menten equation, and for the more general case where $n = 2$ (the 2:2 function). The program given in *Listing 1* was written on an RML 380 Z. Lines $1 - 29$, 34, 36 and 100 are specific graphics commands to the RML computer. Their function is to plot a box around the screen perimeter, and to call the high resolution plotting commands. Users of other computers simply replace these commands by their own specific plotting functions. The user is asked whether a 1:1 (i.e., Michaelis-Menten) or a 2:2 function is required (line 40), and enters M, or another letter, as appropriate. The rate equations to be substituted are on lines 80 (Michaelis-Menten) and 90 (2:2). Line 30 introduces an arc-tangent scaling function. Up to 10 separate graphs may be plotted simultaneously on one screen. The user then enters the parameters required; $K_m$ (line 52) and $V_{max}$ (line 54) for a 1:1 function, with the addition of two further parameters (lines 62 and 66) if a 2:2 function is being followed. The computer will then plot on the screen the curve shape defined by the parameters chosen. The resolution is 318 x 191 pixels. *Figure 1* shows a typical set of graphs produced from a 1:1 function. *Table 1* shows how changes in the parameter values can produce changes in the kinetic curve shapes.

## 2.2 Displaying Haemoglobin and Myoglobin Dissociation Curves

The program in Section 2.1 can be adapted to illustrate the oxygen dissociation curves for myoglobin and haemoglobin. The effect of changing pH, carbon dioxide concentration, and 2,3-diphosphoglycerate concentration on the haemoglobin dissociation can also be shown. A 2:2 equation is used (line 90) to express the required curve shapes. The equation parameters are incorporated into the program (line 50 for haemoglobin, line 53 for myoglobin, line 56 for a right shift in

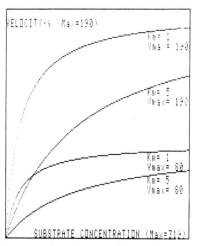

**Figure 1.** Four kinetic plots produced from program *Listing 1*. $K_m$ and $V_{max}$ values were entered as shown.

109

**Table 1.** Parameter Values and Curve Shapes Obtainable from the Kinetic Display Program (*Figure 1*).

| Parameter | | | | Curve shape |
|---|---|---|---|---|
| $K_m$ ($\alpha_1$) | $V_{max}$ ($\beta_1$) | Numerator constant ($\alpha_2$) | Denominator constant ($\beta_2$) | |
| 45 | 23 | 345 | 2 | No maxima or sigmoid inflexions |
| 0.4 | 123 | 23 | 4 | One maximum |
| 0.056 | 5.66 | 3.22 | 0.03 | One sigmoid inflexion |
| 0.056 | 5.66 | 3.44 | 0.003 | Sigmoid inflexion tending to an asymptote of positive slope |

The 2:2 function should be selected.

The rate equation followed is: $V = \dfrac{\alpha_1 x + \alpha_2 x^2}{1 + \beta_1 x + \beta_2 x^2}$

These parameter values serve as examples. Others should be investigated to show the dependence of curve shape upon the parameters (e.g., lowering the $\beta_1$ value will shift the sigmoid curve to the left).

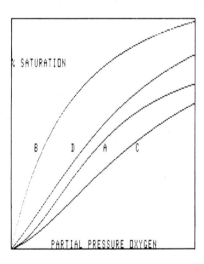

**Figure 2.** Plots of percentage saturation *versus* oxygen partial pressure for haemoglobin (Hb) and myoglobin. A = normal Hb dissociation curve, B = myoglobin dissociation curve, C = Hb dissociation curve with decreased pH, increased $P_{CO_2}$, or increased 2,3 diphosphoglycerate, D = Hb dissociation curve with increased pH, decreased $P_{CO_2}$, or decreased 2,3 diphosphoglycerate.

the haemoglobin dissociation curve, and line 59 for a left shift in the dissociation curve) (*Listing 2*). The output from this program is shown in *Figure 2*, again using an RML 380 Z and an Epson dot-matrix printer.

## 2.3 High Resolution Graphic Display of Molecules

One of the most useful features of computers to the biological scientist is the ability to produce realistic graphic displays. Interactive computer graphics systems can be used in molecular modelling, and to a limited extent, at present, in structure prediction. The hardware required for such graphical modelling normally includes one or more mainframe computers and a specially designed vector graphics terminal. The use of vector graphics enables the user to define lines between specific points anywhere on the screen, and is capable of a resolution of in the order of 4000 x 4000. It is possible, however, to use the general principles of 3-dimensional matrix transformation (1) in a program for microcomputers which has some of the features of the larger machines at a fraction of the cost, and uses conventional raster graphics displays. The following features are programmed into a 3-dimensional display program written for a Sinclair Spectrum with 48k RAM.

(i) The program displays a diagram of a molecule in perspective.
(ii) Intensity depth cueing is provided in six colours and on a grey scale (in six gradations) for monochrome and hard copy.
(iii) The molecule can be panned in the *x*, *y* or *z* directions.
(iv) The molecule can be viewed from any angle in the *x*, *y* or *z* direction.
(v) The magnification can be set independently in the *x*, *y* or *z* directions to provide windowing onto specific parts of the molecule from any direction.
(vi) The program can be used with a joystick to provide control of viewing angle and magnification.
(vii) Any atom can be labelled by a bright cross.
(viii) Any atom can be circled to approximate its Van der Waal's radius.

Limited animation facilities may also be used to give enhanced depth perception. Five separate views of the molecule, differing by 1−2 degrees, are stored separately on tape. A machine code program can then be used to take each separate view, or screen, and replay them one after the other. The impression is of a molecule that is rotating around its midpoint (2).

For a general discussion on computer graphics, the reader is referred to references 1, 3−4.

### 2.3.1 *Graphical Display of Lysozyme*

The program, containing all the co-ordinates to display the alpha carbon backbone of lysozyme, is shown in *Listing 3*. The user is first asked whether a joystick will be used (line 57). A Kempston joystick has been used with success, but any stick with leaf switches interfacing to the IN function should be satisfactory. If a joystick is not required, line 57 and lines 7000−9090 can be omitted.

Lines 100−110 set up the transformation matrix arrays. The user is then asked to provide the scaling factors or degrees of magnification in each *x*, *y* and *z* direction (line 120 to subroutine 8000−8030). For a normal display the magnification should be the same in each dimension. The user then enters the amount of panning in each dimension (lines 141−160). This facility enables the user to centre the molecule, or a part of the molecule, on the screen. This is particularly useful when viewing part of the molecule at high magnification. Lines 170−197 provide inputs for the rotational angle in degrees in the *x*, *y* and *z* directions from which the molecule is to be viewed. The angles are then converted into radians (line 280).

After setting the resolution of the bonds to dotted or continuous lines (line 202) and the colour of the screen border and text (lines 250 – 270), the program jumps to a number of subroutines. The user can set any number of residues to be labelled by a bright cross on the screen (this appears as a cross on hard copy) or by a circle. The radius of the circle can be set to approximate the Van der Waal's radius of the atom or of the space which might be filled by the side chain of a particular residue (lines 9500 – 9546).

Lines 900 – 950 clear the screen and draw a box around the graphics area. Lines 1000 – 1200 set up the dimension arrays and store the co-ordinate data. The number of atoms is stored as the variable np (129 for lysozyme) and the number of bonds between the atoms is stored as ne. Array s contains the $x$, $y$ and $z$ co-ordinates as stored in the data statements, array e contains the line connection data, and array m contains the transformed co-ordinates. The $x$, $y$ and $z$ co-ordinates for lysozyme derived from X-ray crystallographic data are stored in lines 1205 – 1229. The co-ordinates should be entered as: $x$ co-ordinate of first atom, $y$ co-ordinate of first atom, $z$ co-ordinate of first atom, $x$ co-ordinate of second atom, $y$ co-ordinate of second atom, and so on. Lines 1300 – 1322 contain the line connection data. Here, the atom numbers to be joined should be entered. Thus atoms 1 and 2 are connected, then atoms 2 and 3, and so on. For a protein backbone, all the atoms are connected in series, but for other molecular displays, alternative connections may be required (e.g., for display of amino acid side chains). The method for connection data storage used here is therefore more flexible than a simple FOR...NEXT loop. Lines 5000 – 5900 (the next subroutine) find the centre of the shape, and the co-ordinates are then transformed into the required positions, scaled and translated into screen co-ordinates using the equations in lines 3000 – 4900. The shape in perspective is then drawn onto the screen, together with any atom labelling required, by lines 2000 – 2900. As the chain is synthesised on the screen, the residue number is printed (line 2215). Colour and intensity depth cueing are also incorporated.

The user can then view the molecule from a different position, or with different windows, magnification or labelling. *Figure 3* shows a typical output from the program. A magnification factor of 4.8 was entered for each dimension (line 8000), and the molecule was panned 80 pixels in the $x$ direction and 55 pixels in the $y$ direction, and viewed from an angle of 90 degrees to the normal. The solid lines represent bonds nearer to the viewer than the dotted lines. If a colour monitor or television set is used, then the colours appear in order of increasing depth: blue, red, magenta, green, cyan and yellow. Note that on the Spectrum, only one colour per character block is permissible, so that occasionally false colours appear on the display where bonds run closely adjacent to each other. On a monochrome monitor or television, a decreasing grey scale is seen.

*Figure 4* shows the effect of windowing and labelling. A magnification of 9 in each dimension was used. The alpha carbon atom of glutamate residue 35, which acts as a general acid catalyst, is labelled with a cross. On the opposite side of the substrate binding cleft, the alpha carbon of aspartate residue 52, which stabilises the carbonium ion transition state, is labelled by a circle.

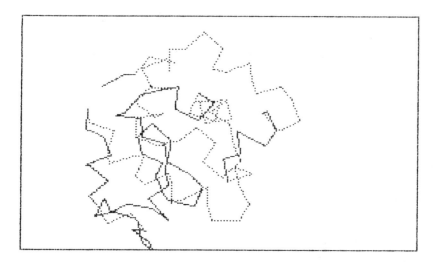

**Figure 3.** Graphical representation of the lysozyme molecule, from program *Listing 3*.

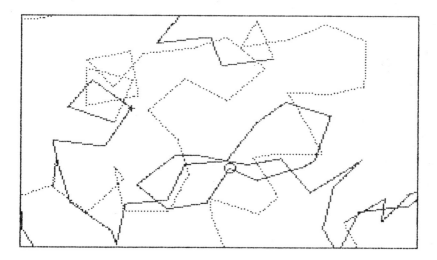

**Figure 4.** Illustration of part of the structure of lysozyme, showing Glu 35 labelled with a cross and Asp 52 labelled with a circle.

### 2.3.2 *Display of the Immunoglobulin Fc Fragment*

The above program can be modified slightly to enable molecules larger than 200 atoms to be displayed. All the co-ordinates should be entered as before, but the array values for np and ne should not exceed 200 with 48k of RAM. Instead of entering separate line connection data for all the atoms, the data starting at line 1300 need only connect about 200 atoms together. After 209 atoms have been plotted and connected as required, a flag variable can be set (e.g., by letting r5 = 1 on line 457) which then enables the arrays to be redefined. *Listing 4* shows how

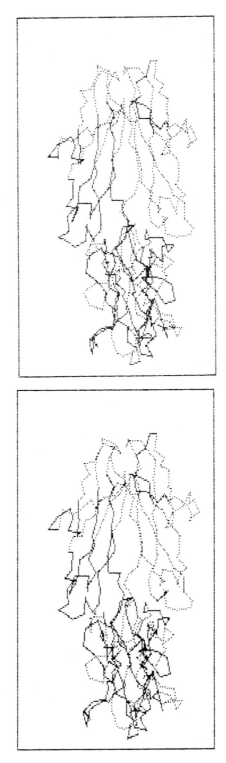

**Figure 5.** A stereo diagram of the alpha-carbon backbone of immunoglobulin Fragment Fc, produced using program *Listing 4.*

lines 50−1170 of the modified program can be written. The data statements for the rest of the molecule start on line 1247. This is then plotted on the screen with the same angles, magnification and labelling as before, so that the whole molecule is drawn in two parts. *Figure 5* shows the result of this modification for the Fc fragment of immunoglobulins, shown here as a stereo pair. Altogether, over 1200 separate co-ordinates were entered. With disc-based microcomputers, co-ordinates can be stored as separate disc files. This is currently being implemented on a BBC version which enables interactive manipulations (M.J.C. Crabbe, unpublished work).

If desired, co-ordinates can be entered from a separate data tape or disc by incorporating a LOAD...DATA command into the program. For producing stereo pair diagrams, two displays should be produced on hard copy, differing by about 3−6 degrees in $x$ axis viewing angle. They can then be mounted side by side and viewed from the appropriate distance ($\sim 30-60$ cm). The molecular diagrams reproduced here were drawn on an Epson FX-80 dot-matrix printer run from a Kempston interface to the Sinclair computer. The software provided by Kempston to run the interface was incorporated as a subroutine to the main programs (lines 9800−9880).

## 3. QUANTITATIVE STUDIES OF LIGAND BINDING AND ENZYME REACTIONS

### 3.1 Calculation of Buffer pH

As enzyme reactions require the pH to be kept stable, it is desirable to maintain hydrogen ion concentration *in vitro* by means of appropriate buffers. A solution of weak acid and its conjugate base (or a weak base and its conjugate acid) can resist pH change at the $pK_a$, where the ratio of acid to base is 1:1. Blood plasma is a mixed buffer system, the major buffers being $HCO_3^-/CO_2$; $HPO_4^{2-}/H_2PO_4^-$ and protein/H protein.

Buffers can be prepared by using the Henderson-Hasselbalch equation, which is derived from the equation for the dissociation of the weak acid HA:

$$K_a = \frac{[H^+][A^-]}{[HA]} \qquad \text{Equation 6}$$

Now pH $= -\log [H]$ and $pK = -\log K_a$, therefore:

$$pH = pK_a + \log \frac{[A]}{[HA]} \qquad \text{Equation 7}$$

This is valid if the concentrations of weak acid and conjugate base are equal to their activities in solution.

Other factors which affect buffer behaviour are the temperature and ionic strength of the medium. Temperature changes affect the $pK_a$ of the buffer, and can be corrected by use of the appropriate temperature co-efficient. Corrections for ionic strength for weak acids can be made by the Debye-Huckel relationship:

$$pK_a' = pK_a - (2n - 1)\left[\frac{0.5\,I^{\frac{1}{2}}}{1 + I^{\frac{1}{2}}} - 0.1\,I\right] \qquad \text{Equation 8}$$

where $I$ is ionic strength (equivalent to concentration for weak acids or bases), and $n$ is the number of charges. The pH of the solution can then be determined from the modified $pK_a$ value.

The program is given in *Listing 5*. The user needs to enter the $pK_a$ value of the buffer at 25°C (line 10), the number of charges (line 40), the buffer concentration (line 70), the temperature in °C (line 100) and the temperature coefficient of the buffer (line 130) which can be found in standard biochemical data books. For example, the temperature coefficient for phosphoric acid ($pK_a = 7.2$) is $-0.0028$, that for Tris ($pK_a = 8.06$) is $-0.028$. The program then calculates and prints the temperature-corrected $pK_a$ (lines 160−170) and substitutes into the appropriate Debye-Huckel equation depending on whether a weak acid or base is being considered (lines 180−240), before printing out the $pK_a$ value (line 250), now corrected for temperature and ionic strength. The user then enters the desired pH (line 260) and the program prints the number of millilitres of a 1 M solution of each species of acid or base to which water is added to make up a final volume of 1 litre (lines 310−340).

This program uses no special graphics commands, and has been run successfully on Sinclair, RML and Commodore PET computers with less than 16k of RAM.

## 3.2 Graphical Analysis of Primary Enzyme Kinetic Data

Having developed a suitable assay for an enzyme reaction, one must verify that the rate of formation of product or utilisation of substrate is linear over a reasonable length of time. *Listing 6* allows the user to enter up to 50 pairs of variables, for example absorbance and time, tabulates the values and asks if any alterations in the data are required, plots the data on a graph with automatic scaling of axes, draws the best fit regression line, and prints the regression data on the screen. The program was written for a Sinclair ZX Spectrum, but the graphics commands used are found on many other microcomputers. Line 10 sets the drawing and background colours, in this case black and white. The user can enter a heading for the graph (line 32), the number of data points (line 40), and the pairs of $x$ and $y$ values (e.g., time and absorbance). The data are then reviewed (subroutine 2000−2240) and altered if required. The next subroutine (3000−3080) determines the maximum and minimum values on each axis. The screen is cleared (line 92), a border drawn around the area of the graph (lines 100−210) and the maximum and minimum values for each axis printed on the graph (lines 215−217). Scaling of the data is then performed to the graph resolution, here about 240 x 150, (lines 230−300) and the scaling factors then translated into point increments (lines 310−320). The points are then plotted and joined with a dotted line (lines 330−450). The linear regression data are calculated (lines 352, and 1000−1050) and printed as slope, $y$ intercept and regression coefficient, with appropriate standard deviations. Finally, the regression line can be plotted on the screen (lines 4002−4050 and 310−385). Subroutine 5000 contains the software for hard copy if desired (supplied by Kempston with their Centronics interface). Other computers may not need software written into the main program in order to obtain hard copy.

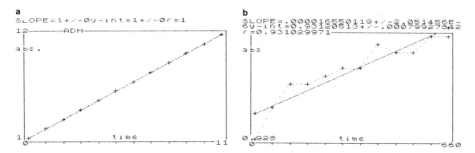

**Figure 6.** Samples of graphs produced from program *Listing 6;* (a) ideal linear regression plot; (b) graph of absorbance at 340 nm *versus* time for the enzyme aldehyde dehydrogenase obtained on a Multistat enzyme analyser.

Two typical graphs produced from the program are shown in *Figure 6*, obtained on an Epson FX-80 dot-matrix printer. *Figure 6* shows an ideal linear regression to 12 determinations of absorbance at 340 nm at different times for the enzyme aldehyde dehydrogenase. Both slope and *y*-intercept values are 1, there are no standard deviations, and the correlation coefficient (r) is also 1. *Figure 6* shows a plot of absorbance at 340 nm against time for aldehyde dehydrogenase obtained using a Multistat enzyme analyser. The absorbances are shown joined by the dotted line, while the continuous line is the best fit linear regression line. The regression data are given above the graph.

One advantage of this program is the automatic scaling of axes and points; the user does not have to provide maximum or minimum values for plotting.

### 3.3 First and Second Order Chemical Kinetics
In order to appreciate the kinetics of enzyme reactions, it is useful to understand the principles of first and second order chemical kinetics.

### 3.3.1 *First Order Kinetics*
If a reactant A is converted to product P:

$$A \xrightarrow{k} P$$

then the rate of formation of product equals the rate constant *k* times the concentration of the reactant A:

$$d[P]/dt = k[A] \qquad\qquad \text{Equation 9}$$

Equation 9 can be integrated and rearranged:

$$\ln[A]/[A - X] = kt \qquad\qquad \text{Equation 10}$$

where [A − X] is the concentration of A at time *t*, and X is the concentration of product at time *t*. The half-life time for a first order reaction can be found from:

$$t = \frac{1}{k} \ln([A]/[A/2]) = \ln 2/k = 0.693k \qquad\qquad \text{Equation 11}$$

When a reaction end-point is not obvious because of other, slower reactions or instrumental drift, *k* can be determined from a simple progress curve using the

Guggenheim method. This is an algebraic procedure which takes the natural logarithm of the difference between early observations (D1) and values approximately three half-times from zero time (D1'). The first order rate constant can then be determined from the slope of the line of (Di − Di') against $t$ for the ith determination.

Apparent first order behaviour does not imply an analogous kinetic mechanism. For example in the reaction:

$$A + B \rightarrow P$$

if one reactant is in excess, pseudo first order kinetics will apply, with velocities dependent upon the concentration of the minor component. Time-dependent enzyme inhibitors can also be analysed by pseudo first order kinetics (see Section 3.6.5). Use of such inhibitors can give information on the topology of substrate binding sites.

The program is given in *Listing 7*. It was written on an RML 380 Z, in less than 16k of RAM, but uses no machine-specific commands, and is suitable for any machine using BASIC. Lines 1−3 set the line print commands for an Epson printer. The user can opt for the Guggenheim method if there is no end-point for the reaction (line 10). Absorbances and times are entered as appropriate (lines 30−40) and 170−180, or 200 if there is no end-point) and regression analysis on the data performed. The program provides a rate constant for the reaction, a regression co-efficient, and the half-life time.

### 3.3.2 *Second Order Kinetics*

Bimolecular reactions involve two similar or different species:

either $$A + A \overset{k}{\rightarrow} P \qquad \text{or} \qquad A + B \overset{k}{\rightarrow} P$$

The rate equation is:

$$d[P]/dt = k\,(A - X)\,(B - X) \qquad \qquad \text{Equation 12}$$

which can be rearranged to:

$$\frac{1}{(A - B)}\ln\left[\frac{B(A - X)}{A(B - X)}\right] = kt \qquad \qquad \text{Equation 13}$$

with definitions as above. If A = B, or [A] = [B], then the equation simplifies to:

$$\frac{X}{A(A - X)^2} = kt \qquad \qquad \text{Equation 14}$$

The program is described in *Listing 8*. It was written on an RML 380 Z, in less than 16k of RAM, but as in the above program, no machine-specific commands are used, and the program could run on any BASIC machine. The principles are very similar to the program in Section 3.3.1. Line 1−4 set the Epson printer commands. The user can select whether the reactants are equal in concentration or otherwise (line 14), and then enter the absorbances and times (lines 30, 60, 240, and 280 or 320). If the initial concentrations are entered in moles per litre (line 110) the rate constants will be given in the appropriate units, per mole per second (line 590) or litre per mole per second (line 610). Where A = B, then the half-life time is calculated as the reciprocal of the product of the rate constant and the initial concentration (lines 680 – 695).

## 3.4 Simple and Rapid Kinetic Analysis in FORTH

Often one requires a program to perform many simple calculations very rapidly. In kinetics, this usually means statistical calculations followed by transformation of the mean initial rate data into one or more graphical spaces, before plotting. This program, in FORTH, calculates mean initial velocities and ratios of initial velocity to substrate concentration ($v$/[S], $1/v$ and $1$/[S]) for plotting into Lineweaver-Burke and Eadie-Hofstee spaces). The rapid parameter stack manipulations and colon definitions used in FORTH mean that calculations are performed much more rapidly than in BASIC, but without the difficulties of programming in machine code or assembler language. The reader wishing to learn about FORTH language programming is referred to two introductory books on the subject (5,6). The program is detailed in *Listing 9*. Lines 2 and 3 on screen 3 set the variables A – H to zero. Double precision is used throughout the calculations. Definition S stores the substrate concentration, V1 the first initial velocity value and V, subsequent initial velocity values. The definition MEAN (screen 4) then calculates the mean velocity and prints the required transformations.

A sample output of the program is shown in *Figure 7*. The text underlined is entered by the programmer.

## 3.5 Distribution-free Analysis in Ligand Binding and Enzyme Reactions

If we assume an enzyme reaction to obey the Michaelis-Menten equation, then in order to obtain accurate estimates of the kinetic parameters $K_m$ and $V_{max}$ (see Section 2.1) we need to transform our data into linearising graphical spaces, for example, Lineweaver-Burke, Hanes or Eadie-Hofstee space. However, the least-squares method of fitting a straight line to the transformed data in such plots is fraught with difficulties. These include the assumptions that random errors are normally distributed, and that only the dependent variable, initial velocity, is subject to experimental errors, while any errors in substrate concentration are not considered. The introduction of a transformation of the Michaelis-Menten equation by Eisenthal and Cornish-Bowden to enable distribution-free plotting of kinetic data has proved valuable when the Michaelis-Menten equation is obeyed (7,8). Such distribution-free methods, where these assumptions are dispensed with, can be applied to both ligand binding and enzyme reactions. They can also be used to give accurate estimates of the initial velocities of enzyme reactions.

```
3 VALUES ok
5.5 S 0.67 V1 0.4 V 0.8 V MEAN   V= 0.6233
V/S= 0.1133
1/V= 1.6043
1/S= 0.1818
S/V= 8.8240 ok
```

**Figure 7.** Simple and rapid kinetic analysis in FORTH; typical output from program *Listing 9*. The user enters the text that is underlined.

### 3.5.1 *Distribution-free Analysis for Ligand Binding*

Assuming equilibrium, the Scatchard equation for ligand binding is:

$$r = \frac{n[A]}{K_d + [A]} \qquad \text{Equation 15}$$

where [A] is the free ligand concentration, r is the bound ligand concentration, $n$ is the concentration of ligand binding sites and $K_d$ is the binding constant. These values can be rearranged and plotted in any of three distribution-free spaces as shown in *Table 2*. Here, $n$ and $K_d$ are treated as variables, and r and [A] as constants. For each pair of r and [A] there are an infinite number of $n$ and $K_d$ values, but only one set will satisfy all values for r and [A] in a given system. The second space, $K_d/n$ against $1/n$ has a number of advantages. For each determination the point [A]/r is plotted on the ordinate axis, the point 1/r is plotted on the abscissa, and a line drawn between them. The lines will intersect at a point corresponding to $K_d/n$ on the ordinate, and $1/n$ on the abscissa. When there are a number of intersections, the median value is taken to eliminate outliers. In this plot, unlike the other two shown in *Table 2*, intersections lie within the axes, and bias arising from intersections in other quadrants is removed, as has been shown for simple enzyme mechanisms (9). As with enzyme kinetics, ligand binding can be described by rational polynomial functions of the form described in Section 2.1. In such complex ligand binding cases the plot of $K_d/n$ *versus* $1/n$ will give a median intersection of $\beta_0/\alpha_1$ on the ordinate axis, and $\beta_m/\alpha_n$ where m = n + r (Section 2.1) on the abscissa, as shown in *Table 2*.

The program, which was written on a Commodore PET 3016 computer, is given in *Listing 10*. Line 5 opens the line to the printer. The user enters the number of observations (line 90) and the variables are dimensioned (line 100). Free and bound ligand concentrations are then entered (lines 110 – 112), and the intercepts on both axes are calculated, sorted and printed (lines 126 – 320). The maximum number of binding sites and the dissociation constant are then calculated and printed. The two routines are necessary as both odd and even numbers of observations must be dealt with (lines 368 – 425). Finally, the program calculates and prints the residual values (i.e., the difference between each intersection calculated from the observations, and the median value). Plots of the residual values can be very informative. For example, they can help to distinguish

**Table 2.** Distribution-free Plots for the Analysis of Ligand Binding.

|   | y axis | x axis | slope | intercept on y axis | intercept on x axis |
|---|--------|--------|-------|---------------------|---------------------|
| 1. | $n$ | $K_d$ | r/[A] | r | −[A] |
| 2. | $K_d/n$ $(\beta_0/\alpha_1)$ | $1/n$ $(\beta_m/\alpha_n)$ | −[A] | [A]/r | 1/r |
| 3. | $n/K_d$ | $1/K_d$ | r | r/[A] | −1/[A] |

[A], free ligand concentration; r, bound ligand concentration; $n$, number of receptor sites; $K_d$, dissociation constant for ligand binding. Alphas and betas are the numerator and denominator binding constants for complex binding mechanisms.

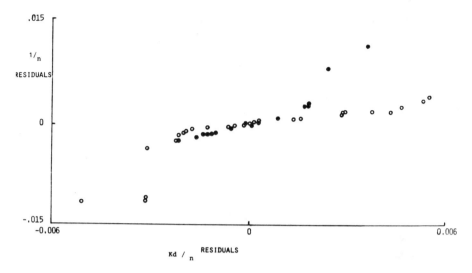

**Figure 8.** Plots of the residuals from intersections in *K/n versus* 1/*n* space, as described in the text, for the binding of tritiated etorphine to bovine retina; $\bigcirc$, data from reference 11, $\bullet$, data from reference 10.

between single and multiple populations of binding sites. Binding experiments for the opiate tritiated etorphine have yielded both linear (10) and biphasic (11) Scatchard plots. However, a plot of $K_d/n$ *versus* 1/*n* of the data from reference 11 indicates a high degree of scatter, with many outlier intersections. The residual plot calculated using the computer program described here shows very little clustering of points in either case (*Figure 8*). This indicates that the binding of tritiated etorphine to bovine retina is probably to a single population of binding sites. This is substantiated by the close agreement between the values for *n* and $K_d$ calculated by the distribution-free analysis with those from reference 10.

A distribution-free plot of the binding data for manganese to 5′ (3/5) tRNA from reference 12 clearly shows two major intersections (*Figure 9*). The residual plot of the intersections (*Figure 10*) shows two major clusters of points, corresponding to the two populations of sites. The values for *n* and $K_d$ calculated by this computer program are in close agreement to those calculated by the original authors using Scatchard analysis.

### 3.5.2 *Distribution-free Analysis for Enzyme Reactions*

Similar arguments for distribution-free analysis apply to enzyme reactions, but here the situation is complicated by the need to obtain accurate initial velocity values. Integrated forms of the Michaelis-Menten equation have been used in combination with Lineweaver-Burke, Eadie-Hofstee and other plots in order to calculate accurate initial velocities and kinetic parameters (13 − 15). We can combine distribution-free analysis and integrated rate equations in order to calculate initial velocities, $K_m$ and $V_m$. The integrated Michaelis-Menten equation:

$$V_m(t) = s_o - s_t + K_m \ln (s_o/s_t) \qquad \text{Equation 16}$$

121

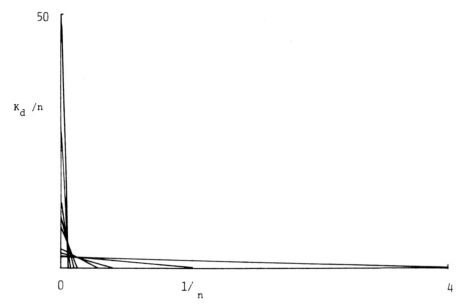

**Figure 9.** Distribution-free plot of the binding of manganese to 5' (three-fifths) tRNA. Data from reference 12.

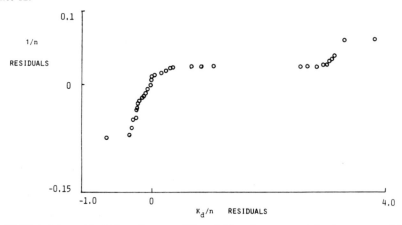

**Figure 10.** Plot of the residuals from the mean $K/n$ and $1/n$ values, computed using program *Listing 10*, for the binding of manganese to 5' (three-fifths) tRNA.

where $V_m$ is apparent maximal velocity, $t$ is time, $s_0$ is initial substrate concentration, $s_t$ is substrate concentration at time $t$ and $K_m$ is the apparent Michaelis constant. This equation can be rearranged into three slope-intercept distribution-free forms, as shown in *Table 3*. For the first plot, a line drawn between the point $K_m$, $V_m$ and $-(s_0 - s_t)/\ln(s_0/s_t) = s_0$ will intersect the $V_m$ axis at $v_0$. Similarly for the second plot, a line of slope $S_0$ drawn through a point $1/V_m, K_m$ will intersect the ordinate at $s_0/v_0$ and the abscissa at $1/v_0$, while for the third plot a line drawn between the point $V_m/K_m$, $1/K_m$ and $-\ln(s_0/s_t)/(s_0 - s_t) = s_0$ will intersect the ordinate at $v_0/s_0$, and be of slope $v_0$. The values found for $v_0$ can then be replotted in distribution-free space, or re-applied to the computer.

**Table 3.** Distribution-free Plots for the Analysis of Enzyme Reactions, from Initial Velocity Determinations and from Progress Curves.

| y axis | x axis | slope | intercept on y axis | intercept on x axis |
|---|---|---|---|---|
| 1. $V_{max}$ | $K_m$ | $v/[S]$ <br> $\dfrac{\ln s_0/s_t}{t}$ | $v$ <br> $\dfrac{(s_0 - s_t)}{t}$ | $-[S]$ <br> $\dfrac{-(s_0 - s_t)}{\ln(s_0/s_t)}$ |
| 2. $K_m/V_{max}$ <br> $(\beta_0/\alpha_1)$ | $1/V_{max}$ <br> $(\beta_m/\alpha_n)$ | $-[S]$ <br> $\dfrac{-(s_0 - s_t)}{\ln(s_0/s_t)}$ | $[S]/v$ <br> $t/\ln(s_0/s_t)$ | $1/v$ <br> $t/(s_0 - s_t)$ |
| 3. $V_{max}/K_m$ | $1/K_m$ | $v$ <br> $\dfrac{s_0 - s_t}{t}$ | $v/[S]$ <br> $\ln(s_0/s_t)$ | $-1/[S]$ <br> $\dfrac{-\ln/s_0/s_t)}{s_0 - s_t}$ |

$V_{max}$, apparent maximal velocity; $K_m$, apparent Michaelis constant; $v$, initial velocity; [S], substrate concentration; $s_0$, initial substrate concentration (i.e., at $t = 0$); $s_t$, substrate concentration at time $t$. Alphas and betas are the numerator and denominator constants for complex mechanisms.

Statistical considerations using steady-state kinetic data indicate that the second plot is the one of choice (9). It is the subject of *Listing 11a* and *b* which give a similar program to that in the previous section. It was written for a Commodore PET computer, but uses no special commands. As before, the user enters the number of observations (line 65), followed by the initial substrate concentration (line 110) and the substrate concentration at various times (line 114). Calculations proceed as before, and values for $v_0$, $K_m$ and $V_m$ are obtained. Values for $K_m$ and $V_{max}$ obtained from this single progress curve will not be accurate. However, the $v_0$ values obtained at a number of substrate concentrations can then be re-applied to the distribution-free program, changing the input parameters, so that V(I) (line 170) represents the initial velocity and S(I) (line 170) represents the substrate concentration. The program will then provide accurate estimates of $K_m$ [K(L) in line 370 or line 400] and $V_{max}$ [M(L) in line 380 or line 410].

If the mechanism is known to exhibit complex kinetics, then lines drawn between *S/V* and *1/V* will intersect at a median point $\beta_0/\alpha_1$ on the ordinate and $\beta_m/\alpha_n$ on the abscissa, as $K_m/V_m$ becomes $\beta_0/\alpha_1$ and $1/V_m$ becomes $\beta_m/\alpha_n$. The values obtained for $\alpha$ and $\beta$ can then be compared with those obtained by polynomial curve fitting. This has been done for the non-Michaelian enzymes polyol dehydrogenase and hexokinase from lens, and shows a close agreement between the methods (16). Statistical estimates of the parameters can be calculated (17).

### 3.6 Steady-state Analysis of Enzyme Reactions

In many cases, it might prove useful to have a single computer program for the analysis of enzyme kinetic data, particularly if the enzyme has been shown to obey the Michaelis-Menten equation under the majority of conditions (18).

The remaining part of this chapter is devoted to such a multi-functional program. Each section is discussed separately, and the user may either treat each subroutine as a separate program, or run them all together to form a single master program.

### 3.6.1 *Kinetic Transformations and Graphical Analyses*

While classical kinetic analysis has largely relied on the Lineweaver-Burke plot, other graphical spaces may be more discerning in disclosing turning points, maxima or minima. The program described here therefore allows the user to plot data in any of the following spaces.

(i)     $v$ *versus* [S]. Classical Michaelian enzymes will give a rectangular hyperbola.

(ii)    $1/v$ *versus* $1/$[S]. Lineweaver-Burke space.

(iii)   $v$ *versus* $v/$[S]. Eadie-Hofstee space; the most discerning for non-hyperbolic behaviour.

(iv)    [S]$/v$ *versus* [S]. Hanes space.

(v)     $v$ *versus* log [S]. Sometimes useful when very wide substrate concentration ranges are being examined.

(vi)    log $v$ *versus* log [S]. Again useful if very wide variations in rate and substrate concentration are being examined.

(vii)   [S] $v$ *versus* [S]. Useful when r $>0$ in the rate equation (see Section 2.1). If, in $v$ *versus* [S] space, v$\to0$ as [S]$\to\infty$, then r$>0$. This plot will then have a horizontal asymptote or straight line of positive slope as [S] if r$=1$ (19).

(viii)  [S] $v$ *versus* [S]. As in plot vii, but now a horizontal asymptote or straight line of positive slope will be obtained as [S]$\to\infty$ if r$=2$.

(ix)    $v/$[S] *versus* v, or r$/$[A] *versus* r (see Section 3.5.1). Scatchard space. For use in ligand binding studies, where r $=$ bound ligand concentration, and [A] $=$ free ligand concentration.

Before transformations into one or more of the graphical spaces, the kinetic data is analysed statistically. Where more than one initial velocity determination at a single substrate concentration has been made, the mean initial velocity, the standard deviation, and the 95% confidence limits are calculated. The 95% confidence limits are given by:

$$v \pm \frac{1.96\sigma}{\sqrt{n}}$$

where $\sigma$ is standard deviation of the population, and $n$ is the number of determinations, assuming the distribution of $v$ is normal.

The program, which was written on a Commodore PET computer, is given in *Listing 12*. The line to the printer (a PET 3022 printer) is opened, and the variables dimensioned (lines $100-150$). Line 180 allows the user to examine the effect of substrate, temperature or inhibitors on the enzyme reaction velocity. This section deals only with the effect of substrate. Only include these lines ($180-195$) if you wish to enter the comprehensive program. The program then jumps to the statistical subroutine (line 1000), where the user enters the total number of s,v data pairs (line 1000), and the individual initial velocity determinations (lines $1026-1110$) at each substrate concentration (line 1005). Note that if the temperature option has been selected, the user is asked to enter the temperature (lines 1004, 1008); the statistical subroutine being an essential feature of the Arrhenius calculations (see Section 3.6.2). Lines 130 and 135 are to prevent entry of non-integer or very large numbers for the number of individual initial velocity determinations. Where only one velocity measurement is made at each substrate concentration, no estimate for standard deviation or 95% confidence limits can be given (lines 1127, 1182, 1185). In other cases these parameters are calculated (lines 1130 – 1181) and, together with the kinetic transformations, can be printed as hard copy (using the PRINT #5 command) if desired (lines 1203 – 1410).

The user can then select the graphical space for data plotting (lines 250 – 980). Note that lines 200 – 230 enable the user with the complete comprehensive program to bypass any data plotting and go on to non-linear regression analysis (see Section 3.6.3). Each part of the program devoted to a particular plot (see above for all the plots which can be used) contains the necessary statistical data transformations, which enable mean values and 95% confidence limits to be plotted. The plotting subroutine starts at line 2000. It is intended for low resolution computers, and for this reason the x axis runs vertically along the paper, while the y axis runs horizontally. The length of the y axis is limited by the width of the output device (line 2050). If a 40-character device is used, then variable B2 on line 2050 should be set to 40 rather than 80. Users with high resolution computers could adapt the plotting program in Section 3.2. With the subroutine shown here, the user must enter upper limit, lower limit and incremental values for both x and y axes (lines 2000 – 2030). Scaling is then performed, the y axis is printed and data is plotted onto the x axis as the paper feeds through the printer. The plot shows both the mean velocity and the 95% confidence limits transformed into the required space. Where the 95% confidence limits are less than the value of one y axis increment, the bar lines are not printed. If the incremental values entered are not sufficient to separate two data points, then double printing may occur. If this happens, replot (line 2890) and change the increment values.

A typical output from this program is shown in *Figure 11*.

### 3.6.2 *The Effect of Temperature on Enzyme Reactions*

In general, enzyme activity increases with increasing temperature up to about 50°C. Above this temperature catalytic activity decreases sharply as the protein denatures. Some enzymes, for example those isolated from thermophilic bacteria, are stable at up to 90°C, possibly because of strong inter-molecular ionic and hydrophobic bonds.

Data are analysed using the Arrhenius equation, based on the transition state theory of chemical reactions:

$$d \ln k/dT = E/RT^2 \qquad \text{Equation 17}$$

where $E$ is the energy of activation, R is the gas constant, $T$ is the temperature in degrees K, and $k$ is the rate constant for the reaction.

$E$ is related to the heat of activation ($\Delta H$) given by the relationship:

$$E = \Delta H + RT \qquad \text{Equation 18}$$

A plot of ln $k$ *versus* $1/T$ will give a line with slope:

$$- \frac{(\Delta H + RT)}{2.303\ R} = E/2.303R$$

```
TOTAL NUMBER  OF POINTS = 6
SUBSTRATE CONCENTRATION = .4
NUMBER OF INITIAL RATE VALUES=              3
SUM=          .0449
SUM OF SQUARES=              6.8393E-04

MEAN V VALUE +/- STANDARD DEVIATION= .0149666667 +/- 2.4419937E-03

MEAN V VALUE +/- 95% CONFIDENCE LIMITS= .0149666667 +/- 2.76337602E-03

VARIANCE=              5.96333325E-06
STANDARD DEVIATION OF THE MEAN=              .163162163

1/MEAN V VALUE= 66.8151448 ;95% CONF. LIMITS ARE: 56.4014435 TO 81.9451104

LOG MEAN V VALUE=-4.20192977 ;95% CONF.LIMITS ARE:-4.40604964 TO-4.03249475

LOG S =            -.916290731
1/S=            2.5
S/V=            26.7260579 ;95% CONF.LIMITS ARE: 22.5605774 TO 32.7780442
V/S=            .0374166667 ;95% CONF.LIMITS ARE: .0305082266 TO .0443251067
SV=            5.98666667E-03 ;95% CONF.LIMITS ARE: 4.88131626E-03 TO 7.09201708E
-03
S†2V=            2.39466667E-03 ;95% CONF.LIMITS ARE 1.95252651E-03
TO 2.83680683E-03
```

```
THIS IS A V VERSUS S PLOT                           THIS IS AN EADIE-HOFSTEE PLOT. THE V AXIS IS HORIZONTAL.
INTERSECTION OF AXES IS AT ( 0 , 0 )                INTERSECTION OF AXES IS AT ( 0 , 0 )

IIIIIIIIIIIIIIIIIIIIIIIIIIIIIIIIIIIIIIIIIIIY:MAX= .02    +IIIIIIIIIIIIIIIIIIIIIIIIIIIIIIIIIIIIIIIIIIIY:MAX= .02
-                                                   -
-                    +                              -                    +
-                         +                         -                       +
-                       +                           -
-                                                   -
-                         +                         -                            +
-                                                   -
-                                                   -
-               +                                   -                            +
-                                                   -                              +
-          +                                        -                          +
-                                                   -                        +
-                                                   -
-                                                   -
+                                                   -
X:MAX= 1                                            X:MAX= .1
```

**Figure 11.** Statistical output from program *Listing 12* together with a *v versus* [S] plot and an Eadie-Hofstee plot with malondialdehyde as a substrate for highly purified bovine lens aldehyde dehydrogenase. Behaviour is clearly non-Michaelian.

Substitution of initial velocities for $k$ values will give the same slope, as the constant factor will only affect the intercept. Occasionally, discontinuities in the graph can occur, for example when an enzyme exists in two interconvertible forms (20).

The program is given in *Listing 13* and should be used in conjunction with the statistical and plotting routines given above. Lines 3020 – 3120 convert the mean velocity and temperature data (calculated using the statistical subroutine in lines 1000 – 1190 given alone) into the axes required for the Arrhenius plot, log $v$ and $1/T$. The data can then be plotted using the plotting routine in lines 2000 – 2885 given above. The slope of the plot, the intercept on the log $v$ axis, and the correlation coefficient for the slope are then calculated and printed (lines 3160 – 3310 and 8000 – 8020). If the correlation coefficient is low, the data should be examined further for discontinuities. *Figure 12* shows a typical output from the program.

### 3.6.3 *Non-linear Regression to the Michaelis-Menten Function*

The theory of non-linear regression to a two-parameter equation in enzyme kinetics has been discussed by several authors (e.g., 21 – 24). This program uses non-linear regression by means of Gauss-Newton iterations and is similar to that described by Duggleby (25), with the additional feature that plots of residuals *ver-*

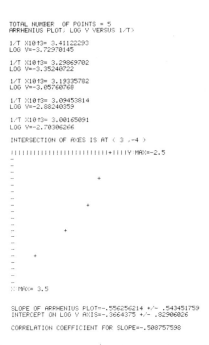

```
TOTAL NUMBER OF POINTS = 5
ARRHENIUS PLOT; LOG V VERSUS 1/T)

1/T X10↑3= 3.41122293
LOG V=-3.72970145

1/T X10↑3= 3.29869702
LOG V=-3.35240722

1/T X10↑3= 3.19335782
LOG V=-3.05760768

1/T X10↑3= 3.09453814
LOG V=-2.88240359

1/T X10↑3= 3.00165091
LOG V=-2.70306266

INTERSECTION OF AXES IS AT ( 3 ,-4 )

||||||||||||||||||||||||||||+||||Y:MAX=-2.5
  -
  -
  -
  -                      +
  -
  -              +
  -
  -        +
  -
  -    +
  -
  -
X:MAX= 3.5

SLOPE OF ARRHENIUS PLOT=-.556256214 +/- .543451759
INTERCEPT ON LOG V AXIS=-.3664375 +/- .82906026

CORRELATION COEFFICIENT FOR SLOPE=-.508757598
```

**Figure 12**. Sample output from program *Listing 13*. The curve shape and low correlation coefficient indicates that the Arrhenius plot is non-linear. (Simulated data.)

*sus* substrate concentration or predicted initial velocity can be obtained. The normalised residual value (*r*) which we have already met in Section 3.5.1, is defined as follows:

$$r = \frac{(\hat{v} - v)}{\sigma}$$

where *v* is the experimentally determined initial velocity, $\hat{v}$ is the predicted value for initial velocity calculated from the equation to which the data have been fitted (in this case the 1:1 or Michaelis-Menten function), and $\sigma$ is the expected standard deviation of *v*.

Where the data is not well fitted to the equation, the values produced for $K_m$ and $V_{max}$ will tend to have large standard deviations and plots of residuals *versus* substrate concentration or predicted initial velocity will not be normally distributed but will show some dependence on the variables. Analysis of the curve shapes may be used to identify the correct higher degree polynomial rate equation (26). Note that as only the shape of the residual plot is important, it is not essential to know $\sigma$, and here it has been given a value of 1.0.

Weighting of observed initial velocity values can be decided by the user from a number of options, including weighting dependent upon the 95% confidence limits calculated by the statistical subroutine. Robust regression by bisquare weighting is also incorporated (27), whereby the large residuals are given less weight than those observations with small residual values. The program is given in *Listing 14*. Partial differentials are calculated by numerical differentiation (25) and iteration continued until the sum of the absolute values of the relative changes in the parameter values is less than $10^{-5}$ (lines 4880−4920), when convergence is considered to have been reached. If convergence is not reached in 10 iterations, the current values of the parameters $K_m$ and $V_{max}$, which until then have appeared on the screen, are printed. The user must enter initial estimates for these parameter values (lines 4385−4480). These should be non-zero and close to the final best-fit values. Estimation should be helped by inspection of the graphical plots detailed in Section 3.6.1. The computer prints out final parameter values with standard deviations (lines 4970−5010) and observed and predicted initial velocity values, with residuals, at each substrate concentration (lines 5030−5080). The user can then obtain plots of predicted *v* values *versus* [S] (lines 5180−5250), residuals *versus* [S] (lines 5310−5360), and residuals *versus* predicted *v* values (lines 5390−5440) if required, using the plotting routine described previously (lines 2000−2880). A typical output from this program is shown in *Figure 13*. The user may also experiment with different methods of data

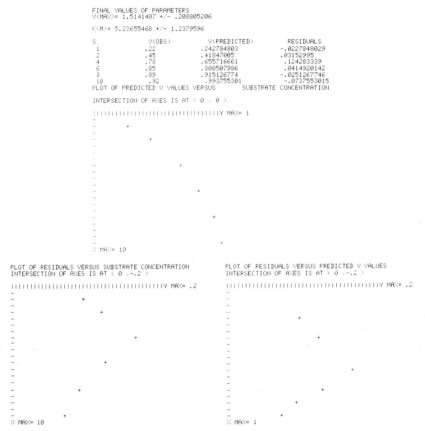

**Figure 13.** Sample output from program *Listing 14*, showing final values of the parameters; a plot of predicted initial velocity *versus* [S]; a plot of residuals *versus* substrate concentration; and a plot of residuals *versus* predicted initial velocity values. Although very few data points are illustrated for clarity, the non-random residual plots indicate that the data may obey a more complex rate equation, and that more experiments are required. (Simulated data.)

weighting (lines 5462). It is interesting to compare this non-linear regression method for estimating kinetic parameters with the distribution-free methods described in Section 3.5.2. A more complex non-linear regression program in BASIC has been developed which allows regression to 1:1 (as here), 1:2, 2:2, 2:3 or 3:3 functions (28).

### 3.6.4 *Co-operativity: the Use of the Hill Plot*

Hill proposed the following equation to account for the sigmoid behaviour in the binding of oxygen to haemoglobin:

$$Y = \frac{K[X]^h}{1 + K[X]^h} \qquad \text{Equation 19}$$

where $Y$ is the fractional saturation, $K$ is the dissociation constant for the single step binding, and h is a constant. The constant h has been taken as an index of co-operativity (the Hill coefficient) and can provide a lower limit for the number of binding sites. The degree of co-operativity is taken to increase as h increases. This equation can be rearranged:

$$\log(Y/(1 - Y)) = h \log X - \log K \qquad \text{Equation 20}$$

so that a plot of $\log(Y/[1 - Y])$ *versus* log [S] (the Hill plot) should be a straight line of slope h. This holds for the middle of the [S] range; at the extremes the slopes tend to $+1$.

The program to draw a Hill plot is given in *Listing 15*. This routine can be entered immediately after the non-linear regression program. Initial velocity data rather than binding data, are used in this plot. The user must enter the required value for $V_{max}$ (line 5222), and the program prints the data in $\log(v/[V_{max} - v])$ *versus* log [S] space as calculated from the statistical subroutine given above. The graph is plotted by the graph plotting routine, and the slope of the plot and the standard deviation of the slope are then calculated and printed (line 5720).

### 3.6.5 *Calculation of Enzyme Inhibition Constants*

Inhibitors may act:

(i)   in a reversible manner, whereby activity can be restored by removing the inhibitor by dialysis or other means;

(ii)  in an irreversible, time-dependent manner.

(i) *Reversible inhibition.* Four main types of reversible inhibition have been described: competitive, uncompetitive, non-competitive and mixed. These may be distinguished by plotting initial velocity values at a number of inhibitor concentrations in double reciprocal space as provided for by the present program. Where double reciprocal plots are linear, $K_i$ values may be obtained by the expression:

$$\text{slope (or intercept) with inhibitor} =$$
$$\text{slope (or intercept) without inhibitor} \times [1 + \frac{[I]}{K_{i(\text{slope or intercept})}}]$$

$K_i$ values can also be obtained from replots of slopes or intercepts (where appropriate) *versus* inhibitor concentration [I], as the intercept of such a replot on the *x* axis is $-K_i$. Any textbook on enzyme kinetics may be consulted for the basic theory behind enzyme inhibition. The method of using slope and intercept replots is employed in the present program (*Listing 16*). Having chosen the reversible inhibition option (line 6000), the user then enters the appropriate *v* and [S] values (lines 6040 – 6060). The double reciprocal plot is plotted as before (line 6100, using subroutine 2000) and slope and/or intercept calculations proceed. $K_i$ (slope) and $K_i$ (intercept) values can then be calculated by least squares regression (lines 6780 and 7170). Standard free energies for the enzyme-inhibitor interactions at 37°C are calculated from the relationship:

$$\Delta G^o = -RT \ln K_{i(\text{slope or intercept})} \qquad \text{Equation 21}$$

and printed (lines 7140 and 7400).

(ii) *Irreversible inhibition.* If inhibition is caused by the irreversible binding of a single molecule of inhibitor the reaction may be represented as:

$$E + I \rightleftharpoons E - I$$

When the inhibitor is present in excess over enzyme, pseudo first order conditions apply, and:

$$v_t/v_o = e^{-k_a t} \qquad \text{Equation 22}$$

where $v_t$ is the initial velocity with inhibitory present, $v_o$ is the initial velocity of uninhibited reaction, $k_a$ is the pseudo first order rate constant for loss of activity and t is time. Thus a graph of $\ln (v_t/v_o)$ *versus* t will have slope $k_a$ (see Section 3.3.1). Non-linear time-dependent inhibition may also be observed, and models have been proposed to account for this (29,30). Using the program described here (*Listing 16*) non-linear time-dependent inhibition can be detected from the shape of the graphical plots, and from the intercept on the y axis, which has a value near to 1.0 for a pseudo first order reaction. Having selected the time-dependent option (line 6000), the user then enters the initial velocity with inhibitor absent (line 7420), the number of velocity values (line 7440) and the velocity values at each incubation time (line 7480). The plotting routine then provides a plot of $\ln (v_t/v_o)$

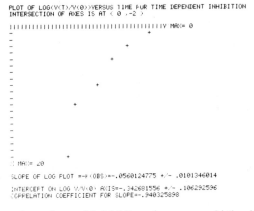

**Figure 14.** Sample output for an irreversible inhibitor using program *Listing 16*. (Simulated data.)

*versus* time, the slope of the line ($= K$obs) and the standard deviation are calculated (line 7635), followed by the intercept and standard deviation on the y axis, and the correlation co-efficient for the slope. *Figure 14* shows a typical output from this program.

## 4. ACKNOWLEDGEMENTS

I would like to thank the technical staff of the Department of Biochemistry, Oxford University, for their invaluable help with the RML 380 Z computers, and Dr. Peter Artymiuk and Dr. Brian Sutton, of the Laboratory of Molecular Biophysics, Oxford University, for providing me with the co-ordinates of lysozyme and fragment Fc. I would also like to thank Dr. H.-H. Ting, Mr. M. Choyce and Mr. Yasnik for expert assistance, Dr. Louise Johnson, Dr. A. Winfield and Dr. John J. Harding for helpful conversations; the Medical Research Council and Fight-For-Sight Inc., New York, U.S.A. for support, and Mr. A.J. Bron for provision of essential laboratory facilities.

## 5. REFERENCES

1. Newman,W.M. and Sproull,R.F. (1981) *Principles of Interactive Computer Graphics,* published by McGraw-Hill, Tokyo.
2. Crabbe,M.J.C. (1984) *Biochem. Soc. Trans., 12,* 1095.
3. Hampshire,N. (1982) *Spectrum Graphics,* published by Duckworth, London.
4. Angell,I.O. and Jones,B.J. (1983) *Advanced Graphics with the Sinclair ZX Spectrum,* published by Macmillan, London.
5. Brodie,L. (1981) *Starting FORTH,* published by Prentice-Hall, New Jersey.
6. Winfield,A. (1983) *The Complete FORTH,* published by Sigma Technical Press, UK.
7. Eisenthal,R. and Cornish-Bowden,A. (1974) *Biochem. J., 139,* 715.
8. Cornish-Bowden,A., Porter,W.R. and Trager,W.F. (1978) *J. Theor. Biol., 74,* 163.
9. Cornish-Bowden,A. and Eisenthal,R. (1978) *Biochem. Biophys. Acta, 523,* 268.
10. Howells,R.D., Groth,J., Hiller,J.M. and Simon,E.J. (1980) *J. Pharm. Exp. Ther., 215,* 60.
11. Osborne,H. and Herz,A. (1981) *Neurochem. Int., 3,* 143.
12. Schrier,A.A. and Schimmel,P.R. (1974) *J. Mol. Biol., 86,* 601.
13. Schwert,G.W. (1969) *J. Biol. Chem., 244,* 1278.
14. Jennings,R.R. and Niemenn,C. (1955) *J. Am. Chem. Soc., 77,* 5432.
15. Wharton,C.W. and Szawelski,R.J. (1982) *Biochem. J., 203,* 351.
16. Crabbe,M.J.C. (1984) *Comput. Biol. Med.,* in press.
17. Crabbe,M.J.C. (1985) in *Methods of Biochemical Analysis Vol. 31,* Glick,D. (ed.), Wiley Interscience, in press.
18. Crabbe,M.J.C. (1982) *Comput. Biol. Med., 12,* 263.
19. Bardsley,W.G. and Childs,R.E. (1975) *Biochem. J., 149,* 313.
20. Londesborough,J. (1980) *Eur. J. Biochem., 105,* 211.
21. Wilkinson,G.N. (1961) *Biochem. J., 80,* 324.
22. Waight,R.D., Leff,P. and Bardsley,W.G. (1977) *Biochem. J., 167,* 787.
23. Mannervik,B., Jakobson,I. and Warholm,M. (1979) *Biochem. Biophys. Acta, 567,* 43.
24. Cornish-Bowden,A. (1975) *Biochem. J., 149,* 305.
25. Duggleby,R.G. (1981) *Anal. Biochem., 110,* 9.
26. Ellis,K.J. and Duggleby,R.G. (1978) *Biochem. J., 171,* 513.
27. Mosteller,F. and Tukey,J.W. (1977) *Data Analysis and Regression,* published by Addison-Wesley, Reading, MA, pp. 353.
28. Crabbe,M.J.C. (1984) *Int. J. Biomed. Comput., 15,* 303.
29. Childs,R.E. and Bardsley,W.G. (1975) *J. Theor. Biol., 53,* 381.
30. Crabbe,M.J.C., Childs,R.E. and Bardsley,W.G. (1975) *Eur. J. Biochem., 60,* 325.

# APPENDIX

## Program listings

**Listing 1.** Program to plot kinetic data in *v versus* [S] space, for either a Michaelis-Menten or 2:2 function.

```
1 LET CO=3
3 GRAPH1
5 CALL "RESOLUTION",0,2
7 CALL "COLOUR",3,7,7,3
9 CALL "FILL",0,0,318,200,5
20 CALL "PLOT",0,0,3
22 CALL"LINE",0,191,3
24 CALL"LINE",318,191,3
26 CALL"LINE",318,191,3
28 CALL"LINE",318,0,3
29 CALL"LINE",0,0
30 A=16*ATN(1)/318
32 B$="VELOCITY-V (Max=190)"
33 C$="SUBSTRATE CONCENTRATION (Max=319)
34 CALL"STPLOT",0,175,VARADR(B$),3
36 CALL"STPLOT",50,0,VARADR(C$),3
40 ?"DO YOU REQUIRE 1:1 (M) OR 2:2 FUNCTION PLOT ?"
50 LET A$=GET$()
51 FOR I=1 TO 10
52 ?"INPUT K(M)";
53 INPUT B:LET H$="Km="+STR$(B)
54 ?"INPUT V(MAX)";
55 INPUT C:LET C=C/1:LET I$="Vmax="+STR$(C)
60 IF A$="M" THEN GOTO 70
62 ?"INPUT NUMERATOR CONST.";
64 INPUT D
66 ?"INPUT DENOMINATOR CONST.";
68 INPUT E
70 FOR X=1 TO 318
75 IF A$<>"M" THENGOTO 90
80 Y= C*(A*X)/(B+(A*X))
85 IF A$="M" THENGOTO 100
90 Y=(C*(A*X)+D*(A*X)^2)/(1+B*(A*X)+E*(A*X)^2)
100 CALL"PLOT",X,Y,CO
102 IF Y>190 OR Y<24 THEN GOTO 110
106 IF X=250 AND A$="M"THEN CALL "STPLOT",X-5,Y-8,VARADR(H$),3
107 IF X=250 AND A$="M"THEN CALL "STPLOT",X-5,Y-16,VARADR(I$),3
110 NEXT X
115 ?"ANOTHER CURVE? IF SO TYPE Y"
116 LET F$=GET$()
117 IF F$<>"Y" OR F$<>"y" THEN GOTO 122
120 NEXT I
122 END
```

**Listing 2.** Program to demonstrate the oxygen binding curves for haemoglobin and myoglobin.

```
1 LET CO=3
2 PRINTER 4,6:PRINT "Check that the Printer is on and it is    'ON LINE'"
3 FOR T=1 TO 200:NEXT T
4 LPRINT "A = Haemoglobin Dissociation Curve":LPRINT "B = Myoglobin Dissociation Curve":LPRINT "
C = HB Curve for - Decreased pH"
5 LPRINT "        "          - Increased pCO2":LPRINT"            - Increased 2,3-DPG"
6 LPRINT "E = HB Curve for - Increased pH":LPRINT"        - Decreased pCO2":LPRINT"
        - Decreased 2,3-DPG"
10 GRAPH 1
20 CALL"RESOLUTION",0,2
21 CALL "FILL",0,0,318,200,1
22 CALL"LINE",0,191,3
24 CALL"LINE",318,191,3
26 CALL"LINE",318,191,3
28 CALL"LINE",318,0,3
29 CALL"LINE",0,0
30 A=16*ATN(1)/318
31 LET A$="PARTIAL PRESSURE OXYGEN"
32 CALL "STPLOT",70,0,VARADR(A$),3
34 LET B$="% SATURATION"
36 CALL"STPLOT",0,150,VARADR(B$),3
40 ?"HAEMOGLOBIN DISSOCIATION CURVE (A)"
50 B=.0056:C=5.66:D=3.22:E=.02
51 GOSUB 70
52 ?"MYOGLOBIN DISSOCIATION CURVE (B)"
53 B=.2:C=55:D=.01:E=.001
54 GOSUB 70
55 ?"HB CURVE FOR DECREASED pH,INCREASEDCO2 OR 2,3 DPG (C)"
```

```
56 B=.05:C=5:D=2:E=.0095
57 GOSUB 70
58 ?"HB CURVE FOR INCREASED pH, DECREASED CO2 OR 2,3 DPG (D)"
59 B=.05:C=15:D=2:E=.0095
60 GOSUB 70
61 LET C$="      B          D        A        C"
62 CALL"STPLOT",0,80,VARADR(C$),3
65 END
70 FOR X=1 TO 318
75 IF A$<>"M" GOTO 90
80 Y= C$(A$X)/(B+(A$X))
85 IF A$="M" GOTO 100
90 Y=(C$(A$X)+D$(A$X)^2)/(1+B$(A$X)+E$(A$X)^2)
100 CALL"PLOT",X,Y,3
110 NEXT X
120 RETURN
```

**Listing 3.** Program to illustrate the alpha-carbon backbone of lysozyme.

```
 50 PRINT "This program illustrates the alpha carbon backbone of lysozyme in
3-dimensions"
 52 PRINT : PRINT "perspective is incorporated"
 55 PRINT : PRINT : PRINT
 57 INPUT "joystick? y/n";j$
 60 PRINT "scaling factors are degrees of magnificationm e.g..5=1/2"
 65 PRINT : PRINT : PRINT
 80 LET z1=1
100 DIM a(4,4)
110 DIM b(4,4)
115 LET s$="n"
120 GO SUB 8000
130 IF s$="y" THEN  GO TO 280
141 PRINT "no.of pixels in x direction from original co-ordinates?"
143 INPUT f: PRINT f
145 PRINT "no.of pixels in y direction?"
147 INPUT g: PRINT g
151 PRINT "no.of pixels in z direction?"
153 INPUT h: PRINT h
160 LET tx=f: LET ty=g: LET tz=h
170 PRINT "x axis rot.angle?"
175 INPUT u: PRINT u
185 PRINT "y axis rot.angle?"
187 INPUT v: PRINT v
193 PRINT "z axis rot.angle?"
197 INPUT w: PRINT w
202 INPUT "near bond steps in pixels (1=continuous";dd
250 INPUT "paper-0-7";a: PRINT : INPUT "border-0-7";b: INPUT "ink for box;-0-7"
;c
270 PAPER a: BORDER b: INK c
280 LET rx=u*3.14159/180: LET ry=v*3.14159/180: LET rz=w*3.14159/180
290 GO SUB 9500
300 GO SUB 900
410 GO SUB 1000
420 GO SUB 5000
430 GO SUB 3000
440 GO SUB 4000
445 GO SUB 2000
452 IF j$="n" THEN  GO TO 457
455 IF IN 31>=16 THEN  GO TO 459
456 IF j$="y" THEN  GO TO 455
457 GO TO 500
459 CLS
475 GO SUB 6000
485 RESTORE : GO TO 280
500 GO SUB 9800
510 STOP
900 CLS
940 PLOT 0,0: DRAW 255,0: DRAW 0,175: DRAW -255,0: DRAW 0,-175
950 RETURN
1000 REM init shape
1010 LET np=129
1020 LET ne=np-1
1040 DIM s(3,np)
1050 DIM e(ne,2)
1060 DIM m(3,np)
1110 FOR n=1 TO np
1120 READ s(1,n),s(2,n),s(3,n)
1130 NEXT n
1150 FOR e=1 TO ne
1160 READ e(e,1),e(e,2)
1170 NEXT e
1200 REM xyzcoord
1205 DATA 22.2,10.3,9.2,22.1,13.6,7.3,18.6,14.9,7.3,17,17,4.5,15.5,20.4,5.5,11.9
,19.4,4.9,12.4,15.9,6.3,13.7,17.2,9.6,10.9,19.8,9.8,8.3,17,9.5
1206 REM
1207 DATA 10.2,14.9,12,10.3,17.7,14.6,6.7,18.7,13.9,5.6,15,14.6,7.7,15,17.8,5.9,
18.1,19.2,8.3,21,18.4,6.2,23.4,16.3,5.4,26,18.9,6.8,24.2,21.9
```

```
1208 REM
1209 DATA 7.2,26.9,24.6,6.3,29.5,21.9,9.1,28.6,19.5,7.9,28.1,15.9,9.2,25.3,13.8,
11.5,27.6,11.9,13.5,28.3,15,14.2,24.6,15.6,15.2,23.8,11.9,17.5,26.9,11.9
1210 REM
1211 DATA 19.2,25.9,15.2,19.8,22.4,13.9,21.2,23.7,10.6,23.9,25.9,12.3,24.6,23.6,
15.1,25.2,20.4,13.2,24.5,20.9,9.5,21.6,18.5,10,24.1,15.7,10.8,22.9,13.4,13.7
1212 REM
1213 DATA 26.6,12.2,14.1,28.1,15.6,14.7,30.4,15.9,17.7,32.4,18.9,18.9,34.8,19.2,
21.9,34.9,22.4,24,37.6,24.1,26.1,35.9,23,29.3,36.6,19.3,28.2,32.9,18.8,27.5
1214 REM
1215 DATA 31.5,17.6,24.1,28.5,18.6,22.1,26.5,15.7,20.5,24.1,15.2,17.7,21.8,17.2,
15.5,21.2,19.7,18.3,24.7,19.7,19.7,23.6,18.9,23.3,26.4,19.4,25.8,27.9,16.6,27.9
1216 REM
1217 DATA 28.6,18.8,30.9,24.8,19.3,31.5,22.5,17,29.5,24.1,13.6,28.8,26.9,11.3,30
,29.8,10.4,27.8,32,9.1,30.7,34.6,11.8,30,33.2,15,31.4,34.5,15.5,34.9
1218 REM
1219 DATA 31.9,17.4,37.1,29,16.4,34.8,25.2,16.6,35.1,23.1,14.2,33,19.8,16.1,33.2
,18.3,14.1,30.3,19.4,10.8,31.9,20.9,9.3,28.8,24.3,8.3,27.4,25.5,10.9,24.9
1220 REM
1221 DATA 25.8,8.3,22.2,22,7.9,22.2,21.9,11.4,20.7,23.8,10.4,17.6,21.2,8,16.3,19
.2,8.3,13,16.1,8.4,15.2,15.9,11.9,16.7,13.5,11,19.5,16.2,11.1,22.1
1222 REM
1223 DATA 17.5,14.5,20.9,14,16.1,20.7,12.9,14.8,24.2,16.2,16.2,25.6,15.7,19.5,23
.8,12.3,19.8,25.3,13.9,19.8,28.7,16.6,22.2,27.7,14.3,24.9,26.2,12.2,24.8,29.3
1224 REM
1225 DATA 15.1,25.4,31.7,14.9,29.2,31.8,17.1,30.6,29,14.8,29.3,26.2,16.6,28.7,22
.9,19.4,31,24,21,27.7,25.2,21.9,27.1,21.5,24.8,29.5,20.7,24.1,29,16.9
1226 REM
1227 DATA 20.5,29.9,17.5,21.3,33,19.5,23.8,34.5,17,22.3,33.3,13.7,18.6,32.7,14.1
,17.2,34.9,16.9,15.5,37.9,15.4,15.7,36.7,11.8,12.8,35.4,9.7,13,31.8,10.8
1228 REM
1229 DATA 9.8,31.2,8.8,12,30.9,5.7,13.4,27.6,7.1,10.1,25.7,6.6,9.1,27.2,3.2,8.1,
24.6,0.5,7.6,22,3.2,4.6,19.7,3.3,3.6,19.8,7
1300 REM conn data
1310 DATA 1,2,2,3,3,4,4,5,5,6,6,7,7,8,8,9,9,10,10,11,11,12,12,13,13,14,14,15,15,
16,16,17,17,18,18,19,19,20
1311 REM
1312 DATA 20,21,21,22,22,23,23,24,24,25,25,26,26,27,27,28,28,29,29,30,30,31,31,3
2,32,33,33,34,34,35,35,36,36,37,37,38,38,39,39,40
1313 REM
1314 DATA 40,41,41,42,42,43,43,44,44,45,45,46,46,47,47,48,48,49,49,50,50,51,51,5
2,52,53,53,54,54,55,55,56,56,57,57,58,58,59,59,60
1315 REM
1316 DATA 60,61,61,62,62,63,63,64,64,65,65,66,66,67,67,68,68,69,69,70,70,71,71,7
2,72,73,73,74,74,75,75,76,76,77,77,78,78,79,79,80
1317 REM
1318 DATA 80,81,81,82,82,83,83,84,84,85,85,86,86,87,87,88,88,89,89,90,90,91,91,9
2,92,93,93,94,94,95,95,96,96,97,97,98,98,99,99,100
1319 REM
1320 DATA 100,101,101,102,102,103,103,104,104,105,105,106,106,107,107,108,108,10
9,109,110,110,111,111,112,112,113,113,114,114,115,115,116,116,117,117,118,118,11
9,119,120
1321 REM
1322 DATA 120,121,121,122,122,123,123,124,124,125,125,126,126,127,127,128,128,12
9
1900 RETURN
2000 REM draw shape
2020 FOR e=1 TO ne
2021 IF m(3,e)<15 THEN  LET ds=dd: GO TO 2030
2022 IF m(3,e)>=14 THEN  LET ds=dd+1: GO TO 2030
2030 LET v1=e(e,1)
2033 LET pe=ABS (300/(m(3,v1)-300))
2040 LET v2=e(e,2)
2043 LET pf=ABS (300/(m(3,v2)-300))
2045 IF v1=0 THEN  GO TO 2240
2050 LET xb=m(1,v1)
2060 LET yb=m(2,v1)
2070 LET xe=m(1,v2)
2080 LET ye=m(2,v2)
2100 LET p=xe-xb
2110 LET q=ye-yb
2120 LET r=SQR (p*p+q*q)
2130 LET lx=p/r
2135 LET ly=q/r
2137 FOR i=0 TO r STEP ds
2140 GO SUB 9700
2142 IF i<>0 THEN  GO TO 2160
2143 IF z1<>99 THEN  GO TO 2160
2144 LET x=xb+i*lx: LET y=yb+i*ly
2146 IF x>255 THEN  GO TO 2230
2147 IF y>175 THEN  GO TO 2230
2149 IF x<0 THEN  GO TO 2230
2151 IF y<0 THEN  GO TO 2230
2154 PLOT x-2,y: DRAW  INK 2; BRIGHT 1;4,0: PLOT x,y-2: DRAW  INK 2; BRIGHT 1;0,
4
2158 GO TO 2230
2160 LET x=xb+i*lx
2170 LET y=yb+i*ly
2180 IF x>255 THEN  GO TO 2230
2190 IF y>175 THEN  GO TO 2230
2200 IF x<0 THEN  GO TO 2230
2210 IF y<0 THEN  GO TO 2230
```

```
2215 PRINT AT 1,10;"residue";e
2216 IF m(3,e)<8 THEN  LET c=1; GO TO 2224
2217 IF m(3,e)<14 THEN  LET c=2; GO TO 2224
2218 IF m(3,e)<20 THEN  LET c=3; GO TO 2224
2219 IF m(3,e)<25 THEN  LET c=4; GO TO 2224
2220 IF m(3,e)<30 THEN  LET c=5; GO TO 2224
2221 LET c=6
2224 INK c; PLOT x,y
2225 IF i=0 AND z2=99 THEN  CIRCLE x,y,a1
2230 NEXT i
2240 NEXT e
2900 RETURN
3000 REM  trans matrix
3010 LET a(1,1)=COS (ry)*COS (rz)
3020 LET a(1,2)=COS (ry)*SIN (rz)
3030 LET a(1,3)=-SIN (ry)
3040 LET a(1,4)=0
3050 LET a(2,1)=COS (rx)*-SIN (rz)+SIN (rx)*SIN (ry)*COS (rz)
3060 LET a(2,2)=COS (rx)*COS (rz)+SIN (rx)*SIN (ry)*SIN (rz)
3070 LET a(2,3)=SIN (rx)*COS (ry)
3080 LET a(2,4)=0
3090 LET a(3,1)=(-SIN (rx))*(-SIN (rz))+COS (rx)*SIN (ry)*COS (rz)
3100 LET a(3,2)=-SIN (rx)*COS (rz)+COS (rz)*SIN (ry)*SIN (rz)
3110 LET a(3,3)=COS (rx)*COS (ry)
3120 LET a(3,4)=0
3130 LET a(4,1)=0
3140 LET a(4,2)=0
3150 LET a(4,3)=0
3160 LET a(4,4)=0
3195 REM
3200 REM scal mat
3210 LET b(1,1)=sx*a(1,1)
3220 LET b(1,2)=sx*a(1,2)
3230 LET b(1,3)=sx*a(1,3)
3250 LET b(2,1)=sy*a(2,1)
3260 LET b(2,2)=sy*a(2,2)
3270 LET b(2,3)=sy*a(2,3)
3290 LET b(3,1)=sz*a(3,1)
3300 LET b(3,2)=sz*a(3,2)
3310 LET b(3,3)=sz*a(3,3)
3330 LET b(4,1)=tx
3340 LET b(4,2)=ty
3350 LET b(4,3)=tz
4000 REM trans
4010 FOR q=1 TO np
4020 LET xt=s(1,q)-xc
4030 LET yt=s(2,q)-yc
4040 LET zt=s(3,q)-zc
4050 LET m(1,q)=xc+(xt*b(1,1)+yt*b(2,1)+zt*b(3,1)+b(4,1))
4060 LET m(2,q)=yc+(xt*b(1,2)+yt*b(2,2)+zt*b(3,2)+b(4,2))
4070 LET m(3,q)=zc+(xt*b(1,3)+yt*b(2,3)+zt*b(3,3)+b(4,3))
4080 NEXT q
4900 RETURN
5000 REM find centroid
5010 LET p=0; LET q=0; LET r=0
5020 FOR i=1 TO np
5030 LET p=p+s(1,i)
5040 LET q=q+s(2,i)
5050 LET r=r+s(3,i)
5060 NEXT i
5070 LET xc=p/np
5080 LET yc=q/np
5090 LET zc=r/np
5900 RETURN
6000 REM rotation
6001 RESTORE
6003 IF j$="y" THEN  GO TO 7000
6005 PRINT AT 20,1;"8=x 7=y 6=z 3=clear"
6008 PAUSE 150; CLS
6010 IF INKEY$="8" THEN  LET u=u+1; PRINT AT 20,1;"x rot.=",u
6015 IF IN 31=1 THEN  LET u=u+1; PRINT AT 20,1;"x rot.=";u
6020 IF INKEY$="7" THEN  LET v=v+1; PRINT AT 20,1;"y rot.=",v
6030 IF INKEY$="6" THEN  LET w=w+1; PRINT AT 20,1;"z rot.=",w
6040 IF INKEY$="3" THEN  GO TO 7080
6050 GO TO 6010
7000 PRINT AT 21,1;"x=right y=up z=down clear=fire"
7005 PAUSE 150; CLS
7015 IF IN 31=1 THEN  LET u=u+1; PRINT AT 20,1;"x rot.=";u
7025 IF IN 31=8 THEN  LET v=v+1; PRINT AT 20,1;"y rot.=";v
7035 IF IN 31=4 THEN  LET w=w+1; PRINT AT 20,1;"z rot.=";w
7045 IF IN 31>=16 THEN  GO TO 9000
7055 GO TO 7015
7080 PRINT AT 20,1;"magnify or reduce ? y/n"
7082 INPUT s$
7084 IF s$="y" THEN  GO TO 120
7090 PRINT AT 20,1;"                              "
7095 RETURN
8000 PRINT "input x scaling factor"; INPUT sx; PRINT sx
8010 PRINT "input y scaling factor"; INPUT sy; PRINT sy
8020 PRINT "input z scaling factor"; INPUT sz; PRINT sz
8030 RETURN
```

```
9000 PRINT AT 20,1;"x y z mag."
9010 PAUSE 150: CLS
9050 IF IN 31=1 THEN  LET sx=sx+.01: PRINT AT 20,1;"x mag.="|sx
9060 IF IN 31=8 THEN  LET sy=sy+0.01: PRINT AT 20,1;"y mag.="|sy
9070 IF IN 31=4 THEN  LET sz=sz+0.01: PRINT AT 20,1;"z mag.="|sz
9080 IF IN 31>=16 THEN  GO TO 280
9090 GO TO 9050
9500 REM mark residues
9505 DIM o(50)
9507 DIM t(f)
9508 DIM z(50)
9510 INPUT "how many residues to label ?";q1
9520 FOR d=1 TO q1
9530 PRINT "residue number?"
9531 INPUT o(d): PRINT o(d)
9535 NEXT d
9537 INPUT "How many residues with van der Waal's radii ?";q2
9539 FOR f=1 TO q2
9540 INPUT "residue number";z(f)
9542 INPUT "radius ?";t(f)
9544 NEXT f
9546 RETURN
9700 REM label?
9701 LET r1=1
9702 LET z1=1: LET a1=1: LET z2=1
9703 FOR f=1 TO q2
9705 FOR d=1 TO q1
9710 IF o(d)=e THEN  LET z1=99
9715 IF z(f)=e THEN  LET z2=99
9717 IF z(f)=e THEN  LET a1=t(f)
9720 NEXT d
9725 NEXT f
9730 RETURN
```

**Listing 4.** Modification to *Listing 3* to enable the co-ordinates of over 400 atoms to be plotted.

```
 50 PRINT "This program illustrates the alpha carbon backbone of fragment Fc in
3-dimensions"
 52 PRINT : PRINT "perspective is incorporated"
 55 PRINT : PRINT : PRINT
 57 INPUT "joystick? y/n";j$
 60 PRINT "scaling factors are degrees of magnificationm e.g..5=1/2"
 65 PRINT : PRINT : PRINT
 80 LET z1=1
 90 LET r5=0
100 DIM a(4,4)
110 DIM b(4,4)
115 LET s$="n"
120 GO SUB 8000
130 IF s$="y" THEN  GO TO 280
141 PRINT "no.of pixels in x direction from original co-ordinates?"
143 INPUT f: PRINT f
145 PRINT "no.of pixels in y direction?"
147 INPUT g: PRINT g
151 PRINT "no.of pixels in z direction?"
153 INPUT h: PRINT h
160 LET tx=f: LET ty=g: LET tz=h
170 PRINT "x axis rot.angle?"
175 INPUT u: PRINT u
185 PRINT "y axis rot.angle?"
187 INPUT v: PRINT v
193 PRINT "z axis rot.angle?"
197 INPUT w: PRINT w
202 INPUT "Near bond steps in pixels (1=continuous";dd
250 INPUT "paper-0-7";a: PRINT : INPUT "border-0-7";b: INPUT "ink for box-0-7";
c
270 PAPER a: BORDER b: INK c
280 LET rx=u*3.14159/180: LET ry=v*3.14159/180: LET rz=w*3.14159/180
290 GO SUB 9500
300 GO SUB 900
410 GO SUB 1000
420 GO SUB 5000
430 GO SUB 3000
440 GO SUB 4000
445 GO SUB 2000
450 PAUSE 50: PRINT AT 21,10;"angles:x=";u;"  y=";v;"  z=";w
451 PRINT AT 0,10;"mag. x=";sx;"  y=";sy;"  z=";sz
452 IF j$="n" AND r5=0 THEN  GO TO 457
453 GO TO 500
455 IF IN 31>=16 THEN  GO TO 459
456 IF j$="y" THEN  GO TO 455
457 LET r5=1: GO SUB 1000: GO SUB 5000: GO SUB 3000: GO SUB 4000: GO SUB 2000
458 GO TO 500
459 CLS
475 GO SUB 6000
485 RESTORE : GO TO 280
500 GO SUB 9800
```

```
 510 STOP
 900 CLS
 940 PLOT 0,0: DRAW 255,0: DRAW 0,175: DRAW -255,0: DRAW 0,-175
 950 RETURN
1000 REM initial shape
1010 LET np=209
1020 LET ne=np-1
1040 DIM s(3,np)
1050 DIM e(ne,2)
1060 DIM m(3,np)
1100 IF r5=1 THEN  RESTORE 1247
1110 FOR n=1 TO np
1120 READ s(1,n),s(2,n),s(3,n)
1130 NEXT n
1135 RESTORE 1300
1150 FOR e=1 TO ne
1160 READ e(e,1),e(e,2)
1170 NEXT e
```

**Listing 5.** Program to calculate amounts of buffer required to attain a certain pH value.

```
10 PRINT "WHAT IS THE pKa VALUE AT 25 DEGREES?"

20 INPUT X

30 PRINT X

40 PRINT "HOW MANY CHARGES?"

50 INPUT Y

60 PRINT Y

70 PRINT "WHAT IS THE BUFFER CONCENTRATION (IONIC  STRENGTH)
?"

80 INPUT Z

90 PRINT Z

100 ENTER TEMPERATURE IN DEGREES C"

110 INPUT T

120 PRINT T

130 PRINT "ENTER TEMPERATURE CO-EFFICIENT OF BUFFER"

140 INPUT D

150 PRINT D

160 LET X=X+D*(T-25)

170 PRINT "TEMPERATURE CORRECTED pKa=";X

180 PRINT "ACID (A) OR BASE (B) ?"


190 INPUTA$

200 LET H=(2*Y-1)*((.5*SQR Z)/( 1+SQR Z))-.1*Z

210 IF A$="B" THEN GOTO 240

220LET X=X-H

230 GOTO 250

240 LET X=X+H

250 PRINT "CORRECTED pKa=";X

260 PRINT "ENTER DESIRED pH"

270 INPUT P

280 LET P=10**(P-X)

290 PRINT "RATIO =";P

300 LET N=P*Z/(1+3*P)

310 PRINT "ml of HA2- =";N*1000

320 LET M=Z/(1+3*P)

330 PRINT "ml OF HA- =";M*1000

340 PRINT "PLUS WATER TO 1 LITRE."
```

**Listing 6.** Graph plotting program, with automatic axis scaling.

```
10 INK 0: PAPER 7
12 LET y$="o"
13 LET ip=0
15 LET A=0: LET B=0: LET C=0: LET D=0
20 LET m1=0: LET n1=0: LET m2=0: LET n2=0: LET z=0
30 DIM x(50): DIM y(50)
32 PRINT "Name of graph?"
34 INPUT a$
40 PRINT "number of data points ?"
50 INPUT n: PRINT n
60 FOR i=1 TO n
70 PRINT "x-axis value?": INPUT x(i): PRINT x(i)
80 PRINT "y-axis value": INPUT y(i): PRINT y(i)
81 NEXT i
82 PRINT "title of x-axis?": INPUT b$: PRINT "title of y-axis?": INPUT c$
85 GO SUB 2000
87 GO SUB 3000
92 CLS
100 LET dn=1: LET dx=n: LET sp=1
110 LET xl=240: LET xr=15
120 LET yt=150: LET yb=10
130 PLOT xr-5,yb-5
140 DRAW (xl-xr+10),0
150 DRAW 0,(yt-yb+10)
160 DRAW -(xl-xr+10),0
170 DRAW 0,-(yt-yb+10)
180 LET xi=(xl-xr)/(dx-dn)
190 FOR x=xr TO xl STEP xi
200 PLOT x,yb-6: PLOT x,yb-7
210 NEXT x
212 PRINT AT 2,7;a$
215 PRINT AT 21,29;xx: PRINT AT 21,1;xu: PRINT AT 20,0;yu: PRINT AT 2,0;yx
217 PRINT AT 20,14;b$: PRINT AT 5,0;c$
230 LET y1=-1000000: LET y2=1000000
240 LET x1=y1: LET x2=y2
250 FOR i=dn TO dx STEP sp
260 IF y1<y(i) THEN   LET y1=y(i)
270 IF y2>y(i) THEN   LET y2=y(i)
280 IF x1<x(i) THEN   LET x1=x(i)
290 IF x2>x(i) THEN   LET x2=x(i)
300 NEXT i
310 LET a=(x1-x2)/(xl-xr)
320 LET b=(y1-y2)/(yt-yb)
330 FOR i=dn TO dx STEP sp
340 LET x=(xr+(x(i)-x2)/a)
350 LET y=((y(i)-y2)/b+yb)
352 LET m1=m1+x(i): LET n1=n1+y(i): LET m2=m2+x(i)*x(i): LET n2=n2+y(i)*y(i): LET z=z+x(i)*y(i)
360 PLOT x-2,y: DRAW 4,0: PLOT x,y-2: DRAW 0,4
365 LET q=i+sp
380 IF q>dx THEN   GO SUB 1000
383 IF q>dx THEN   GO TO 4000
385 IF q>dx AND y$="y" THEN   STOP
388 IF y$="y" THEN   LET ip=(x(n)-x(1))/200
389 IF y$<>"y" THEN   LET ip=(x(n)-x(1))/50
390 FOR j=x(i) TO x(q) STEP ip
400 LET y3=((y(q)-y(i))/(x(q)-x(i)))*(j-x(i))+y(i)
410 LET x=INT (xr+(j-x2)/a)
420 LET y=INT ((y3-y2)/b+yb)
425 IF y>yt+5 THEN   STOP
427 IF y<yb-5 THEN   GO TO 440
430 PLOT x,y
440 NEXT j
450 NEXT i
1000 REM regression
1010 IF y$<>"o" THEN   GO SUB 5000
1015 IF y$<>"o" THEN   STOP
1020 LET m3=m1/n: LET n3=n1/n: LET s1=m2-m1*m3: LET s2=n2-n1*n3: LET s=z-m1*n3
1030 LET w=s/s1: LET w1=n3-w*m3: LET w2=m3-(1/w)*n3: LET s3=s2-w*s: LET s4=s3/(n-2)
1040 PRINT AT 0,0;"SLOPE=";w;"+/-";SQR (ABS (s4/s1));"y-int=";w1;"+/-";SQR (ABS (s4*(1/n+m3*m3/s1)));"r=";s/SQR (ABS (s1*s2))
1050 RETURN
2000 REM review data
2005 PRINT "  "'"";TAB 14;"X";TAB 26;"Y"
2010 FOR i=1 TO n
2020 PRINT i;TAB 14;x(i);TAB 26;y(i)
2030 NEXT i
2040 PRINT "do you want to alter data ? (y/n)"
2050 INPUT d$
2060 IF d$="n" THEN   GO TO 2240
2080 PRINT "enter ` to alter"
2090 INPUT t
2100 PRINT "current values are";TAB 8;x(t);TAB 20;y(t)
2110 PRINT "enter newx and y values"
2220 INPUT x(t),y(t)
2225 PRINT x(t),y(t)
2230 GO TO 2000
2240 RETURN
```

```
3000 REM  max/min
3005 LET i=1
3010 LET xu=x(i): LET xx=x(i): LET yu=y(i): LET yx=y(i)
3020 FOR i=1 TO n
3030 IF xu>x(i) THEN  LET xu=x(i)
3040 IF xx<x(i) THEN  LET xx=x(i)
3050 IF yu>y(i) THEN  LET yu=y(i)
3060 IF yx<y(i) THEN  LET yx=y(i)
3070 NEXT i
3080 RETURN
4000 REM  line
4002 INPUT  "regression line ?";y$
4005 IF y$="n" THEN  STOP
4010 LET y(1)=w*x(1)+w1
4020 LET y(2)=w*x(n)+w1
4030 LET x(2)=x(n)
4040 LET dx=2
4050 GO TO 310
```

**Listing 7.** Program to calculate first order rate constant and half-life time from kinetic data.

```
1 PRINTER 4,6
2 LPRINT CHR$(27);CHR$(69)
3 LPRINT CHR$(14);
4 LPRINT "AFIRST"
5 LPRINT "------------"
10 INPUT "Is there a Reaction End Point?         (1=yes and 2=no).If not, Guggenheim    method
   is used";W
20 IF W=0 THEN GOTO 50
30 INPUT "Enter the Initial Absorbance-";A
40 INPUT "Enter the Final Absorbance-";F
50 LET X1=0
60 LET X2=0
70 INPUT "How many Data Points -";N
72 LPRINT
74 LPRINT "Initial Absorbance = ";A;"  ";"Final Absorbance = ";F
76 LPRINT N;"Data Points"
80 LET Y1=0
90 LET Y2=0
100 LET Z=0
110 DIMQ(25)
120 DIM X(25)
130 DIM T(25)
140 DIM J(25)
142 LPRINT "TIME(seconds)  ABSORBANCE   "
144 LPRINT "------------------------"
150 FOR I=1 TO N
160 PRINT
170 INPUT "Enter Time (in seconds)-";T(I)
180 INPUT "Enter Absorbance at time T-";Q(I)
185 LPRINT T(I);TAB(17);Q(I);"    ";
190 IF W=1 THEN GOTO 250
200 INPUT "Enter Absorbance about 3 half-times from 0 Time";J(I)
210 LET X(I)=(J(I)-Q(I))
220 LET X(I)=LOG(ABS(X(I)))
230 PRINT "LOG (A-A1)=";X(I)
235 LPRINT "Log (A-A1) = ";X(I)
240 GOTO 290
250 LET X(I)=(F-A)-Q(I)
260 LET X(I)=((F-A)/X(I))
270 LET X1=X1+T(I)
280 PRINT "LN(A/(A-X))=";X(I)
285 LPRINT "Log (A/(A-X)) = ";X(I)
290 LET X1=X1+T(I)
300 LET Y1=Y1+X(I)
310 LET X2=X2+T(I)*T(I)
320 LET Y2=Y2+X(I)*X(I)
330 LET Z=Z+T(I)*X(I)
340 NEXT I
350 LET X3=X1/N
360 LET Y3=Y1/N
370 LET S1=X2-X1*X3
380 LET S2=Y2-Y1*Y3
390 LET S=Z-X1*Y3
400 LET B=S/S1
410 LET B1=Y3-B*X3
420 LET S3=S2-B*S
430 LET S4=S3/(N-2)
440 PRINT "Rate Constant=";B;"Seconds"
445 LPRINT "Rate Constant = ";B;"Seconds with S.D. of ";
450 LET V=S4/S1
460 PRINT
470 PRINT "With Std. Dev.=";SQR(ABS(V))
475 LPRINT SQR(ABS(V))
480 PRINT "R for Slope=";S/SQR(ABS((S1*S2)))
485 LPRINT "R for the Slope = ";S/SQR(ABS((S1*S2)))
500 LET G=.693/B
```

```
510 PRINT "Half-Life=";G;"Seconds"
515 LPRINT "Half-Life = ";G;"Seconds"
517 LPRINT:PRINT
520 PRINT "Again (1=yes / 2=no) ?"
525 LET K$=GET$()
530 IF K$="1" THEN RUN
```

**Listing 8.** Program to calculate second order rate constants from kinetic data.

```
1 PRINTER 4,6
2 LPRINT CHR$(27);
3 LPRINT CHR$(69)
4 LPRINT CHR$(14);
5 LPRINT "SECOND ORDER REACTIONS"
6 LPRINT "----------------------------------------------"
7 LPRINT
10 PRINT "For the Second Order Reacion :"
12 PRINT :PRINT "       A = B + P"
14 PRINT:PRINT "Does - A not equal B (1) or "
16 PRINT        "    - A = B (0) ?"
20 INPUT W
30 ?:PRINT "Enter the Initial Absorbance-";:
40 INPUT A
50 IF W=1 THEN GOTO 80
60 ?:PRINT "Enter the Final Absorbance-";
70 INPUT F
80 LET X1=0
90 LET X2=0
100 IF W=0 THEN GOTO 150
110 PRINT "Enter the Initial Concentration of A,  and B (in MOLES)";
120 INPUT U
130 INPUT R
140 PRINT "A=";U;"Molar";" B=";R;"Molar"
150 ?:PRINT "How many Data Points are there ?";: INPUT N
155 LPRINT "A =";U;"Molar and B =";R;"Molar":LPRINT N;"Data Points"
157 LPRINT
160 LET Y1=0
170 LET Y2=0
180 LET Z=0
190 DIM Q(25)
200 DIM X(25)
210 DIMT(25)
220 DIM J(25)
222 IF W=1 THEN LPRINT "TIME(seconds)   ABSORBANCE    Log(B(A-X)/A(B-X))"
223 IF W=0 THEN LPRINT "TIME(seconds)   ABSORBANCE    (X/A(A-x))"
224 LPRINT "----------------------------------------------------------"
230 FOR I=1 TO N
240 PRINT "Enter Time (in Seconds)-";
250 INPUT T(I)
260 PRINT T(I);" Seconds"
270 IF W=1 THEN GOTO 310
280 PRINT "Enter the Absorbance at Time T"
290 INPUT Q(I)
300 IF W=0 THEN GOTO 380
310 PRINT
320 PRINT "Enter the Absorbance at Time T"
330 INPUT J(I)
340 LET X(I)=(R$(U-(J(I)-A))/(U$(R-J(I)-A)))
350 LET X(I)=LOG(X(I))
360 PRINT "log(B(A-x)/A(B-X))=";X(I)
370 GOTO 402
380 LET X(I)=(F-A)-Q(I)
390 LET X(I)=(Q(I)/((F-A)$X(I)))
400 PRINT "(X/A(A-X))=";X(I)
402 LPRINT TAB(5);T(I);TAB(15);
404 IF W=1 THEN LPRINT J(I) ELSE LPRINT Q(I);
406 LPRINT "      ";X(I)
410 LET X1=X1+T(I)
420 LET Y1=Y1+X(I)
430 LET X2=X2+T(I)$T(I)
440 LET Y2=Y2+X(I)$X(I)
450 LET Z=Z+T(I)$X(I)
460 NEXT I
470 LET X3=X1/N
480 LET Y3=Y1/N
490 LET S1=X2-X1$X3
500 LET S2=Y2-Y1$Y3
510 LET S=Z-X1$Y3
520 LET B=S/S1
530 LET B1=Y3-B$X3
540 LET S3=S2-B$S
550 LET S4=S3/(N-2)
560 PRINT
565 LPRINT
570 PRINT "Rate Constant=";B;
575 LPRINT "Rate Constant=";B;
580 IF W=1 THEN GOTO 610
```

140

```
590 LPRINT "Per Mole per Second"
595 LPRINT "Per Mole per Second"
600 ?:GOTO 620
610 PRINT "Litre per Mole per Second"
615 LPRINT "Litre per Mole per Second"
620 LET V=S4/S1
630 PRINT
640 PRINT "With Std. Dev. of ";SQR(V)
645 LPRINT "With Standard Deviation of ";SQR(V)
650 PRINT:PRINT
660 PRINT "R for the Slope=";S/SQR(S1*S2)
665 LPRINT "R for the Slope = ";S/SQR(S1*S2)
670 IF W=1 THEN GOTO 700
680 LET G=1/((F=A)*B)
690 PRINT:PRINT "Half-Life=";G;"Seconds"
695 LPRINT "Half-Life=";G;" Seconds"
697 ?:?
700 LPRINT
710 PRINT "Again (1=yes / 2=no)
720 LET K$=GET$()
730 IF K$="1" THEN RUN
740 IF K$<>"1" THEN LOADGO "Master"
```

**Listing 9.** Simple and rapid kinetic analysis in FORTH. Program in FORTH to calculate mean initial velocities and $1/v$, $1/[S]$, $[S]/v$ and $v/[S]$ values.

```
0 LINK ok
2 LIST
SCR ' 2
  0 ( DOUBLE PRECISION DIVIDE )
  1 ( REM )
  2 ( REM )
  3 : M/ M/MOD ROT DROP ;
  4 : D/10   10 M/ ;
  5 : UD/    DUP 0= IF DROP M/ ELSE
  6 BEGIN 2SWAP D/10 2SWAP D/10 DUP 0= UNTIL
  7 DROP M/ THEN ;
  8 0 VARIABLE K 0 VARIABLE L
  9 -->
 10
 11
 12
 13
 14
 15
ok
3 LIST
SCR ' 3
  0
  1 ( KINETICS )
  2 0 VARIABLE A 0 VARIABLE B 0 VARIABLE C 0 VARIABLE D
  3 0 VARIABLE E 0 VARIABLE F 0 VARIABLE G 0 VARIABLE H
  4 : VALUES DUP B ! C ! ;
  5 : D* E ! F ! G ! H ! H @ F @
  6 U* H @ E @ U* DROP + G @ F @ U* DROP + ;
  7 0 VARIABLE J
  8 : V1 DPL @ 0< IF S->D 0 DPL !
  9 THEN DPL @ DUP 4 < IF 4 SWAP DO 10. D* LOOP
 10 ELSE 4 > IF ." OUT OF RANGE " DROP DROP THEN THEN ;
 11 : F. SWAP OVER DABS <# # # # # 46 HOLD 'S SIGN #>
 12 TYPE SPACE ;
 13 : S V1 A ! J ! ;
 14 : V V1 D+ ;
 15 -->
ok
4 LIST
SCR ' 4
  0
  1 : MEAN C @ M/MOD OVER OVER K ! L !
  2 OVER OVER
  3 ." V= " F. CR
  4 10000. D* J @ A @ UD/ ." V/S= " F.
  5 100000000. L @ K @ UD/ CR
  6 ." 1/V= " F.
  7 100000000. J @ A @ UD/ CR
  8 ." 1/S= " F.
  9 J @ A @ 10000. D* L @ K @ UD/ CR
 10 ." S/V= " F.
 11 ;
 12
 13
 14
 15
ok
```

# Enzyme Reactions

**Listing 10.** Program to calculate parameters for ligand binding using a distribution-free method.

```
5 OPEN5,4
65 PRINT "ENTER NUMBER OF OBSERVATIONS"
90 INPUT N
100 DIM S(30),V(30),M(200),K(200),P(30),A(200),B(200)
105 FOR I=1 TO N
110 INPUT "ENTER FREE LIGAND CONCENTRATION";S(I)
112 INPUT "ENTER BOUND LIGAND CONCENTRATION";V(I)
125 PRINT "FREE =",S(I),"BOUND =",V(I)
126 P(I)=S(I):S(I)=1/V(I):V(I)=P(I)/V(I)
130 NEXT I
140 L=1
145 B=2
150 FOR I=1 TO N-1
160 FOR J=B TO N
170 K(L)=-(V(I)-V(J))/((V(J)/S(J))-(V(I)/S(I)))
180 M(L)=-((V(I)/S(I))*K(L))+V(I)
185 PRINT "K(L)"K(L),"M(L)"M(L),"I"I,"J"J
190 L=L+1
200 NEXT J
205 B=B+1
210 NEXT I
215 I=L-1
217 B=2
220 FOR L=1 TO I-1
230 FOR J=B TO I
240 IF K(L)>=K(J) GOTO 271
250 T=K(L)
260 K(L)=K(J)
270 K(J)=T
271 IF M(L)>=M(J) GOTO280
272 T=M(L)
273 M(L)=M(J)
274 M(J)=T
280 NEXT J
285 B=B+1
290 NEXT L
295 PRINT "K(L)","V(L)""SORTED INTERCEPTS"
300 FOR L=1 TO I
310 PRINT K(L),M(L)
320 NEXT L
325 L=INT(L+.5)
330 X=L
340 X=(X/2)
345 L=INT(L/2)
350 IF(X-L)<=0.1 GOTO395
360 Z=X+(X-L)
365 L=Z
366 A1=1/K(L)
367 B1=M(L)*A1
368 PRINT"1/NUMBER OF BINDING SITES (OR B(N)/A(N)) ="K(L)
369 PRINT#5,"1/NUMBER OF BINDING SITES (OR B(N)/A(N)) ="K(L)
370 PRINT"MAXIMUM NUMBER OF BINDING SITES ="A1
375 PRINT#5,"MAXIMUM NUMBER OF BINDING SITES ="A1
380 PRINT"K(D)/N (OR B(0)/A(1)) ="M(L)
384 PRINT"DISSOCIATION CONSTANT (K(D)) ="B1
386 PRINT#5,"DISSOCIATION CONSTANT (K(D)) ="B1
390 GO TO 430
395 V=(K(L)+K(L+1))/2
400 W=(M(L)+M(L+1))/2
410 A2=1/V
411 B2=W*A2
412 PRINT"NUMBER OF BINDING SITES ="A2
415 PRINT#5,"NUMBER OF BINDING SITES ="A2
420 PRINT"K(D)="B2
425 PRINT#5,"K(D) ="B2
428 GOTO 475
430 FOR L=1 TO I
450 A(L)=K(L)-K(Z)
452 B(L)=M(L)-M(Z)
454 B(L)=B(L)*A1
455 PRINTA1+A(L):B1+B(L)
456 PRINT#5,"RESIDUAL N=":1+A(L),"KD=" B1+B(L)
459 PRINT#5
460 NEXT L
470 END
475 FOR L=1 TO I
480 PRINT K(L)-V,M(L)-W
485 A(L)=K(L)-Y
486 B(L)=M(L)-W
488 B(L)=B(L)*A2
490 PRINTA2+A(L):B2+B(L)
492 PRINT#5,"RESIDUAL N=":A2+A(L),"KD=":B2+B(L)
494 PRINT#5
495 NEXT L
500 END
```

**Listing 11.** Calculation of kinetic parameters for enzymes using a distribution-free method; **(a)** listing of program to calculate initial reaction velocities ($v_o$) using an integrated rate equation method. Estimates of $K_m$ and $V_{max}$ are also obtained; **(b)** listing of program for simple, direct linear calculation of $K_m$ and $V_{max}$ from initial velocity determinations.

```
5 OPEN5,4
30 PRINT"DISTRIBUTION FREE"
40 PRINT
65 PRINT "ENTER NUMBER OF OBSERVATIONS"
90 INPUT N
100 DIM S(30),V(30),M(200),K(200),P(30)
110 PRINT"ENTER INITIAL SUBSTRATE CONCENTRATION"
112 INPUT M:PRINTM
113 FOR I=1 TO N
114 PRINT"ENTER SUBSTRATE CONCENTRATION AT TIME T (BOTH VALUES)"
```

```
116 INPUT S(I),T(I)
118 PRINTS(I),T(I)
120 V(I)=(T(I)/(LOG(M/S(I))))
122 S(I)=T(I)/(M-S(I))
124 PRINT"T/LN(S(0)/S(T))=",V(I)
126 PRINT"T/(S(0)-S(T))=",S(I)
130 NEXT I
140 L=1
145 B=2
150 FOR I=1 TO N-1
160 FOR J=B TO N
170 K(L)=(V(I)-V(J))/((V(J)/S(J))-(V(I)/S(I)))
180 M(L)=((V(I)/S(I))*K(L))+V(I)
185 PRINT "K(L)"K(L),"M(L)"M(L),"I"I,"J"J
190 L=L+1
200 NEXT J
205 B=B+1
210 NEXT I
215 I=L-1
217 B=2
220 FOR L=1 TO I-1
230 FOR J=B TO I
240 IF K(L)>=K(J) GOTO 271
250 T=K(L)
260 K(L)=K(J)
270 K(J)=T
271 IF M(L)>=M(J) GOTO280
272 T=M(L)
273 M(L)=M(J)
274 M(J)=T
280 NEXT J
285 B=B+1
290 NEXT L
295 PRINT "K(L)","V(L)""SORTED INTERCEPTS"
300 FOR L=1 TO I
310 PRINT K(L),M(L)
320 NEXT L
325 L=INT(L+.5)
330 X=L
340 X=(X/2)
345 L=INT(L/2)
350 IF(X-L)<=0.1 GOTO395
360 Z=X+(X-L)
365 L=Z
370 PRINT "KM="K(L)
380 PRINT "V MAX="M(L)
385 PRINT#5,"1/VM="K(L),"KM/VM=",M(L)
387 T=M(L)-M*K(L):P=M/T: PRINT"V(0)=",P:PRINT#5,"V(0)=",P
390 GO TO 430
395 V=(K(L)+K(L+1))/2
400 W=(M(L)+M(L+1))/2
410 PRINT "KM="Y
420 PRINT "V MAX="W
425 PRINT#5,"1/VM="Y,"KM/VM="W
427 T=W-M*Y:P=M/T:PRINT"V(0)=",P:PRINT#5,"V(0)=",P
428 GOTO 475
430 FOR L=1 TO I
440 PRINT K(L)-K(Z),M(L)-M(Z)
450 PRINT#5,"RESIDUALS=",K(L)-K(Z),M(L)-M(Z)
460 NEXT L
470 END
475 FOR L=1 TO I
480 PRINT K(L)-Y,M(L)-W
490 PRINT#5,"RESIDUALS=",K(L)-Y,M(L)-W
495 NEXT L
500 END
READY.


1 PRINTER 4,6
3 LPRINT CHR$(27);CHR$(69)
4 LPRINT CHR$(14);
5 LPRINT "DIRPLOT4"
7 LPRINT "----------------"
8 LPRINT
10 ?"THIS PROGRAM CALCULATES K(M) AND V(MAX) BY THE DIRECT LINEAR PLOT":?
12 LPRINT "Program to calculate K(m) and V(max) by the Direct Linear Plot"
20 ?:?" PLEASE ENTER NUMBER OF OBSERVATIONS"
30 INPUT N
40 DIM S(20),V(20),M(50),K(50)
42 LPRINT
45 LPRINT "  S";TAB(10);"V";TAB(20);"K(L)";TAB(30);"M(L)";TAB(40);"I";TAB(50);"J"
47 LPRINT "----------------------------------------------------------"
50 FOR I=1TON
60 INPUT S,V:S(I),V(I)
70 ?"S="S(I), "V="V(I)
80 NEXT I
90 L=1:B=2
100 FOR I=1TON-1
110 FOR J=BTON
120 K(L)=(V(I)-V(J))/((V(J)/S(J))-(V(I)/S(I)))
130 M(L)=((V(I)/S(I))*K(L))+V(I)
140 ?"K(L)"K(L),"M(L)"M(L),"I"=I,"J"=J
142 LPRINT S(I);TAB(8); V(I);TAB(16);K(L);TAB(29);M(L);TAB(39);I;TAB(48);J
150 L=L+1
160 NEXT J
170 B=B+1
180 NEXT I
190 I=L-1:B=2
200 FOR L=1TOI-2
210 FOR J=BTOI
220 IFK(L)>=K(J)GOTO260
230 T=K(L):K(L)=K(J):K(J)=T
260 IFM(L)>=M(J)GOTO280
270 T=M(L):M(L)=M(J):M(J)=T
280 NEXT J
290 B=B+1
300 NEXT L
310 ?"K(L)","V(L)","SORTED INTERCEPTS"
312 LPRINT:LPRINT "SORTED INTERCEPTS"
313 LPRINT "  K(L)    M(L)":LPRINT "----------------"
320 FOR L=1TOI
330 ?K(L),M(L)
335 LPRINT TAB(3);K(L);TAB(13);M(L)
```

```
340 NEXT L
350 L=INT(L+.5)
360 X=L:X=(X/2)
370 L=INT(L/2)
380 IF (X-L)<=0.1GOTO430
390 Z=X+(X-L):L=Z
400 ?:?:?:?"K(M)="K(L)
405 LPRINT "K(m) = ";K(L)
410 ?:?:?"V(MAX)="M(L)
415 LPRINT "V(max) = ";M(L)
420 GOTO470
430 Y=(K(L)+K(L+1))/2
440 W=(M(L)+M(L+1))/2
450 ?:?:?"K(M)="Y
455 LPRINT "K(m) = ";Y
460 ?:?:?"V(MAX)="W
465 LPRINT "V(max) = ";W
470 END
```

**Listing 12.** Program to obtain statistical analyses of initial velocity data, transformation and plotting into any graphical space.

```
100 OPEN 5,4:PRINT:PRINT:PRINT
150 DIMX(20),Y(20),A(20),B(20),G(20),O(20),W(20):PRINT
180 PRINT"ARE YOU STUDYING THE EFFECT OFSUBSTRATE CONCENTRATION (S),"
185 PRINT"TEMPERATURE (T) OR INHIBTORS (I) ON    ENZYME  REACTION VELOCITY ?"
186 INPUT N$
187 IF N$<>"I"THEN 190
188 IF N$="I" THEN 6000
190 GOSUB 1000
195 IF N$="T" GOTO 3000
200 PRINT"DO YOU REQUIRE KINETIC PLOTS OF YOUR    INITIAL VELOCITY DATA?(Y/N)"
210 INPUT C$
220 IF C$="Y" THEN 250
230 IF C$="N" THEN 4000
250 PRINT"DO YOU REQUIRE A V VERSUS S PLOT ?      (Y OR N)"
255 INPUT D$
258 IF D$="Y" THEN 272
260 IF D$="N" THEN 330
272 PRINT#5," THIS IS A V VERSUS S PLOT"
280 FOR I= 1 TO N
290 X(I)=A(I):Y(I)=B(I):G(I)=D(I):O(I)=D(I)
310 NEXT
320 GOSUB 2000
325 PRINT:PRINT:PRINT#5:PRINT#5
330 PRINT"DO YOU REQUIRE A DOUBLE RECIPROCAL PLOT?(Y OR N)"
340 INPUT E$
350 IF E$="Y" THEN 365
360 IF E$="N" THEN 420
365 PRINT#5,"THIS IS A DOUBLE RECIPROCAL  PLOT. THE  1/V AXIS IS HORIZONTAL"
370 FOR I=1 TO N
380 X(I)=1/A(I):Y(I)=1/B(I)
391 G(I)=(1/(B(I)+D(I)))
392 G(I)=(1/B(I))-G(I)
393 O(I)=(1/(B(I)-D(I)))
394 O(I)=O(I)-(1/B(I))
400 NEXT
410 GOSUB 2000
412 PRINT:PRINT:PRINT#5:PRINT#5
420 PRINT" DO YOU REQUIRE A EADIE-HOFSTEE PLOT ?   (V VS.V/S) (Y OR N)"
430 INPUT F$
440 IF F$="Y" THEN 455
450 IF F$="N" THEN 510
455 PRINT#5,"THIS IS AN EADIE-HOFSTEE PLOT.        THE V AXIS IS HORIZONTAL."
460 FOR I=1 TO N
470 X(I)=B(I)/A(I):Y(I)=B(I):G(I)=D(I):O(I)=D(I)
490 NEXT
500 GOSUB 2000
505 PRINT:PRINT:PRINT#5:PRINT#5
510 PRINT" DO YOU REQUIRE A HANES PLOT ? (S/V VS.S)(Y OR N)"
520 INPUT G$
530 IF G$="Y" THEN 545
540 IF G$="N" THEN 600
545 PRINT#5," THIS IS A HANES PLOT. THE S/V AXIS IS HORIZONTAL."
550 FOR I=1 TO N
560 X(I)=A(I):Y(I)=A(I)/B(I)
572 G(I)=(A(I)/B(I))-(A(I)/(B(I)+D(I)))
574 O(I)=(A(I)/(B(I)-D(I)))-(A(I)/B(I))
580 NEXT
590 GOSUB 2000
595 PRINT:PRINT:PRINT#5:PRINT#5
600 PRINT"DO YOU REQUIRE A V VERSUS LOG S PLOT?    (Y OR N)"
610 INPUT H$
620 IF H$="Y" THEN  635
630 IF H$="N" THEN 690
635 PRINT#5,"THIS IS A V VERSUS LOG S PLOT. THE V AXIS IS HORIZONTAL."
640 FOR I=1 TO N
650 X(I)=LOG(A(I)):Y(I)=B(I):G(I)=D(I):O(I)=D(I)
670 NEXT
680 GOSUB 2000
685 PRINT:PRINT:PRINT#5:PRINT#5
690 PRINT" DO YOU REQUIRE A LOG V VERSUS LOG S      PLOT ? (Y OR N)"
700 INPUT I$
710 IF I$="Y" THEN 725
720 IF I$="N" THEN 780
725 PRINT#5," THIS IS A LOG V VERSUS LOG S PLOT.THE LOG V AXIS IS HORIZONTAL."
730 FOR I=1  TO N
740 X(I)=LOG(A(I)):Y(I)=LOG(B(I))
752 G(I)=LOG(B(I)-D(I)):O(I)=LOG(B(I)-D(I))
760 NEXT
770 GOSUB 2000
775 PRINT:PRINT:PRINT#5:PRINT#5
780 PRINT" DO  YOU REQUIRE AN SV VERSUS S PLOT ?    (Y OR N)"
790 INPUT J$
800 IF J$="Y" THEN 815
810 IF J$="N" THEN 870
815 PRINT#5,"THIS IS AN SV VERSUS S PLOT. THE SV AXIS IS HORIZONTAL."
```

```
820 FOR I=1 TO N
830 X(I)=A(I):Y(I)=A(I)*B(I)
842 G(I)=A(I)*B(I)-A(I)*(B(I)-D(I))
844 O(I)=A(I)*(B(I)+D(I))-A(I)*B(I)
850 NEXT
860 GOSUB 2000
865 PRINT:PRINT:PRINT#5:PRINT#5
870 PRINT" DO YOU REQUIRE AN S-SQUARED V VERSUS S  PLOT ? (Y OR N)"
880 INPUT K$
890 IF K$="Y" THEN 905
900 IF K$="N" THEN 960
905 PRINT#5,"THIS IS AN St2 VERSUS V PLOT. THE St2V AXIS IS HORIZONTAL."
910 FOR I=1 TO N
920 X(I)=A(I):Y(I)=A(I)t2*B(I)
932 G(I)=A(I)t2*B(I)-A(I)t2*(B(I)-D(I))
934 O(I)=A(I)t2*(B(I)+D(I))-A(I)t2*B(I)
940 NEXT
950 GOSUB 2000
955 PRINT:PRINT:PRINT#5:PRINT#5
960 PRINT"DO YOU REQUIRE A SCATCHARD PLOT ?       (V/S VS.V) (Y OR N)"
962 INPUT Y$
963 IF Y$="Y" THEN 968
964 IF A$="Y" THEN 5165
965 IF Y$="N" THEN 4000
968 PRINT#5,"THIS IS A SCATCHARD PLOT. THE V/S AXIS IS HORIZONTAL."
970 FOR I=1 TO N
972 X(I)=B(I):Y(I)=B(I)/A(I)
975 G(I)=(B(I)/A(I))-((B(I)-D(I))/A(I))
976 O(I)=((B(I)+D(I))/A(I))-(B(I)/A(I)))
977 NEXT
978 GOSUB 2000
980 PRINT:PRINT:PRINT#5:PRINT#5
990 GOTO 3000
1000 PRINT"ENTER NUMBER OF S,V DATA POINTS"
1001 INPUT N
1002 PRINT#5,"TOTAL NUMBER  OF POINTS ="N
1003 FOR I=1 TO N
1004 IF N$="T" THEN 1008
1005 PRINT"WHAT IS THE VALUE FOR SUBSTRATE          CONCENTRATION ?"
1006 GOTO 1010
1008 PRINT"WHAT IS THE TEMPERATURE IN DEGREES C ?"
1010 INPUT A(I)
1020 E=0:S=0:S2=0:PRINT
1026 PRINT"HOW MANY INDIVIDUAL V VALUES ARE THERE ?"
1027 INPUT R
1030 IF R<>INT(R) THEN 1026
1035 IF R>10 THEN 1026
1040 PRINT"ENTER INITIAL RATE DATA (V VALUES)        THEN PRESS RETURN"
1045 FOR U= 1 TO R
1050 PRINT
1060 INPUT F
1080 E=E+1:S=S+F:S2=S2+F*F
1110 NEXT
1120 IF E=0 THEN 1280
1125 IF R>1 THEN 1130
1127 IF R=1 THEN 1182
1130 M=S/E:B(I)=M
1140 V=(E*S2-S*S)/E/(E-1)
1150 G=SQR(V):D(I)=1.96*G/SQR(R):D(I)=D:G(I)=G:C=G/M
1181 GOTO 1203
1182 M=F:B(I)=M
1185 V=0:G=0:C=0:D=0
1190 GOTO 1203
1203 PRINT"DO YOU WISH TO PRINT STATISTICS ?        (Y OR N)"
1204 INPUT B$
1205 IF B$="Y" THEN 1207
1206 IF B$="N" THEN 1400
1207 PRINT#5,"SUBSTRATE CONCENTRATION ="A(I)
1208 PRINT#5,"NUMBER OF INITIAL RATF VALUES=",R
1209 PRINT#5,"SUM=",S
1210 PRINT#5,"SUM OF SQUARES=",S2
1220 PRINT#5,
1230 PRINT#5,"MEAN V VALUE +/- STANDARD DEVIATION="M"+/-"G
1233 PRINT#5
1235 PRINT#5,"MEAN V VALUE +/- 95% CONFIDENCE LIMITS="M"+/-"D
1238 PRINT#5
1240 PRINT#5,"VARIANCE=",V
1260 PRINT#5,"STANDARD DEVIATION OF THE MEAN=",C
1262 IF N$="T" GOTO 1400
1265 PRINT#5
1270 PRINT#5,"1/MEAN V VALUE="1/M";95% CONF. LIMITS ARE:"1/(M+D)"TO"1/(M-D)
1280 PRINT#5
1290 H=LOG(M)
1295 PRINT#5,"LOG MEAN V VALUE="H";95% CONF.LIMITS ARE:"LOG(M-D)"TO"LOG(M+D)
1296 PRINT#5
1298 PRINT#5,"LOG S =",LOG(A(I))
1300 PRINT#5,"1/S=",1/A(I)
1310 PRINT#5,"S/V=",A(I)/M";95% CONF.LIMITS ARE:"A(I)/(M+D)"TO"A(I)/(M-D
1320 PRINT#5,"V/S=",M/A(I)";95% CONF.LIMITS ARE:"(M-D)/A(I)"TO"(M+D)/A(I)
1330 PRINT#5,"SV=",A(I)*M";95% CONF.LIMITS ARE:"A(I)*(M-D)"TO"A(I)*(M+D)
1340 PRINT#5,"St2V=",(A(I)t2)*M";95% CONF.LIMITS ARE"(A(I)t2)*(M-D)
1350 PRINT#5,"TO"A(I)t2*(M+D);
1360 PRINT#5
1400 NEXT
1410 RETURN
2000 PRINT"ENTER VALUES FOR LOWER LIMIT,UPPER LIMIT AND INCREMENTS ON X-AXIS"
2005 A1=0:A2=0:A3=0
2010 INPUT A1,A2,A3
2020 PRINT"ENTER VALUES FOR LOWER LIMIT,UPPER LIMIT AND INCREMENTS ON Y-AXIS"
2025 B1=0:B2=0:B3=0
2030 INPUT B1,B2,B3
2040 B2=(B2-B1)/B3
2050 IF B2<=80 THEN 2080
2060 PRINT"Y-RANGE IS TOO LARGE. TRY ANOTHER VALUE"
2070 GOTO 2020
2080 FOR I= 1 TO N
2090 X(I)=INT((X(I)-A1)/A3+.5):Y(I)=INT((Y(I)-B1)/B3+.5)
2103 IF G(I)=0 GOTO  2110
2105 G(I)=INT((G(I)-B1)/B3)
2108 O(I)=INT((O(I)-B1)/B3)
2110 NEXT I
2111 G(R)=G(I):O(R)=O(I)
2120 Y(N+1)=INT(B2+.5)+1
2130 X(N+1)=INT((A2-A1)/A3+.5)+1
```

```
2140 PRINT#5,"INTERSECTION OF AXES IS AT (";
2150 PRINT#5,A1;",";B1;")"
2160 PRINT#5
2170 FOR J=1 TO N
2180 FOR I=1 TO N-J
2190 A=X(I):B=Y(I):C=X(I+1):D=Y(I+1)
2210 IF A<C THEN 2240
2220 X(I)=C:Y(I)=D:X(I+1)=A:Y(I+1)=B
2240 NEXT I
2250 NEXT J
2260 T=1
2270 FOR P=0 TO N-1
2280 IF X(P+1)>=0 THEN Q=P:P=N
2290 NEXT P
2300 P=Q:R=0
2310 FOR I=0 TO INT((A2-A1)/A3+.5)
2320 T=T+P:P=0
2340 IF T>N THEN 2360
2350 IF X(T)=I THEN 2410
2360 IF I=0 THEN 2390
2370 PRINT#5,"-";
2380 GOTO 2860
2390 S=N+1
2400 GOTO 2740
2410 FOR L=T TO N
2420 IF X(L)<=X(T) THEN P=P+1
2430 NEXT L
2440 IF P=1 THEN 2540
2450 FOR J=1 TO P
2460 FOR L=1 TO P-J
2470 D=Y(T+L-1):B=Y(T+L)
2490 IF D<=B THEN 2520
2500 Y(T+L-1)=B:Y(T+L)=D
2520 NEXT L
2530 NEXT J
2540 FOR L=0  TO P-1
2550 Z=Y(T+L)
2560 IF Z>=0 THEN 2580
2570 NEXT L
2580 IF I=0 THEN 2730
2590 IF Z=0 THEN 2700
2600 PRINT#5,"-";
2610 IF L=P-1 THEN 2690
2620 FOR J=L TO P-1
2630 IF Z>B2 THEN 2860
2640 IF Y(T+J)=Z THEN 2680
2645 R=R+1
2648 IF G(R)=0 GOTO 2660
2649 IF G(R)>Z GOTO 2660
2650 PRINT#5,TAB(Z-G(R));"|"TAB(G(R))"+"TAB(O(R))"|";
2655 GOTO 2670
2660 PRINT#5,TAB(Z);"+";
2670 Z=Y(T+J)
2680 NEXT J
2690 IF Z<0 THEN 2860
2700 IF Z>B2 THEN 2860
2705 R=R+1
2708 IF G(R)=0 GOTO 2715
2709 IF G(R)>Z GOTO 2715
2710 PRINT#5,TAB(Z-G(R));"|"TAB(G(R))"+"TAB(O(R))"|";
2712 GOTO 2720
2715 PRINT#5,TAB(Z);"+";
2720 GOTO 2860
2730 S=T+L
2740 FOR J=0 TO B2
2750 IF Y(S)<>J THEN 2830
2760 PRINT#5,"+";
2770 FOR K=S TO T+P-1
2780 IF Y(K)=Y(S) THEN 2810
2790 S=K
2800 GOTO 2840
2810 NEXT K
2820 GOTO 2840
2830 PRINT#5,"|";
2840 NEXT J
2850 PRINT#5,"Y:MAX="B2*B3-ABS(B1);
2860 PRINT#5
2870 NEXT I
2880 PRINT#5,"X:MAX="A2;
2885 PRINT#5
2890 PRINT"WOULD YOU LIKE ANY REPLOTS OF KINETIC DATA ? (Y OR N)"
2900 INPUT A$
2910 IF A$="Y"THEN 250
2920 RETURN
```

**Listing 13.** Program subroutine for calculation of Arrhenius parameters.

```
3000 PRINT#5,"ARRHENIUS PLOT; LOG V VERSUS 1/T)"
3010 PRINT#5
3020 FOR I=1 TO N
3070 X(I)=1000/(A(I)+273.15)
3080 PRINT#5,"1/T X10↑3="X(I)
3090 Y(I)=LOG(B(I))
3095 G(I)=0
3100 PRINT#5,"LOG V="Y(I):PRINT#5
3120 NEXT
3130 GOSUB 2000
3150 PRINT:PRINT#5
3160 FOR I=1 TO N                        3165 X=X(I)
3170 X=1000/(A(I)+273.15)
3180 V=LOG(B(I))
3190 X1=X1+X:Y1=Y1+Y:X2=X2+X*X:Y2=Y2+Y*Y:Z=Z+X*V
3240 NEXT
3250 GOSUB 8000
3260 PRINT#5
3270 PRINT#5,"SLOPE OF ARRHENIUS PLOT="B"+/-"SQR(S4/S1)
3280 PRINT#5,"INTERCEPT ON LOG V AXIS="B1"+/-"SQR(S4*(1/N+X3*X3/S1))
3290 PRINT#5
3300 PRINT#5,"CORRELATION COEFFICIENT FOR SLOPE="S/SQR(S1*S2)
3310 PRINT#5
```

**Listing 14.** Program subroutine for non-linear regression analysis of data to the Michaelis-Menten equation.

```
4000 PRINT" DO YOU REQUIRE NON-LINEAR REGRESSION    TO YOUR DATA ,"
4001 PRINT"AND ESTIMATES OF K(M) AND V(MAX) ?(Y OR N)"
4002 INPUT Z$
4004 IF Z$="Y" THEN 4010
4006 IF Z$="N" THEN 6000
4010 PRINT#5,"NON LINEAR REGRESSION ANALYSIS ON KINETIC DATA"
4055 PRINT
4060 PRINT"WHAT TYPE OF WEIGHTING WOULD YOU LIKE ?"
4065 PRINT
4070 PRINT"CONSTANT STANDARD DEVIATION ? (C)"
4075 PRINT
4080 PRINT"PROPORTIONAL STANDARD DEVIATION ?(P)"
4085 PRINT
4090 PRINT"BEWEEN PROPORTIONAL AND CONSTANT STANDARD DEVIATION ? (B)"
4095 PRINT
4100 PRINT"STANDARD DEVIATION DEPENDENT ON 95%    CONF.LIMITS ? (S)"
4105 PRINT
4110 INPUT W$
4120 PRINT" BISQUARE WEIGHTING ALSO ?(Y OR N)"
4130 INPUT X$
4135 PRINT:PRINT
4190 FOR I=1 TO N
4230 IF W$="S" THEN 4310
4235 X1(I)=A(I):Y(I)=B(I):W(I)=1
4260 IF W$="C" THEN 4330
4270 W(I)=1/Y(I)
4280 IF W$="B" THEN 4330
4290 W(I)=W(I)↑2
4300 GOTO 4330
4310 X1(I)=A(I):Y(I)=B(I):W(I)=1/D(I)↑2
4330 NEXT I
4380 PRINT"THE FORM OF THE FUNCTION IS        G=V(MAX)*S/K(M)+S"
4385 PRINT" ENTER ESTIMATES OF THE PARAMETERS (V(MAX),K(M))"
4390 B=0
4400 INPUT B(1),B(2)
4410 PRINT"    V(MAX)        K(M)        SSQ"
4420 I1=0:I1=I1+1
4430 I1=I1+1
4440 IF I1>10 THEN 5100
4450 S1=0:S2=0:S3=0:S4=0:S5=0:S6=0:R1=0:G=0
4520 FOR I=1 TO N
4540 X=X1(I):G=B(1)*X/(B(2)+X)
4560 Z=Y(I)-G
4570 R5=SQR(W(I))*Z
4580 R1=R1+ABS(R5)
4590 FOR J=1 TO 2
4600 B(J)=1.02*B(J)
4610 G=B(1)*X/(B(2)+X)
4620 U=0:U=G
4640 B(J)=B(J)*.98/1.02
4650 G=B(1)*X/(B(2)+X)
4660 B(J)=B(J)/.98
4670 P(J)=(U-G)/(.04*B(J))
4680 NEXT J
4690 R3=1
4710 IF X$="N" THEN 4740
4720 IF I1=1 THEN 4740
4730 GOSUB 5120
4740 PRINT
4750 S1=S1+R3*W(I)*P(1)↑2
4760 S2=S2+R3*W(I)*P(1)*P(2)
4770 S3=S3+R3*W(I)*P(2)↑2
4780 S4=S4+R3*W(I)*P(1)*Z
4790 S5=S5+R3*W(I)*P(2)*Z
4800 S6=S6+R3*W(I)*Z↑2
4810 NEXT I
4820 R2=6*R1/N
4830 D=S1*S3-S2↑2
4850 Q(1)=(S3*S4-S2*S5)/D
4860 Q(2)=(S1*S5-S2*S4)/D
4870 C=0
4880 C=ABS(Q(1)/B(1))+ABS(Q(2)/B(2))
4890 B(1)=B(1)+Q(1)
4900 B(2)=B(2)+Q(2)
4910 PRINTB(1)B(2)S6
4920 IF C>1.00000E-05 THEN 4430
4940 V=S6/(N-2)
4950 Q(1)=SQR(V*S3/D)
4960 Q(2)=SQR(V*S1/D)
4970 PRINT#5,"FINAL VALUES OF PARAMETERS"
4990 PRINT#5,"V(MAX)="B(1)"+/-"Q(1)
5000 PRINT#5
5010 PRINT#5,"K(M)="B(2)"+/-"Q(2)
5020 PRINT#5
5030 PRINT#5,"S            V(OBS)        V(PREDICTED)        RESIDUALS
5040 FOR I=1 TO N
5060 X=X1(I):G=B(1)*X/(B(2)+X)
5070 PRINT#5,X1(I),Y(I),G,Y(I)-G
5072 M=0:E=0:K=0
5075 M(I)=G:E(I)=Y(I)-G:K(I)=Y(I)
5080 NEXT I
5085 GOTO 5165
5090 PRINT"END OF ITERATIONS"
5100 PRINT#5,"TERMINATED AFTER 10 ITERATIONS"
5110 GOTO 4940
5120 R3=0
5130 R4=(R5/R2)↑2
5140 IF R4>1 THEN 5160
5150 R3=(1-R4)↑2
5160 RETURN
5165 PRINT"DO YOU REQUIRE RESIDUAL  PLOTS ?        (Y OR N)"
5170 INPUT M$
5175 IF M$="N" THEN 5470
5180 PRINT#5,"PLOT OF PREDICTED V VALUES VERSUS        SUBSTRATE CONCENTRATION"
5190 PRINT"PLOT OF PREDICTED V VALUES VERSUS        SUBSTRATE CONCENTRATION"
5195 PRINT
```

```
5200 PRINT#5
5210 FOR I=1 TO (
5220 X(I)=X1(I):Y(I)=M(I):G(I)=0
5240 NEXT
5250 GOSUB 2000
5270 PRINT:PRINT#5:PRINT#5
5310 PRINT#5,"PLOT OF RESIDUALS VERSUS SUBSTRATE CONCENTRATION"
5315 PRINT"PLOT OF RESIDUALS VERSUS SUBSTRATE        CONCENTRATION"
5317 PRINT
5320 FOR I=1 TO N
5330 X(I)=X1(I):Y(I)=E(I):G(I)=0
5350 NEXT
5360 GOSUB 2000
5380 PRINT#5
5390 PRINT#5,"PLOT OF RESIDUALS VERSUS PREDICTED V VALUES"
5395 PRINT"PLOT OF RESIDUALS VERSUS PREDICTED V    VALUES"
5397 PRINT
5400 FOR I=1 TO N
5410 X(I)=M(I):Y(I)=E(I):G(I)=0
5430 NEXT
5440 GOSUB 2000
5450 PRINT:PRINT#5
5460 PRINT#5
5462 PRINT"DO YOU WISH TO ALTER WEIGHTING ? (Y/N)"
5464 INPUT Z#
5466 IF Z#="Y" THEN4010
```

**Listing 15.** Program subroutine for obtaining a Hill plot together with its slope.

```
5470 PRINT"DO YOU REQUIRE A HILL PLOT?LOG(V/V(M)-V)VS.LOG S (Y OR N)"
5480 INPUT J#
5490 IF J#="Y"THEN 5510
5500 IF J#="N"THEN 6000
5510 PRINT#5,"THIS IS A HILL  PLOT.THE LOG(V/(V(MAX)-V)AXIS IS HORIZONTAL,"
5520 PRINT#5,"THE LOG S AXIS IS VERTICAL."
5522 PRINT"ENTER VALUE REQUIRED FOR V(MAX)"
5524 INPUT H
5530 PRINT#5
5540 FOR I=1 TO N
5550 X(I)=LOG(X1(I))
5560 Y(I)=LOG(K(I)/(H-K(I))):G(I)=0
5565 PRINT#5,"LOG(V/VM-V)="Y(I):PRINT#5,"LOG S="X(I):PRINT#5
5570 NEXT
5580 GOSUB 2000
5590 PRINT:PRINT#5:PRINT#5
5610 FOR I=1 TO N
5620 X=LOG(X1(I))
5630 Y=LOG(K(I)/(H-K(I)))
5640 X1=X1+X:Y1=Y1+Y:X2=X2+X*X:Y2=Y2+Y*Y:Z=Z+X*Y
5690 NEXT
5700 GOSUB 8000
5710 PRINT#5
5720 PRINT#5,"SLOPE OF THE HILL PLOT="B"+/-"SQR(ABS(S4)/S1)
5730 PRINT:PRINT#5:PRINT
```

**Listing 16.** Program subroutine for obtaining data from reversible and irreversible inhibition experiments, including the statistical subroutine (lines 8000 – 8020).

```
6000 PRINT"DO YOU REQUIRE REVERSIBLE(R),         IRREVERSIBLE(I)OR NO(N)"
6002 PRINT"INHIBITION PLOTS ?"
6010 INPUT M#
6020 IF M#="R"THEN6040
6030 IF M#="I"THEN7420
6035 IF M#="N" THEN 7660
6040 PRINT"ENTER TOTAL NUMBER OF V,S VALUES-       WITH AND WITHOUT INHIBITOR"
6045 N=0
6050 INPUT N
6051 PRINT#5,"DOUBLE RECIPROCAL  PLOT FOR REVERSIBLE INHIBITION"
6052 FOR I=1 TO N
6055 PRINT"ENTER VALUES FOR S,V"
6060 INPUT X(I),Y(I)
6070 X(I)=1/X(I):Y(I)=1/Y(I):G(I)=0
6090 NEXT I
6100 GOSUB 2000
6105 PRINT:PRINT#5
6110 PRINT"DO YOU REQUIRE SLOPE/INTERCEPT         CALCULATIONS?(Y OR N)"
6120 INPUT N#
6130 IF N#="Y"THEN6150
6140 IF N#="N"THEN7660
6150 PRINT"ENTER  NO.OF DATA SETS"
6160 INPUT P
6170 FOR I=1 TO P
6180 PRINT"ENTER INHIBITOR CONCENTRATION"
6190 INPUT Q(I)
6210 X1=0:X2=0:Y1=0:Y2=0:Z=0
6260 PRINT"ENTER NUMBER OF S,V DETERMINATIONS"
6265 N=0
6270 INPUT N
6280 FOR R=1 TO N
6290 PRINT"ENTER S,V VALUES"
6300 INPUT X,Y
6310 X=1/X:Y=1/Y
6330 X1=X1+X:Y1=Y1+Y:X2=X2+X*X:Y2=Y2+Y*Y:Z=Z+X*Y
6380 NEXT
6390 GOSUB 8000
6480 PRINT#5
6490 PRINT#5,"SLOPE OF DOUBLE RECIPROCAL PLOT="B"+/-"SQR(S4/S1)
6500 PRINT#5
6505 B(I)=B
6510 PRINT#5,"Y-INTERCEPT="B1"+/-"SQR(S4*(1/N+X3*X3/S1))
6511 PRINT#5
6512 PRINT#5,"INTERCEPT ON THE X-AXIS="B2
6513 PRINT#5
```

```
6515 C(I)=B1
6520 PRINT#5
6530 PRINT#5,"F-RATIO FOR SLOPE="B*S/S4
6540 PRINT#5
6550 PRINT#5,"CORRELATION COEFFICIENT="S/SQR(S1*S2)
6560 PRINT#5
6580 NEXT
6590 PRINT"DO YOU REQUIRE A REPLOT OF SLOPES VERSUS I ?(Y OR N)
6600 INPUT O$
6610 IF O$="Y" THEN 6630
6620 IF O$="N" THEN 6690
6630 FOR I=1 TO N
6640 X(I)=Q(I):Y(I)=B(I)
6655 G(I)=SQR(S4/S1):O(I)=G(I)
6670 NEXT
6675 PRINT#5,"REPLOT OF SLOPES VERSUS INHIBITOR CONCENTRATION"
6680 GOSUB 2000
6690 PRINT"DO YOU REQUIRE A REPLOT OF INTERCEPTS VERSUS I ? (Y OR N)
6700 INPUT P$
6710 IF P$="Y" THEN 6730
6720 IF P$="N" THEN 6780
6730 N=P
6735 FOR I=1 TO N
6740 X(I)=Q(I):Y(I)=C(I)
6755 G(I)=SQR(S4*(1/N+X3*X3/S1)):O(I)=G(I)
6760 NEXT
6765 PRINT#5,"REPLOT OF INTERCEPTS VERSUS INHIBITOR CONCENTRATION"
6770 GOSUB 2000
6780 PRINT"DO YOU REQUIRE K(I)(SLOPE) ?(Y OR N)
6790 INPUT R$
6800 IF R$="Y"THEN 6820
6810 IF R$="N" THEN 7170
6820 N=P
6830 FOR I=1 TO N
6840 X=Q(I):Y=B(I)
7000 X1=X1+X:Y1=Y1+Y:X2=X2+X*X:Y2=Y2+Y*Y:Z=Z+X*Y
7050 NEXT
7060 GOSUB 8000
7090 S2=Y2-Y1*Y3
7130 PRINT#5,"K(I)(SLOPE="ABS(B2)
7140 PRINT#5,"AT 37 DEGREES C, THE DELTA G ZERO VALUE FOR THE EFFECT OF"
7150 PRINT#5,"THE INHIBITOR ON THE SLOPE="2579*LOG(ABS(B2*1000))/1000
7160 PRINT
7170 PRINT"DO YOU REQUIRE K(I)(INTERCPT) ?"
7180 INPUTS$
7190 IF S$="Y" THEN 7210
7200 IF S$="N" THEN 7660
7210 N=P
7220 FOR I=1 TO N
7230 X=Q(I):Y=C(I)
7250 X1=X1+X:Y1=Y1+Y:X2=X2+X*X:Y2=Y2+Y*Y:Z=Z+X*Y
7300 NEXT
7310 GOSUB 8000
7380 PRINT#5
7390 PRINT#5,"K(I)(INTERCEPT)="ABS(B2)
7400 PRINT#5,"AT 37 DEGREES C,THE DELTA G ZERO VALUE FOR THE EFFECT OF"
7410 PRINT#5,"THE INHIBITOR ON THE INTERCEPT="2579*LOG(ABS(B2*1000))/1000
7420 PRINT"ENTER INITIAL VELOCITY WITHOUT INHIBITORPRESENT"
7430 E=0
7435 INPUT E
7440 PRINT"ENTER NUMBER OF INITIAL VELOCITY VALUES"
7450 N=0
7460 INPUT N
7465 PRINT#5,"PLOT OF LOG(V(T)/V(0))VERSUS TIME FOR TIME DEPENDENT INHIBITION"
7470 FOR I=1 TO N
7480 PRINT"ENTER VALUES FOR INITAL VELOCITY AND INCUBATION TIME (V,T)"
7482 X=0:V=0
7486 INPUT V(I),X(I)
7490 Y=0:A(I)=X(I)
7500 X(I)=A(I)
7510 Y(I)=LOG(V(I)/E)
7515 G(I)=0
7520 NEXT
7530 GOSUB 2000
7535 PRINT:X1=0:X2=0:Y1=0:Y2=0:Z=0
7540 FOR I=1 TO N
7550 X=A(I)
7553 Y=LOG(V(I)/E)
7555 X1=X1+X:Y1=Y1+Y:X2=X2+X*X:Y2=Y2+Y*Y:Z=Z+X*Y
7580 NEXT
7590 GOSUB 8000
7630 PRINT#5
7635 PRINT#5,"SLOPE OF LOG PLOT =-K(OBS)="B"+/-"SQR(S4/S1)
7640 PRINT#5
7645 PRINT#5,"INTERCEPT ON LOG V/V(0) AXIS="B1"+/-"SQR(S4*(1/N+X3*X3/S1))
7650 PRINT
7655 PRINT#5,"CORRELATION COEFFICIENT FOR SLOPE="S/SQR(S1*S2)
7660 PRINT"END OF PROGRAM"
7670 STOP
8000 X3=X1/N:Y3=Y1/N:S1=X2-X1*X3:S2=Y2-Y1*Y3:S=Z-X1*Y3
8010 B=S/S1:B1=Y3-B*X3:B2=X3-(1/B)*Y3:S3=S2-B*S:S4=S3/(N-2)
8020 RETURN
```

CHAPTER 6

# The Analysis of Nucleic Acid Sequences

R.J. SMITH

## 1. INTRODUCTION

Recombinant DNA technology and advanced sequencing techniques have enabled the establishment of libraries of DNA sequences and yielded descriptions of those elements of sequence structure which are employed in the recognition and the regulation of expression of genetic information. Thus the means to analyse and manipulate the structure of polynucleotide sequences has become important to both teaching and research. However, it is difficult to discern particular sequences within the sequence data since the sequential array of bases has no recognisable punctuation. Also many of the required processes such as those equivalent to transcription, sequence inversion or translation are tedious operations especially when long sequences are involved. Consequently, manual processing is error-prone and the inevitable mistakes are difficult to detect. These repetitive operations are fortunately well suited to computer processing.

Considerable effort has been given to the construction of computer programs that are able to analyse sequence data. The capabilities of these programs and their sophistication is progressing rapidly, as witnessed by two recent collections of program descriptions (1,2) which also provide excellent reference material. Many of the programs have been written for main frame or minicomputers, although the microcomputer is not excluded. This chapter discusses sequence analysis on microcomputers using the programs in the Appendix as examples of the required algorithms. The basic requirements of sequence storage, manipulation and direct sequence searching are included together with some of the more sophisticated approaches such as sequence detection and the location of translatable sequences are included. A brief description of cellular mechanisms is given where they are necessary to explain program requirements, otherwise it is assumed that the reader has a basic knowledge of the processes of DNA replication, transcription and translation.

## 2. PRINCIPLES OF SEQUENCE ANALYSIS BY MICROCOMPUTER

### 2.1 Polynucleotide Sequence Data Storage

In describing polynucleotide sequences the ribonucleoside monophosphate monomers are commonly abbreviated according to their base structures, e.g., A; adenosine, etc. Frequently the sequence is numbered to aid description and location of specific sub-sequences. The convention adopted with transcribed sequences sets the first base transcribed as +1 and numbers the sequence to the right (downstream) as positive and the sequence to the left (upstream) as negative. Often sub-sequences having particular functions are underlined or otherwise accentuated. Translatable sequences are often spaced into triplet codons with the appropriate one or three letter amino acid code placed beneath.

The first choice to be made in writing or choosing sequence analysis programs is the form in which the nucleotide sequence data is to be stored in memory. In BASIC, alphanumeric characters are stored as strings and as text files on magnetic media. Simple string storage suffers from the major disadvantage that, for most types of BASIC, the maximum length of a string is limited to 255 ($FF) characters. Longer sequences could be accommodated by complex restructuring using sub-string concatenation, but this would be unwieldy. The limitation is overcome by the use of dimensioned string arrays in which each element of the array represents one base of the sequence. As each element requires one byte, the length of the sequence is limited only by the memory space available. Sequence data may also be stored as a binary coded file (3). Excluding methylation and the modified bases of tRNA, polynucleotide sequences consist of four variables. Stored as a string array each variable or base uses one byte or eight bits of information. In terms of storage this is inefficient since four variables can be encoded by just two bits of information, i.e., 00, 01, 10, 11. Thus four bases could be encoded for each byte of memory at the maximum permissible data compression (4). The 4-fold increase in storage capacity applies to magnetic media, e.g., disc, as well as RAM. The latter may be particularly important considering the need to store large files in memory alongside the program, the machine and disc operating systems and graphics requirements.

Machine code routines are necessary to encode, decode and manipulate binary coded sequence data files. Although such files may be used from BASIC *via* direct memory access (PEEK and POKE statements) the memory saving benefits of binary storage are diminished by the slower execution times involved. Machine code routines enable the use of binary coded files *via* BASIC programs and may be seen as a small, specialised operating system. The advantages of binary coded storage must be weighed against the disadvantages. Two bit data coding for instance can encode no more than four variables so that modified bases or even uncertainties in a sequence (often denoted by 'N') cannot be encoded. The initial choice of a data storage system will depend largely upon the intended use. Teaching programs intended to demonstrate aspects of molecular genetics and using relatively short sequences and a restricted library may benefit from the simplicity of BASIC programming. However, programs employing the more complex reiterative search routines are likely to require the reduced execution times available with machine coded or compiled programs. These are also likely to employ large data files and a requirement for a random access storage medium (i.e., disc storage) is therefore indicated. An additional benefit is that a disc system will allow the routines comprising an extensive sequence manipulation program to be chained, i.e., each routine is loaded into memory as required. In older machines having restricted memory, or when the more complex and sophisticated techniques which were developed on main frame systems are implemented on a microcomputer, data compression and program chaining may prove essential.

## 2.2 Input — Creating Sequence Data Files

Recent advances have led to a rapid increase in the number of sequences being published, so that the complete sequences of several small viral and organelle genomes are now available. In recognition of the importance of computer analysis, polynucleotide sequence data banks have been established in Europe and America. It seems likely that access to these libraries will increase, but when a main frame computer is not available personal sequence libraries have to be created by entering published sequences *via* the keyboard. There is probably no need to stress that this is a tedious and error-prone process, even with routines designed to aid typing.

In order not to overtax patience and to reduce the number of physically abused microcomputers it is wise to recognise the need for routines able to correct input errors. Essentially, these have the attributes of a word processor. Such programs are now common and circumvent the need to write specific sequence correction routines. It may be necessary to convert the product of a word processor into a form usable by the sequence manipulation program. An example is included in the appendix, *Listing 1.1* which converts the text files produced by a commercial word processor (Screenwriter Apple R) to the binary coded file required by *Listing 1*. A word processor offers other options including the excision, merging and splicing of sequences. These facilities allow removal of specific sequence structure such as restriction sites and the 'mutation' and 'recombination' of sequences. There is, however, a disadvantage in using a word processing program which employs a file storage different from that of the sequence manipulation program, in that the operator must return to the word processor whenever modifications are required.

## 2.3 Sequence Inversion and Complementation

Polynucleotides are orientated polymers. The nucleoside monophosphate residues are joined by a $3'$-$5'$ phosphodiester between the $3'$ carbon of one pentose sugar to the $5'$ carbon of the next. This asymmetry gives the polynucleotide an orientation which is distinguished by molecular processes. For instance, during translation the genetic code is read from the mRNA template in the $5'$-$3'$ direction. Sequence manipulation routines that emulate these molecular processes must obviously observe the correct orientation.

Neither alphanumeric nor binary coded files contain information describing the orientation of the sequence. If files are to be inverted and complemented some means of identifying orientation is necessary to avoid confusion. *Listing 1* sets aside the first byte of the data file for notation of sequence orientation and is also used to identify the source of a sequence, that is whether it is RNA or DNA. This is sufficient providing that the sequence file is maintained as a whole. Subroutines may be appended to the complementation and inversion routines which automatically record the change in orientation. However, if extensive sequence editing options are included which allow sequence files to be spliced or segments to be extracted and established as new files, care must be taken to ensure that correct orientation is maintained during these operations. If the sequence data is not fully compressed in the file it would be possible to record orientation by setting one bit of each byte.

The reason for recording the source of the sequence in a fully compressed file is because the file makes no distinction between an RNA or DNA sequence. Both U and T are encoded as 11 so that expression of a sequence as RNA or DNA depends upon the decoding string employed. Printing a sequence from the file employs the numeric coding of the base composition to determine which component of a decoding string function is sent to printer or screen. Thus if Q\$ = "AGCU" the file is decoded as RNA and if Q\$ = "AGCT" it is decoded as DNA (*Listing 1*, 410 – 470). In all other operations, except the use of 'U' in subsequence searches, the distinction between RNA and DNA is not required.

The transcription and replication of DNA involve polymerases which process their templates in a 3'-5' orientation and produce a 5'-3' complementary product. Thus the product is not only complementary to the template, but also inverted in orientation. The structure of DNA is a double-stranded helix in which the two polynucleotides are anti-parallel, i.e., they have opposite orientations. The complementation routine thus allows the DNA sequence to be stored as a single data file and the expression of the double-stranded sequence is produced by the complement of the file. The orientation of the complement is important to the sense of the sequence, as in translation or sequence searches, and therefore care must be taken to arrange the correct orientation by use of the inversion routine.

When sequence file storage is based on alphanumeric characters a simple BASIC routine using IF statements serves to form the complementary sequence by working through the sequence one base at a time; *Listing 2* (ref. 4). In a binary coded file careful choice of the numeric assignment of bases may simplify the machine code routines required. For instance, in the 2-bit code of the appended program the choice was such that the logical *NOT* operand performs complementation, i.e., 00 (A) becomes 11 (T) and 01 (G) becomes 10 (C) and *vice versa*. A compressed binary file is not, however, as readily inverted as an alphanumeric one since the bases within each byte must also be reorientated. This requires the decoding of each byte and recoding in the opposite orientation prior to inverting the order of the bytes within the file (*Listing 1*).

## 2.4 Translation

Part of the information encoded in the genetic archive describes the primary sequence of polypeptides. One computer program often required translates this information into the corresponding amino acid sequence. The difficulty lies not in the translation routine, which is simple, but in defining the exact start of the translatable sequence. In the cell the information is transcribed from one strand of the DNA helix (the codogenic strand) in the form of mRNA. The transcription process forms the complementary sequence which is therefore a base sequence copy of the other strand of the DNA helix (inappropriately called the nonsense strand) except for the replacement of thymidine by uridine.

Transcription does not merely reiterate the sequence, but acts to select a distinct and complete unit of information from the undistinguished linear array of the DNA sequence. Since the process also selects the codogenic strand of the helix the correct complement of the information is presented for translation. The process depends upon specific identification of signal sequences (Section 2.5). Furthermore, the mRNA also contains non-translated information. For instance, included in the 5′ leader sequence of mRNA is the information required by the ribosome to determine the exact start of the protein-coding region. The detection of these signal sequences is necessary for correct computer translation of the information, but unfortunately it is a complex process. An additional problem when studying the sequence of genomic DNA, as opposed to cDNA reverse transcripts of mRNA, is that, at least in eukaryotes, many genes are split by non-coding sequences called introns. These must be detected if the non-coding sequence is to be successfully translated.

### 2.4.1 *The Genetic Code and Reading Frames*

Each amino acid encoded in the DNA base sequence is represented by three contiguous bases known as the triplet codon. These form the genetic code which appears to be identical in all species with the exception of certain variations found in some eukaryotic organelles. Three bases can combine to yield 64 ($4^3$) different triplet bases which encode some 20 common amino acids. The code is thus said to be degenerate since more than one codon is assigned to each amino acid (*Figure 1*).

THE GENETIC CODE

| 1st ↓ 2nd → | U | C | A | G | ↓ 3rd |
|---|---|---|---|---|---|
| U | Phe | Ser | Tyr | Cys | U |
| | Phe | Ser | Tyr | Cys | C |
| | Leu | Ser | Ochre | Terminate | A |
| | Leu | Ser | Amber | Trp | G |
| C | Leu | Pro | His | Arg | U |
| | Leu | Pro | His | Arg | C |
| | Leu | Pro | Glun | Arg | A |
| | Leu | Pro | Glun | Arg | G |
| A | Ileu | Thr | Aspn | Ser | U |
| | Ileu | Thr | Aspn | Ser | C |
| | Ileu | Thr | Lys | Arg | A |
| | Met * | Thr | Lys | Arg | G |
| G | Val | Ala | Asp | Gly | U |
| | Val | Ala | Asp | Gly | C |
| | Val | Ala | Glu | Gly | A |
| | Val | Ala | Glu | Gly | G |

*Initiation or internal

**Figure 1.** The genetic code displayed in the traditional format. Note that the translator routine of the sequence manipulator (*Listing 1*) employs a different format in which A is encoded as 00 etc. (see Section 2.4.1) (lines 5130 and 5200, *Listing 1*).

The code is read sequentially as a non-overlapping code and the sequence of discrete codons is co-linear with the amino acid sequence of the encoded polypeptide. However, the DNA base sequence is continuous and without punctuation, yet correct translation requires an exact start point.

For example:

CAT CAT CAT CAT

may be read as:

CAT CAT CAT CAT

or ATC ATC ATC ATC

or TCA TCA TCA TCA

only one of which will be the correct 'reading frame'. Reading the code out of 'phase', i.e., in the wrong frame, scrambles the information and produces a nonsense sequence of amino acids.

The genetic code has three codons which are not assigned to amino acids. These are named amber (UAG), ochre (UAA) and opal (UGA) and are used to denote the end of a coding sequence. Another codon (AUG) is used to determine the start of a coding sequence. The ribosome recognises this initiation codon and, by defining methionine (N-formyl methionine in prokaryotes) as the first amino acid of the encoded polypeptide, ensures that both the correct start and the right phase of the encoded sequence is chosen. However the AUG codon is not sufficiently specific to be the only indicator of start and phase − a random sequence of 1000 bases would, for example, contain an average 16 'AUG' codons. The ribosome is normally prevented from recognising spurious AUG codons since the initial binding of a ribosome to mRNA depends on recognition of a longer, more unique piece of information within the 5′ leader sequence. This restricts the ribosome so that the correct AUG codon is automatically chosen.

In practice most published sequence data describe isolated DNA of known function so that the proportion of non-coding DNA sequence is substantially reduced and the seqences are well annotated. Within these defined sequences a search for an AUG codon may be sufficient to define the start of the coding region or yield so few alternatives that the correct reading frame is readily determined. Once correct translation is underway the end of the coding region is denoted by the first stop codon encountered. Where the amino acid sequence of the encoded polypeptide is known, correct translation of the nucleic acid sequence is readily confirmed by direct comparison. Other means of identifying coding regions are described in Section 2.1.

The form of the decoding routine, which formulates the amino acid sequence from the nucleotide sequence, will depend upon the manner in which the nucleotide sequence data is filed in memory, though all such routines will require to assemble the codon units and apply this data to the genetic code. In *Listing 2.9* translation is accomplished by converting each base in the triplet to a number (U, C, A and G = 1, 2, 3 and 4, respectively) and using the three numbers as a subscript to read a three-dimensional array. This array contains the amino acid assignments of the genetic code in the conventional tabulated form. The data is collected as a string and each string concatenated to form the polypeptide sequence.

A similar algorithm is employed with base sequence data encoded as a compressed binary file except that assigning a number to each base is omitted. In binary, six bits may contain between 0 and 63 decimal which become equivalent to the 64 possible codons. Translation is effected by assembling the triplet as the least significant 6 bits of a byte. This contains the unique number used as a subscript to a one-dimensional array containing the amino acid assignment of the genetic code in the appropriate order (*Listing 1*; line 5130). Thus the codon AAA yields the 6-bit binary number 00 00 00 (0) and TTT yields 11 11 11 (63). The use of a machine code routine to return a number directly related to translation simplifies the routine and improves execution time.

## 2.5 Detection of Sub-sequences

### 2.5.1 *The Detection of Signal Sequences*

A significant amount of the information stored in the sequence structure of the genomic DNA does not encode polypeptide sequences, but consists of signal sequences. These are sequence structures which are specifically recognised by proteins and are used to punctuate and regulate the expression of genes. DNA is a continuous sequence structure which has discrete units of information (genes) encoded within it. Some means of recognising these units, by defining the beginning and end of each unit as well as the position of any introns, is necessary, otherwise incomplete and erroneous messages will be expressed to the detriment of the cell. Replication, transcription and translation are all template-directed syntheses. Therefore they all possess the common mechanism of beginning at a particular point, moving along the template while using the information in it to direct the synthetic process and then terminating the synthesis at another defined point.

In addition to this punctuation of the genome, other specific sequences are involved in the regulation of expression of the genetic information. The cell makes some proteins in greater amounts than others so that a means of differential expression of the genes must be involved. Although many proteins are made continuously (constitutive expression of the gene) others are made only when required (regulated expression). These functions also depend upon specific sequence structures which enable specific protein binding and thus an individual regulation of gene expression. Thus signal sequences also provide useful concepts for interpreting the mechanisms of differential gene expression through which cell differention occurs.

The most commonly encountered sub-sequences are described below:

(i)  Promoter sequences define the beginning of a transcriptional unit. The rate of RNA polymerase binding to a promoter site governs the frequency of initiation of transcription and thus the basal rate of expression of the gene. In translated genes (i.e., those from which mRNA is transcribed) the promoter consists of several distinct sections of conserved sequence structure; principally at $-35$ bp and $-10$ bp upstream from the start of transcription. In rRNA genes, somewhat different promoter sequences have been found while in tRNA and 5S RNA genes, part of the promoter sequences are located within the transcribed sequence. The sequence structure of promoters varies though some residues are more conserved than others.

(ii)　Enhancer regions, which often occur more than 100 bp upstream from the initiation site, are also required for the accurate transcription of genes and act as positive control elements.

(iii)　Operator regions occur in genes which display regulated expression. They are sites of specific protein binding which restrict RNA polymerase initiation at the promoter. The sequence structure of operators differs in each regulated gene although sequencing studies suggest they have a common characteristic in that they possess inverted dyad symmetry (inverted mirror image). Inverted dyad symmetry is also found in positive regulation sequences, in which binding of the protein aids RNA polymerase initiation. This implies that regulatory proteins may possess a common DNA binding mechanism.

(iv)　Attenuator sequences occur at the 5′ end of the transcribed region of translated genes and thus form part of the mRNA leader sequence. They regulate the transcription of the latter part of the gene by allowing, under certain conditions, premature termination of transcription.

(v)　On initiating translation, ribosome recognition and binding of mRNA is dependent upon a sequence found in the non-translated 5′ leader sequence of mRNA. This sequence is complementary to the 3′ end of 16S or 18S RNAs which, in protein complexes, form the smaller subunits of prokaryotic and eukaryotic ribosomes, respectively.

(vi)　In eukaryotes many translatable genes are split by non-coding sequences called introns as noted previously (Section 2.4). These are bounded by conserved sequences known as splicing junctions in recognition of the post-transcriptional modification process which removes the introns.

(vii)　The restriction endonucleases form part of a mechanism by which prokaryotes degrade foreign DNA. Their cleavage of double-stranded DNA at specific sites up to six bases long provides one of the most powerful tools of recombinant DNA technology. The detection of known restriction cleavage sites in a sequence is a useful attribute for those planning the construction of chimaeric DNA in which sequences from different sources are joined together.

## 2.5.2 *Direct Comparison Sub-sequence Searches*

The signal sequences described are of two types. Those that are exact and invariable, such as restriction endonuclease sites and the start and stop codons of translation, and those that, although they perform the same function (for example promoters and enhancers), vary in the exact sequence used. The latter are often described by a consensus sequence which is an average sequence deduced from consideration of some large number of known sequences. Sub-sequence searches which detect the presence of a short sequence within a longer one depend upon a comparison of the two sequences. Thus exact sub-sequences are readily detected, but the detection of variable signals is not efficiently performed by direct comparison since the exact sub-sequence structure is unknown.

Sub-sequence search routines are relatively simple. An algorithm is required which sets a window on the main sequence. The 'window' technique is frequently used by routines which sequentially apply a process to a segment of the sequence. A window is a fixed length of sequence within which the operation is performed. When complete, the window is moved along the sequence by one or more bases and the operation repeated, e.g.

|  | CAT CAT CAT CAT |
|---|---|
| 1st (6 base window) | CAT CAT |
| 2nd | ATC ATC |
| 3rd | TCA TCA |

In sub-sequence searches the window is equal in length to the sub-sequence. Each base in each position in the window is compared with the corresponding base in the sub-sequence. On completion of the comparison, or on default if bases do not compare, the window is moved on one base along the main sequence and the comparison repeated. *Listing 2.6* creates a window three bases long by constructing the triplet (CO$) at each position (L) in the sequence RNA$. *Listing 2.14* allows a subsequence of variable length (SS$) and uses a nested FOR/NEXT loop to compare, in the IF statment, each base in the window [DNA$ $(L + J - 1)$] to the corresponding base in the substring array [SS$ (J)].

A very similar process is used in *Listing 1*. The sub-sequence is loaded into page 03 and compared with the main binary coded sequence. The procedure is complicated by the need to disassemble each compacted byte of the main sequence using the disassembler subroutine. Mismatch in any base comparison moves the routine on to the next window *via* the searcher B routine. This subroutine checks if the mismatch is due to a 'wild card' entry. The sub-sequence may contain three other variables besides the four bases (N.B. P$, line 2002) which denote a pyrimidine, a purine or any base (lines 2010 − 2050). The 'searcher' B routine checks whether the appropriate base in the main sequence compares with these characters and if so directs the program back to 'searcher A' to continue comparing that particular window.

The purpose of the 'wild card' characters is to provide some leeway in searching for variable sequences by using an inexact comparison. Although inclusion of the wild card routine improves the sub-sequence search program, allowing for instance searches for AUG and GUG codons simultaneously, it reduces the specificity of the search. An extreme case, for example, would be a sub-sequence composed entirely of the 'F' wild card character which would give a positive comparison in every window. With highly variable sequences, such as the promoters, the number of wild cards required to ensure detection of the sub-sequence reduces its specificity to such an extent that many false detection events are generated. Direct comparison sequence searches are therefore of limited value since most signal sequences of sufficient length to be useful indicators of function in an unknown sequence, are also variable. Direct searches are of use, however, in detecting exact sequences such as restriction sites, in programs dealing with well-defined sequences, and are perhaps valuable for demonstration purposes in teaching.

### 2.5.3 *Indirect Sub-sequence Searches*

The variable signal sequences provide specific binding sites for proteins. The variation dictates the affinity of the protein for that site and may govern the rate of protein binding and thus the rate at which the dependent mechanism functions. For example, variation in a promoter site may change the rate of binding of RNA polymerase and thus the maximum rate of transcription of the gene. Within the sequence some nucleotide bases appear to be more important to the protein binding function than others. These tend to be conserved while those of less importance vary more dramatically. In assessing the consensus sequence of a variable signal a number of functionally comparable sequences are compared. The frequency with which each base occurs in each position within the sequence provides an estimate of its importance. The consensus sequence reflects the frequencies determined with N, Pu or Py indicating nil, purine or pyrimidine preferences, respectively.

A two-dimensional array, four deep to represent each base and equal to the signal sequence length, can be used to provide a frequency table for the signal. Each position in the array records the frequency with which a base occurs at that position in that signal sequence. The frequency table provides a means of distinguishing signal sequences. Using a window algorithm (Section 2.5.2) equal to the length of the signal the similarity of the windowed sequence to the signal may be calculated. Each base in the window is used to access the array according to position and base type. A single value is generated for each window which is a measure of the probability that the window is a signal sequence.

The frequency table is assumed to reflect those elements of the sequence which are important in the protein binding sites. In most cases the binding mechanism is unknown and the frequency table, as a criterion emulating protein binding, is not directly testable. The setting of a cut-off value to exclude unlikely sequences must therefore depend on experience and be approached with care. By applying the frequency table to each of the sequences used in its construction and plotting the results, an indication of suitable cut-off values can be obtained. The range found is high and the technique does not umambiguously identify signals thus indicating that the algorithm does not effectively emulate the protein/binding site recognition (5). Each signal may have unique qualities in terms of recognition which are lost in the averaging effect obtained in calculation of the frequency tables. No account for instance is taken of possible differences in secondary and tertiary conformations of the sequence.

Other criteria may be employed. Three sequence elements could be used in the detection of promoter sites; the −35 region, the −10 region and the +1 region at the start of transcription. The spacing between these regions is known to be of prime importance in RNA polymerase binding. Thus on detection of a window having a high probability of being a −35 region the program may be directed to search for a −10 and then a +1 region at the effective spacing in the sequence (5). Lack of these, at high probability, defaults the initial −35 region detection.

## 2.6 Searching for Function

The analysis techniques so far described are limited to the detection of known sequence elements, but the need may arise for an empirical approach in interpreting new sequences or general investigations of structure and function. Such analyses are based on the effects upon sequence structure imposed by the encoding of particular functions. In other words functional sequences have a non-random sequence structure. In contrast to comparative searches for known sequences this approach has the potential for indicating new sequence elements and is therefore a powerful research tool.

### 2.6.1 Protein-coding Regions

Several techniques have been described for the detection of sequences which encode translatable information. Amino acids differ in the frequency with which they are incorporated into proteins (6). The number of codons assigned to each amino acid differ and certain codons are used in preference to others. This varies not only from one species to another, but also between different proteins. Each of these factors contribute to the unequal use of bases in protein-coding sequences (7).

Codon usage techniques depend upon comparison of the sequence with an expected codon usage and employ a standard reference table which describes the frequency at which different codons occur in a protein-coding sequence. The table may be prepared by analysis of known genes, or from an average amino acid composition of proteins. In the latter case the effect of codon preference is ignored.

In order to distinguish one part of a sequence from another the technique is applied to a sliding window (*Listing 3*). A logarithmic plot of the probability factor indicates those parts of the whole sequence which are likely to encode translatable information. A plot of each of the three possible reading frames is necessary to detect all possible coding regions. The information provided may be supplemented by indicating the presence of low frequency (rare) codons (which should be infrequent in a coding region) and open reading frames (i.e., sequences beginning with AUG and containing no stop codons).

Different genes are expressed at different rates and genes having a low rate of expression may contain more infrequent codons than highly expressed genes (8,9). This implies that the genes chosen to construct codon usage frequency tables should be those encoding proteins which are expressed at high rates so as to optimise the differential effect of codon preference. However, the method depends upon the assumption that the coding regions within an examined sequence are similar to the standard codon frequency table employed. One consequence is that weakly expressed genes, which may contain infrequent codons, are less readily detected. However, it has been shown that the technique is still usable if codon preference is omitted and the frequency table based solely on average amino acid composition (7).

Other techniques (7) are available to assess the frequency with which each of the four bases is found in each of three positions in the codon. Both amino acid composition and codon preference contribute to the unequal use of bases in the codon. One procedure compares the observed with the expected frequencies for each base in each position within the codons generated from a windowed sequence in each of the three possible reading frames. An alternative which dispenses with the use of a standard table and the associated assumptions calculates the differential use of bases in each of the three codon positions. The procedure may be implemented by counting the number of times each base is used in each position of the codons in one reading frame of a windowed sequence. The routine calculates the difference between the positional base frequencies and the average base frequency for all four bases. The value obtained reflects the uneven use of bases in different positions of the codon and this indicates coding regions. While requiring careful interpretation the method has the advantage of being an unbiased indicator of the probability of coding since it dispenses with the use of assumed standard frequency tables.

### 2.6.2 *Assessing Sequence Structure*

When a sequence encodes a particular function its base composition can vary dramatically from the average. Many such sequences are purine-rich, e.g., polyadenylation sites. A plot of the base composition within a windowed sequence will indicate local deviations in the base composition of the sequence. A more sophisticated technique assesses local deviations by comparison of a window with an expected base composition derived from the composition of the whole sequence. The procedure may also be applied to di- and tri-nucleotide frequencies and the alternating purine pyrimidine sequence structure required for the formation of Z conformation DNA.

Searches for direct and inverted repeats also provide information on potentially functional sequence structures; for instance, operator-binding proteins recognise inverted repeats and non-homologous recombination events involve similar structures. Inverted repeats may also form the nucleic acid secondary structures known as hairpin loops. Thus, genes encoding tRNA may be found by searching for inverted repeats conforming to the clover-leaf tRNA structure and containing other conserved sequences (10). Both direct and inverted repeats may be detected by direct comparison search routines by comparing a sub-sequence, obtained directly or by inversion, from the main sequence. The search must be repeated for each sub-sequence generated by a sliding window. Repeats larger than the window size may be noted by adding a subroutine which determines the extent of the comparison. Alternatively, the comparison may be based on a routine which reports the fraction of comparable bases in the window. These are discarded if they fail to exceed a variable cut-off value. This routine includes similar, but inexact, sequence matches (3).

Questions concerning the evolution of genes and the rates of change of sequence structure benefit from routines which assess the degree of homology between two sequences. However, additions or deletions in the sequence will

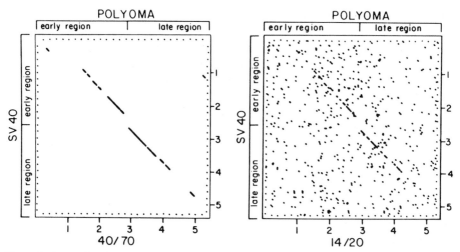

**Figure 2.** Dot matrix plot comparison of SV40 *versus* polyoma virus genomes. Note the effect of window size in reducing background (left, large window; right small window). (Reproduced, with permission, from ref. 2).

place homologous regions out of register. To ensure that all homologous regions are detected, a direct comparison routine would have to be repeated for all possible registers. This program would be rather long winded. Furthermore, the results of the program reported in numeric form would not be easily interpreted. For this reason the dot matrix report has been adopted (11,12). A two-dimensional array is created in which the two sequences are aligned along the $x$ and $y$ axes. A dot is placed at each point in the array at which the bases on the respective $x$ and $y$ axes are comparable (*Figure 2*). Regions of homology appear as 45° continuous diagonal lines. If the homology is in direct register the diagonal is central; otherwise it is offset. Gaps between adjacent diagonals indicate a site within the sequence where disjunction of the register occurs.

Since there are only four variables in the sequence, fortuitous short similarities occur frequently. Thus the dot matrix array has a high background which tends to obscure the more important details. Several programmers have adopted an algorithm in which the fraction of comparable bases in a segment of one sequence and a windowed portion of the other must exceed a default value. This ensures that the matrix is marked only when a substantial homology occurs; the degree of homology depending upon the size of window or segment chosen. The routine provides the opportunities to compress the data into a smaller matrix (12). Dot matrix homology comparisons also serve to provide a readily assimilated visual expression of repeated sequence structure when a sequence is compared with itself.

## 3. CONCLUSIONS

The more advanced nucleic acid sequence analysis programs have been developed on main frame computers. In comparison microcomputers suffer three main disadvantages: limited available free RAM, processor speed and graphics facilities. Limited RAM may cause problems due to the need to store one or more sequences in memory, but with a compressed binary coded file even a substantial sequence of 10 000 bases requires only 2.5k. Due to the reiterative nature of many of the search routines, particularly the common windowing algorithm, processor speed may cause substantial delay in dealing with long sequences. However, algorithms can be employed which reduce the processing required (*Listing 3*) (12,13). Inadequate graphics are more difficult to overcome. Those micro-computers which provide sufficiently high resolution graphics to accommodate the results derived from lengthy sequences do so at the expense of available RAM, but even these problems can be reduced (14).

Recombinant DNA technology and sequencing techniques are not undertaken lightly. Establishments supporting these activities are likely to have access to main frame computer facilities able to support extensive programs. In sequence analysis the major role of the microcomputer is likely to be one of teaching and demonstration. As more sequences are added to the already substantial sequence libraries and more mechanisms are explained in terms of sequence structure the need to demonstrate structure and function will increase. By providing interpretation, manipulation and analysis of sequence data, microcomputers can give the student first hand experience of the relationship between structure and function and the variation of the sequences involved. Since these teaching programs will be concerned with relatively small sequence files many of the problems mentioned are reduced to manageable proportions.

## 4. ACKNOWLEDGEMENTS

I wish to thank Dr. R.J. Beynon for the use of his BASIC routines and Dr. D. Rickwood, Dr. M.K. O'Farrell and Dr. Benyon for their positive critisicm of the manuscript. I also acknowledge Mrs. B. Smith for typing services. *Listings 1* and *3* are reproduced by permission of IRCS, St. Leonards's House, St. Leonard-gate, Lancaster LA1 1PF, England and The Biochemistry Microcomputer Group, c/o Dr. R. Beynon, P.O. Box 147, Liverpool L59 3BX.

## 5. REFERENCES

1. Söll,D. and Roberts,R.J., eds. (1982) *The Application of Computers to Research on Nucleic Acids*, published by IRL Press, Oxford and Washington, DC.
2. Söll,D. and Roberts,R.J., eds. (1984) *The Application of Computers to Research on Nucleic Acids II. Part 2*, published by IRL Press, Oxford and Washington, DC.
3. Spence,H.D. (1983) *Biochemistry Microcomputer Group*, **8**, 12.
4. Smith,R.J. (1983) *IRCS Medical Science Monograph (IRCS Med. Sci.,* **11**, 800.
5. Beynon,R.J. (1982) *Biochemistry Microcomputer Group,* **7**, 28.
6. Staden,R. (1984) *Nucleic Acids Res.,* **12**, 505.
7. Gouy,M. and Goutier,C. (1982) *Nucleic Acids Res.,* **10**, 7055.
7. Staden,R. (1984) *Nucleic Acids Res.,* **12**, 551.
9. Smiley,B.L., Lupski,J.L., Svec,P.S., McMacken,R. and Godsen,G.N. (1982) *Proc. Natl. Acad. Sci. USA,* **79**, 4550.
10. Gribskov,M., Devereux,J. and Burgess,R.R. (1984) *Nucleic Acids Res.,* **12**, 539.
11. Staden,R. (1984) *Nucleic Acids Res.,* **12**, 521.
12. Herter,P.A., Max,E.E., Seidman,J.G., Maizel,J.V. and Leder,P. (1980) *Cell,* **22**, 97.
13. White,C.T., Hardies,S.C., Hutchinson,C.A. and Edgell,M.E. (1984) *Nucleic Acids Res.,* **12**, 751.
14. Staden,R. (1982) *Nucleic Acids Res.,* **10**, 2951.

# APPENDIX
## Program listings

**Listing 1**. Sequence manipulator.

```
90  HIMEM: 8191
100 REM :SEQQ-REQUIRES MC PROGRAM FREDSEQ.CC
105 PRE 0: HOME
110 PRINT "    MENU": PRINT : PRINT
120 PRINT "1.  SEQ. INPUT"
130 PRINT "2.  SEQ. OUTPUT"
140 PRINT "3.  SEQ. SEARCHER"
150 PRINT "4.  SEQ. TRANSCRIBER"
160 PRINT "5.  SEQ. INVERTER"
170 PRINT "6.  SEQ. TRANSLATER"
173 PRINT "7.  SEQ. FILE LOADING"
175 PRINT : PRINT
180 INPUT "PLEASE SELECT 1-7  ":M
190 IF M < 1 OR M > 7 THEN 180
200 ON M GOTO 400,1000,2000,3000,4000,5000,700
400 HOME
410 Q$ = "AGCT": PRINT : PRINT
420 HOME : POKE 50,63: PRINT : PRINT "SEQ. INPUT ROUTINE": POKE 50,255: PRINT
    : PRINT
430 INPUT "IS THE SEQ. DNA OR RNA? ":B$
440 IF LEFT$ (B$,1) = "D" THEN 480          request source and orientation
450 IF LEFT$ (B$,1) = "R" THEN 470          data, encode, place in 1st
460 GOTO 430                                byte of file
470 Q$ = "AGCU"
480 PRINT : PRINT : INPUT "DOES THE SEQ. BEGIN AT THE 5' OR 3' END ";B    set appropriate Q$.
490 IF B = 3 OR B = 5 THEN 510
500 GOTO 480
510 IF LEFT$ (B$,1) = "D" THEN C = 0
520 IF LEFT$ (B$,1) = "R" THEN C = 1
530 POKE 16384,B + C
540 I = 0:P = 0
550 PRINT : PRINT : PRINT "TYPE IN THE SEQ. PLEASE"
555 PRINT : PRINT "USE 'E' TO END INPUT"
557 PRINT : PRINT
560 P = P + 1
570 GET B$: IF B$ = "E" THEN 660            get base seq. check if end "E"
580 PRINT B$;
590 FOR J = 1 TO 4: IF B$ = MID$ (Q$,J,1) THEN 620    encode
600 NEXT
610 GOTO 570                                place in 2 bit buffer
620 POKE 8193 + I,J - 1:I = I + 1: IF I < 4 THEN 570
630 CALL 8280                               call assembler
640 D = PEEK (8192): POKE 16384 + P,D
650 I = 0: PRINT " ";: GOTO 560
660 : PRINT : PRINT : INPUT "SEQ. FILE NAME REQUIRED ";N$
665 D$ = CHR$ (4):P = P + 1
670 PRINT D$;"BSAVE";N$",A16384,L";P         store data file seq. as binary file
680 GOTO 105
700 LL = 1: GOSUB 6400
710 LL = 0: GOTO 105
1000 HOME : POKE 50,63: PRINT : PRINT
1010 PRINT "SEQ. OUTPUT ROUTINE": POKE 50,255
1015 Q$ = "AGCT"
1020 GOSUB 6300                              routine to set start & end bytes for data file
1030 GOSUB 6000                              allows choice of any part of file
1035 PRINT : PRINT N$: PRINT : PRINT         routine, hard copy?
1040 CALL 8663
1050 EN = PEEK (8199) + PEEK (8200) * 256
1060 FOR J = 3 TO 0 STEP - 1:R = PEEK (8193 + J) + 1: PRINT MID$ (Q$,
    R,1);: NEXT
1070 CALL 8673                               call disassembler  print results form 2 bit buffer
1080 IF EN = PEEK (8243) + PEEK (8244) * 256 THEN 1100   check if end byte. loop for next data file byte
1082 KP = KP + 1: IF KP < > 20 THEN 1090
1084 PRINT :KP = 0
1090 GOTO 1060
1100 PRINT "  ": PRE 0
1105 GOTO 6100
2000 N = 0: HOME
2002 P$ = "AGCTPSDF"
2005 PRINT : POKE 50,63: PRINT "SEQ.SEARCHER ROUTINE": PRINT : PRINT
2007 PRINT : PRINT
2010 PRINT : PRINT "THE SUB SEQ. TO BE COMPARED MAY"
2020 PRINT "INCLUDE WILD BASES-IF THE BASE"
```

165

```
2030 PRINT "MAY BE ANY (PU OR PY) TYPE 'S'"
2040 PRINT ";IF EITHER PURINE TYPE 'D';AND"
2050 PRINT "IF EITHER PYRIMIDINE TYPE 'F'."
2053 POKE 50,255
2055 GOSUB 6300
2060 PRINT : PRINT : PRINT "PLEASE TYPE IN SUB SEQ."
2065 PRINT "TYPE 'E' TO BEGIN SEARCH"
2070 I = 0
2080 GET B$: IF B$ = "E" THEN 2135
2090 SB$ = SB$ + B$
2095 PRINT B$;
2100 FOR J = 1 TO 8                                  input subseq. encode & store
2102 IF B$ = MID$ (P$,J,1) THEN  GOTO 2120           in page 03
2105 NEXT
2110 GOTO 2080
2120 POKE 768 + I,J - 1:I = I + 1
2130 GOTO 2080
2132 GOSUB 6030
2135 PRINT : PRINT N$: PRINT : PRINT "SUBSEQ.=";SB$
2137 PRINT : PRINT
2150 POKE 8204,I - 1: POKE 8201,3                    set length of subseq. and Y register
2160 CALL 8205                                       initialize MC routine
2170 EN = PEEK (8199) + PEEK (8200) * 256            load 1st reg. byte of data file
2180 CALL 8242                                       disassemble it.
2190 CALL 8249                                       call researcher
2200 CALL 8752                                       check if end of req. data file.
2210 R = PEEK (8243) + PEEK (8244) * 256
2220 IF EN = R THEN 2290
2230 N = N + 1: IF N > 1 THEN 2250
2240 PRINT "SEQ. MATCH FOUND"
2250 BY = ((R - 16384) * 4) - 4:BP = BY - PEEK (8204) + (4 - PEEK (8202    calculate base position
     ))
2260 PRINT N".  AT BASE "BP                          print number & position
2270 CALL 8777                                       ie. start of subsq. in data file
2280 GOTO 2200
2290 IF N > 0 THEN 2300                              return to searcher
2295 PRINT "NO SEQ. MATCH FOUND"
2300 PRE 0: GOTO 6100
3000 HOME : PRINT : POKE 50,63: PRINT "TRANSCRIBER ROUTINE": POKE 50,255

3005 LL = 1
3010 GOSUB 6300                                      set start & end of data file (whole file)
3015 LL = 0
3020 CALL 8205                                       initialize
3030 CALL 8512                                       call transcripter
3040 PRINT "TRANSCRIPTION COMPLETED"
3045 GOSUB 6210                                      reset orientation in 1st date byte
3050 FOR J = 1 TO 1000: FOR K = 1 TO 2: NEXT : NEXT  wait for a few seconds
3060 PRINT : PRINT : INPUT "DO YOU WANT TO FILE THE TRANSCRIBED SEQ. Y/N   file storage?
     ";B$
3070 IF B$ < > "N" AND B$ < > "Y" THEN 3060          return
3080 IF B$ = "N" THEN 105
3090 IF B$ = "Y" THEN 660
4000 HOME : PRINT : POKE 50,63: PRINT "INVERTER ROUTINE": POKE 50,255
4005 D = PEEK (16384)
4010 LL = 1: GOSUB 6300                              set start & end data file
4020 LL = 0
4030 CALL 8205                                       initialize
4040 CALL 8518                                       call byte inverter
4045 CALL 8545                                       call file inverter
4047 GOSUB 6210
4050 PRINT : PRINT "SEQ. INVERSION COMPLETED"
4070 PRINT : PRINT : INPUT "DO YOU WANT TO FILE THE INVERTED SEQ. Y/N "    file storage?
     ;B$
4080 IF B$ < > "N" AND B$ < > "Y" THEN 4070          return
4090 GOTO 3080
5000 HOME : PRINT : POKE 50,63: PRINT "TRANSLATER ROUTINE": POKE 50,255
5003 GOSUB 6120                                      check orientation provide warning
5005 GOSUB 5100                                      if incorrect
5007 L1 = PEEK (43616) + PEEK (43617) * 256          aa sequence or triplets?
5010 GOSUB 6500                                      set start & end positions in
5017 GOSUB 6000                                      data file
5020 CALL 8205                                       Hard copy?
5022 CALL 8242                                       call initialize load & disassemble
5024 CALL 8249                                       mc routines
5025 EN = PEEK (8199) + PEEK (8200) * 256
5027 PRINT PEEK (8201)
5035 CALL 8855                                       call researcher
```

```
5040 W = 1 + ( PEEK (8192) * 3)
5043 R = PEEK (8243) + PEEK (8244) * 256
5045 IF R = EN THEN 5070
5047 IF R > EN THEN 5070
5050 PRINT MID$ (A$,W,3)".";
5060 GOTO 5035
5070 PRINT : PRINT
5075 PRE 0: PRINT "PRESS ANY KEY TO RETURN TO MENU"
5080 GET B$: GOTO 105
5100 PRINT : INPUT "DO YOU REQUIRE A DISPLAY OF THE AMINO ACID SEQ. OR T
     HE TRIPLET CODON SEQ. A/T ";B$
5110 IF B$ < > "A" AND B$ < > "T" THEN 5100
5120 IF B$ = "T" THEN 5200
5130 A$ = "LYSLYSASNASNARGARGSERSERTHRTHRTHRTHRILEMETILEILEGLUGLUASPASPGL
     YGLYGLYGLYALAALAALAALAVALVALVALVALGLNGLNHISHISARGARGARGARGPROPROPROPR
     OLEULEULEULEUSTPSTPTYRTYRSTPTRPCYSCYSSERSERSERSERLEULEUPHEPHE"
5140 RETURN
5200 A$ = "AAAAAGAACAATAGAAGGAGCAGTACAACGACCACTATAATGATCATTGAAGAGGACGATGG
     AGGGGGTGGCGCAGCGGCCGCTGTAGTGGTCGTTCAACAGCACCATCGACGGCGCCGTCCACCGCCCCC
     TCTACTGCTCCTTTAATAGTACTATTGATGGTGCTGTTCATCGTCCTCTTTATTGTTCTTT"
5210 RETURN
6000 PRINT : PRINT : INPUT "DO YOU REQUIRE A HARD COPY Y/N ";B$
6010 IF B$ < > "Y" AND B$ < > "N" THEN 6000
6020 IF B$ = "N" THEN 6040
6030 PRE 1: POKE 1657,80
6035 PRINT CHR$ (27);"Q"; CHR$ (80)
6040 RETURN
6100 PRINT : PRINT "PRESS ANY KEY TO RETURN TO MENU"
6110 GET B$: GOTO 105
6120 D = PEEK (16384)
6130 IF D = 4 OR D = 3 THEN 6140
6135 RETURN
6140 HOME : FLASH : PRINT : PRINT
6145 FOR J = 1 TO 10: HOME : PRINT "WARNING": CALL  - 198: NEXT
6147 NORMAL
6150 PRINT : PRINT "YOU ARE TRANSLATING THIS SEQ BACKWARDS!!"
6160 PRINT : PRINT "DO YOU WANT TO CONTINUE  Y/N"
6170 GET B$: IF B$ < > "Y" AND B$ < > "N" THEN 6170
6180 IF B$ = "Y" THEN 6200
6190 GOTO 105
6200 RETURN
6210 IF D = 3 THEN  POKE 16384,5
6215 IF D = 5 THEN  POKE 16384,3
6220 IF D = 4 THEN  POKE 16384,6
6225 IF D = 6 THEN  POKE 16384,4
6230 RETURN
6300 PRINT : PRINT : INPUT "DO YOU WANT TO LOAD A NEW SEQ. FILE  Y/N ":
     B$
6310 IF B$ < > "N" AND B$ < > "Y" THEN 6300
6320 IF B$ = "N" THEN 6415
6400 PRINT : PRINT : INPUT "PLEASE TYPE IN SEQ. FILE NAME ";N$
6407 D$ = CHR$ (4)
6410 PRINT D$;"BLOAD";N$
6415 L1 = PEEK (43616) + PEEK (43617) * 256
6418 IF LL = 1 THEN 6440
6420 PRINT : PRINT : INPUT "DO YOU WANT TO USE ALL OF THIS SEQ.? Y/N ";
     G$
6430 IF G$ = "N" THEN 6500
6440 A = PEEK (43634): POKE 8197,A
6450 B = PEEK (43635): POKE 8198,B
6460 L2 = L1 + 16384:L3 =  INT (L2 / 256):L4 = L2 - (L3 * 256)
6470 POKE 8199,L4 - 1: POKE 8200,L3: POKE 8201,0
6480 : RETURN
6500 PRINT : PRINT "THIS SEQ. IS ";L1 * 4" BASES LONG"
6510 PRINT : PRINT : INPUT "WHICH BASE DO YOU WANT TO START FROM ";N1
6520 PRINT : INPUT "AND WHICH BASE DO YOU WANT TO FINISH ON ";N2
6530 IF N1 < 1 OR N2 > L1 * 4 THEN 6510
6540 M1 = N1: GOSUB 6600
6545 POKE 8197,M5: POKE 8198,M4
6550 N3 = 5 - (N1 - ( INT (N1 / 4) * 4)): POKE 8201,N3
6555 IF N3 = 5 THEN  GOSUB 6620
6560 M1 = N2: GOSUB 6600
6570 POKE 8199,M5 + 1: POKE 8200,M4
6575 FOR J = 0 TO 4: PRINT  PEEK (8197 + J): NEXT
6580 RETURN
6600 M3 =  INT (M1 / 4) + 16384:M4 =  INT (M3 / 256):M5 = M3 - (M4 * 256)
```

check of req. and of data file.

print translation

return.

request & set A$ as appropriate

hard copy required?

menu RJS service routine.

orientation check & warning
routine

change orientation code in
1st data byte to opposite.

load new seq. file?

calculate start and end of
file

place variables in buffer

calculate start and end
of the section requested
calculate Y register value

required put in variables
buffer.

```
6610 RETURN
6620 N3 = 1: POKE 8201,N3: POKE 8197,M5 - 1
6630 RETURN
7000 FOR J = 0 TO 63:W = 1 + (J * 3): PRINT MID$ (A$,W,3)".";: NEXT
```

```
2000-  00        BRK                          data file storage byte.
2001-  00        BRK
2002-  00        BRK                          2 bit data storage bytes
2003-  00        BRK
2004-  00        BRK
2005-  05 40     ORA    $40                   data file start bytes
2007-  8D 40 01  STA    $0140                 data file end bytes
200A-  00        BRK                        buffer for variables transfer between
200B-  00        BRK                        routines X, Y, and A.
200C-  02        ???                        sub seq. length byte.
200D-  AC 09 20  LDY    $2009               INIT
2010-  AD 05 20  LDA    $2005
2013-  8D 33 20  STA    $2033               loads & stores from
2016-  AD 06 20  LDA    $2006               variables buffer to
2019-  8D 34 20  STA    $2034               routine INITIALIZING
201C-  AD 07 20  LDA    $2007               ROUTINE
201F-  8D 6C 21  STA    $216C
2022-  8D 73 21  STA    $2173
2025-  AD 08 20  LDA    $2008
2028-  8D 6D 21  STA    $216D
202B-  8D 74 21  STA    $2174
202E-  20 6A 20  JSR    $206A
2031-  60        RTS
2032-  AD 8D 40  LDA    $408D               LOADER
2035-  8D 00 20  STA    $2000             loads data file byte to
2038-  60        RTS                          $2000
2039-  A2 00     LDX    £$00              DISSASSEMBLER
203B-  8A        TXA
203C-  A8        TAY                        takes data byte from
203D-  AD 00 20  LDA    $2000              $ 2000 breaks into 2 bit
2040-  C0 00     CPY    £$00               units stores these in
2042-  D0 0D     BNE    $2051              2 bit data buffer
2044-  29 03     AND    £$03
2046-  9D 01 20  STA    $2001,X
2049-  E0 03     CPX    £$03               orientation $ 2004 → $ 2001
204B-  F0 0A     BEQ    $2057
204D-  E8        INX
204E-  4C 3B 20  JMP    $203B
2051-  4A        LSR
2052-  4A        LSR
2053-  88        DEY
2054-  4C 40 20  JMP    $2040
2057-  60        RTS                        ASSEMBLER
2058-  A2 00     LDX    £$00               takes 2 bit units from
205A-  A9 00     LDA    £$00               2 bit buffer constructs data file
205C-  0A        ASL                        byte leaves this in $ 2000
205D-  0A        ASL                        orientation $ 2001 → $ 2004
205E-  7D 01 20  ADC    $2001,X            1st encoded base in seq. placed in
2061-  8D 00 20  STA    $2000              MSBs of byte
2064-  E8        INX
2065-  E0 04     CPX    £$04
2067-  D0 F3     BNE    $205C
2069-  60        RTS                        INC
206A-  AD 34 20  LDA    $2034             compares data file byte to
206D-  CD 08 20  CMP    $2008             data Rle end bytes if equal
2070-  D0 08     BNE    $207A             RTS to basic.
2072-  AD 33 20  LDA    $2033
2075-  CD 07 20  CMP    $2007
2078-  F0 13     BEQ    $208D
207A-  EA        NOP
207B-  18        CLC
207C-  AD 33 20  LDA    $2033
207F-  69 01     ADC    £$01              increments by 1 data file byte
2081-  20 10 22  JSR    $2210             in loader
2084-  A9 00     LDA    £$00
2086-  6D 34 20  ADC.   $2034
2089-  20 20 22  JSR    $2220
208C-  60        RTS
208D-  68        PLA
208E-  68        PLA
208F-  60        RTS
```

168

```
2090-  A0 03      LDY   £$03
2092-  B9 01 20   LDA   $2001,Y
2095-  DD 00 03   CMP   $0300,X
2098-  D0 24      BNE   $20BE
209A-  EC 0C 20   CPX   $200C
209D-  D0 03      BNE   $20A2
209F-  4C 3B 22   JMP   $223B
20A2-  E8         INX
20A3-  C0 00      CPY   £$00
20A5-  D0 12      BNE   $20B9
20A7-  8E 0B 20   STX   $200B
20AA-  20 6A 20   JSR   $206A
20AD-  20 32 20   JSR   $2032
20B0-  20 39 20   JSR   $2039
20B3-  AE 0B 20   LDX   $200B
20B6-  4C 90 20   JMP   $2090
20B9-  88         DEY
20BA-  4C 92 20   JMP   $2092
20BD-  60         RTS
20BE-  BD 00 03   LDA   $0300,X
20C1-  C9 05      CMP   £$05
20C3-  F0 D5      BEQ   $209A
20C5-  C9 06      CMP   £$06
20C7-  F0 13      BEQ   $20DC
20C9-  C9 07      CMP   £$07
20CB-  F0 1B      BEQ   $20E8
20CD-  E0 00      CPX   £$00
20CF-  F0 D2      BEQ   $20A3
20D1-  20 FA 20   JSR   $20FA
20D4-  AC 09 20   LDY   $2009
20D7-  A2 00      LDX   £$00
20D9-  4C 92 20   JMP   $2092
20DC-  B9 01 20   LDA   $2001,Y
20DF-  F0 B9      BEQ   $209A
20E1-  C9 01      CMP   £$01
20E3-  F0 B5      BEQ   $209A
20E5-  4C 7F 22   JMP   $227F
20E8-  B9 01 20   LDA   $2001,Y
20EB-  C9 03      CMP   £$03
20ED-  F0 AB      BEQ   $209A
20EF-  C9 02      CMP   £$02
20F1-  F0 A7      BEQ   $209A
20F3-  BD 00 03   LDA   $0300,X
20F6-  4C CD 20   JMP   $20CD
20F9-  EA         NOP
20FA-  A9 00      LDA   £$00
20FC-  E0 00      CPX   £$00
20FE-  F0 11      BEQ   $2111
2100-  C8         INY
2101-  C0 04      CPY   £$04
2103-  F0 04      BEQ   $2109
2105-  CA         DEX
2106-  4C FC 20   JMP   $20FC
2109-  A0 00      LDY   £$00
210B-  18         CLC
210C-  69 01      ADC   £$01
210E-  4C 05 21   JMP   $2105
2111-  20 54 22   JSR   $2254
2114-  EA         NOP
2115-  EA         NOP
2116-  EA         NOP
2117-  EA         NOP
2118-  EA         NOP
2119-  EA         NOP
211A-  EA         NOP
211B-  EA         NOP
211C-  EA         NOP
211D-  EA         NOP
211E-  EA         NOP
211F-  38         SEC
2120-  AD 33 20   LDA   $2033
2123-  ED 0A 20   SBC   $200A
2126-  20 10 22   JSR   $2210
2129-  AD 34 20   LDA   $2034
212C-  E9 00      SBC   £$00
212E-  20 20 22   JSR   $2220
2131-  20 6C 22   JSR   $226C
2134-  60         RTS
```

SEARCHER A

compares data in 2 bit buffer.
to subseq. data in page $ 0300
loops if equal to searcher B if not.

Y reg controls use of 2 bit buffer
if all buffer used jumps to inc load
and disassembler in that order saves
& resets X & Y reg as required.
if end of subseq. reached ie X = $ 2009
to basic service routine to report
saves Y reg & resets on RTS.

SEARCHER B
entry on subseq. not equal to file.
checks wild cards returns to searcher
A if equal & meet pyrimidine or
purine requirements.
direct return if 1st base of subseq.
otherwise reset file position.

check if file base a purine

check if file base a pyrimidine

reset file data byte and Y register
for next subsequence comparison.

169

```
2135-   AD 00 20    LDA   $2000
2138-   49 FF       EOR   £$FF
213A-   8D 8D 40    STA   $408D
213D-   20 6A 20    JSR   $206A
2140-   20 32 20    JSR   $2032
2143-   4C 35 21    JMP   $2135
2146-   20 32 20    JSR   $2032
2149-   20 79 22    JSR   $2279
214C-   A2 00       LDX   £$00
214E-   0A          ASL
214F-   0A          ASL
2150-   7D 01 20    ADC   $2001,X
2153-   8D 8D 40    STA   $408D
2156-   E8          INX
2157-   E0 04       CPX   £$04
2159-   D0 F3       BNE   $214E
215B-   20 6A 20    JSR   $206A
215E-   4C 46 21    JMP   $2146
2161-   20 0D 20    JSR   $200D
2164-   20 32 20    JSR   $2032
2167-   AD 00 20    LDA   $2000
216A-   AA          TAX
216B-   AD 8D 40    LDA   $408D
216E-   8D 8D 40    STA   $408D
2171-   8A          TXA
2172-   8D 8D 40    STA   $408D
2175-   20 7B 20    JSR   $207B
2178-   38          SEC
2179-   AD 6C 21    LDA   $216C
217C-   E9 01       SBC   £$01
217E-   8D 6C 21    STA   $216C
2181-   8D 73 21    STA   $2173
2184-   AD 6D 21    LDA   $216D
2187-   E9 00       SBC   £$00
2189-   8D 6D 21    STA   $216D
218C-   8D 74 21    STA   $2174
218F-   CD 34 20    CMP   $2034
2192-   EA          NOP
2193-   EA          NOP
2194-   D0 0B       BNE   $21A1
2196-   AD 33 20    LDA   $2033
2199-   CD 6C 21    CMP   $216C
219C-   10 02       BPL   $21A0
219E-   D0 01       BNE   $21A1
21A0-   60          RTS
21A1-   4C 64 21    JMP   $2164
21A4-   AC 09 20    LDY   $2009
21A7-   A2 00       LDX   £$00
21A9-   A9 00       LDA   £$00
21AB-   0A          ASL
21AC-   0A          ASL
21AD-   79 01 20    ADC   $2001,Y
21B0-   EA          NOP
21B1-   EA          NOP
21B2-   8D 00 20    STA   $2000
21B5-   E8          INX
21B6-   E0 03       CPX   £$03
21B8-   F0 16       BEQ   $21D0
21BA-   C0 00       CPY   £$00
21BC-   D0 0E       BNE   $21CC
21BE-   8D 09 20    STA   $2009
21C1-   4C 85 22    JMP   $2285
21C4-   AD 09 20    LDA   $2009
21C7-   A0 03       LDY   £$03
21C9-   4C AB 21    JMP   $21AB
21CC-   88          DEY
21CD-   4C AB 21    JMP   $21AB
21D0-   8C 09 20    STY   $2009
21D3-   60          RTS
21D4-   60          RTS
21D5-   EA          NOP
21D6-   EA          NOP
21D7-   20 0D 20    JSR   $200D
21DA-   20 32 20    JSR   $2032
21DD-   20 39 20    JSR   $2039
21E0-   60          RTS
21E1-   20 6A 20    JSR   $206A
21E4-   4C DA 21    JMP   $21DA
21E7-   A2 03       LDX   £$03
```

TRANSCRIBER

form logical NOT of each
data file byte restore in file.

INVERTER A

disassemble each byte with
disassembler reassemble in
opposite orientation.

INVERTER B

take each byte and interchange position
first with last second with next to
last etc.

calculate next byte to operate on
the latter part of file.

check if all bytes shifted.

TRANSLATER

disassemble each byte in turn
reassemble data as a 'triplet'
rts to basic with triplet in $ 2000
saving Y reg and resetting on
reentry.

2 bit data buffer usage controlled by
Y loops - calls inc loader and
disassembler as required.

```
21E9-  20 39 20   JSR   $2039
21EC-  AC 09 20   LDY   $2009
21EF-  0A         ASL
21F0-  0A         ASL
21F1-  7D 01 20   ADC   $2001,X
21F4-  E0 01      CPX   £$01
21F6-  F0 14      BEQ   $220C
21F8-  E8         INX
21F9-  C0 03      CPY   £$03
21FB-  F0 04      BEQ   $2201
21FD-  C8         INY
21FE-  4C EF 21   JMP   $21EF
2201-  8D 8D 40   STA   $408D
2204-  20 7B 20   JSR   $207B
2207-  A0 00      LDY   £$00
2209-  4C EF 21   JMP   $21EF
220C-  8C 09 20   STY   $2009
220F-  60         RTS
2210-  8D 33 20   STA   $2033
2213-  8D 3B 21   STA   $213B
2216-  8D 54 21   STA   $2154
2219-  8D 6F 21   STA   $216F
221C-  8D 02 22   STA   $2202
221F-  60         RTS
2220-  8D 34 20   STA   $2034
2223-  8D 3C 21   STA   $213C
2226-  8D 55 21   STA   $2155
2229-  8D 70 21   STA   $2170
222C-  8D 03 22   STA   $2203
222F-  60         RTS
2230-  A2 00      LDX   £$00
2232-  AC 09 20   LDY   $2009
2235-  4C 92 20   JMP   $2092
2238-  EA         NOP
2239-  8E 09 20   STX   $2009
223C-  8C 0A 20   STY   $200A
223F-  60         RTS
2240-  AE 09 20   LDX   $2009
2243-  AC 0A 20   LDY   $200A
2246-  4C FB 20   JMP   $20FB
2249-  AC 0A 20   LDY   $200A
224C-  AE 0C 20   LDX   $200C
224F-  A9 00      LDA   £$00
2251-  4C FA 20   JMP   $20FA
2254-  C0 00      CPY   £$00
2256-  D0 0C      BNE   $2264
2258-  38         SEC
2259-  E9 01      SBC   £$01
225B-  A0 03      LDY   £$03
225D-  8C 09 20   STY   $2009
2260-  8D 0A 20   STA   $200A
2263-  60         RTS
2264-  88         DEY
2265-  8C 09 20   STY   $2009
2268-  8D 0A 20   STA   $200A
226B-  60         RTS
226C-  8E 0B 20   STX   $200B
226F-  20 32 20   JSR   $2032
2272-  20 39 20   JSR   $2039
2275-  AE 0B 20   LDX   $200B
2278-  60         RTS
2279-  20 39 20   JSR   $2039
227C-  A9 00      LDA   £$00
227E-  60         RTS
227F-  B9 01 20   LDA   $2001,Y
2282-  4C C9 20   JMP   $20C9
2285-  8E 0A 20   STX   $200A
2288-  20 6A 20   JSR   $206A
228B-  20 32 20   JSR   $2032
228E-  20 39 20   JSR   $2039
2291-  AE 0A 20   LDX   $200A
2294-  4C C4 21   JMP   $21C4
2297-  AC 09 20   LDY   $2009
229A-  A2 00      LDX   £$00
229C-  A9 00      LDA   £$00
229E-  4C BA 21   JMP   $21BA
22A1-  03         ???
```

SERVICE ROUTINES

INIT SUB ROUTINE RESETS.
PROGRAM VARIABLES
NB.

entry end exit routines

for MC routines- interfacing between
basic program & MC routines

sub routine for seq. searcher
reset routine.

```
22A2-   4C BA 21   JMP   $21BA
22A5-   4C AD 21   JMP   $21AD
```

Listing 1 consists of a machine code program and a BASIC driver program. The former contains three service routines: 'init' which initialises variables in the machine code routines, 'Loader' which collects data from the file and 'inc' which directs the program to the next byte of the data file. Four bytes comprise a 2-bit data buffer and a further seven transfer variables between separate routines.

The program encodes sequence data as a compressed binary coded file; each variable is represented by 2 bits. 'Assembler' and 'Disassembler' are the routines which encode and decode the compressed file. They support the other machine code routines as well as the BASIC 'input' and 'output' routines.

'Transcriber' forms the complement of the sequence file. 'Inverter A' and 'Inverter B' invert the sequence, first inverting the four bits of data in each byte and then the bytes within the file. 'Translater' assembles 2-bit data as a 6-bit binary number which the BASIC program uses to translate the codon. 'Searcher A' compares an input sequence with the data file through a window routine. 'Searcher B' checks on wild card entries.

**Listing 1.1.** File converter

```
3 D$ = CHR$ (4): PRINT D$;"BLOADFREDSEQ"
5 Q$ = "AGCT": REM  TEXT FILE READER
10  INPUT "FILE NAME";A$
20  INPUT "FILE LENGTH";N
30  INPUT "NEW BINARY FILE NAME";N$
35  INPUT "DOES THE SEQ BEGIN 5' OR 3'";C
40  PRINT D$;"OPEN";A$
50  PRINT D$;"READ";A$
55 I = I + 1
57  GET B$
59  FOR J = 1 TO 4: IF B$ = MID$ (Q$,J,1) THEN 61: NEXT
60  NEXT
61  POKE 32768 + I,J
63  IF I = N THEN 65
64  GOTO 55
65  PRINT D$;"CLOSE";A$
100 I = 0:P = 0:G = 0
105 P = P + 1
110 G = G + 1
115 HOME : PRINT " "
120 J =  PEEK (32768 + G)
130 POKE 8193 + I,J
132 I = I + 1
134 IF I < 4 GOTO 110
140 CALL 8280
150 D =  PEEK (8192): POKE 16384 + P,D
165 IF G > N THEN 180
167 HOME : PRINT P,G,N
170 I = 0: GOTO 105
180 HOME : PRINT : PRINT "BEGINING CONVERSION"
185 FOR H = 1 TO 100: NEXT
194 POKE 16384,C + 1
200 P = P + 1
210 PRINT D$;"BSAVE";N$",A16384,L";P
220 PRINT "ANOTHER FILE CONVERSION ?"
230 GET B$
240 IF LEFT$ (B$,1) = "Y" THEN  GOTO 5
250 END
500 GET B$
510 STR$ (B$)
520 GOTO 500
```

This short program converts text files to compressed binary coded files thus allowing a word processor with editing facilities to be used to construct sequence data files.

**Listing 2.** (1 – 14) BASIC routines

1.
```
20000  REM          REPLICATION
20010  REM          NEED DNA$(LN)
20020  REM          FORMS CDNA$(LN)
20030  :
20040  FOR L = 1 TO LN
20050  B$ = DNA$(L)
20060  IF B$ = "A" THEN B$ = "T": GOTO 20110
20070  IF B$ = "T" THEN B$ = "A": GOTO 20110
20080  IF B$ = "G" THEN B$ = "C": GOTO 20110
20090  IF B$ = "C" THEN B$ = "G": GOTO 20110
20100  B$ = "*"
20110  CDNA$(LN - L + 1)  = B$
20120  NEXT
20130  :
20140  RETURN
```

2.
```
20200  REM          PRINT DNA AND C-DNA
20210  REM          NEED DNA$(LN),CDNA$(LN)
20220  REM          ASSUMES WW COLUMNS
20230  :
20240  L = 1
20250  :
20260  FOR J = L TO L + WW
20265  IF J = LN THEN 20290
20270  PRINT DNA$(J);
20280  NEXT J
20290  PRINT
20300  FOR K = L TO L + WW
20305  IF K = LN THEN 20380
20310  PRINT CDNA$(LN - K + 1);
20320  NEXT K
20330  PRINT
20340  PRINT
20350  L = L + WW
20360  GOTO 20260
20370  :
20380  RETURN
```

3.
```
20400  REM          TRANSCRIPTION
20410  REM          NEEDS DNA$(LN)
20420  REM          FORMS RNA$(LN)
20430  :
20440  FOR L = 1 TO LN
20450  B$ = DNA$(L)
20460  IF B$ = "A" THEN B$ = "U": GOTO 20510
20470  IF B$ = "T" THEN B$ = "A": GOTO 20510
20480  IF B$ = "G" THEN B$ = "C": GOTO 20510
20490  IF B$ = "C" THEN B$ = "G": GOTO 20510
20500  B$ = "*"
20510  RNA$(L) = B$
20520  NEXT
20530  :
20540  RETURN
```

4.
```
20600  REM          EXCHANGE DNA STRANDS
20610  REM          NEED DNA$(LN),CDNA$(LN)
20620  :
20630  FOR L = 1 TO LN
20640  B$ = DNA$(L)
20650  DNA$(L) = CDNA$(L)
20660  CDNA$(L) = B$
20670  NEXT L
20680  :
20690  RETURN
```

5.
```
20700  REM          REVERSE TRANSCRIPTION
20710  REM          NEEDS RNA$(LN)
20720  REM          FORMS DNA$(LN)
20730  :
20740  FOR L = 1 TO LN
20750  B$ = RNA$(L)
20760  IF B$ = "A" THEN B$ = "T": GOTO 20810
20770  IF B$ = "U" THEN B$ = "A": GOTO 20810
20780  IF B$ = "G" THEN B$ = "C": GOTO 20810
20790  IF B$ = "C" THEN B$ = "G": GOTO 20810
20800  B$ = "*"
20810  DNA$(LN - L + 1) = B$
20820  NEXT
20830  :
20840  RETURN
```

6.
```
21000  REM          FIND INITIATION CODON
21010  REM          IN RNA$(LN) FROM (?
21020  REM          IC=0:NO INITIATION FOUND
21030  :
21040  LE = LN - 2: IC = 0
21050  FOR L =   0? TO LE
21060  CO$ = RNA$(L) + RNA$(L + 1) + RNA$(L + 2)
21070  IF CO$ = "AUG" OR CO$ = "GUG" THEN 21100
21080  NEXT L
21090  GOTO 21110
21100  IC = L
21110  :
21120  RETURN
```

## Nucleic Acid Sequence Analysis

7.
```
50000  REM        ASSEMBLE GENETIC CODE
50010  REM          IN GC$ (3-L CODE)
50020  :
50030  FOR L = 1 TO 4
50040  FOR L1 = 1 TO 4
50050  FOR L2 = 1 TO 4
50060  READ GC$(L,L1,L2)
50070  NEXT L2
50080  NEXT L1
50090  NEXT L
50100  :
50110  RETURN
50120  REM        5' BASE = U
50130  DATA PHE,PHE,LEU,LEU: REM   MID BASE U
50140  DATA SER,SER,SER,SER: REM   MID BASE C
50150  DATA TYR,TYR,STP,STP: REM   MID BASE A
50160  DATA CYS,CYS,STP,TRP: REM   MID BASE G
50170  REM        5' BASE = C
50180  DATA LEU,LEU,LEU,LEU
50190  DATA PRO,PRO,PRO,PRO
50200  DATA HIS,HIS,GLN,GLN
50210  DATA ARG,ARG,ARG,ARG
50220  REM        5' BASE = A
50230  DATA ILE,ILE,ILE,MET
50240  DATA THR,THR,THR,THR
50250  DATA ASN,ASN,LYS,LYS
50260  DATA SER,SER,ARG,ARG
50270  REM        5' BASE = G
50280  DATA VAL,VAL,VAL,VAL
50290  DATA ALA,ALA,ALA,ALA
50300  DATA ASP,ASP,GLU,GLU
50310  DATA GLY,GLY,GLY,GLY
```

8.
```
50400  REM        ASSEMBLE GENETIC CODE
50410  REM          IN GC$ (1-L CODE)
50420  :
50430  FOR L = 1 TO 4
50440  FOR L1 = 1 TO 4
50450  FOR L2 = 1 TO 4
50460  READ GC$(L,L1,L2)
50470  NEXT L2
50490  NEXT L1
50490  NEXT L
50500  :
50510  RETURN
50520  DATA F,F,L,L,S,S,S,S,Y,Y,*,*,C,C,*,W
50530  DATA L,L,L,L,P,P,P,P,H,H,Q,Q,R,R,R,R
50540  DATA I,I,I,M,T,T,T,T,N,N,K,K,S,S,R,R
50550  DATA V,V,V,V,A,A,A,A,D,D,E,E,G,G,G,G
```

9.
```
22000  REM        TRANSLATION
22010  REM          NEEDS RNA$(LN) AND SP(START)
22020  REM          GIVES PP$() (3-L CODE)
22030  AA = 0:TC = 0
22040  FOR L = SP TO LN STEP 3: REM  MOVE 1 CODON AT A TIME
22050  IF (LN - L) < 3 THEN 22190: REM  FINISHED ?
22060  FOR J = 0 TO 2
22070  IF RNA$(L + J) = "U" THEN B(J + 1) = 1
22080  IF RNA$(L + J) = "C" THEN B(J + 1) = 2
22090  IF RNA$(L + J) = "A" THEN B(J + 1) = 3
22100  IF RNA$(L + J) = "G" THEN B(J + 1) = 4
22110  NEXT J
22120  AA$ = GC$(B(1),B(2),B(3))
22130  IF AA$ = "STP" THEN 22180
22140  AA = AA + 1
22150  PP$(L) = AA$:PP$(L + 1) = "":PP$(L + 2) = ""
22160  NEXT L
22170  GOTO 22190
22180  TC = L
22190  RETURN
```

10.
```
23000  REM        TRANSLATION
23010  REM          NEEDS RNA$(LN) AND SP(START)
23020  REM          GIVES PP$() (1-L CODE)
23030  AA = 0:TC = 0
23040  FOR L = SP TO LN STEP 3: REM   MOVE 1 CODON AT A TIME
23050  IF (LN - L) < 3 THEN 23190: REM   FINISHED ?
23060  FOR J = 0 TO 2
23070  IF RNA$(L + J) = "U" THEN B(J + 1) = 1
23080  IF RNA$(L + J) = "C" THEN B(J + 1) = 2
23090  IF RNA$(L + J) = "A" THEN B(J + 1) = 3
23100  IF RNA$(L + J) = "G" THEN B(J + 1) = 4
23110  NEXT J
23120  AA$ = GC$(B(1),B(2),B(3))
23130  IF AA$ = "*" THEN 23180
23140  AA = AA + 1
23150  PP$(L) = AA$:PP$(L + 1) = "":PP$(L + 2) = ""
23160  NEXT L
23170  GOTO 23190
23180  TC = L
23190  RETURN
23200  :
23210  REM        AA=NO OF AMINO ACIDS
23220  REM        TC=1ST BASE OF TERM CODON
23230  REM        TC=0:COMPLETE TRANSLATION
```

11.
```
50600  REM        CLEAR PP$(LN)
50610  :
50620  FOR L = 1 TO LN
50630  PP$(L) = "-"
50640  NEXT L
```

12.
```
24000  REM            PRINT RNA,PROTEIN
24010  REM            NEEDS RNA$(),PP$()
24020 :
24030 L = 1
24040  IF L > LN THEN 24170
24050 AA$ = PP$(L)
24060  IF AA$ = "" OR AA$ = "-" THEN 24130
24070  FOR J = L TO L + 2
24080  PRINT RNA$(J);
24090  NEXT J
24100  PRINT "      ";PP$(L)
24110 L = L + 3
24120  GOTO 24040
24130  PRINT RNA$(L);"      ";PP$(L)
24140 L = L + 1
24150  GOTO 24040
24160 :
24170  RETURN
```

13.
```
1000  REM            DEMO NUCLEOTIDE ROUTINES (RJB)
1010  LN = 400:::::: REM      LENGTH OF DNA
1020  DIM DNA$(LN),CDNA$(LN),RNA$(LN),PP$(LN),GC$(4,4,4)
1030  GOSUB 50600: REM   SET UP PP$
1040  GOSUB 50000: REM   READ 3-L CODE
1050  REM            SET UP RANDOM DNA
1060 :
1070  FOR L = 1 TO LN
1080 A =  INT ( RND (.9) * 4 + .5)
1090  IF A = 1 THEN B$ = "A": GOTO 1130
1100  IF A = 2 THEN B$ = "T": GOTO 1130
1110  IF A = 3 THEN B$ = "G": GOTO 1130
1120  IF A = 4 THEN B$ = "C": GOTO 1130
1130 DNA$(L) = B$
1140  NEXT L
1150 :
1160  GOSUB 20000: REM      REPLICATE DNA
1165 :
1170  WW = 20:::::: REM      SCREEN WIDTH
1175 :
1180  GOSUB 20200: REM      PRINT DNA,CDNA
1185 :
1190  GOSUB 20600: REM      EXCHANGE STRANDS
1195 :
1200  GOSUB 20400: REM      TRANSCRIBE DNA (WAS CDNA)
1205 :
1210  OG = 1:::::::: REM      START POSITION
1215 :
1220  GOSUB 21000: REM      FIND INITIATION CODON
1225 :
1230  PRINT "INITIATION CODON AT ";IC
1235 :
1240  SP = IC:::::: REM      SET UP START
1245 :
1250  GOSUB 22000: REM       TRANSLATE 3-L CODE
1255 :
1260  GOSUB 24000: REM      PRINT RNA/PROTEIN
1265 :
1270  END
```

14.
```
26000  REM            SUBSTRING SEARCH IN DNA$()
26010  REM            NEEDS SS$(),LS,SO
26020 :
26030 MF = 0:LE = LN - LS
26040  FOR L = SO TO LE
26050  FOR J = 1 TO LS
26060  IF DNA$(L + J - 1) <  > SS$(J) THEN 26100
26070  NEXT J
26080 MF = L
26090  GOTO 26120
26100  NEXT L
26110 :
26120  RETURN
```

These routines for manipulating nucleic acid sequences are suitable for demonstration and teaching purposes. They were constructed by R.J.Beynon (ref.5) and are reproduced with permission.

**Listing 3**. Window

```
10   REM :MAKE 3D ARRAY OF CODON P
     REF.
50   DIM Z(4,4,4)
60   FOR J = 1 TO 4: FOR K = 1 TO
     4: FOR L = 1 TO 4
70   READ X:Z(J,K,L) =  LOG (X)
80   NEXT L: NEXT K: NEXT J
900  INPUT "WINDOW SIZE IN CODONS
     ";C
905  INPUT "SCALE";SC
910  L = C * 3
920  A = 24576
925  GOTO 1000
929  REM :MAKE RANDOM SEQ.
930  FOR J = 1 TO 600:X =  RND (1
     ): POKE 24576 + J, INT (X *
     4): NEXT
940  END
999  REM :SET FIRST WINDOW
```

```
1000  FOR K = 1 TO L STEP 3
1010  FOR J = 1 TO 5
1020  P(J) =  PEEK (A + K + J) + 1

1030  NEXT J
1040  S(1) = S(1) + Z(P(1),P(2),P(
      3))
1050  S(2) = S(2) + Z(P(2),P(3),P(
      4))
1060  S(3) = S(3) + Z(P(3),P(4),P(
      5))
1070  NEXT K
1090  GOSUB 4000
1099  REM  WINDOW UPDATE
1100  I = I + 3
1110  FOR N = 1 TO 5:P(N) =  PEEK
      (A + I + N) + 1:PE(N) =  PEEK
      (A + I + L + N) + 1: NEXT
1120  FOR K = 1 TO 3:S(K) = S(K) -
      Z(P(K),P(K + 1),P(K + 2)) +
      Z(PE(K),PE(K + 1),PE(K + 2))
      : NEXT
1130  DIV = S(1) + S(2) + S(3)
1140  FOR J = 1 TO 3:PF(J) = S(J)
      / DIV: NEXT
1150  PS = PS + 1: IF PS > 278 THEN
      5000
1160  FOR J = 1 TO 3
1170  PF(J) = PF(J) - 0.25
1180  IF PF(J) < 0 THEN PF(J) = 0
      .001
1190  PP(J) = (60 * J) - (PF(J) *
      SC)
1200  NEXT J
1210  FOR D = 1 TO 3: IF PP(D) >
      189 THEN PP(D) = 189: NEXT
1220  FOR T = 1 TO 3: IF PP(T) <
      0 THEN PP(T) = 0: NEXT
1230  FOR B = 1 TO 3: HCOLOR= 3: HPLOT
      PS,PP(B) TO PS,PX(B):PX(B) =
      PP(B): NEXT
1240  GOTO 1100
2999  REM :LOAD SEQ. SET LENGTH
3000  A =  PEEK (43634): POKE 8197
      ,A
3010  B =  PEEK (43635): POKE 8198
      ,B
3015  L1 =  PEEK (43616) +  PEEK (
      43617) * 256
3020  L2 = L1 + 16384:L3 =  INT (L
      2 / 256):L4 = L2 - (L3 * 256
      )
3030  POKE 8199,L4 - 1: POKE 8200
      ,L3: POKE 8201,0
3040  RETURN
3999  REM :SET UP HGR GRAPHICS
4000  HGR
4010  POKE 49234,0
4030  FOR J = 1 TO 279 STEP 10: HPLOT
      J,190 TO J,180: NEXT
4040  FOR J = 1 TO 3: HPLOT 0,J *
      60 TO 279,J * 60: NEXT
4050  HPLOT 0,0 TO 0,190
4060  RETURN
5000  END
6999  REM :MAKE SEQ. OF CAT REPEA
      T FOR TEST
7000  A = 24576
7010  NU = NU + 1
7020  POKE A + NU,2:NU = NU + 1
7030  POKE A + NU,0:NU = NU + 1
7040  POKE A + NU,3
7050  IF NU > 1000 THEN 7070
7060  GOTO 7010
7070  END
9999  REM :CODON PREFERENCE DATA
10000 DATA 30,29,26,18,12,8,14,9
      ,14,8,22,7,9,26,23,20
10020 DATA 32,29,27,25,15,11,20,
      24,19,14,22,27,12,22,14,18
10030 DATA 16,24,13,10,4,5,11,12
      ,14,11,10,13,8,33,13,13
10040 DATA 10,13,21,18,12,6,15,1
      5,1,1,18,14,1,14,10,8
```

This program provides a plot of potential coding function in a sequence which is based on codon preference (Section 2.5.2) and employs a codon frequency table taken from reference b. The program serves as an example of a windowing routine and could be used for the development of several different BASIC programs emulating those described in references 7 and 10. The routine calculates a value required for the first window. For each subsequent window the value is derived by subtracting the contribution provided by the codon lost from the left-hand side of the window and adding that provided by the incoming right-hand codon. All three phases of translation are treated at the same time. The sequence is filed in binary code as in *Listing 1* except that it is not compressed, one base being encoded per byte. Each codon is assembled from three bytes which provide three numbers between 1 and 4 (A to T). These are used to access a three-dimensional array, e.g., Z (1,2,3) and return the appropriate codon preference value. Five values are collected P(1) to P(5) which provide the three codon phases, i.e., 1,2,3; 2,3,4; 3,4,5. Therefore, to update each window, five 'left-hand' values and five right-hand values are required, cf. variable P and PE, respectively. Note that this type of in/out window updating cannot be employed with direct search routines or those requiring positional matches.

**Listing 3.1.** Seq. shift

```
90   REM :SEQ SHIFT REDUCES 2 BIT
     BINARY CODE TO 8 BIT BINARY
     CODE
100  D$ =  CHR$ (4): PRINT D$;"BLO
     ADFREDSEQ.CC
110  INPUT "SEQ. FILE NAME ?";N$
120  PRINT D$;"BLOAD";N$
125  GOSUB 3000
130  CALL 8663
150  FOR J = 3 TO 0 STEP  - 1:Q =
     Q + 1: POKE 24576 + Q, PEEK
     (8193 + J)
158  NEXT
160  CALL 8673
170  IF Q > L1 * 4 THEN 200
180  GOTO 150
200  END
3000 A =  PEEK (43634): POKE 8197
     ,A
3010 B =  PEEK (43635): POKE 8198
     ,B
3015 L1 =  PEEK (43616) +  PEEK (
     43617) * 256
3020 L2 = L1 + 16384:L3 =  INT (L
     2 / 256):L4 = L2 - (L3 * 256
     )
3030  POKE 8199,L4 - 1: POKE 8200
     ,L3: POKE 8201,0
3040  RETURN
```

This program facilitates the use of 'Window' (*Listing 3*) by converting 2-bit binary coded sequence files, such as those used by 'sequence manipulator' (*Listing 1*), into an 8-bit binary code.

CHAPTER 7

# Microcomputers in Spectrophotometry

## A. LODOLA

## 1. INTRODUCTION AND GENERAL CONSIDERATIONS

The availability of low cost yet powerful microcomputers for use in the laboratory has expanded the potential of a wide range of equipment, not least spectrophotometers. Commercial instruments are now available with an integral microcomputer. With this type of instrument the software is not usually directly accessible to the user, hence new or different software based uses are dependent on the manufacturer. The purpose of this chapter is to discuss those applications where the spectrophotometer is controlled by a stand alone microcomputer, with complete access to the software. It is limited to the systems used by the author, nevertheless the general principles involved are widely applicable and where appropriate alternative possibilities are highlighted.

A number of programs are described which relate primarily to solution spectrophotometry but are also applicable to the densitometry of gels. Programs are written in Applesoft BASIC and require modification for use on other systems; shape tables are written in 6502 ASSEMBLER. The assembler may also vary with implementation; at least 16k of RAM are required to use the programs. The PEEK and POKE statements used to control the A/D (analogue to digital) and D/A (digital to analogue) boards are unique to the author's system; all other PEEK and POKE statements are described fully in the documentation supplied with the Apple. Full program listings are given in the Appendix at the end of this chapter.

### 1.1 Equipment

*Figure 1* describes the basic features of a typical system. A dual beam scanning spectrophotometer is interfaced to an Apple ITT 2020 microcomputer which is used to control the monochromator and input data from the photomultiplier (*via* a log ratio amplifier). Data are displayed on a video terminal before dumping onto floppy disc and/or hard copy production on a standard x/y chart recorder. Data input and output to the microcomputer are *via* 8-bit converters (a 2 channel A/D and 3 channel D/A).

In establishing a system the following points should be considered (1).

(i) *Microcomputers.* Any of the microcomputers commonly available are suitable for use (e.g., Apple, BBC Acorn). The choice of machine is dictated by the expertise of the user and the technical backup available. If these are limited one of the more popular machines, with as wide a range of hardware and software as possible, should be used. A disc drive or tape recorder is required for program and

179

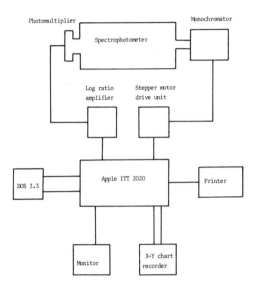

**Figure 1.** Diagrammatic representation of a microcomputer controlled dual beam scanning spectrophotometer. The stepper motor which drives the monochromator is controlled directly by the microcomputer; output from the photomultiplier is accessed by the microcomputer *via* a log-ratio amplifier and an 8-bit A/D converter. The monitor and x/y recorder are used to display the spectrum and produce a hard copy respectively. A floppy disc system is used for storing programs and data files.

data storage. The extra speed and flexibility of floppy discs makes them the best choice. Two disc drives are advantageous but not essential (one for 'program floppys' and the other for 'data floppys').

(ii) *Spectrophotometer*. Most laboratory spectrophotometers are suitable for interfacing to a microcomputer. However, the more sophisticated the use the greater the expertise required. Thus, to monitor and store absorbance output requires only the location of a convenient point to measure the photomultiplier output signal (preferably after amplification, and subtraction of the reference value). This could be at a display (i.e., meter) or chart recorder output line. If automatic cuvette change or scanning facility are used it is also necessary to identify, monitor and/or control a location regulating the event.

(iii) *Interface units and ports*. These enable the microcomputer to communicate with and control equipment. A number of interface ports are available and in general all microcomputers are supplied with a number of internal busses which can be used for this type of application. Some of the more common (parallel) busses are:

(i)    the IEEE programmable instrumentation bus;
(ii)   the Apple bus, which is based on seven slots in the main microcomputer board to which external devices can be connected;
(iii)  the Z-80 microcomputer bus, which is present on a range of machines which use the Z-80 chip (e.g., Tandy and Sharp).

Additionally a number of microcomputers have a serial interface bus (e.g., RS232) which is generally used for producing hard copy. The bus used is dependent on the interface unit and except where it is custom built, is not specified by the user. A/D and D/A converters are commercially available for a number of machines with either 8-bit or 12-bit resolution. The choice is dependent on the application. For routine scanning spectrophotometry or single wavelength measurements 8-bit resolution ($0 - 255$ bits) is usually sufficient. For spectrum derivitisation or detailed spectrum analysis 12-bit resolution ($0 - 1620$ bits) is essential. The Model B BBC microcomputer is supplied with four A/D converters in place with inputs in the range $0 - 1.8$ V. The digitised input is sampled by use of ADVAL. The digital output is in the range $0 - 65\ 520$ and therefore requires scaling for use with the plotting routines.

Many converters do not have a facility for distinguishing negative going signals. Although output from the author's log ration amplifier varies in the range $- 10$ V to $+ 10$ V, in operation signals below 0 V are recorded as zero. To ensure that the complete spectrum is captured it is necessary to set starting conditions such that the signal does not fall below 0 V at any point on the spectrum. A more systematic solution is the use of converters which are able to distinguish these voltages, and produce a sign recognition bit.

(iv) *Hard copy production.* An x/y chart recorder or dot matrix printer, with a graphics capability, can be used. If a matrix printer is not available, a printer to supplement the chart recorder is useful because it can be integrated into programs to produce a hard copy of numerical data.

(v) *Relay devices.* If the microcomputer is used to control remote units directly (e.g., stepper motors) a buffer device drawing low current, but capable of activating systems drawing relatively high current, is required. This can be achieved using relay switches.

## 1.2 Software

The more complex the system the greater the flexibility but the greater the expertise required. Using relatively simple programs the potential of the equipment can be greatly expanded in terms of data handling and presentation. If commercial software is available it will not usually meet individual requirements, although it is often of higher quality in terms of data display and use of memory. Program development is central to establishing this type of system, but is not as daunting a task as it may appear. For inexperienced programmers BASIC is simple and flexible enough to allow control and manipulation routines to be written without detailed knowledge of computer programming. As expertise increases other languages (e.g., ASSEMBLER, PASCAL) can be used to increase the flexibility and speed of the program. Complete hardware/software packages are commercially available for common laboratory spectrophotometers.

It is useful to establish a package of programs under central control from a 'directory' which automatically calls the relevant programs each time the system is activated. The programs listed here are presented as individual units for ease of presentation. *Figure 2* illustrates one approach with reference to *Listing 1* in the

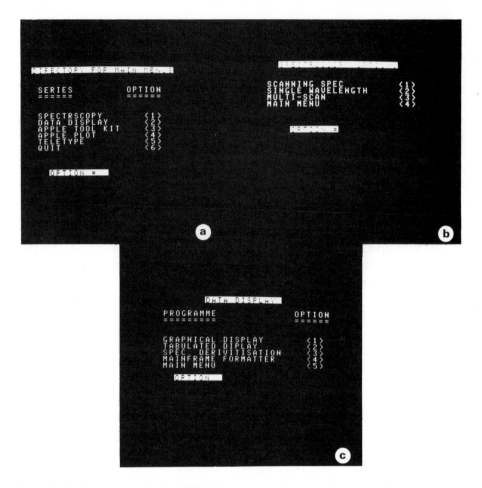

**Figure 2.** Display sequence for the 'HELLO' program used to control program access. Use of programs is under the control of a directory, on booting DOS a main menu is presented (**a**) from which a number of functions may be selected. The requisite programs are then loaded automatically or a series of suboptions are offered (**b** and **c**).

Appendix. On booting DOS a control program is loaded automatically and run (the Apple 'HELLO' program); it directs the user to the appropriate function and, more importantly, to the program required. Initially a menu is presented (lines 50−160) (*Figure 2a*) which prompts the user for a function. Where appropriate the program(s) required are loaded into the microcomputer and run (e.g., option 4 Apple Plot); if there are subfunctions a new menu is presented (lines 190−250 and 310−410) (*Figure 2b* and *c*). This allows a multi-user/function approach and requires no knowledge of microcomputers or programming on the part of the user. An obvious disadvantage is that users are not required to understand the software to use the system. The 'program floppys' can be write protected to prevent accidental program overwriting or modification. *Listing 2* is the 'core' program and contains all the features which the other input

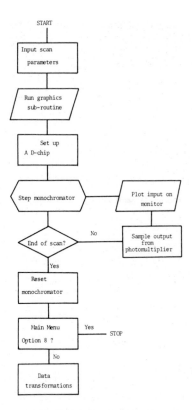

**Figure 3.** Flow diagrams for *Listing 2*. The major features of the program are the synchronisation of data capture with the position of the monochromator and its subsequent transfer to the screen for display.

programs use, it is therefore described in more detail than the other programs. No examples of hard copy output are provided, it is sufficient to realise that the x/y chart recorder produces accurately scaled copies of the screen displays shown in *Figures 4d, 5a* and *9a*.

## 2. APPLICATIONS

A variety of spectrophotometers are available for performing specialist tasks, for example, single or dual wavelength monitoring at fixed or scanning wavelength. With the use of a microcomputer all of these functions are possible using a single instrument, albeit with some limitations.

### 2.1 Scanning Spectrophotometry

This type of instrument produces absorption difference spectra of the material under study. In operation two identical samples are placed in the spectrophotometer and a spectrum obtained of the region of interest. After appropriate additions to the reaction cuvette the spectrum scan is repeated and the baseline minus corrected spectrum obtained. The flow diagram in *Figure 3*

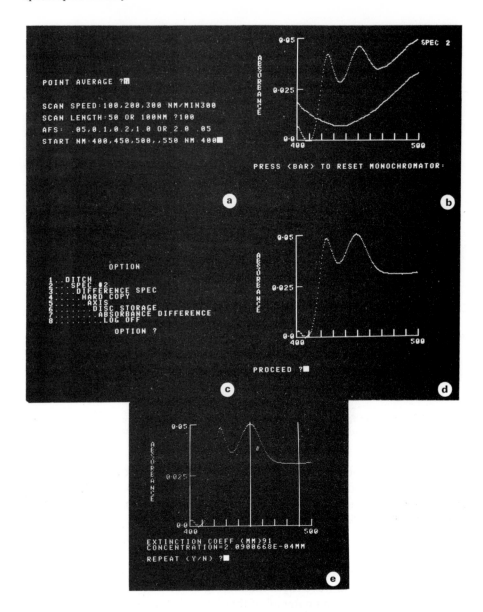

**Figure 4.** Input sequence for *Listing 2*. On entering the program the run parameters are established **(a)**, after which the microcomputer inputs the baseline (not shown) followed by the action spectrum **(b)**. A series of options are offered **(c)**; **(d)** shows the difference spectrum of (carbon monoxide reduced minus reduced) rat liver microsomes, used to determine the concentration of cytochrome P450 **(e)**.

describes *Listing 2* which can be used to control these operations. There are two main components to the program, one relates to the control of the monochromator drive unit and its synchrony with data input/storage and the other to data manipulation. A typical spectrum capture display sequence is shown in *Figure 4*.

### 2.1.1 *Monochromator Drive and Input Synchrony*

Data input must occur in sequence with each increment of the monochromator. This can be achieved using the microcomputer to control the stepper motor driving the monochromator. Given the high current which these motors draw it is not practical to power them directly from the microcomputer. A spare output line on the D/A converter may be used to control a remote motor drive unit. An alternative source for the signal is provided in the Apple by the games I/O connector (socket J14). Pins 12 − 15 generate a TTL compatible signal for uses where the current drain does not exceed 1.6 mA. In either case the only requirement is that the state of the line (i.e., lo or hi) can be controlled directly from within the program (e.g., for Pin 14 of the Apple J14 socket, a POKE − 16294, 1 sets the output high and POKE − 16295, 0 sets it low). If direct control is not possible two other approaches can be used.

(i) By locating the phasing pulse for the motor and determining how many pulses per nm there are; the microcomputer can use this information to regulate its input sequence.

(ii) A simple device can be constructed to monitor the position of the monochromator using a variable resistor (2). The vernier on monochromators rotates in synchrony with the movement of the grating. Therefore if the slide wire of a variable resistor is brought into contact with the vernier its resistance will change in direct proportion to the degree of rotation of the vernier. If a constant current is applied to the resistor its output voltage can then be calibrated in terms of volts per nm.

Once input synchrony has been obtained a sequence of events can be established. This is shown below with reference to *Listing 2*.

*Event 1*. Prepare the screen display.

On entering the program two machine language subroutines (SHAPE9 and AXIS; *Listings 2.1* and *2.2*) are loaded (line 1710) into memory. These are the shape tables which are used to format and annotate the screen display. Discussion of these programs is outside the scope of this chapter, and it is dealt with elsewhere (3,4). The subroutines are not activated until the running parameters have been established using a second subroutine which prompts the user for details of the run (lines 1400 − 1650) (*Figure 4a*).

*Event 2*. Step the monochromator motor drive forward one unit.

The monochromator drive unit is controlled from the microcomputer directly by the statement POKE 49666, 0, which sets the output of the D/A converter channel controlling the stepper motor to lo (a POKE 49666, 128 sets it hi; line 90). Each lo to hi cycle (minimum interval time 50 nsec) increments the monochromator by 0.5 nm. Line 90 also contains a time wasting loop (counting B from 1 to X) which is used to set the scan speed for the spectrum. Its precise value can be determined empirically; in the author's system values of X which provide scan rates of 100, 200 and 300 nm/min are 100, 50 and 20, respectively.

*Event 3*. Input the photomultiplier output.

Signal input and conversion relies on a standard 8-bit A/D chip. Its sampling and conversion rate is controlled from within the program. After each increment of the monochromator the A/D chip samples the output from the log ratio amplifier and digitises the signal (line 120), a PEEK to lccation 50176 allows the digitised signal to be sampled.

*Event 4.* Display and store the digitised signal.

Once the input parameters have been established the screen clears and displays annotated axes for the spectra which are to be collected (lines 1510 − 1650). The digitised absorbance value for each point of the spectrum, obtained from line 200 or 210, is displayed directly onto the screen (line 220) (*Figure 4b*). Since the memory location containing this value is plotted directly, i.e., by PEEK(50176), no distinction has to be made between the baseline and action spectrum. Storage (volatile) of each spectrum is as an integer array (lines 200 and 210). To allow repetitive scanning using the same baseline, the elements are allocated to different arrays; A%(A) is used for the baseline and B%(A) for the action and difference spectrum. The arrays are specified using the constant R (line 190); R = 1 for the baseline and R = 2 for the action spectrum.

*Event 5.* Examine whether the maximum permissible number of inputs is exceeded, if so then go to event 6, if not then repeat event 2.

Each spectrum is recorded at 2 points per nm. Two factors govern the minimum wavelength interval between inputs; the gearing of the monochromator drive motor and the speed at which the program can perform the input/storage and display steps. *Listing 2* has been used by the author at four inputs per nm, but should be usable at up to 10 inputs per nm. Incrementation is regulated using a FOR...NEXT loop (lines 80 and 250). Two standard scan lengths are used, 50 or 100 nm, and are specified by the constant W (which must be doubled to provide the correct loop size). Since the program uses a variable (W) in this FOR...NEXT loop a spectrum of varying length can be obtained up to a maximum of 250 points (i.e., the maximum permissible value which can be plotted on the *x* axes using this program). While spectra of less than 50 nm can be accommodated directly by this program without modification, longer scans require that the matrix space be extended (line 20) and the lines controlling the plot function altered so that not more than 250 elements are plotted. Since the SHAPE and AXIS subroutines are for 100 nm scans with a 650 nm maximum value these would also have to be altered.

*Event 6.* Present the main menu with manipulative options.

At the end of the spectrum the monochromator is reset (line 270), the screen is cleared, the menu displayed and the user prompted for an option (lines 290 − 390) (*Figure 4c*).

### 2.1.2 *Data Manipulation*

Any number of data handling routines can be used to transform and analyse the data post-capture to meet individual needs. *Listing 2* was written for use with a scanning spectrophotometer, the functions thus centre on the calculation of a baseline corrected difference spectrum prior to storage, and/or hard copy production.

*Calculation of a difference spectrum (Option 3)*. An iterative procedure is used in which each element is recalled sequentially from the storage array, the difference (action − baseline) is calculated and stored in an array. To minimise memory usage the uncorrected action spectrum is overwritten by the corrected spectrum (i.e., back into B%(A); lines 570−790) and the derivative spectrum is re-displayed on the screen (lines 720−770) (*Figure 4d*). In displaying the data two factors must be considered.

(i) *Screen size.* Use of Apple Page 1 of high resolution graphics limits the display to a 280 (*x* axis) by 160 (*y* axis) matrix, however, the data requires 200 by 255 point matrix for each 100 nm scan.

(ii) *Negative going spectra.* No facility is available on the Apple to plot positive and negative going points simultaneously. These could arise from the presence of a signal sign bit on the A/D output or on calculating the difference spectrum.

Both of these factors must be dealt with by the program and can be achieved by testing the value of each spectrum element and comparing it with standard values which define the display parameters (lines 570−610). By comparison with 0, negative values can be identified, the largest negative value determined, its sign changed and added to each element to make all negative values positive (lines 620−630). A new cycle must then be initiated whereby the maximum element value is determined and a scaling factor calculated (255 for an 8-bit chip, 1260 for a 12-bit chip etc.; lines 640−660). If necessary the elements are scaled down (lines 670−710) and the division factor (K) used (lines 680 and 710) is displayed on the screen (line 770). The routine described formats the spectra for output to an x/y recorder (a 200 by 255 display), thus for screen display the absorbance values are reduced further by 50%. If an accurate screen representation of the spectrum is required for dumping to a dot matrix printer, the same approach can be used but the scaling factor for the display must be determined accurately. Under these conditions it may be worth using the largest possible graphics screen available for formatting the spectra (i.e., HGR2 on the Apple).

With the BBC microcomputer a number of display modes are available, and can be accessed by the MODE command. The highest resolution display provided by MODE(0), is 640 by 256 pixels and 80 by 32 test field, and would seem to be the most appropriate for spectrum display. An additional advantage of the BBC microcomputer is the ability to move the graphics origin (using VDU 29,X;Y;) which eliminates the need to make provision for negative going signals.

*Wavelength difference measurement (Option 7)*. Interpreting a difference spectrum relies on the form and position of the peaks and/or the absorbance difference between two points on the spectrum. A subroutine which permits this type of comparison is used by Option 7 (lines 1210−1390). After prompting for the wavelengths of interest the program determines whether they fall within the range of the spectrum (lines 1240−1270). Their position is displayed on the screen, and by subtraction of the appropriate spectrum elements (lines 1280−1310) the optical difference between the two points is calculated and displayed. If an extinction coefficient is supplied the molar concentration that this represents (lines 1320 and 1360) (*Figure 4e*) is also given.

*Storage of the spectrum (Option 6).* Both the baseline and difference spectra are stored as arrays. After a spectrum has been obtained there is an option to transfer the spectrum (baseline corrected or uncorrected action spectrum) on to floppy disc (lines 1090 – 1200) as a text file. The user is prompted for a file name each time the function is used, however, the listing could be changed to include a variable which increments each time the option is used as shown below.

M = M + 1
G$ = G$ + STR$(M)

M is used to increment the file and is converted to a string value M$ before addition to the string G$ (the file name). This produces a new string which is the incremented file name. For the first spectrum of any set a file is automatically initialled (e.g., SPECTRUM) and subsequent spectra would then be incremented .. SPECTRUM 1,..... SPECTRUM n.

Transfer of data to floppy disc not only reduces the amount of RAM which is required for a given set of analyses but produces a permanent record of the spectrum, which can be re-entered into the microcomputer for re-analysis or transfer to other machines [e.g., microcomputer to microcomputer (5) or microcomputer to mainframe (Section 3.3)].

*Hard copy (Options 4 and 5).* Using a D/A chip each spectrum element is regenerated as a voltage directly proportional to its absorbance value [i.e., A% of A%(M)], or wavelength [i.e., M of A%(M)]. The output lines from the D/A converter can be controlled directly by POKE statements; this allows the pen of an x/y recorder to be positioned from within a program. With reference to *Listing 2* a POKE to 49664 is used to control one output channel on the D/A converter (the x position) and a POKE to 49665 controls the other channel (y position). An iterative routine which POKE's these locations with the wavelength and absorbance values is used to draw the spectrum (lines 800 – 920). Interrupt statements are used to allow time to position the pen on the recorder and operate the penlift (lines 840 and 900). Since the values plotted are relative voltages an axis or other scaling routine must also be included. Lines 930 – 1080 plot both the $x$ and $y$ axes with subdivisions. If a dot matrix printer, with a graphics ability, is used the screen contents can be dumped directly onto the printer. While this is a highly flexible system which allows the transfer of axis labels, it means that greater care must be exercised in formatting the screen display. The same spectrum formatting routines can be used as described above and annotation is possible on the Apple using shape tables or high resolution character generators (Section 3). This is laborious and largely avoidable since commercial software which allows mixed graphics on the Apple are available. With some microcomputers (e.g., the BBC Acorn) mixed graphics are built into the system which eliminates this problem.

*Leaving the program (Option 8).* When either a new analysis is initiated or upon exiting from the program all variables are reset and/or the data lost. A useful safety net is provided if the user is asked to verify the exit or reset command, which is commonly found to be a vital component of any such program. If the command is not verified the user can be returned to the main menu with all set variables and constants intact (lines 410 – 420).

## 2.2 Dual Wavelength Spectrophotometry

Where there is an overall increase in the spectrum it may be necessary to relate the change at a particular wavelength to a reference point which is relatively stable. This function can be achieved using a purpose-built dual wavelength spectro-photometer. Operationally a dual wavelength instrument can be considered a variant of a single wavelength instrument. With both, the log ratio amplifier produces a continuous signal which represents the action minus reference absorbance for the latter and absorbance at wavelength 1 minus absorbance at wavelength 2 for the former. Data capture is therefore continuous and, in a manner analogous to that described below for single wavelength instruments, a time base can be introduced by the insertion of a calibrated counting loop in the input sequence. If the microcomputer has an internal clock function this can be sampled to provide a time base for the input. For the Apple a number of companies offer add-on boards with this function.

### 2.2.1 *Use of a Scanning Split Beam Spectrophotometer as a Dual Wavelength Machine*

Since a scanning spectrophotometer produces a spectrum of the material under study it is able to provide absorbance differences at different wavelengths; in effect the same information produced by dual wavelength machines. A microcomputer can be used to control and format this information and a number of wavelength pairs can be followed simultaneously. The major disadvantage of this approach is that data input is not continuous thereby reducing the time resolution for measurements. *Listing 3* is able to utilise the spectrum information generated during a scan to produce dual wavelength measurements. In operation it has many features in common with *Listing 2*.

(i) *Monochromator drive and input synchrony.* This is identical in *Listings 2* and *3* both in terms of data capture and display. In the dual wavelength mode one addition has been made to the input sequence. In the FOR.....NEXT loop of line 70 which is used to repeatedly scan the spectrum, a user prompt is employed as a means of repeated scanning. Alternatively a calibrated counting loop or clock could be used. The data is formatted for screen display as in *Listing 2,* the only difference is that a set of spectra are produced for each experiment (*Figure 5a*). To accommodate the multiscan function the run parameter prompt sequence is altered; the user is prompted for two extra parameters, the time intervals between scans (line 690) and the number of repeat scans (line 700). The system is limited to a maximum of eight spectra per sample, the only restriction is storage mode. With 32k of memory up to 10 spectra can be stored in RAM. By increasing the amount of RAM or by dumping the spectra onto floppy disc the number can be further increased. The latter operation requires a separate spectrum manipulation program to recover the spectra and calculate absorbance differences.

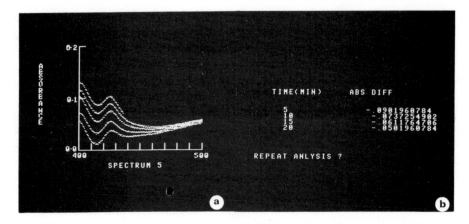

**Figure 5.** Use of a single wavelength spectrophotometer as a dual wavelength instrument. Repetitive scanning of a sample allows the use of a single wavelength instrument in a dual wavelength mode. The time course of the O-demethylation of *p*-nitroanisole by suspensions of isolated hepatocytes is shown **(a)**. After spectrum capture the absorbance difference at given wavelength pairs can be determined **(b)** as a function of time.

(ii) *Data manipulation and hard copy production.* Unlike *Listing 2* this routine does not offer a menu at the end of the input sequence, instead two fixed options are available. Lines 330 − 370 allow the transfer of data to floppy disc and lines 380 − 490 allow dual wavelength analysis in a manner analogous to *Listing 2*. This prompts for the wavelength of interest, calculates the absorbance difference and displays it as a table of absorbance change with time (*Figure 5b*). The formatting of the data can obviously be changed to meet individual needs; for example, absorbance changes could be expressed in terms of concentration or as velocity plots. Similarly data may be recorded manually or alternatively sent to a printing device by inserting a CALL statement to the printer after the display commands. After each analysis it is possible to repeat the analysis at a different wavelength pair (lines 480 − 490), to recycle, or to log out of the program (lines 510 − 540). By the addition of the plotting routine used in *Listing 2* each spectrum set could also be dumped to an x/y recorder (or matrix printer), the only modification required is the inclusion of a FOR....NEXT loop to generate each spectrum in turn.

### 2.3 Single Wavelength Spectrophotometry

This is potentially the simplest data acquisition function to establish and it does not have the added complication of input/event synchrony. Using an ordinary chart recorder the chart speed can be used to provide the time base while the microcomputer provides the absorbance value. *Listing 4* enables the user to monitor absorbance change at a fixed wavelength with a fixed cuvette pair. The input control statements for this program are identical to those in *Listing 2* (lines 40 − 100). Rather than displaying the absorbance change on the screen as a velocity plot, numerical data is displayed on screen and the velocity plot is produced simultaneously by the chart recorder (lines 110 − 360) (*Figure 6a* and *b*). The data are displayed as a table of absolute absorbance and time plus the absorbance and

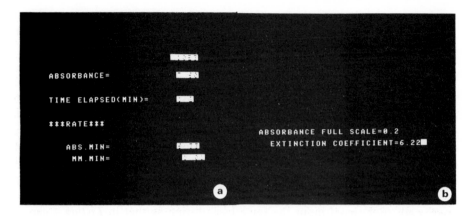

**Figure 6.** Fixed wavelength spectrophotometry. When used at a fixed wavelength, absolute absorbance values can be determined (**a**) prior to calculation of reaction rates (**b**).

molar concentration (if an extinction coefficient is supplied). The time base for the program is generated by a calibrated counting loop (lines 220 and 230). An interrupt facility is included in the input sequence (line 90) to allow it to be reset (i.e., to Time = 0) or to initiate a new cycle. Since the absorbance change is not retained within RAM there is no possibility of post-capture manipulation, however, this could easily by achieved by modifying *Listing 4*. The number of input points would need to be limited and a matrix could then be established (absorbance/unit time) for storing the velocity plot.

If the spectrophotometer is equipped with an automatic cuvette change facility *Listing 5* could be used in a 'passive mode'. That is, as the cuvette being monitored is changed, the absorbance alters producing a sharp deflection on the chart recorder as the light beam is obscured. Obviously the screen display sequence (lines 140 − 360) is inappropriate under these circumstances. If it were not possible to control or monitor the cuvette changer directly, the simple expedient of timing the interval between cuvettes would allow synchronised input of absorbance values. If such a procedure is employed, or if the operation is controlled by the microcomputer, then data input may be directly synchronised with each cuvette in a manner analogous to the input sequence used in scanning spectrophotometry. The absorbance change in each cuvette could be stored as a matrix of optical change *versus* time and this would allow mathematical transformation prior to displaying the velocity plot on the screen and/or dumping to a chart recorder (6).

### 2.4 Densiometry of Polyacrylamide Gels

Polyacrylamide gel electrophoresis is a very powerful tool in the rapid analysis of protein mixtures and with the development of 2-dimensional gel electrophoresis the resolving power of the technique has greatly increased (7). To aid in the interpretation of the electrophoretic patterns and to facilitate comparisons, densiometric scanning of the gels was introduced. Using relatively simple programs the densiometric readings can be transferred directly to a microcomputer and subjected to a number of transformations. A distinction must be drawn between the analysis of 1- and 2-dimensional gels.

### 2.4.1 *1-Dimensional Gels*

1-Dimensional gels, using either slabs or sticks of acrylamide (or other suitable support material), resolve proteins into a series of discrete bands which are separated along the longitudinal axis of the gel. In determining the relative concentration of each band it is common practice to scan the gel (at 550 nm with Coomassie Blue stained gels for example) to produce an absorbance profile. In spectrophotometric terms this is strictly analogous to single wavelength scanning, except that the position of the gel relative to the detector varies rather than the wavelength. For signal input the same basic listing as that in *Listing 4* can be used, except that the display functions need to be changed to correspond to that of *Listing 2*. Input and gel position synchrony could be achieved by determining the maximum number of inputs possible over the full span of the carriage movement. A time wasting loop could then be used in the program to ensure that the maximum number of points to be collected are spread evenly over the length of the gel. A more systematic approach can be adopted by locating and monitoring the carriage control line. The variable resistor monitor described above (Section 2.1.1) could also be used in this situation. Data transformation would employ the same procedures as those shown in *Listing 2,* and depending on the number of data points generated by each scan, the data could be stored as an integer array for direct processing or transferred to floppy disc.

One feature not shown in *Listing 2* which would be of use in interpreting gel data would be a facility to integrate the peaks produced. Essentially the principles and approach would be similar to those used in integration of chromatograph peaks discussed in Chapter 8. A number of different strategies could be adopted, although peak integration itself (in relative terms) would be quite simple since addition of the individual elements of which each peak is composed would produce a value directly related to peak area. This could be achieved automatically with routines to search the spectrum for maxima and minima and identification of peaks prior to integration. A program with these functions has been published (8). An alternative approach is to direct peak integration interactively. The microcomputer could display the (blank corrected) densitometer profile and prompt the user for peak parameters which would define the start and finish of a peak. The advantage of this approach is that shoulders on peaks would be easy to deal with and the analysis limited to groups of peaks within a gel.

### 2.4.2 *2-Dimensional gels*

In 2-dimensional gel electrophoresis a protein spot pattern is produced which is characterised with reference to two axes. Along the $x$ axis separation is based on isoelectric criteria and along the $y$ axis on molecular weight. A typical gel can result in up to 2000 individual protein spots appearing on a gel. A single densiometric scan cannot, therefore, be used to define a 2-dimensional gel. Instead the gel (usually 15 x 10 cm) must be scanned repeatedly; the greater the number of lines derived per cm of gel the more precise the digital profile obtained (9). Because of the variation inherent in the technique, spot patterns of the same protein mix on different gels are not usually exactly superimposable. In order to compare gels it is therefore necessary to vary the computerised gel display, this requires sophisticated interactive graphics. Given the large amount of memory required for data input and analysis it is impractical to implement this facility using the more common (and inexpensive) microcomputers to which this chapter refers. With the recent introduction of high-powered microcomputers the situation may soon change.

Examples of computer controlled 2-dimensional gel analysis systems are to be found in references $10-12$. Typically a single gel scanned at a resolution of 100 $\mu$m produces $1.5-2.5$ x $10^6$ 8-bit numbers. Analysis of the data requires transfer of the data to a large capacity disc storage module, in reference 9 for example, a Digital Corporation PDP-11/60 minicomputer is used.

## 2.5 Signal to Noise Ratio

With all the programs discussed two features can be included which greatly reduce the signal to noise ratio of the input.

(i) *Signal averaging*. This can be achieved by repeated scanning of the spectrum then averaging the spectra to produce a composite. A simpler approach is to point average the signal at the input stage. The two major programs presented (*Listing 2*, lines $100-160$; *Listing 3,* lines $110-170$) both contain this feature. At the signal input stage there is a loop to sample the signal from 1 to $n$ times after which it is averaged prior to transfer to the storage matrix. The use of this facility does reduce the maximum possible scanning rate of a spectrum and may distort kinetic plots.

(ii) *Curve smoothing*. Once the complete spectrum has been stored the noise level can be reduced by averaging the value of adjacent points. A routine for this is given in *Listing 6* and discussed in Section 3.2. Its use can, however, produce a shift in absorbance maxima which must be allowed for in plotting routines, it may also result in a loss of resolution.

## 3. DATA RETRIEVAL AND MANIPULATION

A major advantage of spectrum capture using microcomputers is the potential to regenerate and submit the data to further analysis. In this section two routines are illustrated which rely to some extent on user development and one which uses the Appleplot package of programs. Although the discussion is limited to Apple software, similar packages are available for other machines.

## 3.1 Data Formatting using Commercial Software

With the Apple, two packages are available for improving the quality of data display, which may be of use in preparing data for publication. Of the two

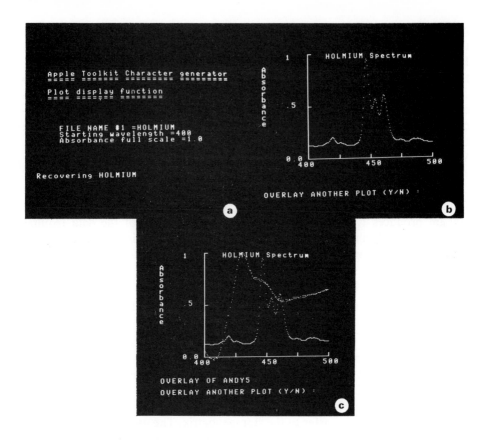

**Figure 7.** Use of Apple Tool Kit high resolution graphics. Data can be retrieved from floppy disc (**a**) and redisplayed using commerical software packages (**b** and **c**).

systems one can be incorporated directly into the input program (Apple Tool Kit character generator) while the other (Appleplot) is used exclusively with data retrieved from floppy disc.

### 3.1.1 *Character Generator*

This allows mixed graphics and both upper and lower case characters. Since it forms part of a separate package it can be used as a subroutine of the main control program and called to format the screen display. *Figure 7* is an example of data which has been retrieved from floppy disc and re-displayed using this utility (*Listing 5*). While it is able to improve data display it nevertheless requires the development of a control program to take full advantage of its capabilities if it is to be used with TEXT files. An alternative approach would be to incorporate this feature directly into the input and display sequence of *Listing 2* for example. This would remove the need to use shape tables to define and label the axes and would make the display more flexible given that the graphics screen can be written to directly.

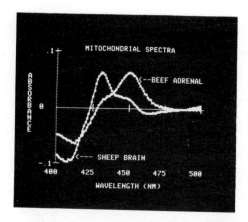

**Figure 8.** Use of Appleplot. Appleplot is a graphics package for the Apple. This figure illustrates the graph plotting with overlay and labelling facilities which it provides. The diagram shows the (carbon monoxide, reduced minus reduced) spectra of beef adrenal and rat brain mitochondria.

### 3.1.2 *Appleplot*

This program accepts stored data and replots it in a number of different ways. The data must however conform to the following sequence.

Number of data points
x(1)
y(1)
x(2)
y(2)
etc.

A simple BASIC program can be used to retrieve spectra stored as TEXT files and then re-format them for use with Appleplot. *Figure 8* shows the type of detail which is possible; obviously velocity data could also be used in these plots and the overlay facility of Appleplot allows the multiscan data to be used.

With the BBC microcomputer mixed graphics are standard, which simplifies the formatting of the graphics prior to dumping to hard copy. Use of the VDU 4 command, which causes the text to be written at the cursor position, is of great value here. As with the Apple a number of commercial graphics packages are available (e.g., The Acorn Graphs and Charts package).

For both the graphics generator and Appleplot enhanced data it is advantageous to have a dot matrix printer to which the screen can be dumped. If one is not available the simple expedient of photographing the screen display (as the author has done here) provides a cheap and acceptable alternative. Techniques for this are described in Chapter 4 (Section 4.1.1).

### 3.2 Spectrum Derivitisation

Derivative analysis provides a powerful technique in resolving complex spectra (13). The analysis involves computing the difference between the original spectrum and the same spectrum which has been shifted a finite distance along its

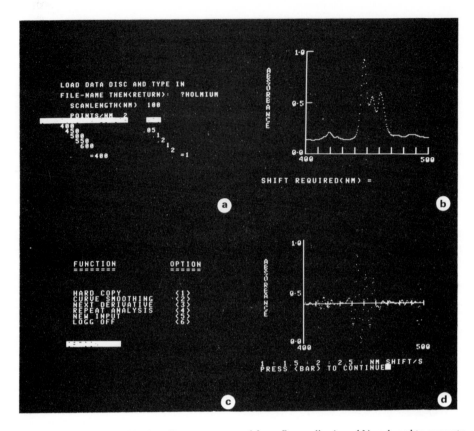

**Figure 9.** Spectrum derivitisation. Data are recovered from floppy disc (**a** and **b**) and used to generate a series of difference spectra (**c** and **d**) up to the 4th derivative. This simple example shows how the three central components of the Holmium spectrum can be isolated.

*x* axis. The calculated difference is assigned to the wavelength corresponding to the midpoint of wavelength 1 and 2 (the offset distance between the spectra). Higher derivatives can be obtained by repeating the procedure. An analysis of this type can be performed immediately after data capture or form part of a separate 'off-line' facility.

Since digitised spectra are stored in a matrix it is a relatively simple procedure to 'move' the spectrum. This can be achieved by adding *n* elements to the matrix element specifying the wavelength prior to subtraction from the original element. For example:

$$A\%(M) - A\%(M+1)$$

This has moved the spectrum one unit prior to subtraction from the original spectrum. The difference is stored in a separate array prior to display and/or dumping to an x/y recorder. The program used by the author (*Listing 6*) also contains a curve smoothing routine to reduce the background noise generated by the analysis. The screen formatting routines are those used in *Listings 2.1* and *2.2*. Spectra are retrieved from floppy disc (lines 50 – 340) and displayed on the screen

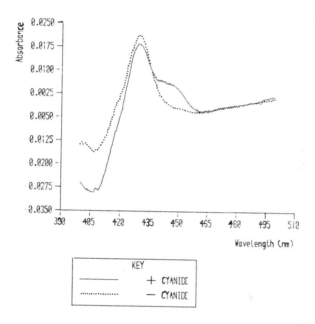

**Figure 10.** Use of a mainframe plotting macro after data transfer from a microcomputer. Using an Apple to mainframe interface a spectrum is transferred to the mainframe and replotted using a graphics macro.

(line 350), a typical analysis sequence is shown in *Figure 9*. After derivitisation (from the 1st to the 4th derivative) subroutines are available to produce a hard copy or re-analyse the data (lines 720 – 820), as shown in *Figure 9c*.

### 3.3 **Transfer to Mainframe Computers**

One obvious advantage of spectra stored on floppy discs is the ability to transfer it from machine to machine, not only from microcomputer to microcomputer but also from microcomputer to mainframe. The details of transfer, and program description, are outside the scope of this chapter. Both the hardware and software required are available for Apple and BBC microcomputers. The author employs a system in which Apple TEXT files are transferred direct to a mainframe computer (ICL 2960), which enables the use of a range of facilities. For example, mainframe BASIC can be used to reformat the data prior to use with a plotting macro as shown in *Figure 10*. This in effect is a sophisticated form of the Appleplot facility. One more obvious application is the possibility of more complex spectrum analysis, for example curve fitting programs to isolate spectrum components. In general the microcomputer and mainframe link is of great value both in terms of data presentation and in the more complex analytical protocols allowed.

## 4. ACKNOWLEDGEMENTS

I thank Mr P. Welch (Computing Laboratory, The University of Kent) for the Apple to mainframe transfer programs and Mr R. Newsam (Biological Laboratory, The University of Kent) for the photography. The programs described were developed for projects funded by the Medical Research Council.

## 5. REFERENCES

1. Unsworth,W.D. (1982) *Laboratory Microcomputers,* **4**, 11.
2. Butler,W.L. (1972) in *Methods in Enzymology Vol XXXIV,* Pietro,A.S. (ed.), published by Academic Press. p. 3.
3. Zaks,R. (1979) in *Programming the 6502.*
4. Applesoft II Basic Programming Reference Manual, p. 91.
5. Stockwell,P.A., van Eerten,M.T.W. and Forrester,I.T. (1982) *Biochem. Group Newsletter,* **6**, 13.
6. Maskill,H. and Thompson,J.J. (1982) *Laboratory Microcomputers,* **1**, 11.
7. O'Farrell,P.H. (1975) *J. Biol. Chem.,* **250**, 4007.
8. Crosby,I.M. (1982) *Biochem. Microcomputer Newsletter,* **6**, 7.
9. Taylor,J., Anderson,N.L., Coulter,B.P., Scandora,A.E. and Anderson,J. (1979) in *Electrophoresis '79: Analytical Methods of Clinical Applications,* Radola,B.J. and de Gruyter,W. (eds.), p. 329.
10. Kronberg,H., Zimmer,H.G. and Neuhoff,V. (1980) *Electrophoresis,* **1**, 27.
11. Manabe,T., Kojima,K., Kitzukawa,S., Hoshino,T. and Okuyama,T. (1981) *J. Biochem.,* **89**, 841-855.
12. Vo,K.-P., Miller,M.J., Geidoschek,E.D., Nielsen,C., Olson,A. and Xuong,N.H. (1981) *Anal. Biochem.,* **112**, 258.
13. Butler,W.L. (1979) in *Methods Enzymol.,* **16**, 501.

## APPENDIX
### Program listings

**Listing 1.** Apple 'HELLO' program to control user functions.

```
10  ONERR  GOTO 30
20  D$ = CHR$ (4)
30  TEXT : HOME
40  HTAB 7: VTAB 3: INVERSE : PRINT "DIRECTORY FOR MAIN MENUS": NORMAL
50  VTAB 6: HTAB 8: PRINT "SERIES          OPTION"
60  VTAB 7: HTAB 8: PRINT "======      ======"
70  VTAB 10: HTAB 8: PRINT "SPECTRSCOPY       <1>"
80  VTAB 11: HTAB 8: PRINT "DATA DISPLAY      <2>"
90  VTAB 12: HTAB 8: PRINT "APPLE TOOL KIT    <3>"
100 VTAB 13: HTAB 8: PRINT "APPLE PLOT        <4>"
110 VTAB 14: HTAB 8: PRINT "TELETYPE          <5>"
120 VTAB 15: HTAB 8: PRINT "QUIT              <6>"
130 VTAB 19: HTAB 10: INVERSE : PRINT "OPTION = ";: NORMAL : GET A
140 IF A < 1 THEN 130
150 IF A > 6 THEN 130
160 ON A GOTO 180,290,420,430,440,170
170 HOME : VTAB 10: HTAB 15: INVERSE : PRINT "BYE BYE!": NORMAL : END
180 HOME
190 HTAB 11: VTAB 2: INVERSE : PRINT "SPECTROSCOPY OPTIONS": NORMAL
200 HTAB 9: VTAB 5: PRINT "SCANNING SPEC      <1>"
210 HTAB 9: VTAB 6: PRINT "SINGLE WAVELENGTH  <2>"
220 HTAB 9: VTAB 7: PRINT "MULTI-SCAN         <3>"
230 HTAB 9: VTAB 8: PRINT "MAIN MENU          <4>"
240 HTAB 13: VTAB 12: INVERSE : PRINT "OPTION =";: NORMAL : GET B
250 ON B GOTO 260,270,280,30
260 PRINT : PRINT D$;"EXEC SCANNING"
270 PRINT : PRINT D$;"RUN SINGLENM"
280 PRINT : PRINT D$;"EXEC MULTISCAN"
290 HOME
300 VTAB 4: HTAB 15: INVERSE : PRINT "DATA DISPLAY ": NORMAL
310 VTAB 6: HTAB 8: PRINT "PROGRAMME          OPTION"
320 VTAB 7: HTAB 8: PRINT "=========      ======"
330 VTAB 10: HTAB 8: PRINT "GRAPHICAL DISPLAY   <1>"
340 VTAB 11: HTAB 8: PRINT "TABULATED DIPLAY    <2>"
350 VTAB 13: HTAB 8: PRINT "MAINFRAME FORMATTER <4>"
360 VTAB 12: HTAB 8: PRINT "SPEC. DERIVITISATION <3>"
```

```
370   VTAB 14: HTAB 8: PRINT "MAIN MENU              <5>"
380   VTAB 16: HTAB 10: INVERSE : PRINT "OPTION :";: NORMAL : GET B
390   IF B < 1 THEN 290
400   IF B > 5 THEN 290
410   ON B GOTO 490,500,510,520,30
420   PRINT : PRINT D$;"RUN TOOLKIT"
430   PRINT : PRINT D$;"RUN HELLOPLOT"
440   HOME
450   VTAB 8: HTAB 6: INVERSE : PRINT "LOADING TELETYPE PROGRAMME": NORMAL
460   PRINT : PRINT D$;"BLOAD TELE"
470   HOME : VTAB 8: HTAB 6: PRINT "TELETYPE LOADED": END
480   PRINT : PRINT D$;"RUN TABDISP"
490   PRINT : PRINT D$;" RUN GRAPHICSDISP"
500   PRINT : PRINT D$;"RUNTABDISP"
510   PRINT : PRINT D$;"RUNMAINFORM"
520   PRINT : PRINT D$;"RUNDERIVATIVE"
```

**Listing 2.** Control program for a single wavelength scanning spectrophotometer.

```
5     REM: LOAD GRAPHICS AND PROMPT FOR RUN CONDITIONS
10    GOSUB 1660
20    DIM A%(200),B%(200)
30    GOSUB 1400
40    DRAW 2 AT 280,5:R = 1: GOTO 70
50    DRAW 3 AT 280,5:R = 2
60    HOME : POKE   - 16304,0: POKE 16297,0
70    POKE 49667,129: POKE 50179,154
80    FOR A = 1 TO W * 2
90    FOR AA = 1 TO 2: POKE 49666,0: FOR B = 1 TO X: NEXT : POKE 49666,128: NEXT
100   IF Z < > 1 GOTO 120
110   FOR BB = 1 TO Y
120   POKE 50178,0: POKE 50178,8: WAIT 50178,32,1
130   IF Z < > 1 GOTO 190
140   VV = PEEK (50176):V = V + VV: NEXT BB
150   V = V / Y
160   A%(A) = V: GOTO 180
170   B%(A) = V
180   HPLOT 70 + A,(144 - (V * .56)): GOTO 230
190   IF R = 2 THEN 210
200   A%(A) = PEEK (50176): GOTO 220
210   B%(A) = PEEK (50176)
220   HPLOT A + 70,(144 - PEEK (50176) * .56)
230   IF PEEK ( - 16384) < 127 THEN 250
240   POKE  - 16368,0: GOSUB 1730
250   V = 0: NEXT A
260   HOME : VTAB 23: PRINT "PRESS <BAR> TO RESET MONOCHROMATOR:";: GET A$
270   FOR A = 1 TO W * 4: POKE 49666,0: FOR B = 1 TO 25:  : POKE 49666,128: NEXT
      NEXT
290   TEXT : HOME : VTAB 6: HTAB 14: PRINT "OPTION": PRINT
300   PRINT "  1..DITCH"
310   PRINT "  2...SPEC #2"
320   PRINT "  3....DIFFERENCE SPEC"
330   PRINT "  4.....HARD COPY"
340   PRINT "  5......AXIS"
350   PRINT "  6.......DISC STORAGE"
360   PRINT "  7........ABSORBANCE DIFFERENCE"
370   PRINT "  8.........LOG OFF": PRINT
380   HTAB 15: PRINT "OPTION ?";: GET A
390   ON A GOTO 410,470,530,800,930,1090,1210,400
400   HOME : VTAB 10: HTAB 10: PRINT "LOGGED OUT": END
410   HOME : VTAB 10: HTAB 10: PRINT "ARE YOU SURE?";: GET A$
420   IF A$ = "N" THEN 290
430   VTAB 12: HTAB 10: PRINT "SAME PARAMETERS ?";: GET A$
440   IF A$ = "N" THEN 30
450   GOSUB 1510
460   GOTO 40
470   IF R = 1 THEN 50
480   IF R > = 2 THEN  GOSUB 1510
490   FOR A = 1 TO W * 2
500   HPLOT A + 70,(144 - A%(A) * .56)
510   NEXT A
520   GOTO 50
525   REM: START OF DIFFERENCE SPECTRUM
530   IF R < 2 THEN 290
540   IF R = 3 THEN 720
550   HOME : VTAB 10: HTAB 5:KL = 0:GG = 0:H = 255
560   PRINT "CALCULATING DIFFERENCE SPECTRUM"
570   FOR A = 1 TO W * 2
580   B%(A) = B%(A) - A%(A)
590   IF B%(A) < GG THEN GG = B%(A)
600   IF B%(A) > H THEN H = B%(A)
610   NEXT A
620   IF GG > = 0 THEN 670
630   GG = GG * - 1:H = 255
640   FOR A = 1 TO W * 2
650   B%(A) = B%(A) + GG: IF B%(A) > H THEN H = B%(A)
660   NEXT A
```

199

```
670  IF H < = 255 THEN 720
680  FOR K = 2 TO 5:KK = H / K
690  IF KK < = 255 THEN 710
700  NEXT
710  FOR A = 1 TO W * 2:B$(A) = B$(A) / K: NEXT :KL = 1
720  GOSUB 1510
730  FOR A = 1 TO W * 2
740  HPLOT A + 70,(144 - B$(A) * .56)
750  NEXT
760  HOME : IF KL < > 1 THEN 780
770  VTAB 23: INVERSE : PRINT "DIVISION BY  ";: PRINT K: NORMAL
780  VTAB 24: PRINT "PROCEED ?";: GET A$
790  R = 3: GOTO 290
795  REM: START OF SPECTRUM PLOT
800  HOME : VTAB 10: HTAB 7: PRINT "SPECTRUM PLOT"
810  IF R < 2 THEN 830
820  POKE 49664,1: POKE 49665,B$(1): GOTO 840
830  POKE 49664,1: POKE 49665,A$(1)
840  VTAB 20: HTAB 5: PRINT "PRESS <BAR> TO CONTINUE:";: GET A$
850  FOR A = 1 TO W * 2
860  IF R < 2 THEN 880
870  POKE 49664,A: POKE 49665,B$(A): GOTO 890
880  POKE 49664,A: POKE 49665,A$(A)
890  NEXT
900  HOME : VTAB 23: PRINT "PRESS <BAR> TO CONTINUE: ";: GET A$
910  POKE 49664,255: POKE 49665,0
920  GOTO 290
930  HOME : VTAB 10: HTAB 10: PRINT "AXIS-PLOT"
940  POKE 49664,200: POKE 49665,0
950  VTAB 23: HTAB 5: PRINT "PRESS <BAR> TO CONTINUE:";: GET A$
960  FOR X = 200 TO 0 STEP  - 20
970  POKE 49664,X: FOR F = 1 TO 150: NEXT
980  POKE 49665,10: FOR F = 1 TO 150: NEXT : FOR F = 10 TO 0 STEP  - 1: POKE
     49665,F: NEXT
990  FOR F = 1 TO 150: NEXT
1000 NEXT
1010 FOR Y = 0 TO 255 STEP 51
1020 POKE 49665,Y: FOR F = 1 TO 500: NEXT
1030 POKE 49664,20: FOR F = 1 TO 300: NEXT : FOR F = 20 TO 0 STEP  - 1: POKE
     49665,F: NEXT
1040 FOR F = 1 TO 300: NEXT
1050 NEXT
1060 VTAB 23: HTAB 5: PRINT "PRESS <BAR> TO CONTINUE:";: GET A$
1070 POKE 49664,255: POKE 49665,0
1080 GOTO 290
1085 REM: START OF FLOPPY TRANSFER
1090 HOME : VTAB 10: PRINT "DISC STORAGE"
1100 VTAB 13: PRINT "PUT A DATA DISC IN NOW"
1110 VTAB 20: INPUT "FILE NAME: ";G$
1120 PRINT D$;"OPEN";G$
1130 PRINT D$;"WRITE";G$
1140 FOR A = 1 TO W * 2
1150 IF R < 2 THEN 1170
1160 PRINT B$(A): GOTO 1180
1170 PRINT A$(A)
1180 NEXT A
1190 PRINT D$;"CLOSE";G$
1200 GOTO 290
1205 REM: DIFFERENCE CALCULATION
1210 IF R < 2 THEN 290
1220 POKE  - 16304,0: POKE  - 16297,0
1230 HOME : VTAB 23: PRINT "ABSORBANCE DIFFERENCE...W1 - W2"
1240 INPUT "W1= ";FG
1250 IF FG < FF THEN 1240: IF FG > (FF + (W*2)) THEN 1240
1260 INPUT "W2= ";GF
1270 IF GF < FF THEN 1260: IF GF > (FF + (W*2)) THEN 1260
1280 MA = (FG - FF) * 2:MB = (GF - FF) * 2
1290 HPLOT MA + 70,0 TO MA + 70,144
1300 HPLOT MB + 70,0 TO MB + 70,144
1310 CC = (B$(MA) - B$(MB)) * (EE / 255)
1320 HOME : VTAB 23: PRINT "ABS DIFF=";: PRINT CC
1330 INPUT "EXTINCTION COEFF (MM)";I
1340 IF I = 0 THEN 1370
1350 C = CC / I
1360 PRINT "CONCENTRATION=";: PRINT C;: PRINT "MM"
1370 PRINT : PRINT "REPEAT (Y/N) ?";: GET A$
1380 IF A$ = "Y" THEN 1210
1390 GOTO 290
1395  REM: INPUT RUN CONDITIONS
1400 HOME : VTAB 5: HTAB 10:R = 0:V = 0:Z = 0
1410 VTAB 4: HTAB 4: PRINT "POINT AVERAGE ?";: GET A$: FLASH : PRINT A$: NORMAL
     : IF A$ = "N" GOTO 1440
1420 Z = 1: VTAB 6: HTAB 4: PRINT "HOW MANY POINT AVERAGES(1-4) ?";: GET Y: FLAS
H : PRINT Y: NORMAL
1430 X = 1: GOTO 1480
1440 VTAB 8: HTAB 4: INPUT "SCAN SPEED:100,200,300 NM/MIN";B$
1450 IF B$ = "200" THEN X = 50: GOTO 1480
1460 IF B$ = "100" THEN X = 100: GOTO 1480
1470 X = 20
1480 VTAB 10: HTAB 4: INPUT "SCAN LENGTH:50 OR 100NM ?";W
```

200

```
1490  VTAB 12: HTAB 4: INPUT "AFS: .05,0.1,0.2,1.0 OR 2.0 ";EE
1500  VTAB 14: HTAB 4: INPUT "START NM:400,450,500,,550 NM ";FF
1510  HGR : HCOLOR= 7: SCALE= 10: ROT= 0
1520  POKE 232,200: POKE 233,84
1530  DRAW 1 AT 80,3
1540  POKE 232,128: POKE 233,80: SCALE= 1
1550  DRAW 14 AT 50,142: DRAW 1 AT 10,30
1560  IF FF = 400 THEN   DRAW 5 AT 65,153: DRAW 6 AT 263,148
1570  IF FF = 450 THEN   DRAW 11 AT 64,154: DRAW 12 AT 264,148
1580  IF FF = 500 THEN   DRAW 6 AT 63,148: DRAW 7 AT 263,148
1590  IF FF = 550 THEN   DRAW 12 AT 64,148: DRAW 13 AT 264,148
1600  IF EE = .05 THEN   DRAW 15 AT 33,75: DRAW 16 AT 42,8
1610  IF EE = .1 THEN   DRAW 17 AT 51,5: DRAW 16 AT 42,77
1620  IF EE = .2 THEN   DRAW 17 AT 52,75: DRAW 18 AT 50,5
1630  IF EE = 1 THEN   DRAW 19 AT 50,77: DRAW 20 AT 55,7
1640  IF EE = 2 THEN   DRAW 20 AT 55,77: DRAW 21 AT 49,1
1650  RETURN
1655  REM: INPUT GRAPHICS SUBROUTINES
1660  HOME : VTAB 10: HTAB 7: PRINT "SPECTRAL CAPTURE AND MANIPULATION"
1670  VTAB 12: HTAB 7: PRINT "USING AN ITT 2020"
1680  VTAB 14: HTAB 7: PRINT "A. LODOLA: UNIVERSITY OF KENT"
1690  VTAB 20: HTAB 5: PRINT "PRESS <BAR> TO STOP SPECTRUM CAPTURE"
1700  HTAB 5: PRINT "ANY TIME DURING THE RUN"
1710  D$ =  CHR$ (4): PRINT D$;"BLOAD SHAPE9": PRINT D$;"BLOAD AXIS"
1720  RETURN
1730  HOME : VTAB 23: PRINT "<1> TO CONTINUE,<2> FOR MAIN MENU:";: GET A$
1740  IF A$ = "1" THEN  HOME : RETURN
1750  HOME : GOTO 290
```

**Listing 2.1.** Shape table subroutine for *Listing 2*.

Starting address for program: $5080

| *Shape* | *Hexadecimal starting address* | |
|---|---|---|
| | lo-bit | hi-bit |
| Absorbance | 2D | 00 |
| Spec1 | CO | 00 |
| Spec2 | 00 | 01 |
| Proceed ? | 3E | 01 |
| 400 | AE | 01 |
| 500 | D7 | 01 |
| 600 | 03 | 02 |
| 420 | 30 | 02 |
| 520 | 58 | 02 |
| 620 | 81 | 02 |
| 450 | AA | 02 |
| 550 | D5 | 02 |
| 650 | 02 | 03 |
| 0.0 | 2E | 03 |
| 0.025 | 4E | 03 |
| 0.05 | 89 | 03 |
| 0.1 | B6 | 03 |
| 0.2 | D2 | 03 |
| 0.5 | F0 | 03 |
| 1.0 | 01 | 04 |
| 2.0 | 1C | 24 |

```
5080:   15   00   2D   00   C0   00   00   01
5088:   3E   01   AE   01   D7   01   03   02
5090:   30   02   58   02   81   02   AA   02
5098:   D5   02   02   03   2E   03   4F   03
50A0:   89   03   B6   03   D2   03   F0   03
50A8:   0E   04   20   04   2D   04   36   DE
50B0:   1B   20   24   2C   28   A8   15   76
50B8:   92   1A   3B   3F   36   36   36   2D
50C0:   2D   20   18   3F   47   49   8C   92
50C8:   92   1A   1C   3F   17   76   6D   32
50D0:   1E   FF   20   12   12   32   36   36
50D8:   29   0D   20   24   24   3B   07   92
50E0:   92   92   37   36   36   6E   09   1C
50E8:   1C   1F   28   2D   01   04   E4   3F
50F0:   3F   11   09   49   92   92   1A   3B
50F8:   3F   36   36   36   2D   2D   20   18
5100:   3F   47   49   8C   92   92   92   D2
5108:   D8   03   2D   2D   36   DE   1B   20
5110:   24   2C   28   A8   15   76   92   D2
5118:   32   36   36   07   38   38   38   24
5120:   94   32   36   16   48   49   D2   3C
5128:   FF   32   36   56   2D   25   04   91
5130:   92   92   12   3B   3F   27   24   24
5138:   2C   2D   95   1A   3F   07   00   1C
5140:   3F   17   76   6D   32   1E   FF   20
5148:   49   89   4A   24   24   24   2D   AD
5150:   F6   3F   07   59   8A   49   4A   24
5158:   24   24   2D   20   95   1A   3F   97
5160:   2A   2D   05   49   09   48   1E   FF
5168:   20   24   44   6D   32   59   8A   59
5170:   49   52   49   49   49   09   3F   7F
5178:   21   24   24   A4   13   05   00   1C
5180:   3F   17   76   6D   32   1E   FF   20
5188:   49   89   4A   24   24   24   2D   AD
5190:   F6   3F   07   59   8A   49   4A   24
5198:   24   24   2D   2D   95   1A   3F   97
51A0:   2A   2D   05   49   09   48   1E   FF
51A8:   20   24   44   6D   32   49   49   09
51B0:   48   49   09   0C   2D   15   F6   37
51B8:   F7   2E   2D   2D   01   AA   24   24
51C0:   24   2D   AD   F6   3F   17   41   48
51C8:   48   49   37   36   36   6E   09   1C
51D0:   1C   1F   28   2D   01   20   1C   3F
51D8:   3F   49   49   49   12   36   36   29
51E0:   0D   20   24   24   3B   07   49   49
51E8:   49   92   12   49   1E   FF   20   24
51F0:   44   6D   32   92   52   49   08   24
51F8:   24   24   2D   2D   95   1A   3F   97
5200:   2A   2D   05   01   09   01   24   24
5208:   24   2D   2D   95   1A   3F   97   2A
5210:   2D   05   01   09   01   24   24   24
5218:   2D   AD   36   36   1E   3F   07   49
5220:   49   48   48   48   49   18   0C   6D
5228:   F6   17   B6   1D   07   VV   04   24
5230:   24   3C   1E   1E   1E   2E   2D   0D
5238:   49   76   2D   05   20   24   E4   3F
5240:   17   36   76   0C   0C   04   09   12
5248:   49   76   2D   05   20   24   E4   3F
5250:   17   36   76   0C   0C   04   00   3F
5258:   3F   36   2D   0D   32   36   1B   3F
5260:   28   08   49   49   76   2D   05   20
5268:   24   E4   3F   17   36   76   0C   0C
5270:   04   09   12   09   01   76   2D   05
5278:   20   24   E4   3F   17   36   76   0C
5280:   0C   04   00   3F   17   1E   36   76
5288:   2D   05   24   1C   3F   07   49   4A
5290:   49   76   2D   05   20   24   E4   3F
5298:   17   36   76   0C   0C   04   09   12
52A0:   09   01   76   2D   05   20   24   E4
52A8:   3F   17   36   76   0C   0C   04   00
52B0:   04   24   24   3C   1E   1E   1E   2E
52B8:   2D   05   08   08   08   01   0C   2D
52C0:   15   F6   37   F7   2E   2D   2D   01
52C8:   08   08   76   2D   05   20   24   E4
52D0:   3F   17   36   76   0C   0C   04   00

52D8:   3F   3F   36   2D   0D   32   36   1B
52E0:   3F   28   08   08   08   48   09   0C
52E8:   2D   15   F6   37   F7   2E   2D   2D
52F0:   01   08   08   76   2D   05   20   24
52F8:   E4   3F   17   36   76   0C   0C   04
5300:   00   3F   17   1E   36   76   2D   05
5308:   24   1C   3F   07   41   49   09   08
5310:   0C   2D   15   F6   37   F7   2E   2D
5318:   2D   01   08   08   76   2D   05   20
5320:   24   E4   3F   17   36   76   0C   0C
5328:   04   00   04   24   24   3C   1E   1E
5330:   1E   2E   2D   05   08   08   08   08
5338:   09   09   3F   3F   36   2D   0D   32
5340:   36   1B   3F   28   08   49   49   76
5348:   2D   05   20   24   E4   3F   17   36
5350:   76   0C   0C   04   00   3F   3F   36
5358:   2D   0D   32   36   1B   3F   28   08
5360:   08   08   08   08   09   09   09   3F
5368:   3F   36   2D   0D   32   36   1B   3F
5370:   28   08   49   49   76   2D   05   20
5378:   24   E4   3F   17   36   76   0C   0C
5380:   0C   00   3F   17   1E   36   76   2D
5388:   05   24   1C   3F   07   40   09   08
5390:   49   49   09   3F   3F   36   2D   0D
5398:   32   36   1B   3F   28   08   49   49
53A0:   76   2D   05   20   24   E4   3F   17
53A8:   36   76   0C   0C   04   00   76   2D
53B0:   05   20   24   E4   3F   17   36   76
53B8:   0C   0C   04   89   09   3D   09   89
53C0:   76   2D   05   20   24   E4   3F   17
53C8:   36   76   0C   0C   04   00   76   2D
53D0:   05   20   24   E4   3F   17   36   76
53D8:   0C   0C   04   89   09   3D   09   89
53E0:   76   2D   05   20   24   E4   3F   17
53E8:   36   76   0C   0C   04   49   48   0C
53F0:   2D   15   F6   37   F7   2E   2D   2D
53F8:   01   40   40   40   49   3F   3F   36
5400:   2D   0D   32   36   1B   3F   28   00
5408:   76   2D   05   20   24   E4   3F   17
5410:   36   76   0C   0C   04   89   09   3D
5418:   09   89   76   2D   05   20   24   E4
5420:   3F   17   36   76   0C   0C   04   49
5428:   48   48   09   3F   3F   36   2D   0D
5430:   32   36   1B   3F   28   00   76   2D
5438:   05   20   24   E4   3F   17   36   76
5440:   0C   0C   04   89   89   3D   91   49
5448:   49   3F   7F   21   24   24   A4   13
5450:   05   00   76   2D   05   20   24   E4
5458:   3F   17   36   0C   0C   0C   89   91
5460:   3D   48   48   01   0C   2D   15   F6
5468:   37   F7   2E   2D   2D   01   00   76
5470:   2D   05   20   24   E4   3F   17   36
5478:   76   0C   0C   04   89   09   3D   48
5480:   48   48   49   3F   3F   36   2D   0D
5488:   32   36   1B   3F   28   00   3F   7F
5490:   21   24   24   A4   13   05   89   89
5498:   3D   09   89   76   2D   05   20   24
54A0:   E4   3F   17   36   76   0C   0C   04
54A8:   00   0C   2D   15   F6   37   F7   2E
54B0:   2D   2D   01   08   40   3D   09   89
54B8:   76   2D   05   20   24   E4   3F   17
54C0:   36   76   0C   0C   04   00   00   00
```

**Listing 2.2.** AXIS-shape table for *Listing 2.*

```
POINTER TO AXIS START   :   E8 : C8      POKE 232,204
                            E9 : 50      POKE 233,84
```

| 54C8 : | 01 | 00 | 04 | 00 | 3" | 36 | 36 | 36 |
|--------|----|----|----|----|----|----|----|----|
| 54D0 : | 1D | 36 | 36 | 36 | 2E | A5 | 2D | 14 |
| 54D8 : | 2D | 14 | 2D | 14 | 2D | 14 | 2D | 14 |
| 54E0 : | 2D | 14 | 2D | 14 | 2D | 14 | 2D | 04 |
| 54E8 : | 00 |

**Listing 3.** Use of a single beam scanning spectrophotometer to generate dual wavelength data.

```
10   GOSUB 870: REM   LOAD GRAPHICS
20   DIM A$(5,200),B$(10)
30   GOSUB 560: REM   SCAN PARAMETERS
40   REM   SET UP A/D AND D/A CHIPS
50   HOME : POKE 49667,129: POKE 50179,154
60   REM INPUT SEQUENCE
70   FOR MA = 1 TO Q
80   HOME : VTAB 21: HTAB 14: PRINT "SPECTRUM ";: PRINT MA
90   FOR A = 1 TO W * 2
100  FOR AA = 1 TO 2: POKE 49666,0: FOR B = 1 TO X: NEXT : POKE 49666,128: NEXT
AA
110  IF Z < > 1 THEN 130
120  FOR BB = 1 TO Y
130  POKE 50178,0: POKE 50178,8: WAIT 50178,32,1
140  IF Z < > 1 THEN 190
150  VV =   PEEK (50176):V = V + VV: NEXT BB
160  V = V / Y: IF R = 2 THEN 210:A$(MA,A) = V: GOTO 180
170  B$(MA,A) = V
180  HPLOT A + 70,(144 - (V * .56)): GOTO 230
190  IF R = 2 THEN 210
200  A$(MA,A) =   PEEK (50176): GOTO 220
210  B$(MA,A) =   PEEK (50176)
220  HPLOT A + 70,(144 - ( PEEK (50176) * .56))
230  IF   PEEK ( - 16384) < 127 THEN 250
240  POKE   - 16368,0: GOSUB 930
250  V = 0: NEXT A
260  REM   RESET MONOCHROMATOR
270  HOME : VTAB 23: PRINT "PRESS <BAR> TO REVERSE MONOCHROMATOR:";: GET A$
290  FOR A = 1 TO W * 4: POKE 49666,0: FOR B = 1 TO 25: NEXT : POKE 49666,128: N
EXT
300  IF MA = Q THEN 330
310  HOME : VTAB 23: PRINT "PRESS <BAR> FOR NEXT SPECTRUM";: GET A$
320  NEXT MA
330  HOME : VTAB 21: PRINT  SPC( 5): PRINT "DO YOU WANT TO STORE"
340  PRINT "THIS SPECTRUM SET ON DISC ?";: GET A$: IF A$ = "N" THEN 390
360  HOME : VTAB 21: INVERSE : INPUT "FILE NAME=";G$: NORMAL
370  D$ =   CHR$ (4): PRINT D$"OPEN";G$: PRINT D$"WRITE";G$: FOR D = 1 TO Q: FOR A
 = 1 TO W * 2: PRINT A$(D,A): NEXT A,D
380  REM   START OF DIFFERENCE CALCULTION
390  HOME
392  VTAB 22: HTAB 6: INVERSE : PRINT "ASSAY WAVELENGTHS...A-B": NORMAL
410  HTAB 15: INPUT "A(NM)=";FA: PRINT : HTAB 15: INPUT "B(NM)=";FB
420  FA = (FA - FF)  * 2:FB = (FB - FF) * 2
430  HOME : TEXT : VTAB 9: PRINT  SPC( 7): PRINT "TIME(MIN)";:: PRINT  SPC( 5): P
RINT "ABS DIFF": PRINT : PRINT
440  FOR MA = 2 TO Q
450  B$(MA) = (A$(MA,FA) - A$(1,FA)) - (A$(MA,FB) - A$(1,FB))
460  PRINT  SPC( 9): PRINT QQ * (MA - 1);;: PRINT  SPC( 14): PRINT B$(MA) * (EE /
255)
470  NEXT
480  VTAB 20: HTAB 5: PRINT "REPEAT ANLYSIS ?";: GET A$
490  IF A$ = "N" THEN 510
500  HOME : POKE   - 16304,0: POKE 16297,0: GOTO 390
510  HOME
520  HTAB 6: VTAB 9: PRINT "R)ECYCLE"
521  HTAB 6: VTAB 10: PRINT "L)OGOFF"
530  HTAB 10: VTAB 15: INVERSE : PRINT "OPTION :";: GET A$: NORMAL : IF A$ = "R"
THEN 30
540  HOME : VTAB 5: HTAB 10: PRINT "LOGGED-OFF": END
550  HOME : PRINT "LOGGED-OFF": END
```

```
560  HOME :R = 0:V = 0:Z = 0: REM  INPUT PARAMETERS
570  VTAB 4: HTAB 4: PRINT "POINT AVERAGE ?";: GET A$
580  IF A$ = "N" THEN 610
590  Z = 1: VTAB 6: HTAB 4: PRINT "HOW MANY POINT AVERAGES(1-4)? ";: GET Y
600  X = 1: GOTO 650
610  VTAB 8: HTAB 4: INPUT "SCAN SPEED:100,200,300 NM ";B$
620  IF B$ = "200" THEN X = 50: GOTO 650
630  IF B$ = "100" THEN X = 100: GOTO 650
640  X = 20
650  VTAB 10: HTAB 4: INPUT "SCAN LENGTH:50 OR 100NM?";W
660  POKE 232,128: POKE 233,80
670  VTAB 12: HTAB 4: INPUT "AFS:.05,.1,.2,1, OR 2 ";EE
680  VTAB 14: HTAB 4: INPUT "START NM:400,450,500,550NM ";FF
690  VTAB 16: HTAB 4: INPUT "SCAN INTERVALS(MIN)";QQ
700  VTAB 18: HTAB 4: INPUT "NUMBER OF SCANS(1-5 ):";Q: IF Q > 5 THEN 700
710  HGR : HCOLOR= 7: SCALE= 10: ROT= 0
720  POKE 232,200: POKE 233,84
730  DRAW 1 AT 80,3
740  POKE 232,128: POKE 233,80: SCALE= 1
750  DRAW 14 AT 50,142: DRAW 1 AT 10,30
760  IF FF = 400 THEN  DRAW 5 AT 65,153: DRAW 6 AT 263,148
770  IF FF = 450 THEN  DRAW 11 AT 64,154: DRAW 12 AT 264,148
780  IF FF = 500 THEN  DRAW 6 AT 63,148: DRAW 7 AT 263,148
790  IF FF = 550 THEN  DRAW 12 AT 64,148: DRAW 13 AT 264,148
800  IF EE = .05 THEN  DRAW 15 AT 33,75: DRAW 16 AT 42,8
810  IF EE = .1 THEN  DRAW 17 AT 51,5: DRAW 16 AT 42,77
820  IF EE = .2 THEN  DRAW 17 AT 52,75: DRAW 18 AT 50,5
830  IF EE = 1 THEN  DRAW 19 AT 50,77: DRAW 20 AT 55,7
840  IF EE = 2 THEN  DRAW 20 AT 55,77: DRAW 21 AT 49,1
850  RETURN
860  REM  GRAPHICS SUBROUTINE
870  HOME : VTAB 10: HTAB 7: PRINT "DUAL WAVELENGTH ASSAY"
880  VTAB 12: HTAB 7: PRINT "USING AN APPLE ITT 2020"
890  VTAB 14: HTAB 7: PRINT "A. LODOLA:UNIVERSITY OF KENT"
900  INVERSE : HTAB 7: VTAB 20: PRINT "SPEC 1 IS THE BASELINE": NORMAL
910  D$ =  CHR$ (4): PRINT D$"BLOAD SHAPE9": PRINT D$"BLOAD AXIS"
920  RETURN
930  HOME : VTAB 22: PRINT "<1> TO CONTINUE <2> TO RESTART INPUT ";: GET A$
940  IF A$ = "1" THEN  HOME : RETURN
950  TEXT : GOTO 30
```

**Listing 4.** Use of a scanning spectrophotometer in a single wavelength mode.

```
10   GOSUB 470
20   DD = 0: DIM Q(1)
30   GOSUB 100
40   POKE 49667,129: POKE 50179,154
50   POKE 50178,0: POKE 50178,8: WAIT 50178,32,1
60   POKE 49665, PEEK (50176)
70   GA =  PEEK (50176): GOSUB 210
80   IF  PEEK ( - 16384) < 127 THEN 50
90   POKE  - 16368,0: NORMAL : GOTO 370
100  HOME
110  VTAB 18: HTAB 3: INPUT "ABSORBANCE FULL SCALE=";AA:AB = AA / 255 * 100
120  VTAB 20: HTAB 5: INPUT "EXTINCTION COEFFICIENT=";BB
130  HOME
140  VTAB 3: HTAB 26: INVERSE : PRINT "X10E3": NORMAL
150  VTAB 6: HTAB 4: PRINT "ABSORBANCE="
160  VTAB 10: HTAB 4: PRINT "TIME ELAPSED(MIN)="
170  VTAB 14: HTAB 4: PRINT "***RATE***"
180  VTAB 18: HTAB 7: PRINT "ABS.MIN="
190  VTAB 20: HTAB 8: PRINT "MM.MIN="
200  RETURN
210  POKE 32,24: POKE 33,10: POKE 34,5: INVERSE
220  DD = DD + 1: IF DD < 40 THEN 240
230  D = D + 1:DE = D / 10:DD = 0
240  GB = GA * AB: IF D = 1 THEN Q(1) = GB
250  GB = GB - QA:GB$ =  STR$ (GB)
260  IF DE = 0 THEN 300
270  GC = GB / DE:GC$ =  STR$ (GC)
280  IF BB = 0 THEN 300
290  GD = GC / BB:GD$ =  STR$ (GD)
300  VTAB 6: HTAB 3: PRINT  LEFT$ (GB$,4)
310  VTAB 10: HTAB 3: CALL  - 868
320  VTAB 10: HTAB 3: PRINT DE
330  VTAB 18: HTAB 3: PRINT  LEFT$ (GC$,4)
340  IF BB = 0 THEN 360
350  VTAB 20: HTAB 4: PRINT  LEFT$ (GD$,4)
360  RETURN
370  TEXT : HOME : VTAB 6: HTAB 8: PRINT "FUNCTION     OPTION"
380  VTAB 9: HTAB 8: PRINT "RETURN       <1>"
390  VTAB 10: HTAB 8: PRINT "RESET        <2>"
400  VTAB 11: HTAB 8: PRINT "LOGGOFF      <3>"
410  HTAB 10: VTAB 15: INVERSE : PRINT "OPTION :";: GET A: NORMAL
420  ON A GOTO 430,440,460
430  D = 0:DD = 0:DE = 0:GB$ = "0": GOSUB 130: GOTO 50
440  D = 0:DD = 0:DE = 0:GB$ = "0": GOTO 30
450  RETURN
```

```
460   HOME : VTAB 10: HTAB 10: PRINT "BYE BYE": END
470   HOME : VTAB 3: HTAB 4: PRINT "SINGLEWAVELENGTH SPECTROPHOTOMETRY"
480   VTAB 4: HTAB 3: PRINT " =============== ================="
490   VTAB 10: HTAB 4: PRINT "A. LODOLA;BIOLOGICAL LABORATORY"
500   VTAB 12: HTAB 4: PRINT "UNIVERSITY OF KENT"
510   FOR M = 1 TO 1000: NEXT
520   RETURN
530   HOME
```

**Listing 5.** Formatting TEXT files using the high resolution (Hi Res) generator of the Apple Tool Kit.

```
10    HGR : HCOLOR= 7
20    HOME :0 = 0
30    VTAB 3: HTAB 7: PRINT "APPLE TOOLKIT CHARACTER GENERATOR"
40    VTAB 6: HTAB 7: PRINT "PLOT DISPLAY FUNCTION"
50    VTAB 4: HTAB 7: PRINT "===== ======= ========= ========="
60    VTAB 7: HTAB 7: PRINT "==== ======= ========"
70    DIM A$(200)
80    D$ = CHR$ (4)
90    VTAB 12: HTAB 9
100   INPUT "FILE NAME #1 =";AA$
110   HTAB 9: INPUT "STARTING WAVELENGTH =";B
120   HTAB 9: INPUT "ABSORBANCE FULL SCALE =";C
130   VTAB 20: HTAB 5: PRINT "RECOVERING ";: PRINT AA$
140   PRINT D$;"OPEN";AA$: PRINT D$;"READ";AA$
150   FOR M = 1 TO 200
160   INPUT A$(M)
170   NEXT
180   PRINT D$;"CLOSE";AA$
190   HOME
200   HGR : HCOLOR= 7
210   HPLOT 70,0 TO 70,140
220   HPLOT   TO 270,140
230   FOR M = 270 TO 70 STEP  - 50: HPLOT M,140 TO M,135: NEXT
240   FOR M = 0 TO 140 STEP 70: HPLOT 70,M TO 75,M: NEXT
250   VTAB 19: HTAB 7: PRINT B;: HTAB 19: PRINT B + 50;: HTAB 30: PRINT B + 100
260   A$ = "ABSORBANCE"
270   VTAB 2: HTAB 2: FOR N = 1 TO  LEN (A$): PRINT  MID$ (A$,N,1): NEXT N
280   HOME : HTAB 5: PRINT C
290   VTAB 9: HTAB 5: PRINT C / 2
300   VTAB 18: HTAB 5: PRINT "0.0"
310   FOR M = 1 TO 200
320   HPLOT M + 70,144 - A$(M) * .59
330   NEXT M
340   IF 0 = 1 THEN 370
350   HTAB 12: VTAB 1: PRINT AA$;: PRINT " SPECTRUM"
360   GOTO 380
370   VTAB 22: PRINT "OVERLAY OF ";: PRINT AA$
380   POKE 34,23
390   VTAB 24: PRINT "OVERLAY ANOTHER PLOT (Y/N) :";: GET A$
400   IF A$ = "Y" THEN  GOSUB 450
410   PRINT
420   PRINT "NEW INPUT (Y/N) :";: GET A$
430   IF A$ = "Y" THEN 10
440   TEXT : HOME : END
450   PRINT
460   INPUT "NAME OF FILE #2 =";AA$
470   PRINT D$;"OPEN";AA$: PRINT D$;"READ"AA$
480   FOR M = 1 TO 200
490   INPUT A$(M)
500   NEXT
510   PRINT D$;"CLOSE";AA$
520   VTAB 22: CALL  - 958
530   0 = 1: GOTO 310
```

**Listing 6.** Spectrum derivitisation.

```
10    ONERR  GOTO 720
20    GOSUB 1300: REM  LOAD GRAPHICS
30    D$ =  CHR$ (4)
40    DIM A$(400),B$(400),C$(400),D(4)
50    HOME : VTAB 8: HTAB 5: PRINT "LOAD DATA DISC AND TYPE IN"
60    VTAB 10: HTAB 5: PRINT "FILE-NAME THEN<RETURN>: ";: INPUT A$
70    IF A$ = "" THEN 50
80    HTAB 7: VTAB 12: INPUT "SCANLENGTH(NM) ";SS
90    HTAB 7: VTAB 14: INPUT "POINTS/NM ";PP
100   INVERSE : PRINT "STARTING WAVELNGTH";: NORMAL : PRINT
110   HTAB 5: PRINT "400"
120   HTAB 6: PRINT "450"
130   HTAB 7: PRINT "500"
140   HTAB 8: PRINT "550"
```

```
150  HTAB 9: PRINT "600"
160  PRINT : HTAB 11: INPUT "=";FF
170  INVERSE : VTAB 15: HTAB 23: PRINT "AFS": NORMAL : PRINT
180  HTAB 22: PRINT ".05"
190  HTAB 23: PRINT " .1"
200  HTAB 24: PRINT " .2"
210  HTAB 25: PRINT " 1"
220  HTAB 26: PRINT " 2"
230  HTAB 30: INPUT "=";EE
240  SP = SS * PP: IF SP < = 200 THEN 300
250  INVERSE : HOME : VTAB 7: HTAB 5: PRINT "NUMBER OF SPECTRUM ELEMENTS"
260  VTAB 9: HTAB 5: PRINT "OUT OF MEMORY RANGE,   PRESS <1> "
270  VTAB 11: HTAB 5: PR    INT "TO EXIT, <2> TO RECYCLE      ";: GET A$: NORMAL :
     IF A$ = "2" THEN 50
280  IF A$ = "2" THEN 50
290  HOME : END
300  HOME : VTAB 10: HTAB 8: INVERSE : PRINT "RECOVERING ";: PRINT A$: NORMAL
310  PRINT D$;"OPEN";A$
320  PRINT D$;"READ";A$
330  FOR M = 1 TO SP: INPUT A%(M): NEXT
340  PRINT D$;"CLOSE"A$
350  HOME : GOSUB 1150
360  DD = 0
370  FOR M = 1 TO SP: HPLOT 70 + M,(144 - A%(M) * .56): NEXT
380  AB = 0:DD = DD + 1
390  G = 0:H = 255:KL = 0: HOME : VTAB 23: INPUT "SHIFT REQUIRED(NM) =";D(DD):
     D(DD) = D(DD) * 2:AB = AB + D(DD)
400  FOR M = 1 TO SP - AB
410  IF DD > 1 THEN 430
420  B%(M) = A%(M + D(DD)) - A%(M): GOTO 440
430  B%(M) = B%(M + D(DD)) - B%(M)
440  IF B%(M) < G THEN G = B%(M)
450  IF B%(M) > H THEN H = B%(M)
460  NEXT
470  GOTO 500
480  IF DD < 4 THEN 380
490  GOTO 720
500  IF G > = 0 THEN GG = G: GOTO 560
510  GG = G * - 1:H = 255
520  FOR M = 1 TO SP - AB
530  B%(M) = B%(M) + GG
540  IF B%(M) > H THEN H = B%(M)
550  NEXT
560  IF H < = 255 THEN 600
570  FOR K = 2 TO 5:KK = H / K: IF KK < = 255 THEN 580: NEXT
580  FOR M = 1 TO SP - AB:B%(M) = B%(M) / K: NEXT
590  GG = GG / K:KL = 1
600  HGR : HCOLOR= 7
610  FOR M = 1 TO SP - AB
620  MN = ((2 * M) + AB) / 2
630  HPLOT 70 + MN,144 - B%(M) * .56
640  NEXT
650  GH = 144 - GG * .56:GI = GH + 3:GJ = GH - 3
660  HPLOT 70,GH TO 270,GH
670  FOR M = 70 TO 270 STEP 20: HPLOT M,GI TO M,GJ: NEXT : HPLOT 70,0 TO 70,144
680  GOSUB 1180: HOME
690  VTAB 22: FOR R = 1 TO DD: PRINT D(R) / 2;: PRINT " : ";: NEXT : PRINT
     "NM SHIFT/S"
700  IF KL < 1 THEN 710: VTAB 23: PRINT "DIVISION BY ";: PRINT K
710  VTAB 23: PRINT "PRESS <BAR> TO CONTINUE";: GET A$
720  TEXT : HOME
730  VTAB 6: HTAB 7: PRINT "FUNCTION";: HTAB 25: PRINT "OPTION"
740  HTAB 7: PRINT "========";: HTAB 25: PRINT "======"
750  VTAB 11: HTAB 7: PRINT "HARD COPY";: HTAB 26: PRINT "<1>"
760  HTAB 7: PRINT "CURVE SMOOTHING";: HTAB 26: PRINT "<2>"
770  HTAB 7: PRINT "NEXT DERIVATIVE";: HTAB 26: PRINT "<3>"
780  HTAB 7: PRINT "REPEAT ANALYSIS";: HTAB 26: PRINT "<4>"
790  HTAB 7: PRINT "NEW INPUT";: HTAB 26: PRINT "<5>"
800  HTAB 7: PRINT "LOGG OFF";: HTAB 26: PRINT "<6>"
810  VTAB 20: HTAB 6: INVERSE : PRINT "OPTION   ";: NORMAL : GET B: ON B GOTO
     910,830,480,350,50,820
820  HOME : VTAB 5: HTAB 10: PRINT "LOGED-OFF": END
830  HGR : HCOLOR= 7
840  FOR M = 1 TO SP - AB:AA = M + 1:BB = M + 2:MN = (M + M + AB) / 2
850  C%(M) = (B%(M) + B%(AA) + B%(BB)) / 3
860  HPLOT 70 + MN,144 - (C%(M) * .56)
870  NEXT
880  GOSUB 1180
890  CS = 1: GOTO 660
900  REM  HARD COPY START
910  HOME : POKE - 16304,0: POKE 16297,0: VTAB 21: HTAB 11: INVERSE : PRINT
     "SPECTRUM PLOT": NORMAL
920  POKE 34,22
930  POKE 49667,129: IF CS < > 1 THEN 950
940  POKE 49664,1: POKE 49665,C%(1): GOTO 960
950  POKE 49554,1: POKE 49665,B%(1)
960  HOME : PRINT "PRESS <BAR> TO CONTINUE";: GET A$
970  FOR M = 1 TO SP - AB
980  NM = ((2 * M) + AB) / 2
```

```
990   IF CS = 1 THEN 1010
1000  POKE 49664,NM: POKE 49665,B%(M): GOTO 1020
1010  POKE 49664,NM: POKE 49665,C%(M)
1020  NEXT
1030  POKE 49664,200: POKE 49665,GG: FOR F = 1 TO 200: NEXT
1040  FOR M = 200 TO 0 STEP  - 20
1050  POKE 49665,(GG + 10): FOR F = 1 TO 200: NEXT : POKE 49665,GG: FOR F = 1 TO
      200: NEXT
1050  POKE 49664,M: FOR F = 1 TO 200: NEXT
1070  NEXT
1080  POKE 49665,(GG + 10)
1090  HOME : PRINT "ABSORBANCE SCALE BAR (Y/N) ?";: GET A$: PRINT : IF A$ = "N"
      THEN 1130
1100  POKE 49664,200: POKE 49665,255: VTAB 15: PRINT "PRESS <BAR> TO CONTINUE";:
      GET A$: PRINT
1110  POKE 49664,180: FOR MM = 1 TO 100: NEXT : POKE 49664,200: FOR MM = 1 TO
      100: NEXT : POKE 49665,191: FOR MM = 1 TO 400: NEXT : POKE 49664,180
1120  HOME : PRINT "PRESS <BAR> TO CONTINUE";: GET A$
1130  POKE 49654,0: POKE 49665,0:CS = 0: GOTO 720

1140  CS = 0: GOTO 720
1150  HOME : HGR : HCOLOR= 7: SCALE= 10: ROT= 0
1160  POKE 232,200: POKE 233,84
1170  DRAW 1 AT 80,3
1180  POKE 232,128: POKE 233,80: SCALE= 1
1190  DRAW 14 AT 50,142: DRAW 1 AT 10,30
1200  IF FF = 400 THEN  DRAW 5 AT 65,153: DRAW 6 AT 263,148
1210  IF FF = 450 THEN  DRAW 11 AT 64,154: DRAW 12 AT 264,148
1220  IF FF = 500 THEN  DRAW 6 AT 63,148: DRAW 7 AT 263,148
1230  IF FF = 550 THEN  DRAW 12 AT 64,148: DRAW 13 AT 264,148
1240  IF EE = .05 THEN  DRAW 15 AT 33,75: DRAW 16 AT 42,8
1250  IF EE = .1 THEN  DRAW 17 AT 51,5: DRAW 16 AT 42,77
1250  IF EE = .2 THEN  DRAW 17 AT 52,75: DRAW 18 AT 50,5
1270  IF EE = 1 THEN  DRAW 19 AT 50,77: DRAW 20 AT 55,7
1280  IF EE = 2 THEN  DRAW 20 AT 55,77: DRAW 21 AT 49,1
1290  RETURN
1300  HOME : VTAB 10: HTAB 7: PRINT "SPECTRUM DERIVITISATION"
1310  VTAB 12: HTAB 7: PRINT "USING AN APPLE ITT 2020"
1320  VTAB 14: HTAB 5: PRINT "A. LODOLA: UNIVERSITY OF KENT"
1330  D$ =  CHR$ (4): PRINT D$"BLOAD SHAPE9": PRINT D$"BLOAD AXIS"
1340  RETURN
```

CHAPTER 8

# Microcomputers in Chromatography

R.J. SMITH

## 1. INTRODUCTION

The use of computers for instrument control and data manipulation in chromatography has resulted in reduced operation time and increased reproducibility and accuracy. These benefits were first recognised in the 1950s and the subsequent development of computerised chromatography paralleled that of computer architecture. Before microcomputers became available the cost of main frame and minicomputer systems prevented the proliferation of computer integrators. Commercial enterprises undertook much of the microcomputer integrator development and produced a variety of dedicated machines.

The most recent development stems from the improved processing speed and enlarged RAM of the more recent personal microcomputers. Suitably programmed, these equal the performance of the dedicated machines, facilitate storage of the digitised chromatogram and allow use of the machine for other purposes if required. A number of commercial programs are available; Apple based systems predominating. The rekindled interest in integration software is probably motivated in part by economic considerations; systems based on personal microcomputers may halve the cost of using dedicated machines.

Continued development has resulted in integrators and, to a lesser extent, controllers becoming standard components of the modern chromatograph. Consequently chromatographers need to be aware of the characteristics and limitations of these devices, in order to choose a system appropriate to their needs and to optimise their own system. Although on occasion the effort required to write the software addressing a particular problem may be justified, this is not often the case. Modification of an existing program, however, may be justified. A few enlightened manufacturers are allowing users access to their software. Thus a knowledge of the theory and practice of automated data analysis in chromatography is an important requisite for the chromatographer. This chapter attempts to meet these requirements and provide some insight into the working of integrators and controllers by discussing their characteristics and limitations. The appendix contains a collection of simple programs which are used to provide programming examples. A brief discussion of peripheral routines concludes the chapter.

Microcomputers are used for two purposes in chromatography; integration and machine control. The integrator is the most familiar. In the sophisticated form its function is to detect peaks within a chromatogram, assess the peak area and provide a quantitative mass estimate for the compound producing the peak.

An instrument controller is essentially a microprocessor timing device controlling the switching of taps and pumps in a pre-set sequence. This chapter concentrates upon integrator software which is the more complex. Ideally, however, both controller and integrator should be facets of one program.

Integration software consists of peak detection routines, peak area summation routines and peripheral routines governing such things as display and data presentation. Degrees of sophistication exist of course. A manually controlled program may merely summate the integral of a peak which is defined by the operator. On the other hand, peak detection routines allow automated integration and real-time analysis of data (i.e., as it is acquired). Peak detection algorithms employ an analysis of first or second derivatives (1 – 4).

Alternatively, integration may employ an analysis of the statistical moments of a frequency distribution to model the peak (5 – 7). An iterative analysis is employed to improve the parameters of the model continually until an acceptable match to the peak is obtained. Although complex and involving assumptions concerning peak shape, only programs of this type are able to deconvolute merged peaks.

## 2. CHROMATOGRAPH CONTROLLERS

The purpose of the controller program is to automate the operation of the chromatograph. The program has a simple theme. An array in memory, called an event table, is used to link an event code with a time. The program sequentially accesses this list of events performing each one at the time dictated by an internal clock. Multiple tables may provide a different sequence of events for each cycle of the chromatograph and may include those variables required by integration routines for precise integration of different chromatograms. By including integration parameters full automation of the chromatograph may be obtained.

For sequential isocratic analyses the only essential event required is automated injection of the sample. Preloaded samples are injected onto the column at programmed intervals. If the position of multiway taps can be programmed then different eluents, columns or detectors may be selected in each cycle. For example, in *Figure 1* taps at A and B allow selection of different eluents and columns. More specialised requirements might employ taps at C and D to provide a selection of different detectors or a recycle facility. A programmable delay between cycles may be required to allow equilibration to the new conditions.

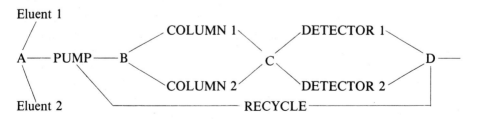

**Figure 1.** Diagram of a chromatographic system operated by taps (A, B, C, D) which are potentially under microcomputer control. See text for explanation.

Programmed eluent flow rate (by controlling pump speed) may be used to accommodate different procedures. This facility may also extend the capabilities of the chromatograph. Stepwise or continuous adjustment provides the facility known as flow programming, which is useful in reducing the retention time of strongly retained compounds and thus shortening the analysis time. Using two controlled pumps gradient elution can be performed. Both facilities are available on electronic gradient formers, but these do not usually allow simultaneous gradient and flow programming.

Controllers are obviously useful in dealing with large numbers of routine analyses. Preferably these should utilise the same or a similar procedure in order to reduce wasteful equilibration time. The commercial development of controllers has been enhanced by the industrial and clinical markets where the potential for continuous operation and reduced operative requirements are attractive. Keying in numerous event tables is laborious, but is offset by storage as files on magnetic media. Thus the operator may acquire a library of routines which are readily accessed.

Since each procedure must be keyed in, the controller program has an intrinsic inertia towards rapid change. The variations inherent in complex mixtures (e.g., biological extracts) or resulting from column ageing or different batches of column packing, are not therefore readily accommodated. In addition the adoption of new procedures may be hindered (8). The automation provided by a controller is an expensive facility due to the necessary peripheral actuater devices. Financial justification will depend upon the intended use of the chromatograph.

## 3. PEAK DETECTION

The following sections provide examples by reference to *Listing 1* in the appendix. The annotated listings describe the function of the routines. The program provides the routines required to effect automated integration of a digitised chromatogram and demonstrates the principles of peak detection and integration. The modular construction is designed to aid program modification and to encourage experimentation. While unsuitable for fast, real-time integration it is a useful post-chromatography integration system.

### 3.1 Detectors – Data Format and Noise-to-Signal Ratio

Despite the variety of chromatographic detectors they all generate the same form of data; the familiar peaks and valleys of the conventional chromatogram. This arises because they operate sequentially on a discrete volume of eluent or area of a chromatogram. Thin-layer and paper chromatograms and electrophoretograms also yield a similar format when analysed by scanning spectrophotometry. Consequently the same principles of peak detection and integration may be applied to the data obtained from a wide range of procedures and detectors. However it is recognised that while they are similar in gross characteristics the chromatograms differ in detail especially in peak width (PW), peak shape and resolution (8, 9). This requires that sensitive routines such as data collection, peak detection and baseline notation are adjusted to accommodate the differences. Some formats demand different data handling routines (e.g., molecular exclusion and simulated distillation chromatography). These differences explain the need, on occasion, to modify a program to a particular purpose.

There is an intrinsic random fluctuation (called noise) in the analogue signal generated by detectors (10). As the sensitivity of detectors has been increased so inevitably has the noise-to-signal ratio. The detector signal is one which is randomly and continuously variable, over which is superimposed the large, non-random and discontinuous variation of the chromatogram. The function of the algorithms of peak detection routines is to distinguish between these random and non-random components of the signal. As might be expected the greater the random fluctuation, the greater the compensation that is required. In consequence the sensitivity of peak detection will be reduced.

## 3.2 Analogue to Digital (A/D) Conversion

The analogue signal of a detector must be converted to a digital value for use by a microcomputer (see Chapter 2). The conversion chops the signal into discrete units which represent the value of the signal during a definite time period. The chromatogram may be envisaged as being sliced and each unit is often called a data slice. The chromatogram is thus represented in the computer memory as a sequential array of numbers. A/D conversion may result in the loss of information if the frequency of conversion is insufficient. At the lower extreme a peak occurs within a slice and all the information defining it is lost. It might seem therefore that there should be no upper limit to the frequency of conversion because definition increases with frequency. Both the memory available for data storage and the time required to process the data argue otherwise. More important, however, is that as the number of data slices increases the differential between adjacent slices decreases. At some point this differential equals that of the average random noise fluctuation. Since the peak detection routines depend on analysis of the differential, (i.e., the first derivative), they would become severely limited. This problem increases with detector attenuation.

A compromise must be made between the frequency of digital conversion necessary for peak definition and that for peak detection. A standard convention describes PW as the peak width measured at half peak height from the baseline of the chromatogram. Ten conversions per PW is generally sufficient. For a peak approximating a Gaussian distribution this equals about 30 conversions across the whole peak. Statistical methods may be used to evaluate the first derivative over a group of data slices (11,12), in which case higher frequencies of conversion are desirable. However, both are limited by the increased program execution time required (10).

## 3.3 Theory of Peak Detection by First and Second Derivatives

Several methods have been devised for detecting peaks within a digitised chromatogram. The majority rely upon an analysis of the first or second derivatives (4,10,13 – 15). These correspond to the differential between two or more adjacent data slices and the rate of change of those differentials (*Figure 2*).

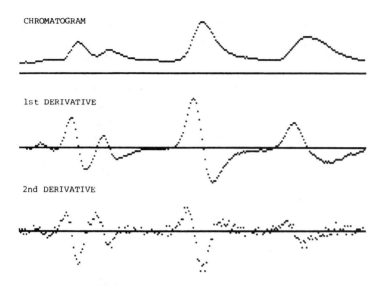

**Figure 2.** The first and second derivation of a chromatogram generated with *Listing 3* using an eleven point weighted digital filter (11). Note that the derivatives become less distinct as the peak becomes broader and flatter and that the second derivative exhibits considerable variance despite the smoothing routine.

*Listing 3* in the appendix calculates first and second derivatives and plots them on the screen. It may be used to gain insight into the operation of peak detection algorithms.

In the simplest form the first derivatives may be considered as a positive or negative trend. If the trend is positive, rising from the baseline, the start of a peak is noted. On the positive to negative inflection the top of the peak is detected. The first derivative continues on a diminishing negative trend towards zero at which point the peak ends and the chromatogram resumes a baseline. If the signal and the baseline were perfectly stable the peak detection routines would require merely to note the positive and negative trends. However, random noise fluctuations also generate positive and negative signals which must be distinguished from those derivatives attributable to a peak.

### 3.4 Noise Rejection Parameter

The signal recording noise and a peak differ in two respects. Firstly, the signal changes rapidly with time during a peak whereas the amplitude of the noise fluctuation is small and relatively constant. Secondly, noise is a pseudo-random variation while the signal recording a peak is non-random. Both factors are used to distinguish a peak signal from noise. The first employs a noise rejection parameter (NR). This is a variable which could be set to equal the maximum deviation between adjacent data slice values encountered on the baseline (i.e., the maximum noise fluctuation). The first derivative is compared with this value and if smaller is discounted in peak detection. NR may also be referred to as a peak detection 'threshold' (e.g., reference 2) especially when the first derivative is computed in a more complex form. In either case a peak cannot be detected before the threshold parameter is exceeded.

NR reduces the sensitivity of a peak detection routine and thus reduces the accuracy of integration. Since the first derivative must have exceeded the parameter before peak detection is made, the start of the peak is noted late and thus part of the peak is not included in the area integration. Routines determining the end of a peak may also employ NR so that early termination may occur. This is more serious because most chromatogram peaks tail and a larger peak area may be excluded. These problems are increased with high digital conversion frequencies and small broad peaks. The use of NR to reduce detection of spurious peaks must therefore be balanced against the intrinsic reduced sensitivity. Its value should always be kept as small as possible within the limit dictated by the noise-to-signal ratio.

### 3.5 Signal Smoothing

The sensitivity of peak detection routines may be improved by excluding the effects of noise through the use of signal smoothing procedures. These involve the analysis of groups of data over a time period which tends to exclude high frequency oscillations (11) and thus distinguish between the random and non-random attributes of noise and signal. Within limits such procedures benefit from high rates of A/D conversion. Two techniques are commonly used: group averaging and the weighted digital filter (2,16) (see *Listing 3*).

Briefly 'group' or 'box car' averaging takes the average of a contiguous group of data points in a sequential array to represent the value of the central datum. For each successive average the box car containing the group is moved along the array by one datum. The improvement in the signal-to-noise ratio is proportional to the square root of the number of data points in the box car. An extension of the group average which is more frequently employed in chromatography was implemented by Savitsky and Golay (12). Group averaging techniques reduce high frequency noise, but low frequency noise and random spikes may persist. The digital weighted filter is capable of suppressing these effects. The technique is similar to group averaging, but each datum is multiplied by a convoluting integer. Providing an appropriate convoluting function is employed, the technique is equivalent to a least squares correction of the central data point and may be used to evauate directly the first derivative of the least squares best function (10,12). Compare, for example, *Figures 2* and *3*.

Smoothing techniques must be used with caution. They may be employed to obtain a corrected first derivative or include smoothing of the raw data for area integration. Both results can be distorted by use of an inappropriate convoluting function. In practice the size of the data group is limited. The program time required to process a large group is likely to be excessive, particularly when real-time analysis is required. In addition no more than one inflection point should be contained within the data group. Small narrow peaks containing few data slices are less likely to be detected as the size of the data group increases. Thus a balance must be achieved between the size of the group and the smoothing necessary for a

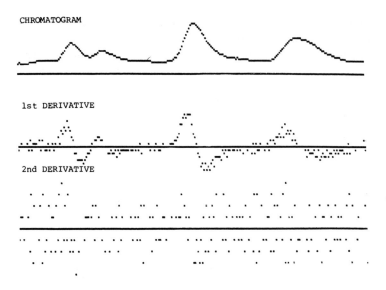

CHROMATOGRAM

1st DERIVATIVE

2nd DERIVATIVE

**Figure 3.** The first and second derivation of the chromatogram as in *Figure 2* except the derivatives were not subject to smoothing.

particular signal-to-noise ratio and between the frequency of A/D conversion and PW.

### 3.6 Peak Detection Threshold

Peak detection routines employ peak detection thresholds as a further means of distinguishing between random noise and the non-random signal recording a peak. To detect any event within a peak the program tests the first or second derivative against certain criteria. For instance, the start of a peak is signalled when the criteria for a positive first derivative are met. To exclude random positive derivatives, generated by noise, the criteria are required to be met not once, but several times in succession. In *Listing 1* this procedure is facilitated by accumulating positive criteria:

    1510 IF SGN (N(1)) < = 0 THEN GOTO 1540

If the derivative is positive the program proceeds by default to line 1520:

    1520 E = E + 1 : IF E >P1 THEN 1570

The variable E acts as an accumulator for positive derivatives and if it exceeds a pre-programmed overflow value (threshold) the start of a peak is recognised. The overflow vaue reflects the size of the data group being tested and obviously it must exceed that likely to accumulate from random noise alone.

Re-setting an accumulator to zero is useful if a trend is reversed before an overflow value is reached (line 1540). The accumulator routine is very sensitive to the frequency of A/D conversion as are smoothing techniques (Section 4.4). Given a constant A/D conversion rate the overflow value for individual accumulators may be related to the PW value (lines 8100 − 8120), though the optima will vary with different peak shapes. In practice most peak detection routines employ PW and NR although PW is the more important. These parameters compliment each other such that one acts to guard the function of the other. In consequence both may be minimised and the sensitivity of peak detection thereby increased.

### 3.6.1 *Peak Detection by First Derivative*

Three aspects of a peak need to be detected; the start, the top and the end (17). The algorithms required differ for each aspect and display different sensitivities to noise. Chromatogram peaks are not often symmetrical. In column chromatography the peak shape is frequently that of an exponentially modified Gaussian distribution (1,8,18). Thus the leading edge of the peak rises sharply while the trailing edge declines more gently and gradually merges with the baseline. When the profile at any point in a peak is of a low angle the first derivative is correspondingly small *(Figure 2)*. Consequently it is prone to the influence of noise. The sharp rise at the beginning of a peak and the inflection from a positive to negative derivative at the top of the peak are thus more readily detected than the small derivatives generated by the gradual decline at the end of the peak (3,4).

The structure of peak detection routines requires that the value of the derivative be tested against definite criteria. If the criterion is met the derivative contributes towards a peak detection event. In *Listing 1* the criteria and the accumulation of acceptable derivatives are separate routines. The criteria direct the increment of two variables, D and E. If either of these exceed a threshold related to the PW value program execution is re-directed to subroutines. For example, in *Listing 1*, lines 1500 – 1550, positive first derivatives are allowed to increment E, otherwise D is incremented. The program assumes peak initiation occurs on the baseline so that overflow of E denotes the start of a peak. Overflow of D accesses the subroutine for baseline notation. The succession of criterion testing is ensured by re-setting the accumulator to zero if the sequence of accumulation is interrupted. A similar format is employed to detect all three aspects of the peak.

The first derivative describes the positive or negative trend of the digitised chromatogram. The value of the trend is described by the second derivative. Thus the start of a peak is denoted by a succession of positive first derivatives, though that value may be constrained by comparison with NR. In a similar way the top of the peak is found by a succession of negative first derivatives (line 1610). These simple criteria suffice because both events are usually clear cut and only exceptional noise obscures them. However detection of the end of a peak is more difficult (2) because the first derivatives are small and thus prone to noise. The effective criteria accumulate zero derivatives or those falling within defined limits (e.g., NR; line 1090). NR may therefore have a disproportionate effect, accentuating premature peak end detection. Consequently the overflow value for this accumulator must be larger than those previously mentioned. Even so, the algorithm is sensitive to peak tailing which is often encountered.

Several devices may be used to supplement the basic criteria, but they must be chosen with care. For instance, the signal might be required to return to a value equivalent to the baseline at the beginning of the peak, but this would cause complications (and may fail) if a drifting baseline is encountered. One common device is based on peak shape. The routine counts the number of data points that occur between the start and the top of the peak. Two or three times that number are required to occur after the top of the peak before peak end detection is allowed (15). This simple device ensures that peak end detection takes place well after the end of the peak. Providing that the baseline notation is accurate, integration of the peak area does not suffer from the inclusion of a few baseline data points. These are removed on subtraction of the baseline from the total peak integral. The routine also has a second function in that it allows detection of skewed peaks which is important in the resolution of merged peaks. The criterion involved here tests whether the peak end can be detected when the requisite number of data slices, after the peak top, has occurred. If the first derivative still has a substantial negative value, a skewed peak is indicated.

### 3.6.2 *Peak Detection by Second Derivative*

The second derivative of a digitised chromatogram provides an estimate of the rate of change of the first derivative. The use of the second derivative for peak detection is attractive since, unlike the first derivative, it is independent of baseline drift. However all authorities agree that the second derivative is more prone to noise fluctuations than the first. It may be demonstrated both in theory and practice that the probability of detecting a peak in a chromatogram, with a given noise-to-signal ratio, is greater with algorithms employing the first derivative than those using the second (2). It is preferable to employ smoothing procedures when using the first derivative for peak detection, whereas it is essential to do so when using the second derivative (cf. *Figures 2* and *3*).

Peak detection routines using algorithms based on the second derivative have the same general structure as those described for the first derivative. Each decision point will test for specific criteria and employ a threshold value to restrict premature or spurious events. The criteria required to test the second derivative for the detection of the peak start, top and end are respectively a positive trend, a negative inflection (or noted as the most negative value) and a return to zero.

Difficulties may be encountered in detecting the start of rapidly accelerating peaks (i.e., those having a very steep leading stage). In this case the initial positive phase of the second derivative may be virtually non-existent because the leading edge contains few data slices. Note that a minimum of three data points are required to formulate a second derivative. For this reason the accumulation of positive second criteria may be insufficient to mark the start of a peak especially where narrow peaks are the norm, for example in gas chromatography. A criterion which tests for negative second derivatives or indeed any deviation from zero is not necessary, but is a useful addition. As with the first derivative the detection of the maximum data point (if not the peak maximum) is relatively straightforward, but the detection of the end of the peak may be more troublesome. Providing the deviation is constant, baseline drift is of no account and the second derivative will equal zero. Although the probem encountered with the first derivative at peak end detection is thus removed, that of detecting zero

217

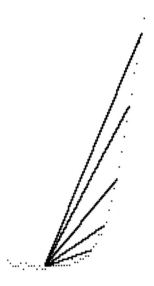

**Figure 4.** Tangential skimming. The angle subtended from a fixed point to subsequent data points is calculated. A succession of increasing angles is indicative of the start of a peak. The angle may be calculated from the horizontal, but is more sensitive if sloping baselines are taken into account.

derivatives in the presence of noise is exacerbated. One solution is the use of a comparative NR, suitably adjusted for use with the second derivative. However, the problems associated with the use of the NR parameter will then occur.

### 3.6.3 *Alternative Criteria*

The basic principles of peak detection using first and second derivatives are not new. While the combinations of criteria and threshold values differ widely between different auto-integrators (rightly so if these are tailored to specific use), they all follow the general principles described above. A more recent alternative described in the literature is based on a tangent search (2,15). This is a pseudo-second derivative test with reduced sensitivity to noise. The procedure employed calculates the angle returned between any fixed data point and succeeding points (*Figure 4*).

The test criteria for peak start require that the tangents of the angles subtended by successive data points are increasing and that the number of these exceeds a threshold value. The technique may also be used in skimming rider peaks. Unlike criteria based on the first derivative the technique, known as tangential skimming, is not susceptible to baseline drift. In practice it is particularly useful in detecting small, broad and flat peaks and yet may miss rapidly accelerating peaks in which the leading edge contains few data slices. As the first derivative algorithms readily detect sharp peaks, but tend to fail with small broad peaks, the two algorithms complement each other and are profitably used in conjunction. In this case one acts as confirmation of the other and may be further bolstered by use of the second derivative.

Another alternative, which is restricted to post-chromatography analysis, dispenses with the use of first and second derivatives altogether (16). The procedure detects peaks by analysis of the greatest values of the data points. Each value detected relates to a group of data points encompassing a peak, while merged peaks are separated on the minima found between peaks. A fitting line is calculated, which describes the linear dependence of PW and retention time, against which each peak is checked and which is used in detecting shoulder peaks. The procedure relies upon fine definition of the baseline and employs a 'rubber band technique' in which the baseline is first drawn through minimum base points. This is modified until a continuous curve is obtained in which joined parabolas pass through all defined base points. The method requires definition of only two variables for peak detection in any one chromatogram — sensitivity and minimum PW. In this respect the technique has advantages over those employing first and second derivatives.

## 3.7 Scoop Back Procedures

The necessity of using threshold values means that by the time a characteristic of a peak is detected the event has already passed (14). This requires the use of 'scoop back' procedures which make allowance for the number of data slices which occur between the start of a peak and its detection. In real-time integration this allows the collection of that data and its inclusion in the peak integral. Some form of short-term memory must therefore be present to store the most recent data and facilitate scoop back, even in those real-time auto-integrators which do not have any long-term memory. Data smoothing techniques increase the delay before detection and thus the amount of data to be recovered. This provides a further reason why extensive smoothing should be matched with high frequency A/D conversion.

The program given in *Listing 1* acts on a digitised chromatogram stored in a binary coded file. Unlike many commercial programs peak detection and integration are separate events. The notation of peak events is placed into the data file. Scoop back in this case requires placing the notation relative to the current position in the file. The number of data included in the scoop back process is directly governed by the threshold value. This in turn is calculated from the variable PW, so that both are automatically adjusted. The demonstration program places peak notation in the odd numbered bytes while even numbered bytes store the 8-bit data.

## 3.8 PW Parameter Adjustment

The broadening of peaks as the retention time increases is a common feature of chromatography. As peaks become broader and lower their first and second derivatives diminish. In consequence they become more prone to distortion by noise fluctuation, which remains constant. If the frequency of A/D conversion is constant the number of data slices included in an early narrow peak may be a small fraction of those present in a late broad peak. The criteria and threshold values which allow optimum detection of one peak shape are likely to be less than adequate for detection of the other extreme. For example, a tall narrow peak will produce a small number of large derivatives upon which noise has little effect. Criteria tests give strong positive results and threshold values need to be small. In contrast, low broad peaks are much more difficult to detect given the pedantic nature of computer routines. Derivatives will be small and more readily affected by noise. The results of the tests will be less well defined and threshold values need to be larger to exclude noise fluctuations triggering peak events.

As well as coping with peak broadening an auto-integration program should be adaptable to a variety of chromatograms. Although PW is normally proportional to retention time certain procedures exhibit variable PW (e.g., stepped elution as in amino acid analysers). Two factors may be used to accommodate such variance in a program; either the criteria or the threshold parameters are varied. The former are not readily adjusted since this requires re-programming, although multiple criteria may be employed. However, the threshold values are readily adjusted since they can be linked to the PW parameter so that it sets the threshold values for all the decision loops throughout the program. Consequently the PW parameter is the most powerful variable in peak detection logic. To accommodate PW variation during chromatography a secondary routine allows re-setting of the threshold values (*via* PW) at defined times. This is accomplished within the program using an array equivalent to an event table. On each loop of the peak detection routine the time is checked against the current element of the array. On matching, a subroutine is accessed which re-calculates the threshold variables.

*Listing 1* uses a 2-dimensional array as an event table which links the new PW value and the time at which it is to be implemented (lines 130−150). As the PW and NR parameters are interactive a similar procedure could be adopted for NR, but normally it is re-set *via* the baseline notation routine (lines 2000−3000).

### 3.9 Resolution of Merged Peaks using First and Second Derivatives

Merged peaks are a common component of chromatograms. Unfortunately the two techniques used to detect and integrate merged peaks are neither simple nor fully adequate. One uses first and second derivatives and may include area apportioning routines (4,10,11,13,15,17). The other is a deconvolution process which uses a modified Gaussian or other distribution as a model to which component peaks may be fitted (5,17).

The first derivative alone may be used to distinguish merged peaks where a distinct valley occurs between them. The criterion involved is based on the negative to positive inflection of the derivative across the valley *(Figure 4)*. The point of inflection marks the bottom of the valley. Normally this point is used to apportion area between the two peaks using a perpendicular divide from the valley to the baseline (13). The method has been considered as an acceptable approximation providing that the height of the valley from the baseline is less than 5% of the peak height and both peaks are of a similar height. This is frequently not the case.

A problem arises in apportioning areas between detected peaks. Techniques based on the second derivative or peak masking require extensive programming and yield indifferent results. Techniques for the deconvolution of merged peaks (see Section 3.10) provide a more satisfactory answer. A shoulder peak, where no

CHROMATOGRAM

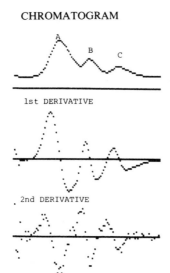

**Figure 5.** First and second derivatives from a merged peak group. Peak B may be considered as a rider peak of peak A while B and C constitute merged peaks. In this case the distinction is not readily apparent.

valley exists between the peaks, can be detected using the second derivative, though the technique is sensitive to noise fluctuations. Unusual skew in a peak is indicative of the presence of more than one component. A crude estimate of skew is simply derived by the method described in Section 3.6.1. This technique does not aid resolution, but may be used to warn the operator.

As distinct from shoulder peaks, rider peaks are clearly defined peaks present on the tail of a larger peak (*Figure 5*). Calculation of the area of the rider peak requires a correction which takes account of the excessive contribution of the main peak. Normally a linear correction is made across the bottom of the rider peak. Since a distinct valley is present the start of the peak is readily detected, but the end of the peak is more difficult to define. The criterion, in methods employing first or second derivatives, is based on a search for derivatives of equal or less value than that detected immediately prior to the start of the rider peak. The precision of the technique is very susceptible to noise.

A more effective procedure is tangential skimming (see Section 3.6.3) in which the area of the rider peak is assessed for each data point after the top of the peak by inserting a baseline from the start of the peak to the current data point. The end of the peak is detected when the assessed area is not further significantly incremented by including more data points.

There is no simple distinction between two merged peaks and a substantial rider on the back of a skewed peak (*Figure 5*). The models described represent two extremes and between these exist a gradation of intermediate forms which are not uniformly defined by different chromatographers. The decision to evoke rider peak skimming may be made on detection of a skewed peak or, more commonly, on the relative heights of the two peaks. The larger the putative rider peak the more likely that a perpendicular divide will yield a more accurate apportionment of area (2). However, uncertainties and approximations cannot be avoided in the detection and area apportionment of merged peaks using first and second derivatives. Thus several authorities have suggested that the analysis of poorly resolved peaks is best accomplished by improved chromatography rather than by reliance upon mathematical resolution (2,15).

### 3.10 Deconvolution of Merged Peaks

The deconvolution of overlapping peaks has been widely discussed in the literature (6,9,20,21). The techniques described employ an analysis of the statistical movements of a peak profile (18). They are based on the concept that the composite curve caused by the merging peaks may be dissected by fitting suitable model peaks. A non-linear least squares method is used to fit the model to each peak detected in the composite curve. Fitting is an iterative process which is halted when convergence of model and composite cannot be further improved. The speed of convergence is increased by excluding unreasonable solutions such as negative peak areas or widths. The difference in the area of the composite and the sum of the model peaks may be used as a criterion of satisfactory fit.

The technique has two main disadvantages. First, the assumed shape of the peak (normally a Gaussian or modified Gaussian distribution) may be a poor representation of the true peak shape and result in significant errors in area apportionment. Second, the technique employs an extensive program and iterative procedures which require relatively long execution times. Despite these disadvantages and the complexity of the technique it can provide deconvolution of peaks and an area apportionment far superior to the approximations resulting from analyses using first and second derivatives.

### 4. BASELINE DETECTION

Baseline detection within a chromatogram is based on the assumption that any area not within a peak is a justifiable baseline. The criteria used require consideration. Inaccurate baseline notation yields inaccurate integration (14,15). Most frequently the baseline beneath peaks is assumed to be a line drawn between the nearest baseline notations which encompass the peak(s). Other schemes have been described, including a least squares fit to points within a narrow, defined band throughout the chromatogram (16) and a process employing linear and parabolic fitting between defined points. In all cases the process depends upon an initial definition of parts of the chromatogram which represent the true baseline. In complex chromatograms large peak groups frequently obscure the baseline over an extended period. There can be no satisfactory means of positioning the baseline beneath such a group even though some guidance might be assumed by consideration of the baseline generated by the procedure in the absence of a sample. For an internally compensated, real-time integrator even this poor substitute does not exist.

Baseline detection is part of the overall peak detection routine. Inaccurate peak detection may cause inaccurate baseline detection (15). For example, premature peak end detection and consequent misplacement of the baseline is a common fault. In older integrators with little data storage capacity large peak groups could force peak integration using forward projection of the baseline. This process may result in inaccurate integration with divergent baselines.

## 4.1 Accelerating Baselines

For the purposes of baseline detection two kinds of sloping baseline require consideration; consistent slow acceleration and rapid acceleration. Accelerating baselines interfere with peak detection. Positive baselines trigger incorrect peak and merged peak detection while negative baselines may thwart peak end detection. Peak detection with first and second derivatives are sequential routines based on the assumption that the start, top and end of a peak follow in regular order. If one part of the routine does not function the whole fails and incorrect merged peak detection is a common consequence. For this reason, incorporation of an escape route, which limits the width of a peak and forces peak end detection, is a useful additional routine. It may be based on the format described for skewed peak detection.

The second derivative is not sensitive to consistently accelerating baselines. Criteria based on it and the tangent search routine may be used to confirm and limit the first derivative criteria, though particular care is required to balance peak end and merged peak criteria to prevent false baseline notation between peaks. Providing that the second derivative of the baseline does not exceed NR it may act as the first line of defence, since the first derivative can be set in comparison as a zero deviation. If NR is re-set during baseline notation some buffer capacity against further acceleration in the baseline is maintained. However, any large peak group will obscure the baseline and may outwit this device.

Rapidly accelerating baselines are encountered in gradient elution procedures. They cannot be distinguished from peak start conditions except by the ill-defined criteria which compare the second derivative with the expected acceleration of a peak. More often the 'rubber band technique' is employed (16), in which the minimum data in an arbitrary group (e.g., valleys between detected peaks) are assumed to represent the baseline; the imagery arises from the view of a rubber band stretched around fixed points. This process is completed by linear extrapolation between the minima.

In real-time analysis this procedure is of limited use and manual override routines are often substituted. The selection of suitable minimal data points can be improved by linear and non-linear least squares techniques (15,16) and tangent skimming processes. In all cases, however, the accuracy is governed by the criteria used to select the minima. If the rapidly accelerating baseline is also heavily populated with peaks no effective means of distinguishing a baseline exists. In such cases the baseline generated in the absence of a sample may be assumed. From the analytical viewpoint improved chromatography, perhaps employing a suitable isocratic elution, is a better alternative.

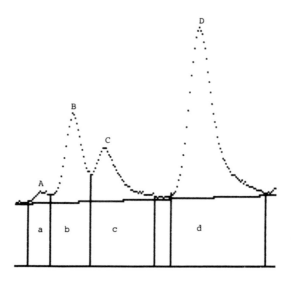

**Figure 6.** Peak integrals. The labelled peaks (A, B, C, D) have the baseline areas denoted by the corresponding lower case letters (a, b, c, d). The integral of the peak depends on the subtraction of the baseline area from the total peak integral, therefore accurate baseline notation is essential. The area of merged peaks (A, B, C) is normally apportioned by a vertical divide from the valley between the peaks as shown.

## 5. INTEGRATION

### 5.1 Calculation of Peak Integrals

To provide some leeway for baseline drift a detector is normally offset from the zero voltage or ground state signal by up to 10% of the detection range (attenuation). An appreciable difference therefore exists between the baseline of the chromatogram and the zero detector response. Integration routines formulate the area of a peak by simple summation of the data included within the peak detection marks (*Figure 6*). This sum includes the area below the baseline which, due to the spread of the peak, may easily exceed the area of the peak above the baseline. The true peak area is resolved from the sum by subtraction of the baseline area. The routines which derive the baseline and thus the area beneath it are of prime importance in preserving the accuracy of integration (2, 14 − 16).

If viewed as a histogram it is apparent that the vertical rectangular strips only approximate the curve of the peak (*Figure 7*). As the number of strips increases so their sum approaches the real area of the peak, but the number of data taken is limited by other considerations. Thus simple summation only approximates the area of the peak. More accurate techniques are available in the form of the trapezoidal rule and Simpson's rule which view the strips as trapezoid and parabolic approximations of the peak curve respectively (a comparison of the two techniques is given by *Listing 4*). However, noise and the resultant small errors occurring in peak detection are likely to produce a deviation which exceeds the approximation involved in the simple summation of data. Program time may be better employed with other routines such as data smoothing.

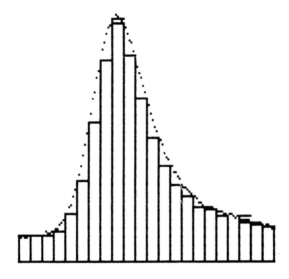

**Figure 7.** Histogram of a peak demonstrating how the simple summation of digitised data only approximates the true area.

## 5.2 Real-time versus Post-run Integration

The first dedicated microcomputer integrators had small memories. They and their commercial counterparts did not store the raw data and were of necessity, real-time integrators. The bias thus created in the design of integration programs has tended to be perpetuated. Only recently have commercial systems become available which create a data file of the chromtogram. Such storage allows manipulatory routines not available in real time. In addition real-time integration is constrained particularly when very short data intervals are required. For instance, as noted previously, the need to scoop back data pertinent to a peak detection decision requires that some form of short-term, transient data storage is available (14).

Infrequently accessed routines, such as baseline notation, increase the execution time for the loop in which they are called. Without data storage the loop time cannot exceed the data acquisition interval. The problem is in part resolved by accessing the central decision loops on interrupt routines and providing temporary data storage which is necessary for data smoothing. However, with few exceptions, such routines may only be employed in machine code programs. The problem is only acute when rapid data acquisition is required (in which case high level language programs are inappropriate anyway). As a rough guide the minimum peak width likely to be encountered is perhaps $3-5$ sec and would require a data acquisition interval of about 0.1 sec.

The strategy of a real-time integration program must include peak detection with scoop back of data. The total peak integral is accumulated in the peak detection loop and corrected for baseline by horizontal extrapolation back from the first baseline encountered after a peak, or peak group, ends. The total peak integral will be temporarily stored in an array prior to baseline correction. After correction the integral, peak retention time and peak type (e.g., merged, unique, rider) are stored in a memory array to await printing at the end of the run. In contrast post-run integration requires only real-time data acquisition. Since the analytical routines may act upon the data file of the chromatogram, execution time for each piece of data is of no consequence other than the normal considerations for overall program execution time. The major disadvantage is that analytical routines exclude data acquisition and therefore reduce chromatograph operation time. Such problems are not confined to chromatography and one commercially available answer is a portable data logging system which separates the functions of data acquisition and analysis (see Chapter 3). A similar device is employed in recently marketed integration systems which are able to log data from several input channels while simultaneously providing auto or manual integration.

Data file storage offers advantages in the practice of chromatography. In optimising the integration of a chromatogram the effect of varying the integration parameters is readily observed by using a data file. Without such data storage real-time analysis requires that the chromatograph be run to generate data each time the parameters are tested. In complex chromatograms this may be a time consuming and expensive operation. Data storage also allows direct comparison of chromatograms so that variations due to column ageing or differences in packing materials are readily detected. It is also possible that errors in chromatography or integration may be recovered by re-integration of the stored data.

The structuring of the integration program may be organised to take advantage of data filing. The program may be allowed the opportunity to backtrack should a program decision indicate re-analysis of data which has already passed through the decision loop. One example is *Listing 1* in which the peak detection and integration functions are split; using one pass through the data file for peak detection and a second for integration. Since the peak detection loops have similar execution times and the main infrequent routine is merely placement of a flag within the data file to mark peak decisions, a valid compromise in program structure would consist of real-time data acquisition and peak detection followed by post-run integration. However, it must be a compromise since baseline notation in real time is still required. In seeking to reduce the execution time of program loops some routines may be removed. For example, real-time display of chromatograms on a VDU are attractive, but a program is easily relieved of this burden by twinning the detector signal to a flat bed recorder.

## 5.3 Manual Integration Programs

Although data file storage aids the treatment of problems encountered in peak integration it does not remove them. The problems are no less severe and in many cases are the same as those met in real-time analysis. Manual integration programs are of limited application because of the operator and machine time tied up in the analysis. However, they are a useful adjunct to an auto-integration program since they replace the manual override routines found in real-time analysis (Section 6.5). In a simple form, manual integration consists of routines which allow the operator to define the limits of the integration required. Secondary routines calculate the integral and subtract a manually defined baseline. Numerous other manipulative routines may be appended such as direct comparison of two filed chromatograms placed in register and the removal of an unfortunate baseline deviation or skewed peaks (4). Deconvolution of merged peaks could also be usefully included in this category. Full development should incorporate manual integration and auto-integration in a suite of programs. The routines for integration and baseline correction could serve both auto and manual integration options. In addition files resulting from manipulative routines could be addressed through the auto-integration program.

The major practical disadvantage of manual integration on microcomputer systems stems from inadequate screen display (see Section 6.2). Operator guidance of the program is dependent upon the information available in the screen display. High resolution screens are limited both by hardware design and available memory. In consequence neither the quantity nor the quality of the display are adequate for the purpose. This problem may be eased by the adoption of appropriate routines such as compression of the data to give a foreshortened display of the chromatogram. The appendix contains an example of a manual integration program and includes the concept of a floating pointer (*Listing 2*). This device is a simple means of communicating to the program the quantitative data required for integration.

## 6. SUPPLEMENTARY ROUTINES

This section describes the peripheral routines of an integration program which include data calculation and presentation, chromatogram display and printing and the manual override routines. It is in such routines that the greatest diversity is found. To some extent they govern the user friendliness of the program and so bear careful consideration by the prospective purchaser. The routines of peak detection and integration are constrained to meet stringent criteria, so that modification of these interactive routines is not a task to be undertaken lightly. In contrast the peripheral routines, particularly those for presentation and display, are more readily adapted to suit particular requirements.

### 6.1 Data Calculation and Presentation

In the simplest format an auto-integration program needs to report only two correlated pieces of data, the peak retention time and the peak area (or height). In practice the usual basic report mode presents for each peak a calculation of percentage composition, that is the percentage fraction of the total peak area. Often this report mode is of limited use, but is retained perhaps as a vestige of earlier integration systems. It forms the basic report mode because the calculation is simple and requires no peak identification (see Section 6.3).

In order to generate a quantitative report, a calibrating calculation is required which relates the area of the peak to the mass of the component. For example, with a spectrophotometric detector the calibration would employ an extinction coefficient for the component in question, relative to the wavelength used (see Chapter 7). Thus the calibration rests upon a response factor obtained from the analysis of a known amount of a standard and logically employing the same chromatographic procedure and integration parameters as those applied to the unknown sample. Two procedures are common; internal and external standardisation. External standardisation employs one or more standards which are analysed separately from the unknown and may include analysis of several different concentrations to yield a standard calibration curve. An internal standard is a compound of similar chromatographic characteristics as the sample which is included in the sample at a known concentration. Variation in the determined peak area of the internal standard compared to that expected provides a basis by which peak area of samples may be corrected to account for sample losses and errors during extraction, preparation and purification.

## 6.2 Peak Determination

The more sophisticated integrator systems incorporate calibration routines which perform calculation upon the peak area data and present the results in the data format. Area percent reports require nothing more than summation of the total area and the report for each peak of the appropriate fraction. However, to apply calibration routines the program must be capable of identifying peaks in order to apply the correct response factor or selecting the appropriate peak as the internal standard. The characteristic normally employed to identify peaks is their retention time. Minor variation in the retention time may be expected even for the most reproducible procedures, especially if the integration program is manually initiated. Consequently, simple comparison of the determined retention times with absolute pre-programmed values is not a fruitful approach. In practice, peaks are deciphered by their occurrence within a particular period of the chromatogram which is delimited by a set variance (tolerance) about the pre-programmed value (22). Obviously this limits the sensitivity of the routine though it may be regained, in part, through the use of secondary routines employing other criteria such as the order of retention.

## 6.3 Peak Identification

The identification of peaks by analysis of peak shape has been explored and provides a possible alternative. Analysis may employ either the moments of peak distribution or be based on the first and second derivatives (12,18). The concept arises from the observation that the skew and excess parameters of the peaks produced by an homologous series of compounds have particular values. Thus one type of compound may be distinguished from another according to its position within a skew-excess co-ordinate system. However this could not be readily applied without considerable operator guidance.

Given a peak selection routine a number of sophisticated supplementary routines may be attached to the basic integration program. These would enable automated calibration from an external standard, including offset for those calibrations which do not extrapolate through zero, and automated standardisation using a defined internal standard. A central component of the calculation routine is the response factor table. This is a 2-dimensional array in memory relating retention time to the response factor. For each peak encountered the routine matches the detected retention time to a value in the array, employing the criteria noted above. If a match is not found the peak is reported as an unknown. If the peak is matched the corresponding response factor in the array is used to calculate the mass of the component producing the peak. By allowing each element of the array to be used once only, the order of the array superimposes the order of retention on the peak identification routine. False peak identification may occur if the chromatogram is densely populated with peaks or the retention time is variable. In such cases the user should check peak identification carefully. For ease of use the report format should include a clear presentation of the retention time and response factor used for each peak.

One component of the report format frequently encountered is an abbreviation which indicates the type of peak reported. This information might include, for example, whether the peak was skewed, merged or unique. Other characteristics which may be reported include baseline resolved peaks, rider peaks, negative, reference and group peaks. Information may also be included concerning the type of baseline correction which has been applied to the peak integral. Such information is useful in ensuring the correct operation of the integration program and allows a qualitative assessment of the probable accuracy of the data, particularly with reference to the resolution of merged peaks.

## 6.4 Chromatogram Display

The routines for the display of a chromatogram in the conventional profile format are the least satisfactory in microcomputer auto-integration programs. The dissatisfaction arises from the restrictions imposed on converting the sequential digital information of the data file into a chromatogram profile. These restrictions stem from the limited size of the VDU screen, the lack of scrolling on most high resolution graphic screens and the dot-matrix print format.

High resolution graphics screens use a block of memory to store the display. In essence each bit in the assigned area of memory which is high (equivalent to binary one) is displayed on the screen as a point of light. Each bit that is low (equivalent to zero) is dark. Thus the amount of memory space required is directly proportional to the resolution of the graphics screen. Microcomputers vary in the degree of resolution they can support and this is a prime consideration when purchasing a machine for use in chromatography. For example, the Apple Europlus II uses 8k of memory to support a graphics screen resolution of 190 x 280 pixels. Other machines support higher resolutions. However the prime consideration is not the resolution itself, but the amount of memory left available for use when supporting high resolution graphics. Space in memory is needed for both the integration program and storage of the chromatogram data file. In calculating the available free memory, that required to support disc operating systems and high level language interpreters must also be taken into account.

Each data point is normally represented by an 8-, 10- or 12-bit binary number (i.e., $0-255$, 1024, 4096 respectively). In plotting such values to a high resolution graphics screen it is possible that 8-bit data can be accommodated. However 12-bit data would require compression entailing an eight-fold loss in resolution.

Note that this affects the display alone and not the raw data present in memory. The loss of resolution is not serious if the display is merely being used to follow the progress of a chromatographic procedure, but may have more impact if fine detail is necessary to the integration. Resolution is particularly important to manual integration programs which depend upon operator manipulation of a chromatogram display.

The size of the graphics screen may constitute a severe limitation. Given the A/D conversion frequency necessary for smoothing and peak detection routines, the number of data points taken for even a short procedure will exceed that which may be plotted on a high resolution screen. If the format of the high resolution screen is software controlled it may be possible to cause the high resolution screen to scroll in similar manner to the text screen. The display routine may then present a pan across the chromatogram. If the format is hardware defined, scrolling of the screen is unlikely to be obtainable. In this case it must be cleared and the next section of the data file written into the display memory. The process thus becomes one of paging through each section of the chromatogram. This is generally unsatisfactory because the user finds it difficult to appreciate the continuity of the chromatogram and edge effects frequently occur where an important peak is split between one page and the next. In theory the whole page of memory could be re-written for each data point; moving the group of data points along by one each time. This routine would mimic the scrolling effect, but even with machine code routines there is a discernable time lapse in writing each group of data. The effect is one which is slow, jerky and visually offensive. The scrolling effect can be achieved on the text screen providing the low resolution and vertical orientation of the chromatogram is aceptable. The resolution depends on the text screen facilities, but is unlikely to exceed 80 x 30, so that resolution of 12-bit data is reduced by a factor of 50.

Auto-integration programs may accommodate the variation in PW either by adjusting program threshold values, in which case the frequency of A/D conversion is fixed, or by altering the frequency of conversion. In the latter case a plot

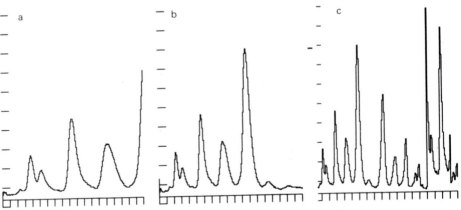

**Figure 8.** An example of compressed data plotting. **(A)** every third datum plotted; **(B)** every fifth datum plotted; **(C)** every tenth datum plotted. (Most figures in this chapter have a compression factor of 2.)

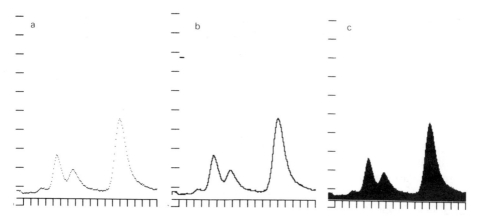

**Figure 9.** The three formats for chromatogram presentation on the screen or dot-matrix hard copy. **(A)** point plot; **(B)** line plot; **(C)** infilled histogram.

of all the data points yields a corrupt version of the chromatogram in which all peaks tend towards the same width. In either case the necessary frequency of conversion will give a display in which the peaks appear unnaturally wide. The problem may be overcome by selective plotting of data points (*Figure 8*). If only every third or fourth point is used the chromatogram is compressed to a more manageable size. The process is akin to reducing the chart speed on a chart recorder, but differs in that significant data is lost from the display. It should be employed with care if the information content is important. *Listing 5* allows compressed data plotting.

The third limitation arises from the dot matrix structure of the VDU screen and dot-matrix printers. Three formats are available for the display of chromatograms; a point plot, infilled histograms or a line plot (*Figure 9*). The first merely plots a single point on the screen for each piece of data. When some 30 points cover each peak the profile is well defined, but if the number is reduced, or a hard copy is made using a dot-matrix printer set to full page width, visual definition of the profile deteriorates. This may be inadequate and is particularly poor on photographic reproduction. The second technique plots a bar histogram from zero (however defined) to the data point. The chromatogram is presented as an infilled histogram. Although the visual definition of the profile is improved, the effect can be visually tiring and disturbing. It is particularly so when blocks of light are flashing on and off the screen as a program re-writes each block of data in paging through the data file. Dot-matrix printers often vary in intensity due to the misalignment of paper and a hard copy of this format may be of poor quality. It is not a format seen in publications and may not be acceptable to editorial staff.

Line plotting is a halfway stage between point and infilled formats. For each data point a line is plotted vertically between the value of the previous datum and the present one. This produces a line profile similar to the conventional chart recorder output, but with a slightly stepped effect. In the author's opinion this is the best of the available formats because the visual profile is maintained on compression and there is less discomfort on extended use or serial re-plotting of pages of data. It also provides probably the most acceptable hard copy for publication.

High resolution plotting from high level languages is often characteristic of a particular microcomputer as it depends on the interpreter routines. These commands are probably the least consistent in the various forms of BASIC, see, for example, the programs listed in the appendix. Note that in *Listing 1* the screen print of the chromatogram is delayed. This allows the peak detection to be incorporated and it is marked by a short spike; this constitutes a common feature which is an important aid in monitoring and improving peak detection routines.

Manual integration programs are dependent upon a screen display of the chromatogram profile. The operator uses the display to direct the program to areas of the chromatogram which are to be integrated. To input the start and end of a peak in the chromatogram the appropriate data points and baseline values must be defined. These values are not easily discerned from the screen even if the display is provided with some type of scale. One means of easing the use of manual routines is by a pointer, the position of which is controlled by the operator (see *Listing 2*). The pointer may be positioned to indicate the start and end points for integration. The appropriate values can be taken directly by the integration routine or displayed to the screen as required.

Screen and printer plotting routines are notoriously slow when accessed from high level languages and are therefore prime candidates for conversion to machine code. The configuration of memory and screen is often complex requiring an extensive program to accommodate it. However, considerable improvement may be obtained by machine code routines which convert and limit the data and pass this to the plotting routines of a high level interpreter. An example is provided by *Listing 5*; note that interpreter routines and their location are machine dependent.

## 6.5 Hard Copy Printing

The ideal peripheral is an x/y data plotter, but a dot-matrix printer with graphics capabilities is a cheaper alternative. The formats described above are obtainable on a dot-matrix printer. However the printing suffers from all the disadvantages described. Computer drawn dot-matrix figures are often unacceptable for publication and this may be equally true of dot-matrix printed chromatograms. An alternative is to drive a chart recorder from a microcomputer *via* D/A conversion. The problem here lies in the speed of conversion. If the raw data is used to drive the recorder pen a stepped profile will be the likely result as each piece of data re-positions the pen. The stepping can be smoothed by rapid conversion combined with high chart speed. Equally, the first derivative could be subdivided and each division converted as rapidly as possible. However D/A conversion must be adjusted so as to create the illusion of a continuously variable signal by approaching the pen response time.

## 6.6 Integration Override Routines

Integration programs are based on logical assumptions which exclude unlikely events. Not infrequently these assumptions and the resultant criteria prove inadequate or invalid. Therefore many programs include manual override routines which are designed to support auto-integration. In one sense the routines are props which enable auto-integration to cope, often inadequately, with poorly resolved chromatograms. One example already mentioned is the updating of PW parameters during integration. This is the most useful override routine and serves as a programming example. Override routines frequently direct or modify program operation on a timed event basis within clearly defined regions of a chromatogram. Thus a detailed knowledge of the chromatogram is required by the operator. The two most common override routines are briefly described below, but many others exist.

Program inhibition serves to inhibit peak detection/integration in a defined area of the chromatogram allowing data logging to continue in real time. The device may be used to avoid areas which disturb automated correction routines, for example initial skewed peaks of non-retained material. In analysis of a data file the routine reduces integration time by allowing selection of desired areas. Suppression of baseline notation may be used to prevent incorrect notations such as may occur in valleys between peaks. However, valley to valley baseline determination, as a manual override routine, may provide the optimum response in following non-uniform baselines.

Normally integration will attempt to resolve all peaks within the chromatogram. Group peak integration causes summation of the group integral, which may allow isomers to be usefully quantified as a single compound. A similar routine named 'forced integration' directs the program into peak detection mode. This routine also allows group peak integration and may be used to integrate small peaks not normally detected.

## 7. CONCLUSION

Chromatographers are fortunate that auto-integration developed alongside computer architecture so that the principles have been thoroughly researched. Continued improvements in the power and memory capacity of microcomputers are likely to herald further developments in integration procedures. It would seem likely that peak integration routines will become generally available to all forms of chromatography. However there are dangers as well as benefits. Integration routines are complex so that inaccurate integration may readily occur. It is easy to be lulled into a false sense of security and care must be taken to guard against the ready assumption that the integrator is infallible. More subtle yet equally insidious is the tendency to rely upon the integrator rather than the chromatograph. The former should never be allowed to supplant efficient use of the latter.

## 8. REFERENCES

1. Guichard,M. and Sicard,G. (1972) *Chromatographia*, **5**, 83.
2. Fozard,A., Franses,J.J. and Wyatt,A.J. (1972) *Chromatographia*, **5**, 130.
3. Chilcote,D.D. and Mrochek,J.E. (1971) *Clin. Chem.*, **17**, 751.
4. Weimann,B. (1974) *Chromatographia*, **7**, 472.
5. Van Rijswick,M.H.J. (1974) *Chromatographia*, **7**, 491.
6. Anderson,A.H., Gibb,T.C. and Littlewood,A.B. (1969) *Chromatographia*, **2**, 466.
7. Yamaoka,K. and Naka Gawa,T. (1974) *J. Chromatogr.*, **92**, 213–222.

8. Klinowski,R.J. and Hoberecht,H.D. (1974) *Chromatographia,* **7**, 452.
9. Stockwell,P.B. and Telford,I. (1980) *Chromatographia,* **13**, 665.
10. Smit,H.C. and Waig,H.L. (1975) *Chromatographia,* **8**, 311.
11. Binkley,D. and Dessy,R. (1979) *J. Chem. Educ.,* **53**, 148.
12. Savitsky,A. and Golat,M.J.E. (1964) *Anal. Chem.,* **36**, 1627.
13. Back,H.L., Buttery,P.J. and Gregson,K. (1972) *J. Chromatogr.,* **68**, 103.
14. Herlicska,E., Brown,A.C. and Hendrickson,J. (1971) *Am. Lab.,* **3**, 29.
15. Woerlee,E.F.G. and Mol,J.C. (1980) *J. Chromatogr. Sci.,* **18**, 258.
16. Caesar,F. and Klier,M. (1974) *Chromatographia,* **7**, 526.
17. Scott,C.D., Chilcote,D.D. and Pitt,W.W.,Jr. (1970) *Clin. Chem.,* **16**, 637.
18. Grushka,E. (1975) *Chromatographic Peak Slope Analysis. Methods of Protein Separation,* Vol. **1**, Catsinpoolas,N. (ed.), published by Plenum, p. 161.
19. Gladney,H.M., Dowden,B.F. and Swalen,J.D. (1969) *Anal. Chem.,* **41**, 883.
20. Westerberg,A.W. (1969) *Anal. Chem.,* **41**, 1770.
21. Hancock,H.A.,Jr., Dahm,L.A. and Muldoon,J.F. (1970) *J. Chromatogr. Sci.,* **8**, 57.
22. Chilcote,D.D. (1974) *J. Chromatogr.,* **99**, 243.

# APPENDIX
## Program listings

The following programs are written in Applesoft BASIC-notation, decimal; no prefix, hexidecimal; $ prefix. In Applesoft a memory array of less than 10 units need not be dimensioned, note variable N(1) *Listing 1.*

### Listing 1. Auto-integrator

```
50 A = 16384:B = 8192: DIM BG(100
   ,1): DIM IN(50,3):BN = 2:CF =
   1
60 HIMEM: B
70 HOME : PRINT : PRINT : INPUT
   "TYPE IN THE CHROMATOGRAM FI
   LE NAME";F$
75 HOME : PRINT : PRINT "LOADING
   ";F$
80 D$ = CHR$ (4): PRINT D$;"BLOA
   D";F$
85 DT = PEEK (43616) + PEEK (43
   617) * 256
90 HOME : PRINT : PRINT : INPUT
   "DO YOU WISH TO CHANGE PW DU
   RING ANALYSIS Y/N";P$
100 IF P$ = "Y" THEN 130
110 IF P$ = "N" THEN 160
120 GOTO 90
130 HOME : PRINT : PRINT : INPUT
   "TYPE IN TIME (,) THEN PW RE
   QUIRED FOR EACH CHANGE (MAX
   10 TYPE 0,0 TO END)";TT,PP
140 TJ = TJ + 1:T(TJ,0) = TT:T(TJ
   ,1) = PP: IF TT = 0 THEN 120

150 GOTO 130
160 HOME : PRINT : PRINT : INPUT
   "TYPE IN INITIAL PW";PW: GOSUB
   8100
170 HOME : PRINT : PRINT : INPUT
   "TYPE IN A SENSITIVITY FACTO
   R FOR NR (0.1 TO 10)";SEN: IF
   SEN < 0.1 OR SEN > 10 THEN 1
   70
180 GOSUB 8000
190 FOR F = 0 TO 10 STEP 2:BO =
   BO + PEEK (A + F): NEXT
200 BC = INT (BO / 5):NR = INT
   (BC / 10) * SEN
1010 BO = 0
1020 I = I + 2
1030 IF I < TX(CF) THEN 8090
1040 FOR F = 9 TO 1 STEP - 1:N(
   F + 1) = N(F):M(F + 1) = M(F
   ): NEXT
```

```
1050 N(1) =  PEEK (A + I) -  PEEK
   (A + I - 2):M(1) = (N(1) + N
   (2) + N(3) + N(4) + N(5)) /
   5
1060 POKE A + I - 1,0
1070 IF I < 10 THEN 1020
1080 IF I > DT THEN  GOTO 5000
1090 IF N(1) < NR AND N(1) >  -
   NR THEN N(1) = 0
1100 IF I > 20 THEN  GOSUB 3000
1110 ON Q + 1 GOSUB 1500,1600,17
   00,1800
1120 GOTO 1020
1500 IF M(1) > 0 THEN 1510
1510 IF  SGN (N(1)) < = 0 THEN
   GOTO 1540
1520 E = E + 1: IF E > P1 THEN 15
   70
1530 RETURN
1540 D = D + E + 1:E = 0
1550 IF D > P1 THEN 2000
1560 RETURN
1570 Q = 1:D = 0:E = 0: POKE A +
   I - 3 - (P1 * 2),1: RETURN
1600 IF  SGN (N(1)) > 0 THEN  GOTO
   1630
1610 E = E + 1: IF E > P1 THEN  GOTO
   1650
1620 RETURN
1630 D = D + E + 1:E = 0: IF D >
   P4 THEN  GOTO 1850
1640 RETURN
1650 Q = 2:D = 0:E = 0: POKE A +
   I - 3 - (P1 * 2),2: RETURN
1660 RETURN
1700 IF  SGN (N(1)) > 0 OR M(1) >
   1 THEN  GOTO 1740
1710 IF  SGN (N(1)) = 0 AND M(1)
   > - .5 THEN 1760
1720 RETURN
1730 REM  -VE NOT USED
1740 E = E + 1:D = 0: IF E > P1 THEN
   GOTO 1780
1750 RETURN
1760 D = D + 1:E = 0: IF D > P1 THEN
   GOTO 1810
1770 RETURN
1780 Q = 1:E = 0:D = 0:
1790 POKE A + I - 3 - (P1 * 2),4
```

```
1800  RETURN
1810  IF  PEEK (A + I) > BC + 5 THEN
      GOTO 1840
1820  Q = 0:E = 0:D = 0
1830  POKE A + I - 1,3
1840  D = 0
1850  RETURN
2000  REM  BASELINE NOTATION
2020  FOR F = PW TO 0 STEP  - 2
2030  B =  PEEK (A + I - F)
2040  U =  PEEK (A + I + 2)
2050  L = B - U: IF  SGN (L) < 0 THEN
      L =  - L
2055  IF L1 < L THEN L1 = L
2060  B1 = B1 + B
2070  NEXT
2080  BC =  INT (B1 / (PW / 2 + 1)
      )
2085  BN = BN + 1:BG(BN,0) = BC:BG
      (BN,1) = I
2100  NR = L1 * SEN
2105  D = 0:L = 0:L1 = 0:U = 0:B1 =
      0
2110  RETURN
3000  P = P + 1
3010  IF P > 275 THEN 8000
3020  HPLOT P,185 -  INT ( PEEK (
      A + I - 20) * (185 / 255))
3030  IF  PEEK (A + I - 21) = 0 THEN
      3050
3040  HPLOT P,185 -  INT ( PEEK (
      A + I - 20) * (185 / 255)) TO
      P,180 -  INT ( PEEK (A + I -
      20) * (185 / 255))
3050  RETURN
5000  I = 1: GOSUB 5500
5010  I = I + 2
5020  IF I > DT THEN 4200
5030  A1 =  PEEK (A + I)
5040  IF A1 = 1 THEN F1 = 1
5050  IF A1 = 1 THEN IN(RR,1) = I
5060  IF A1 = 2 THEN F1 = 2
5070  IF A1 = 2 THEN IN(RR,2) = I
5080  IF A1 = 3 THEN F1 = 3
5090  IF A1 = 3 THEN IN(RR,3) = I
5100  IF A1 = 4 THEN IN(RR,3) = I
5110  IF A1 = 4 THEN F1 = 4
5120  IF A1 = 4 THEN IN(RR + 1,1)
      = I
5130  ON F1 + 1 GOSUB 5160,5170,5
      190,5210,5250
```

```
5140  GOTO 5010
5150  RETURN
5160  RETURN
5170  IT = IT +  PEEK (A + I + 1)
5180  RETURN
5190  IT = IT +  PEEK (A + I + 1):
      F1 = 1
5200  RETURN
5210  IN(RR,0) = IT:IT = 0
5220  F1 = 0
5230  GOSUB 5310
5240  RETURN
5250  REM  :MERGED PEAK
5260  IN(RR,0) = IT:IT = 0
5270  IT = IT +  PEEK (A + I + 1)
5280  F1 = 1
5290  GOSUB 5310
5300  RETURN
5310  FOR T = 4 TO 100
5320  IF BG(T,1) > IN(RR,3) THEN
      5350
5330  IF BG(T,1) = 0 THEN 5440
5340  NEXT
5350  IC =  (BG(T,0) - BG(T - 1,0))
      / (BG(T,1) - BG(T - 1,1))
5360  SB = BG(T - 1,0) + ((IN(RR,1
      ) - BG(T - 1,1)) * IC)
5370  SE = BG(T - 1,0) + ((IN(RR,3
      ) - BG(T - 1,1)) * IC)
5380  BB =  (SB + SE) / 2
5390  TT =  (IN(RR,3) - IN(RR,1)) /
      2
5410  PRINT RR,IN(RR,2),IN(RR,0) -
      (BB * TT)
5420  PR# 0:RR = RR + 1
5430  RETURN
5440  BB = BG(T - 1,0):TT =  (IN(RR
      ,3) - IN(RR,1)) / 2: GOTO 54
      00
5500  PRINT "PEAK NO.","PEAK RT",
      "INTEGRAL"
5510  RETURN
8000  HGR : POKE 49234,0
8010  HPLOT 0,0 TO 0,185 TO 279,1
      85 TO 279,0 TO 0,0: FOR J =
      0 TO 279 STEP 10: HPLOT J,19
      0 TO J,185: NEXT
8020  P = 0: RETURN
8090  PW = T(CF,1):CF = CF + 1
8100  PW =  INT (PW / 2) * 2: IF P
      W < 4 THEN PW = 4
8110  P2 = PW / 2:P1 =  INT (P2 /
      2) * 2:P4 = P1 * 3
8120  RETURN
```

This program works on a chromatogram stored as a digitised binary coded file; stored in memory from 16384 ($4000). It detects peaks within the chromatogram (including merged peaks) and records the baseline. The retention time and the integral of the peak are reported.

*Lines 50−200:* place file in memory, input and store the changes in PW variable required during analysis, input initial PW variable, input sensitivity factor for NR variable: note lines 200 and 2100. The variables which control the sensitivity of the peak detection routine are PW and NR. PW is used to set the accumulator values. NR is automatically set by the baseline detection routine, but is controlled if required by the sensitivity factor.

*Lines 1010−1120:* Calculation module; this routine sequentially updates the position in the data file, checks if end of file has been reached, calculates first and second derivatives, re-sets PW if required and re-sets the first derivative to Ø if this falls within NR.

*Line 1030* checks if PW re-set required. 1040−1150 calculate first and second derivatives (N(1) and M(1)); note the implementation of box car averaging based on the previous 9 calculated first derivatives. Smoothing routines as shown in *Listing 3* may be inserted here, but as these delay peak detection the scoop back routine will require appropriate adjustment.

*Lines 1500−1840:* Peak detection routine; three modules at 1500, 1600 and 1700 respectively detect peak start, peak top, and peak end. Each module consists of criteria in the form of 'if' statements (i.e., 1500 and 1510) accumulators (D + E) which register sequential or non-sequential events determined by the criteria (e.g., 1540 and 1520), and an overflow routine for each accumulator (e.g., 1570).

On overflow of an accumulator the flag Q is re-set which directs the program in the next loop to access a different peak detection module. The peak detection event is recorded in the data file by a poke statement (e.g., line 1570). Note variable P1 in 1520, 1530 and 1570. P1 is set by the PW factor thus governing sensitivity of the routine (e.g., line 1520) and the scoop back required. As data is stored in every other (even) byte, notation is recorded in an odd byte. The routine was written in this way to accommodate 12-bit data with few changes.

*Lines 2000—2110:* baseline notation accessed from 1550 (i.e., outside a peak) calculates an average baseline and the maximum variation in signal, to which it sets NR, the baseline is stored in the dimensioned array BG (100,1).

*Lines 3000—3040* plot the chromatogram to a graphics screen (8192 — 16384; $2000 — $4000) including a spike denoting peak detection events.

*Lines 5000—5510* make a second pass of the data; integrate digits between peak detection marks by summation, calculate baseline beneath peak (lines 5310—5390) print results to screen, store results in array IN (50,3). Note that the stored data provides for simple routines which could be inserted to calculate results in other forms such as peak width at half height, percentage composition or absolute mass.

*Lines 8000—8120* access graphics, draw lines around page, calculate or re-calculate accumulator values from PW input.

## Important variables

| | |
|---|---|
| PW | Peak width |
| NR | Noise rejection |
| A | Start byte for data file ($4000) |
| DT | Length of data file |
| I | Position in data file |
| D and E | Accumulators |
| P1 and P4 | Accumulator scoop back variables |
| Q | Flag for peak detection routine (line 1110) |
| BB | Average baseline value beneath peak |
| TT | Number of data points in peak. |

The program plots a point chromatogram. *Listing 2* plots an infilled histogram. The line plot is demonstrated in *Listing 2* in the hard copy option from the menu.

Although the program may be used to integrate laboratory data, given a suitable A/D conversion and file storage, its primary purpose in this context is to demonstrate the principles of computer integration. In particular the 'IF' statements expressing peak detection criteria can be readily changed and the effect noted. The program was originally written as a test rig to determine the requirements of a machine code program which is under construction.

## Listing 2. Manual Integration

```
10 F$ = CHR$ (20):E$ = CHR$ (4)

20 INPUT "INPUT NAME OF DATA FIL
   E-";F$
30 K = - 1
40 PRINT E$;"BLOAD"F$" "
50 REM **********MENU***********
   *****
60 K = - 1
70 DIM X(40): DIM P(40): DIM Z(4
   0): DIM W(40)
80 K = - 1
90 PRINT : PRINT : PRINT : PRINT
   "             MENU."
100 PRINT "            ****"
110 PRINT "1. FOR FULL PLOT AND
    INTEGRATION."
120 PRINT "2. FOR SAVING RESULTS
    FOR REFERENCE."
130 PRINT "3. FOR RETRIEVING SAV
    ED RESULTS."
140 PRINT "4. FOR HARD COPY OF P
    LOT."
150 PRINT "5. FOR HARDCOPY OF DA
    TA."
160 PRINT "6. FOR DISPLAY OF DAT
    A."
170 PRINT "7. FOR END."
180 PRINT E$;"BLOAD"F$" "
190 LB = PEEK (43634) + PEEK (4
    3635) * 256

200 PL = PEEK (43616) +  PEEK (4
    3617) * 256
210 INPUT "INPUT 1 TO 7.";V
220 ON V GOTO 250,1290,1470,1740
    ,2030,2050,230
230 END
240 REM *********PLOT /INT******
    ******
250 P = 0:I = 0:A = 16384
260 R = 1:K = - 1
270 D$ =  CHR$ (4)
280 POKE 232,252: POKE 233,29
290 PRINT D$;"BLOAD ARROW"
300 SCALE= 1
310 GOSUB 1160
320 IF PI > PL THEN 560
330 GOSUB 700
340 P = 0
350 X = P
360 Y = 160 - ( PEEK (A + (X + (K
     * 279)) * 2) * (160 / 256))
     - 11
370 IF Y < 0 THEN 2500
380 DRAW 1 AT X,Y
390 PRINT "LOCATION OF ARROW= ";
    X + (279 * K)
400 GET IN$
410 IF  LEFT$ (IN$,1) = "L" THEN
    470
420 IF  LEFT$ (IN$,1) = "R" THEN
    490
430 IF  LEFT$ (IN$,1) = "T" THEN
    510
```

```
440  IF LEFT$ (IN$,1) = "F" THEN
     320
450  IF LEFT$ (IN$,1) = "A" THEN
     560
460  GOTO 370
470  IF X + 1 > 279 THEN 370
480  XDRAW 1 AT X,Y:X = X + 1:Y =
     160 - ( PEEK (A + (X + (K *
     279)) * 2) * (160 / 256)) -
     11: GOTO 370
490  IF X - 1 < 0 THEN 370
500  XDRAW 1 AT X,Y:X = X - 1:Y =
     160 - ( PEEK (A + (X + (K *
     279)) * 2) * (160 / 256)) -
     11: GOTO 370
510  Q = X * 2 + (K * 279)
520  P(R) = PEEK (A + Q)
530  X(R) = X + (K * 279)
540  R = R + 1
550  GOTO 370
560  TEXT
570  X(R) = 6969
580  R = 1
590  I = X(R) * 2
600  Z = 0
610  FOR L = X(R) TO X(R + 1)
620  Z = Z + PEEK (A + I)
630  I = I + 2
640  NEXT
650  Z = Z - (P(R) + P(R + 1)) / 2
     * (X(R + 1) - X(R))
660  W = (P(R) + P(R + 1)) / 2
670  Z(R) = Z:W(R) = W
680  GOSUB 880
690  END
700  HGR
710  A = 16384
720  K = K + 1:P = 0
730  HPLOT P,160 - ( PEEK (A + I)
     * (160 / 256))
740  P = P + 1:I = I + 2:PI = PI +
     1
745  HPLOT P,159
750  IF PEEK (A + I) > 190 THEN
     810
760  HPLOT TO P,160 - ( PEEK (A +
     I) * (160 / 256))
770  IF P > 277 THEN 800
780  IF PI > PL THEN 800
790  GOTO 740
800  RETURN
810  GOSUB 825
820  GOTO 730
825  HPLOT P,160 TO P,0
830  P = P + 1:PI = PI + 1:I = I +
     2
835  HPLOT P,160 TO P,0
840  IF PI > PL THEN 800
850  IF PEEK (A + I) > 190 THEN
     825
860  IF P > 279 THEN 800
870  RETURN
880  IF R > 1 THEN 950
890  PRINT ; TAB( 17);"RESULTS"
900  PRINT ; TAB( 17);"*******"
910  PRINT : PRINT
920  PRINT "PEAK POINT1 POINT2 AR
     EA     MEAN B/LINE"
930  PRINT "**** ****** ****** **
     **    ***********"
940  PRINT : PRINT
950  KL = 0: PRINT
960  IF X(R) = 6969 THEN 1150
970  E = X(R): GOTO 1020
980  E = P(R): GOTO 1020
990  E = P(R + 1): GOTO 1020
1000 E = Z: GOTO 1020
1010 E = W: GOTO 1020
1020 PRINT E;
1030 KL = KL + 1
1040 ON KL GOTO 1070,1090,1110,1
     130
1050 IF X(R) = 6969 THEN 1150
1060 R = R + 2: GOTO 590
1070 PRINT TAB( 6);
1080 GOTO 980
1090 PRINT TAB( 13);
1100 GOTO 990
1110 PRINT TAB( 20);
1120 GOTO 1000
1130 PRINT TAB( 30);
1140 GOTO 1010
1150 GOTO 90
1160 PRINT "TYPE L TO MOVE LEFT.
     "
1170 PRINT "TYPE R TO MOVE RIGHT
     "
1180 PRINT "TYPE T TO READ A POI
     NT ON THE "
1190 PRINT "SCREEN TO BE INTEGRA
     TED."
1200 PRINT "(AN EVEN NUMBER MUST
     BE READ.)"
1210 PRINT "TYPE F TO GET NEXT P
     AGE."
1220 PRINT "TYPE A TO END."
1230 PRINT : PRINT : PRINT : PRINT
     "TYPE S TO START."
1240 PRINT : PRINT : PRINT
1250 GET IN$
1260 IF LEFT$ (IN$,1) = "S" THEN
     1280
1270 GOTO 1250
1280 RETURN
1290 G$ = CHR$ (20):D$ = CHR$ (
     10)
1300 B$ = "■"
1310 INPUT "INPUT NAME OF FILE."
     ;G$
1320 REM ********SAVING RESULTS*
     ******
1330 INPUT "INPUT DATE.";D
1340 PRINT B$;"OPEN "G$
1350 PRINT B$;"WRITE "G$""
1360 PRINT D
1370 R = 1
1380 IF X(R) = 6969 THEN 1420
1390 PRINT X(R): PRINT P(R): PRINT
     P(R + 1): PRINT Z(R): PRINT
     W(R)
1400 R = R + 2
1410 GOTO 1380
1420 PRINT X(R)
1430 PRINT B$;"CLOSE"G$""
1440 PRINT : PRINT : PRINT "**DA
     TA SAVED IN ";G$
1450 GOTO 90
1460 REM ********RETRIEVE RESULT
     S*****
1470 R = 1
1480 Q$ = CHR$ (4)
1490 G$ = CHR$ (20):D$ = CHR$ (
     10)
1500 INPUT "INPUT FILE NAME.";G$
1510 B$ = "■"
1520 PRINT B$;"OPEN"G$""
1530 PRINT B$;"READ"G$""
1540 INPUT D: PRINT : PRINT : PRINT
     "***FILE ";G$;" CREATED ON "
     ;D: PRINT : PRINT : PRINT
1550 INPUT X(R)
1560 IF X(R) = 6969 THEN 1610
1570 INPUT P(R): INPUT P(R + 1):
     INPUT Z(R): INPUT W(R)
1580 R = R + 2
1590 IF X(R) = 6969 THEN 1610
1600 GOTO 1550
1610 R = 1
1620 PRINT ; TAB( 17);"RESULTS"
1630 PRINT ; TAB( 17);"*******"
1640 PRINT "PEAK POINT1 POINT2 A
     REA    MEAN B/LINE"
1650 PRINT "**** ****** ****** *
     ***    **** ******"
1660 PRINT
1670 PRINT X(R); TAB( 6);P(R); TAB(
     13);P(R + 1); TAB( 20);Z(R);
     TAB( 30);W(R)
1680 R = R + 2
1690 IF X(R) = 6969 THEN 1710
1700 GOTO 1670
1710 PRINT B$;"CLOSE"G$""
1720 GOTO 90
1730 REM ********HARDCOPY PLOT**
     ******
1740 HGR : POKE 49234,0
1750 F = 0
1760 GOSUB 1930
1770 A = 16384:I = 0:P = 0
1780 GOSUB 1970
```

237

```
1790  IF  PEEK (A + I) > 190 THEN
      1820
1800  IF P > 190 THEN 1880
1810  HPLOT  PEEK (A + I),P TO  PEEK
      (A + I - 2),P
1820  HPLOT 0,P
1830  I = I + 2:P = P + 1:F = F +
      1:L = L + 1
1840  IF P > 190 THEN 1880
1850  IF I > PL THEN 2000
1860  IF  PEEK (A + I) > 190 THEN
      1820
1870  GOTO 1790
1880  POKE 1913,1
1890  PR# 1: PRINT  CHR$ (17);
1900  PR# 0
1910  P = 0: HGR : POKE 49234,0
1920  GOTO 1790
1930  FOR J = 0 TO 279 STEP 10
1940  HPLOT J,0 TO J,10
1950  NEXT
1960  RETURN
1970  L = 0
1980  HPLOT 0,0 TO 279,0
1990  RETURN
2000  TEXT
2010  GOTO 90
2020  REM ********HARDCOPY DATA**
      ******
2030  GOSUB 2210
2040  REM ********DISPLAY DATA***
      ******
2050  I = 0:A = 16384
2060  PI = 0
2070  PRINT : PRINT : PRINT : PRINT
      "DISPLAY OF DATA TO BE PLOTE
      D."
2080  PRINT
2090  FOR C = 1 TO 9
2100  IF  PEEK (A + I) < 10 THEN
      2140
```

```
2110  IF  PEEK (A + I) < 100 THEN
      2160
2120  PRINT  PEEK (A + I);" ";
2130  GOTO 2170
2140  PRINT "  "; PEEK (A + I);"
      ";
2150  GOTO 2170
2160  PRINT " "; PEEK (A + I);"  "
      ;
2170  I = I + 2
2180  NEXT
2190  IF I > PL THEN 2230
2200  GOTO 2080
2210  PR# 1
2220  RETURN
2230  PR# 0
2240  GOTO 90
2500  IF  LEFT$ (IN$,1) = "R" THEN
      2600
2510  O = X
2520  IF X + 1 > 279 THEN 2570
2530  X = X + 1:Y = 160 - ( PEEK (
      A + (X + (K * 279)) * 2) * (
      160 / 256)) - 11
2540  IF Y < 0 THEN 2520
2560  GOTO 370
2570  X = 0
2580  GOTO 370
2600  O = X
2620  IF X - 1 < 0 THEN  THEN 267
      0
2630  X = X - 1:Y = 160 - ( PEEK (
      A + (X + (K * 279)) * 2) * (
      160 / 256)) - 11
2640  IF Y < 0 THEN 2620
2660  GOTO 370
2670  X = 0
2680  GOTO 370
```

This program was written by Mr.S.Bhogal as a third year undergraduate project at the University of Lancaster. The primary aim was to provide a simple visual system which could be used by the operator to define areas of the chromatogram (i.e., peaks) for integration. An arrow is positioned above the chromatogram to indicate the start and end of the integral required. The arrow uses the Applesoft X DRAW command and the simple integration process is listed at 560–680. Results can be saved to, or retrieved from, a text file and a hard copy of the chromatogram in line form is also available.

**Listing 3. S + G DERIV**

```
30   INPUT "TYPE IN DATA FILE NAME
     ";F$
40   D$ =  CHR$ (4): PRINT D$"BLOAD
     ";F$
50   CLEAR : HOME : DIM C(11):A =
     16384:M = 0:P = 0
100  HOME : PRINT : PRINT : INPUT
     "TYPE IN THE NUMBER OF DATA
     ITEMS TO BE TREATED-N.B. 279
     PER PAGE";D:DT = D * 2
150  HOME : PRINT : PRINT : INPUT
     "CHOOSE SMOOTHING FUNCTION-5
     ,7,9";SM
160  IF SM < 5 OR SM > 9 THEN 150

170  ON SM - 4 GOSUB 1500,150,160
     0,150,1700
180  X = 3:Y = 10
190  GOSUB 1000
200  I = 1
210  I = I + 2:P = P + 1
215  IF P > 279 THEN  GOSUB 1000
225  IF I > DT THEN 2000
250  N = 0:N1 = 0:S = 0:M = 0
260  FOR H = 1 TO SM STEP 2
265  C1 =  PEEK (A + I - H):C2 =  PEEK
     (A + I + H)
```

```
270  S = S + (C1   - C(H)) + (C2 *
     C(H))
280  NEXT
290  N1 = S / CN:M = N1 - N2:N2 =
     N1:N = N1
300  T = 110 -  INT (N * X):U = 16
     0 -  INT (M * Y)
305  IF T < 0 OR T > 189 THEN T =
     0
308  IF U < 0 OR U > 189 THEN U =
     0
310  HPLOT P,65 - ( INT ( PEEK (A
     + I)) * (65 / 256))
320  HPLOT P,110 -  INT (N * X)
330  HPLOT P,160 -  INT (M * Y)
340  GOTO 210
1000 HGR : POKE 49234,0: HPLOT 0
     ,65 TO 279,65
1010 HPLOT 0,110 TO 279,110
1020 HPLOT 0,160 TO 279,160
1030 P = 0: RETURN
1500 C(1) = 5:C(3) = 15:C(5) =  -
     3:CN = 35: RETURN
1600 C(1) = 1:C(3) = 3:C(5) = 5:C
     (7) =  - 2:CN = 21: RETURN
1700 C(1) =  - 21:C(2) =  - 35:C(
     5) = 25:C(7) = 15:C(9) = 5:C
     N = 231: RETURN
2000 END
```

This small program demonstrates the effectiveness of smoothing function by allowing a choice of three smoothing convolutes (11). The results are presented graphically by plotting the chromatogram, first derivative and second derivative as shown for example in *Figure 2*.

Lines 260–290 provide a 'basic' routine for implementing the Savitsky and Golay computation of a smoothed first derivative (12) which may be incorporated into *Listing 1*.

### Listing 4. Simpson v Trapezoid

```
1000  HOME : PRINT "
      ***********************
      *SIMPSON V.TRAPEZOID*
      ***********************
      "
1010  PRINT : PRINT "APPLIED TO I
      NTEGRAL ENTERED ON LINE 1020
      AS FOLLOWS :- ": LIST 1020
      : PRINT : PRINT "DERIVED FRO
      M CURVE GIVEN BY
      ' Y = SIN(.22X + 125)'"
1020  DEF FN A(X) = .22 * COS (
      (.22 * X) + 125)
1030  PRINT : INPUT "STARTING LOW
      ER AND UPPER LIMITS (L,U) ?
      ";L,U
1040  PRINT : INPUT "NUMBER OF IN
      CREMENTS  ? ";C
1050  PRINT : INPUT "NUMBER OF ST
      RIPS EACH TIME ? ";N
1060  PRINT
1070  PRINT : INVERSE : PRINT "IN
      CREMENT ";"SIMPSON AREA  ";"
      TRAPEZOIDAL AREA": NORMAL : PRINT

1080  FOR D = 1 TO C
```

```
1090  H = (U - L) / N
1100  S =  FN A(L) +  FN A(U)
1110  FOR I = 2 TO N - 2 STEP 2
1120  Y = Y +  FN A(L + I * H)
1130  NEXT I
1140  FOR I = 1 TO N - 1 STEP 2
1150  Z = Z +  FN A(L + I * H)
1160  NEXT I
1170  A = (H / 3) * (S + 2 * Y + 4
      * Z):B = (H / 2) * (S + 2 *
      Y + 2 * Z)
1180  PRINT D - 1;" - ";D; TAB( 1
      2);A; TAB( 26);B
1190  L = L + 1:U = U + 1: NEXT D
1200  PRINT : PRINT : VTAB 24:V$ =
      "          TO CONTINUE PRESS A
      NY KEY
1210  FOR I = 1 TO  LEN (V$): POKE
      1999 + I, ASC ( MID$ (V$,I,1
      )): NEXT : GET T$: GOTO 1000

]CATALOG

DISK VOLUME 254

A 002 HELLO
T 005 MC AD
```

This program was written by Dr.A.R.Wellburn, Department of Biological Sciences, University of Lancaster. It allows comparison of the Simpson and trapezoid techniques for the integration of the area beneath a derived peak.

### Listing 5. Chromatogram plotter

```
5 D$ =  CHR$ (4): PRINT D$;"BLOAD
    BPLOTCC"
10  INPUT "CHROMATOGRAM DATA FILE
    NAME";F$
20  D$ =  CHR$ (4): PRINT D$;"BLOA
    D";F$
30  INPUT "DATA POINT AT WHICH PL
    OT TO START";N
40  INPUT "PITCH OF DATA PLOTTING
    ";P
50  N = N + 16384:N1 =  INT (N / 2
    56):N2 = N - (N1 * 256)
60  POKE 24583,N1: POKE 24584,N2
70  POKE 24582,F
80  CALL 24587
90  POKE 49234,255
100  GOTO 30
```

```
6000-   00          BRK
6001-   BE 10 00    LDX     $0010.Y
6004-   18          CLC
6005-   01 02       ORA     ($02,X)
6007-   40          RTI
6008-   00          BRK
6009-   00          BRK
600A-   00          BRK
600B    A9 00       LDA     #$00
600D-   8D 04 60    STA     $6004
6010-   8D 05 60    STA     $6005
6013-   AD 08 60    LDA     $6008
6016-   8D 41 60    STA     $6041
6019-   AD 07 60    LDA     $6007
601C-   8D 42 60    STA     $6042
601F-   20 E2 F3    JSR     $F3E2
6022-   A9 FF       LDA     #$FF
6024-   8D 52 C0    STA     $C052
6027-   20 40 60    JSR     $6040
```

```
602A-   AE 04 60    LDX     $6004
602D-   AC 05 60    LDY     $6005
6030-   AD 01 60    LDA     $6001
6033-   20 57 F4    JSR     $F457
6036-   20 B4 60    JSR     $60B4
6039-   20 99 60    JSR     $6099
603C-   4C A2 60    JMP     $60A2
603F-   60          RTS
6040-   AD 18 41    LDA     #4118
6043-   A2 08       LDX     #$08
6045-   8D 02 60    STA     $6002
6048-   A9 0A       LDA     #$0A
604A-   8D 03 60    STA     $6003
604D-   A9 00       LDA     #$00
604F-   8D 01 60    STA     $6001
6052-   8D 00 60    STA     $6000
6055-   0A          ASL
6056-   2E 00 60    ROL     $6000
6059-   0E 03 60    ASL     $6003
605C-   90 09       BCC     $6067
605E-   18          CLC
605F-   6D 02 60    ADC     $6002
6062-   90 03       BCC     $6067
6064-   EE 00 60    INC     $6000
6067-   CA          DEX
6068-   D0 EB       BNE     $6055
606A-   8D 01 60    STA     $6001
606D-   A2 08       LDX     #$08
606F-   A9 10       LDA     #$10
6071-   8D 02 60    STA     $6002
6074-   8D 00 60    LDA     $6000
6077-   0E 01 60    ASL     $6001
607A-   2A          ROL
607B-   CD 02 60    CMP     $6002
607E-   90 06       BCC     $6036
6080-   ED 02 60    SBC     $6002
6083-   EE 01 60    INC     $6001
6086-   CA          DEX
6087-   D0 EE       BNE     $6077
9089-   8D 03 60    STA     $6003
608C-   38          SEC
608D-   A9 BE       LDA     #$BE
608F-   ED 01 60    SBC     $6001
6092-   B0 02       BCS     $6096
6094-   A9 BE       LDA     #$BE
6096-   8D 01 60    STA     $6001
```

```
6099-   EE 04 60   INC   $6004          60B1-   4C 27 60   JMP   $6027
609C-   D0 03      BNE   $60A1          60B4-   18         CLC
609E-   EE 05 60   INC   $6005          60B5-   AD 41 60   LDA   $6041
60A1-   60         RTS                  60B8-   6D 06 60   ADC   $6006
60A2-   AD 05 60   LDA   $6005          60BB-   8D 41 60   STA   $6041
60A5-   F0 0A      BEQ   $60B1          60BE-   AD 42 60   LDA   $6042
60A7-   AD 04 60   LDA   $6004          60C1-   69 00      ADC   #$00
60AA-   C9 18      CMP   #$18           60C3-   8D 42 60   STA   $6042
60AC-   D0 03      BNE   $60B1          60C6-   60         RTS
60AE-   4C 3F 60   JMP   $603F
```

A machine coded program to display a chromatogram file graphically. The machine code accesses Applesoft interpreter routines and would require changes at $6021 – $6024 and $6041, $6042 for use on another machine, otherwise it can be used by any 65XX processor (i.e., most 8-bit machines). The program displays one page of a chromatogram at a time from any start point in the file and compresses the data by any factor required. These inputs are made via the short basic program which 'calls' the MC routine.

Note that the machine code routine re-writes itself during operation ($60B5 – $60C6) to update the position in the data file recorded. In transferring the code to a new location this must be taken into account.

CHAPTER 9

# Microcomputers in Centrifugation

## J. STEENSGAARD and D. RICKWOOD

## 1. INTRODUCTION

The term 'centrifuges' covers a wide range of instruments from simple low-speed bench centrifuges to the very sophisticated preparative and analytical ultracentrifuges capable of speeds in excess of 60 000 r.p.m. Another volume in the *Practical Approach Series* (1) gives a detailed description of all aspects of centrifugation. For quantitative studies employing density gradient separations one usually uses an ultracentrifuge. However, the nature of the data obtained is dependent on the type of ultracentrifuge. In the case of analytical centrifuges it is possible to monitor the sedimentation of the sample during centrifugation. A detailed description of the analytical ultracentrifuge, its optical systems and its applications has been published previously in the *Practical Approach Series* (2).

It is possible to interface an analytical ultracentrifuge directly to a microcomputer to allow the on-line processing of data. However, the method of interfacing depends on the type of instrument, its optical system and its application (2). Moreover, analytical ultracentrifuges are not widely available. In this chapter the discussion will therefore be limited to preparative ultracentrifuges which are to be found in most laboratories.

External microcomputer control of preparative ultracentrifuges has been developed for some types of machine. Features of these machines include automatic timed speed control, re-run facilities and electronic rotor logbook. Although such features are marginally useful, little is gained in user convenience or enhanced performance of the centrifuge. While the user may well take advantage of such features if they are built in, it is not usually worthwhile considering special interfacing, which is both expensive and complex, to allow the attachment of an on-line external microcomputer for control purposes. However, in the future it is likely that it will be possible to extend the capacity of microcomputers associated with centrifuges to allow them to test rotors and hence reduce the risk of accidents.

For preparative centrifuges the most important application of the microcomputer is the processing of the data obtained manually from the analysis of gradients after centrifugation in order to obtain quantitative data on the sedimentation coefficient, molecular weight or buoyant density of the sample. In addition, it is possible to use computer simulation techniques for optimising rate-zonal gradient separations in terms of gradient shape or centrifugation conditions. This chapter presents a number of programs currently in use for centrifugation studies and describes their applications.

## 2. THEORY OF CENTRIFUGATION

The sedimentation coefficient, $s$, of a particle is a quantity which defines its sedimentation velocity in a unit centrifugal field (3). Thus:

$$s = \frac{dR/dt}{\omega^2 R} \qquad \text{Equation 1}$$

where $R$ is the radial distance of the particle from the axis of rotation in centimetres, $dR/dt$ is the particle velocity and $\omega$ is the angular speed of the rotor in radians per second. For practical purposes, sedimentation coefficients are expressed in Svedberg units (S), which are equivalent to $10^{-13}$ seconds.

The sedimentation coefficient is a function of the size, density and shape of particles. For macromolecules, the size is related to its molecular weight ($M$). The density is given in terms of its partial specific volume ($\bar{v}$) which is the reciprocal particle density. Variations in shape are reflected by the frictional ratio ($f/f_o$) which describes the deviation in shape of a particle from a perfect sphere. The exact relationships between these parameters are given by the equation:

$$s = M^{2/3}(\frac{1 - \bar{v}\varrho}{\sqrt[3]{v}})/[(N \, \pi 6 \eta \, \sqrt{0.75/(N\pi)})(f/f_o)] \qquad \text{Equation 2}$$

where N is Avogadro's number.

The relative centrifugal force (RCF) is given by:

$$RCF = \frac{\omega^2 R}{g} \qquad \text{Equation 3}$$

If expressed in terms of revolutions per minute ($Q$) one obtains the expression:

$$RCF = 11.18 \, R \left(\frac{Q}{1000}\right)^2 \qquad \text{Equation 4}$$

Particles can be separated on the basis of their sedimentation rate by differential centrifugation. This involves pelleting the fastest sedimenting particles from an initially homogeneous solution (*Figure 1*). It is possible to calculate the

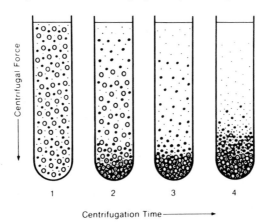

**Figure 1.** Fractionation of particles by differential pelleting. Reproduced from reference 4 with permission.

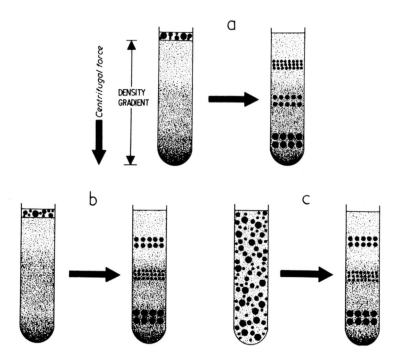

**Figure 2.** Types of density gradient centrifugation. **(a)** Rate-zonal centrifugation. The sample is loaded onto the top of a preformed density gradient (left) and centrifugation results in a series of zones of particles sedimenting at different rates depending upon the particle sizes (right). **(b)** Isopycnic centrifugation using a preformed density gradient. The sample is loaded on top of the gradient (left) and each sample particle sediments until it reaches a density in the gradient equal to its own density (right). Therefore the final position of each type of particle in the gradient (the isopycnic position) is determined by the particle density. **(c)** Isopycnic centrifugation using a self-forming gradient. The sample is mixed with the gradient medium to give a mixture of uniform density (left). During subsequent centrifugation, the gradient medium re-distributes to form a density gradient and the sample particles then band at their isopycnic positions (right). From reference 15 with permission.

pelleting efficiency of rotors numerically (4). The higher centrifugal force a rotor can withstand the more efficient it is considered to be. However, pathlength is also important, in that rotors with shorter sedimentation pathlengths are more efficient for pelleting particles. The pelleting efficiency of a rotor can be determined from its K-factor, which is a constant relating the time in hours ($t$) required to pellet a given particle of sedimentation coefficient ($s$). Thus:

$$K = s\,t \qquad \text{Equation 5}$$

The K-factor is related to the speed in revolutions per minute ($Q$) and the dimensions of the rotor by the expression:

$$K = \frac{2.53 \times 10^{11}(\ln R_{max} - \ln R_{min})}{Q^2} \qquad \text{Equation 6}$$

Hence swing-out rotors which have longer pathlengths usually have higher K-factors even though the maximum centrifugal force generated is the same as that of a fixed-angle rotor. In fact because of the poor resolution of differential pelleting methods (5) one usually needs to use a gradient to optimise the fractionation of biological samples.

Two kinds of gradient centrifugation are widely used in biological research and these are illustrated in *Figure 2*. In *isopycnic* centrifugation, the particles sediment in the gradient until they encounter a density in the gradient that is equal to their own. A separation between different particles is therefore based on differences in density of the particles. In *rate-zonal* centrifugation experiments, the gradient stabilises the zones of particles as they are sedimenting down the gradient. The gradient is designed so that the particles do not reach their isopycnic limit, and the separation between different bands of particles therefore depends on the sedimentation coefficients of the particles in question. It should not be forgotten that the sedimentation coefficient is itself dependent on several factors including size, density and shape of the particles (Equation 2). For a detailed overview see references 1, 6 and 7.

Particles will sediment in a gradient with a velocity that is different for the corresponding sedimentation velocity in standard conditions (water at 20°C). At each point in the gradient, provided that the density of the particle ($\varrho_p$) is known, the actual sedimentation coefficient can be calculated using the equation:

$$s_{T,M} = s_{20,w} \frac{(\varrho_p - \varrho_{T,M})}{(\varrho_p - \varrho_{20,w})} \frac{\eta_{20,w}}{\eta_{T,M}} \qquad \text{Equation 7}$$

where $\varrho_{T,M}$, $\varrho_{20,w}$ and $\eta_{T,M}$, $\eta_{20,w}$ are the densities and viscosities of the solutions, at the experimental and standard conditions respectively.

The density ($\varrho$) of the solution, w/w % and w/v % of any gradient medium are interrelated as follows:

$$\text{w/w \%} = \varrho \, (\text{w/v \%}) \qquad \text{Equation 8}$$

One advantage of using sucrose density centrifugation is that it allows the calculation of sedimentation coefficients by numerical integration of the following equation:

$$s_{20,w} \int_0^t \omega^2 dt = \frac{\varrho_p - \varrho_{20,w}}{\eta_{20,w}} \int_i^R \frac{\eta_{T,M}}{\varrho_p - \varrho_{T,M}} \frac{dR}{R} \qquad \text{Equation 9}$$

The integration of Equation 9 is relatively straightforward. The force-time integral is displayed automatically on some centrifuges; otherwise it can be approximated by the equation:

$$\int_0^t \omega^2 \, dt = (\pi \, Q)^2 \, [P + (A + D)/3]/15 \qquad \text{Equation 10}$$

where $Q$ is the rotor speed (r.p.m.), $P$ is the duration of the run (min) at the chosen rotor speed, $A$ is the acceleration period (min) and $D$ is the deceleration period (min). This formula for the approximation of the force-time integral is based on the assumption that the rates of acceleration and deceleration are constant. This is the case with all better ultracentrifuges, but because the sum of $A$ and $D$ is usually much smaller than $P$, the error which is introduced by variations in the acceleration and deceleration rates will be relatively small. The constant part of the right side of Equation 9 can be evaluated directly if the particle density in the gradient solution is known. Thus, the main problem is to evaluate the integral on the right-hand side of Equation 9, and this is facilitated by the gradient centrifugation technique employed.

Irrespective of the rotor used, at the end of the run the contents of the tubes or zonal rotor are divided into a series of fractions. The volume of each fraction can be determined as well as the concentration of gradient material (usually sucrose) present. The geometry of ultracentrifuge rotors is defined mathematically, so that relationships between rotor radius and accumulated fraction volume can be established for all types of rotor. The term $dR/R$ can then be taken as the calculated radial step through one fraction divided by the radius corresponding to its mid-volume. Moreover, the viscosity and the density of the corresponding radial step can be obtained from measurement of the concentration of gradient material in each fraction, allowing calculation of the buoyancy term inside the integral. The complete polynomials for this purpose can be found in the SUC1 program in the appendix. This technique was originally described by Martin and Ames (8). Detailed descriptions of the numerical procedures have also been published elsewhere (9,10).

In isopycnic centrifugation the particles are separated only on the basis of their density. The size of the particle only affects the time required for the particle to reach equilibrium and the width of the band when the particle is at its isopycnic position. Although this chapter refers to isopycnic centrifugation in terms of gradient formation (see Section 4.3), most of this chapter is concerned with rate-zonal separations and the reader should consult other publications for detailed descriptions of the theory and applications of isopycnic centrifugation (1).

## 3. EVALUATION OF CENTRIFUGE ROTORS

Rotors are primarily characterised by their geometry (*Figure 3*) and by the maximum speed they can withstand. The choice of a particular rotor for a given purpose depends on the nature of the sample, the nature of the desired separation (*Table 1*) and on which rotors are available. Given the values of the minimum and the maximum radial distances of the spinning tubes in the rotor in question, together with the maximum speed of rotation, using Equation 4 one can calculate the centrifugal force at the top, middle and bottom of the tube. Moreover, using Equation 6 the required time to pellet a particle with a sedimentation coefficient of unity (1.0S) can be computed, assuming that the density and viscosity of the medium is similar to that of pure water at 20°C; this is the K-factor of the rotor. This also allows calculation of the time required to pellet a particle with a known sedimentation coefficient as this time will be proportionally shorter.

In the case of methods which involve the use of a supporting sucrose gradient, particles sedimenting in the gradient are retarded to a significant degree by the viscosity and density of the gradient medium. To calculate the pelleting time for particles sedimenting in a gradient it is necessary to account for the braking effect of the gradient by a numerical procedure which is closely related to the procedure for calculating sedimentation coefficients from experimental data (cf. Section 5).

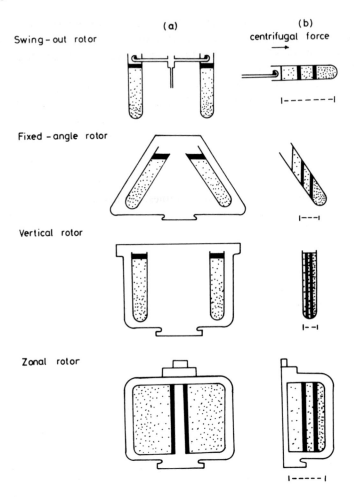

**Figure 3.** Types of rotor used for preparative ultracentrifugation. This figure shows the geometry of swing-out, fixed-angle, vertical and zonal rotors and the effect of rotation on the gradients. The sedimentation pathlength (⊢----⊣) is shown in each case.

**Table 1.** Types of Rotor and Their Applications.

| Type of rotor | Type of separation | | |
| --- | --- | --- | --- |
| | *pelleting* | *rate-zonal* | *isopycnic* |
| Fixed-angle | excellent | poor | good |
| Vertical | poor | good | excellent |
| Swing-out | inefficient | good | adequate |
| Zonal | poor | excellent | adequate |

This can be done by calculating the sedimentation of particles with a range of densities in a 5−20% (w/w) sucrose gradient at 5°C and hence obtaining a set of $K'$-factors (4). However, it is simpler to express the sedimentation rate of particles with a density of 1.3 g/ml since this closely corresponds to the density of ribosomes, DNA and proteins in sucrose solutions; this calculation yields the parameter termed the K*-factor. The program KFAC1 in the appendix calculates the pelleting time of a particle of 1.0S in a $5-20\%$ (w/w) sucrose gradient at a temperature of 5°C; this value is equivalent to the K*-value. Since $5-20\%$ sucrose gradients are essentially isokinetic (i.e., particles move at a constant velocity) centrifugation for half of the pelleting time will sediment the particles of interest about half-way down the gradient. The KFAC1 program also contains the complete polynomials for calculations of densities and viscosities of sucrose as used in the program SUC1, and hence it may be easily modified for computation of K*-values using other types of sucrose gradient.

The following shows some output examples. Inputs (not shown) are the name of the rotor and the minimum and maximum radius (RMIN and RMAX, respectively) together with maximum rotor speed.

```
KONTRON TZT 48.640
RMIN=  3.40    RMAX=   6.62 (CM)
MAX RPM= 48000
RCF MAX= 170502, AV.= 129035, MIN=  87569 (XG)
K-VALUE=    73. (H)
K*-VALUE=   194. (H)

SRU        0.720 UNTS.

   RUN COMPLETE.

MY OWN DREAM
RMIN=  9.00    RMAX= 19.00 (CM)
MAX RPM= 65000
RCF MAX= 897364, AV.= 661215, MIN= 425067 (XG)
K-VALUE=    45. (H)
K*-VALUE=   118. (H)
```

It should be noted that K′ and K* values do not give any indication as to the resolving power of rotors. Fritsch (11) has developed a method by which one can calculate the resolving power of swing-out rotors in terms of a factor, $\Lambda$. The resolving power of rotors can also be compared by computer simulation methods (12). Using the programs given in Section 5 for calculating sedimentation coefficients of particles it is possible to compare the resolving power of swing-out and vertical rotors (12). This method uses a similar model as that used for calculating K*-values from which one calculates the sedimentation coefficient ($s_m$) and rate of increase in sedimentation coefficient ($\Delta s$) at the centre of the gradient after centrifugation for 60 min at maximum speed. The value $\Delta s/s_m$ reflects the resolving power of rotors, the smaller the value the greater the degree of resolution that can be obtained.

## 4. GRADIENT PROGRAMS

### 4.1 General Programs

In work employing gradients for isopycnic separations two related problems are frequently encountered. The first of these is to be able to calculate the density of a defined concentration of gradient material, irrespective of whether the concentration of the gradient material is given as w/w % or as w/v %. Secondly, it is often required that one type of concentration notation be converted to the other. The density, w/w % and w/v % concentrations are interrelated as shown in Equation 8. There is no direct method for all these calculations. In the present program, a series of now classical data relating density (at 25°C) to w/w concentrations has been used to generate a new series of polynomial coefficients by statistical means. The data were originally compiled by Myron Brakke, but here they are quoted from Sober (13). The four kinds of computations in program DENS1 are performed by using third degree polynomials, which are sufficient to reproduce the original table to within three significant figures. Limits of concentrations are given in the program in order not to exceed the maximum solubilities of the materials in question.

The following shows an example of use of the program:

```
GRADIENT PROGRAMS.   DATA FROM M. BRAKKE. AT 25 DEGREES.
----------------------------------------------------------

THIS PROGRAM CAN CALCULATE
   1. DENSITY FROM CONCENTRATION  (W/W PERCENT)
   2. DENSITY FROM CONCENTRATION  (W/V PERCENT)
   3. W/W PERCENT FROM W/V PERCENT
   4. W/V PERCENT FROM W/W PERCENT

SELECT A PROGRAM BY ITS NUMBER
? 1

SELECT GRADIENT MATERIAL

     LICL    1      CSSO4        8
     LIBR    2      K-ACETATE    9
     KBR     3      K-CITRATE   10
     NABR    4      K-TARTRATE  11
     RBBR    5      GLYCEROL    12
     CSCL    6      SUCROSE     13
     CSBR    7
? 8
INPUT
? 10.0
DENS. G/ML : 1.086
CONTINUE: SAME MATERIAL INPUT 1, OTHER  2; STOP 3
? 1
INPUT
? 20.0
DENS. G/ML : 1.190
CONTINUE: SAME MATERIAL INPUT 1, OTHER  2; STOP 3
? 1
INPUT
? 30.0
DENS. G/ML : 1.309
CONTINUE: SAME MATERIAL INPUT 1, OTHER  2; STOP 3
? 1
INPUT
? 40.0
INPUT MUST BE BETWEEN  0   AND   30
TRY AGAIN
INPUT
? 0
DENS. G/ML :  .997
CONTINUE: SAME MATERIAL INPUT 1, OTHER  2; STOP 3
? 3
```

For all quantitative work involving either rate-zonal or isopycnic fractionations it is also important to analyse the shape of the gradient. This is done after fractionation of the gradients usually by measuring the refractive index of each fraction. All gradient solutes increase the refractive index (RI) of solutions in a linear fashion with concentration and hence density ($\varrho$). This relationship can be expressed by the equation:

$$\varrho = a\mathrm{RI} - b \qquad\qquad \text{Equation 11}$$

where $a$ and $b$ are coefficients which are constant for each type of gradient medium. *Table 2* lists the values of $a$ and $b$ for some common gradient solutes.

**Table 2.** Coefficients for the Calculation of Density from Refractive Index.

### 1. Ionic Gradient Media

| Gradient solute | Temperature (°C) RI | Temperature (°C) ϱ | Coefficients a | Coefficients b | Valid density range (g/cm³) |
|---|---|---|---|---|---|
| CsCl | 20 | 20 | 10.9276 | 13.593 | 1.2 – 1.9 |
| | 25 | 25 | 10.8601 | 13.497 | 1.3 – 1.9 |
| Cs₂SO₄ | 25 | 25 | 12.1200 | 15.166 | 1.1 – 1.4 |
| | 25 | 25 | 13.6986 | 17.323 | 1.4 – 1.8 |
| Cs(HCOO) | 25 | 20 | 13.8760 | 16.209 | 1.8 – 2.3 |
| CsTCAᵃ | 20 | 20 | 7.6232 | 9.1612 | 1.1 – 1.7 |
| CsTFAᵇ | 20 | 20 | 23.041 | 29.759 | 1.2 – 1.8 |
| NaBr | 25 | 25 | 5.8880 | 6.852 | 1.0 – 1.5 |
| NaI | 20 | 20 | 5.3330 | 6.118 | 1.1 – 1.8 |
| KBr | 25 | 25 | 6.4786 | 7.643 | 1.0 – 1.4 |
| KI | 25 | 25 | 5.8356 | 6.786 | 1.1 – 1.7 |
| RbBr | 25 | 25 | 9.1750 | 11.241 | 1.1 – 1.7 |
| RbCl | 25 | 25 | 9.3282 | 11.456 | 1.0 – 1.4 |
| RbTCA | 20 | 20 | 6.5869 | 7.7805 | 1.1 – 1.6 |

### 2. Nonionic Gradient Media

| Gradient solute | Temperature (°C) RI | Temperature (°C) ϱ | Coefficients a | Coefficients b |
|---|---|---|---|---|
| Sucrose | 20 | 0 | 2.7329 | 2.6425 |
| Ficoll | 20 | 20 | 2.381 | 2.175 |
| Metrizamide | 20 | 5 | 3.453 | 3.601 |
| Metrizamide/D₂O | 25 | 25 | 3.0534 | 2.9541 |
| Nycodenz® | 20 | 20 | 3.242 | 3.323 |
| Metrizoate | 25 | 5 | 3.839 | 4.117 |
| Renografin | 24 | 4 | 3.5419 | 3.7198 |
| Iothalamate | 25 | 25 | 3.904 | 4.201 |
| Chloral hydrate | 4 | 4 | 3.6765 | 3.9066 |
| Bovine serum albumin | 24 | 5 | 1.4129 | 0.8814 |

ᵃTCA is the trichloroacetate salt.
ᵇTFA is the trifluoroacetate salte. CsTFA is a registered trademark of Pharmacia Ltd.

The program RI/DENSITY listing illustrates the type of very simple program that can be devised for calculating the densities of solutions from their refractive indices. Example outputs from this program are given here.

```
READY.
RUN
LIST OF GRADIENT MEDIA
1) SUCROSE
2) FICOLL
3) METRIZAMIDE
4) NYCODENZ
5) CSCL
6) CSSO4
7) NAI
8) NONE OF THESE
WHICH MEDIUM (1-8)? 5
INSERT VALUE OF REFRACTIVE INDEX
? 1.4000
  1.4       1.70674
INSERT VALUE OF REFRACTIVE INDEX
? 1.3960
  1.396     1.6632996
INSERT VALUE OF REFRACTIVE INDEX
?
```

```
RUN
LIST OF GRADIENT MEDIA
1) SUCROSE
2) FICOLL
3) METRIZAMIDE
4) NYCODENZ
5) CSCL
6) CSSO4
7) NAI
8) NONE OF THESE
WHICH MEDIUM (1-8)? 8
REFRACTIVE INDEX(RI) AND DENSITY(D) ARE RELATED BY THE EQUATION
D=A*RI-B
ENTER VALUE OF A
? 10.8601
ENTER VALUE OF B
? 13.497
INSERT VALUE OF REFRACTIVE INDEX
? 1.4000
  1.4        1.70714
INSERT VALUE OF REFRACTIVE INDEX
? 1.3960
  1.396      1.6636996
INSERT VALUE OF REFRACTIVE INDEX
```

## 4.2 Program for Sucrose Gradients

Sucrose gradients are frequently used for rate-zonal centrifugations, and in such experiments it is necessary to be able to calculate the viscosity as well as the density for a given concentration of sucrose at a defined temperature. Program SUC1 calculates the w/v % mole fraction of sucrose, density and viscosity (in mPa.s) for a list of w/w % of sucrose at a given temperature (in °C). The method for performing these calculations has been developed by Barber (14). It is based on the use of a series of very accurate polynomials. A typical example of the use of this program is as follows:

```
SELECT TEMPERATURE                      SELECT TEMPERATURE
? 10.0                                  ? 20.0
 W/W PC   W/V PC   MOL.FR.  DENS.  VISC.    W/W PC   W/V PC   MOL.FR.  DENS.  VISC.
------------------------------------------  -----------------------------------------
  0.       .00    .0000   1.000   1.308      0.       .00    .0000    .999   1.004
  5.      5.10    .0028   1.020   1.506      5.      5.09    .0028   1.018   1.148
 10.     10.40    .0058   1.040   1.771     10.     10.38    .0058   1.038   1.337
 15.     15.92    .0092   1.061   2.134     15.     15.88    .0092   1.059   1.592
 20.     21.67    .0130   1.083   2.642     20.     21.61    .0130   1.081   1.946
 25.     27.66    .0173   1.106   3.377     25.     27.58    .0173   1.103   2.449
 30.     33.90    .0221   1.130   4.481     30.     33.80    .0221   1.127   3.189
 35.     40.42    .0276   1.155   6.225     35.     40.29    .0276   1.151   4.323
 40.     47.21    .0339   1.180   9.167     40.     47.06    .0339   1.177   6.163
 45.     54.31    .0413   1.207  14.541     45.     54.13    .0413   1.203   9.376
 50.     61.71    .0500   1.234  25.173     50.     61.49    .0500   1.230  15.421
 55.     69.43    .0605   1.262  48.868     55.     69.18    .0605   1.258  28.073
 60.     77.48    .0732   1.291 110.785     60.     77.20    .0732   1.287  58.496
 65.     85.89    .0891   1.321 312.464     65.     85.57    .0891   1.316 147.045
 70.     94.65    .1095   1.352 *1204.633   70.     94.29    .1095   1.347 481.788
 75.    103.79    .1365   1.384 *7397.437   75.    103.39    .1365   1.379 *2325.123
```

## 4.3 Program for Self-forming Gradients

Self-forming gradients are widely used for isopycnic centrifugation of macromolecules. Usually the gradients used for banding macromolecules are of one of the ionic media such as CsCl. The characteristics of these gradient solutes are well known in terms of gradient formation and it is possible to calculate the slopes of gradient as well as the time required to band particles of a known size using the program GRADIENT PROFILE. Knowing the dimensions of the rotor the pro-

**Table 3.** Values of $\beta°$ for Ionic Gradient Media.

| Gradient solute | $\beta°$ values (x $10^{-9}$) for solutions with initial densities (g/cm³) of | | | | | | | |
|---|---|---|---|---|---|---|---|---|
| | 1.1 | 1.2 | 1.3 | 1.4 | 1.5 | 1.6 | 1.7 | 1.8 |
| CsCl | − | 2.04 | 1.55 | 1.33 | 1.22 | 1.17 | 1.14 | 1.12 |
| Cs$_2$SO$_4$ | − | 1.06 | 0.76 | 0.67 | 0.64 | 0.66 | 0.69 | 0.74 |
| CsTCA[a] | − | − | − | 1.18 | − | − | − | − |
| CsTFA[b] | − | − | − | − | − | 1.29 | − | − |
| KBr | 6.20 | 3.80 | 3.05 | − | − | − | − | − |
| KI | 4.28 | 2.55 | 1.96 | 1.73 | − | − | − | − |
| NaBr | 7.70 | 5.20 | − | − | − | − | − | − |
| NaI | 5.10 | 3.19 | 2.82 | − | − | − | − | − |
| RbBr | − | 2.15 | 1.56 | 1.34 | 1.22 | − | − | − |
| RbCl | − | 3.42 | 2.76 | 2.25 | − | − | − | − |
| RbTCA[a] | − | − | − | − | 1.33 | 1.38 | − | − |

[a]TCA is the trichloroacetate salt.
[b]TFA is the trifluoroacetate salt. CsTFA is a registered trademark of Pharmacia Ltd.

gram calculates the isoconcentration point ($R_c$) of the gradient using the equation:

$$R_c = [\tfrac{1}{3}(R_m^2 + R_mR_b + R_b^2)]^{1/2} \qquad \text{Equation 12}$$

where $R_m$ is the distance from the axis of rotation to the meniscus and $R_b$ is the distance from the axis of rotation to the bottom of the tube.

The gradient program is then able to calculate the density at any distance from the axis of rotation using the equation:

$$\varrho_2 - \varrho_1 = \frac{1.1 \times 10^{-2}\ Q^2}{2\beta°}(R_2^2 - R_1^2) \qquad \text{Equation 13}$$

where $\beta°$ is the density gradient proportionality constant (15). This equation can be used to calculate the maximum and minimum densities of any gradient at any speed provided that the $\beta°$ value of the gradient medium is known. *Table 3* lists some $\beta°$ values for common gradient media used in the program.

The program also calculates the time in hours ($t$) taken to band a particle of known sedimentation coefficient ($s$) and density ($\varrho_p$) using the equation:

$$t = \frac{9.83 \times 10^{13}\ \beta°\ (\varrho_p - 1)}{Q^4\ R_p\ s} \qquad \text{Equation 14}$$

where $R_p$ is the distance of the particle from the axis of rotation. This equation is valid for a self-forming gradient; in a preformed gradient particles will band about twice as fast (15). An example of a typical printout for the banding of 20S DNA in CsCl gradients in half-full tubes of the Beckman 80Ti fixed-angle rotor is given:

```
     PLEASE INPUT THE FOLLOWING

Z
ZZZZZZZZZZZZZZZZZZZZZZZZZZZZZZZZZZZZZZZZZZZZ
MAXIMUM RADIUS (CENTIMETRES)=? 8.4
Z
ZZZZZZZZZZZZZZZZZZZZZZZZZZZZZZZZZZZZZZZZZZZZ
MINIMUM RADIUS (CENTIMETRES)=? 6.3
```

```
Z
ZZZZZZZZZZZZZZZZZZZZZZZZZZZZZZZZZZZZZZZZZZZZ
Z DENSIY OF MEDIUM (G/CC)     =? 1.72
Z (LESS THAN 1.8G/CC)
ZZZZZZZZZZZZZZZZZZZZZZZZZZZZZZZZZZZZZZZZZZ
Z ROTOR SPEED (RPM)           =? 35000
Z
ZZZZZZZZZZZZZZZZZZZZZZZZZZZZZZZZZZZZZZZZZZ
Z ARE THE ABOVE CORRECT(YES/NO)?
Z


PLEASE INPUT THE S20,W OF YOUR SAMPLE     S=.........? 20

....AND THE BUOYANT DENSITY               G/CC=......? 1.70

THE TIME TAKEN FOR THE GRADIENT TO FORM
WILL BE APPROXIMATELY
          ..... 24.69 HOURS

USE AN ESTIMATE IF YOU DO NOT KNOW THE   CORRECT VALUE
THE TIME REQUIRED FOR THE SAMPLE TO
REACH EQUILIBRIUM WILL BE APPROXIMATELY
          ..... 51.25 HOURS


AT EQUILIBRIUM THE SAMPLE WILL BE AT
AN APPROXIMATE RADIUS OF
          ..... 7.14CM

THE ABOVE FIGURES ARE ONLY A GUIDE AND

TO CALCULATE THE EXACT GRADIENT PROFILE
          PRESS ANY KEY

DENSITY = 1.72RG/CC)IS AT A RADIUS OF THE
          7.37495763CM


  PLEASE INPUT THE RADIUS FOR WHICH A   DENSITY IS REQUIRED

RADIUS (CM).....? 8.4
DENSITY AT  8.4 CM ....  1.81527271

RADIUS (CM).....? 6.3
DENSITY AT  6.3 CM ....  1.63338845

RADIUS (CM).....? 7.35
DENSITY AT  7.35 CM ....  1.71783471

RADIUS (CM).....?

  1030 END
```

## 5. CALCULATION OF SEDIMENTATION COEFFICIENTS

As can be seen from Equation 1 the sedimentation coefficient of a particle is defined by its sedimentation rate in a unit centrifugal field. For practical purposes one uses a gradient separation method and hence it is necessary to use Equation 9 where, knowing the properties of the gradient medium, the total centrifugal force applied, the density of the particle in the gradient medium and the distance sedimented one can calculate the sedimentation coefficient ($s_{20,w}$). In fact, the distance sedimented is usually obtained by measuring the volume of gradient through which the particle has passed and then calculating the distance using the volume/radius relationship. The volume/radius relationship varies with the type of rotor (*Figure 4*). In the case of swing-out rotors there is a linear relationship between the distance moved and the volume from the top of the gradient. Using the program SWINGOUT it is necessary to input the maximum radius of the rotor ($R_1$), the radius of the tube ($r_2$), the run time ($T2$), centrifugation speed ($Q$), acceleration and deceleration rates, the density of the particle, the total volume of the gradient (U1) and the sample and fraction volumes, U2 and U3 respectively.

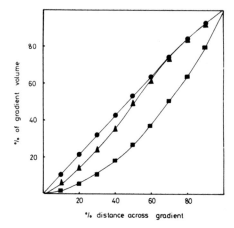

**Figure 4.** Volume/radius relationships of various rotors. The relationships between distance across a gradient and the accumulated volume is shown for the Sorvall AH650 swing-out rotor ( ●——● ), the Sorvall vertical rotor ( ▲——▲ ) and the MSE BXV zonal rotor ( ■——■ ).

It should be noted that this program is very sensitive to errors in the radius of the tube and this problem is exacerbated by the fact that some tubes stretch when subjected to large centrifugal forces. An example printout for the sedimentation of native DNA in a 5 – 20% sucrose gradient in a Beckman SW41 swing-out rotor is given:

```
 BECKMAN SW41
AT 30000 RPM
FOR 6 HOURS
AT 5 DEG/C.
PARTICLE DENSITY= 1.3 G/CC


FRACT      %      S VALUE    MOL WT

  1        5       4.65      79018
  2       6.07    11.31      1912727
  3       7.14    17.83      6274722
  4       8.21    24.27      13195478
  5       9.28    30.64      22707918
  6      10.35    37         34875203
  7      11.42    43.36      49797943
  8      12.5     49.76      67628393
  9      13.57    56.23      88545156
 10      14.64    62.8       112782190
 11      15.71    69.49      140626600
 12      16.78    76.33      172425312

BREAK IN  3000
READY.
```

In the case of zonal rotors there is not a linear relationship between the distance moved ($R$) and the volume ($V$) through which the particles have passed (*Figure 4*). In this case the distance moved is expressed by the relationships:

$$R = 0.5947 + (1.394 + 0.05495\,V)^{\frac{1}{2}}$$
$$R = 0.5126 + (1.480 + 0.0404\,V)^{\frac{1}{2}}$$

for the B XIV and B XV rotors respectively. Hence, by using the appropriate equation it is possible to calculate the sedimentation coefficients of particles in either type of zonal rotor. The SEDCOF program listing given is an example of

*Centrifugation*

The type of program that is routinely used by the authors for sedimentation in zonal rotors, an example of the output from this program is given here:

```
        ****    SEDCOF PROGRAM   ****

THIS PROGRAM MAKES IT POSSIBLE TO CALCULATE EQUIVALENT
SEDIMENTATION COEFFICIENTS BY A PHYSICALLY CORRECT METHOD
FROM SUCROSE DENSITY GRADIENT CENTRIFUGATION DATA.

THIS VERSION IS FOR USE WITH A B-14 (OR EQUIVALENT) ZONAL
ROTOR. CHANGE RADIUS-VOLUME SUBROUTINE IF ANOTHER
ROTOR IS USED.

TWO TYPES OF INPUTS ARE REQUIRED TO RUN THIS PROGRAM,
NAMELY$ A. GENERAL CENTRIFUGE DATA, AND
        B. VOLUME AND SUCROSE CONC. OF EACH FRACTION.

INPUT OF PART A DATA$
INPUT EXPERIMENT NO., AND DATE (DDMM.YY)
? 2,1602.84
INPUT ROTOR SPEED (RPM), AND RUN DURATION (MINS)
? 47629,291
INPUT PERIODS OF ACCELERATION AND DECELERATION (MINS)
? 15,10
INPUT SAMPLE VOLUME AND OVERLAY VOLUME (ML)
? 2,150
INPUT PARTICLE DENSITY (G/ML) AND ROTOR TEMP. (DC)
? 1.400,0.8
INPUT ROTOR DESIGNATION
? tzt48
INPUT OF PART B DATA
INPUT TOTAL NUMBER OF FRACTIONS
? 75
INPUT NUMBER, VOLUME AND SUCROSE CONCENTRATION FOR EACH FRACTION
? 1,10.0,0
? 2,10.0,0.
? 3,10.0,0.
? 4,10.0,0.
? 5,10.0,0.
? 6,10.0,0.
? 7,10.0,0.
? 8,10.0,0.
? 9,10.0,0.
? 10,10.0,0.
? 11,10.0,0.
```

etc.

```
? 64,10.5,24.3
? 65,10.5,25
? 66,10.5,25.4
? 67,10.5,25.9
? 68,10.5,26.4
? 69,10.5,26.9
? 70,10.5,27.4
? 71,10.5,27.9
? 72,10.5,28.3
? 73,10.5,29.0
? 74,10.5,29.9
? 75,10.5,30.0
? 76,10.5,31.1
    ****    ACTIVATE PRINTER AND INPUT SOMETHING   ****
?


    x


--------------------------------------------------------
EXPERIMENT NO.    2                    DATE 1602.84
ROTOR SPEED$ 47629 RPM        RUN DURATION   291 MIN.
ACCELERATION PERIOD   15 MIN  DECELERATION PERIOD  10 MIN
SAMPLE VOLUME    2 ML         OVERLAY VOLUME 150 ML
PARTICLE DENSITY 1.400 G/ML   ROTOR TEMPERATURE   .8 DEG.
--------------------------------------------------------

 NO    VOL    SUC    AVOL    RAD    DENS   VISCOS   S-VAL

  1    10.0    .0
  2    10.0    .0
  3    10.0    .0
  4    10.0    .0
  5    10.0    .0
  6    10.0    .0
  7    10.0    .0
  8    10.0    .0
  9    10.0    .0
 10    10.0    .0
```

```
11   10.0     .0
12   12.7    5.0
13   10.1    6.6
14   10.5    7.7
15   10.5    8.7    153.8   3.73   1.0355   2.2788     .4
16   10.5    9.7    164.3   3.82   1.0397   2.3627    1.8
17   10.5   10.2    174.8   3.91   1.0419   2.4068    3.2
18   10.6   11.1    185.4   4.00   1.0457   2.4898    4.5
19   10.0   11.8    195.4   4.08   1.0487   2.5578    5.8
20   10.5   12.3    205.9   4.16   1.0508   2.6084    7.1
21   10.5   12.7    216.4   4.24   1.0526   2.6501    8.4
22   10.5   13.1    226.9   4.32   1.0543   2.6930    9.7
23   10.1   13.4    237.0   4.39   1.0556   2.7259   10.9
24   10.5   13.7    247.5   4.47   1.0569   2.7595   12.1
25   10.5   14.0    258.0   4.54   1.0582   2.7938   13.3
26   10.5   14.2    268.5   4.61   1.0591   2.8170   14.5
27   10.5   14.6    279.0   4.68   1.0608   2.8645   15.7
28   10.5   14.8    289.5   4.75   1.0617   2.8888   16.8
29   10.0   15.1    299.5   4.82   1.0630   2.9258   17.9
30   10.5   15.5    310.0   4.89   1.0648   2.9764   19.0
31   10.5   15.5    320.5   4.95   1.0648   2.9764   20.1
32   10.5   15.8    331.0   5.02   1.0661   3.0152   21.1
33   10.1   16.0    341.1   5.08   1.0670   3.0416   22.1
34   10.5   16.2    351.6   5.15   1.0679   3.0684   23.2
35   10.5   16.4    362.1   5.21   1.0688   3.0955   24.2
36   10.5   16.6    372.6   5.27   1.0697   3.1231   25.2
37   10.5   16.8    383.1   5.33   1.0706   3.1510   26.2
38   10.5   16.9    393.6   5.39   1.0710   3.1651   27.1
39   10.0   17.2    403.6   5.45   1.0724   3.2081   28.1
40   10.5   17.3    414.1   5.51   1.0728   3.2226   29.0
41   10.5   17.5    424.6   5.57   1.0737   3.2520   30.0
42   10.5   17.7    435.1   5.62   1.0746   3.2818   30.9
43   10.1   17.9    445.2   5.68   1.0755   3.3121   31.8
44   10.5   17.9    455.7   5.74   1.0755   3.3121   32.7
45   10.5   18.2    466.2   5.79   1.0769   3.3583   33.6
46   10.5   18.4    476.7   5.85   1.0778   3.3897   34.5
47   10.5   18.5    487.2   5.90   1.0782   3.4056   35.4
48   10.5   18.7    497.7   5.96   1.0791   3.4337   36.2
49   10.0   18.8    507.7   6.01   1.0796   3.4539   37.1
50   10.5   18.9    518.2   6.06   1.0800   3.4703   37.9
51    9.6   19.2    527.8   6.11   1.0814   3.5201   38.7
52   10.4   19.5    538.2   6.16   1.0828   3.5711   39.5
53   10.1   19.6    548.3   6.21   1.0832   3.5883   40.4
54   10.5   19.9    558.8   6.26   1.0846   3.6408   41.2
55   10.5   20.1    569.3   6.31   1.0855   3.6765   42.0
56   10.5   20.5    579.8   6.36   1.0873   3.7495   42.9
57   10.5   20.8    590.3   6.41   1.0887   3.8058   43.7
58   10.5   21.4    600.8   6.46   1.0915   3.9224   44.6
59   10.0   22.3    610.8   6.51   1.0957   4.1080   45.5
60   10.5   23.3    621.3   6.56   1.1003   4.3305   46.5
61   10.5   23.3    631.8   6.60   1.1003   4.3305   47.4
61   10.5   23.3
62   10.5   24.0
63   10.5   24.3
64   10.5   25.0
65   10.5   25.4
66   10.5   25.9
67   10.5   26.4
68   10.5   26.9
69   10.5   27.4
70   10.5   27.9
71   10.5   28.3
72   10.5   29.0
73   10.5   29.9
74   10.5   30.0
75   10.5   31.1
------------------------------------------------------------
TZT48
```

In contrast to sedimentation in swing-out and zonal rotors, the relationship between radius and volume in vertical rotors is more complex. The basic shape is sigmoidal (*Figure 4*) but the exact shape depends on whether the tube has a hemispherical (Beckman Quickseal) or flat (Sorvall and MSE) top. One can define the volume in terms of distance across the tube (16), but there is no convenient way of expressing distance in terms of volume, hence it is necessary to use a successive approximation technique. This necessitates some changes in the program. An example of a program that has been used for calculating sedimentation coefficients in vertical rotors, called VERT-ROTOR, is given in the appendix to this chapter.

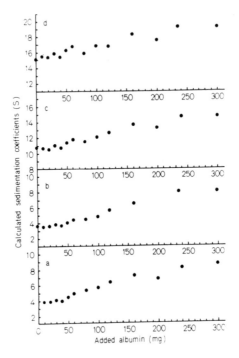

**Figure 5.** Effect of sample loading on the observed sedimentation coefficient of proteins. (**a**) Unlabelled human serum albumin alone; (**b**) samples of 0.3 mg [125]I-labelled human serum albumin (alkylated and monomerised before use); (**c**) 0.5 mg of beef-liver catalase; and (**d**) 0.1 mg of *E. coli* β-galactosidase mixed separately with increasing amounts of human serum albumin were loaded onto separate 3–23% (w/w) isokinetic gradients. The gradients were centrifuged in a titanium MSE BXIV zonal rotor at 47 000 r.p.m. for 5 h (force-time integral of 4.5 x 10¹¹ rad²/sec). Reproduced from ref. 18 with permission.

If on using the program the calculated sedimentation coefficients differ from those expected, errors may have arisen for a number of reasons. For example, errors may occur in inputting the rotor dimensions or the centrifugation conditions or in determining the profile of the gradient from the refractive indices of fractions. However, the major source of error in using this method arises as a result of overloading the gradient with sample (10). This can give values which over-estimate the correct sedimentation coefficient by more than 50% (*Figure 5*). Another possible source of error is that of temperature control during centrifugation. In preparative centrifuges the temperature is at best only accurate to within 1°C. Such variations in temperature can have a significant effect on the viscosity of the gradient and hence the sedimentation of the sample. Also the temperature control system may be incorrectly calibrated. It is possible to check if such errors are occurring by sedimenting a standard sample with a known sedimentation coefficient simultaneously with the test sample. Errors from overloading may obviously be minimised by loading as small amount of sample as is compatible with the analytical procedures to be used.

## 6. INTER-RELATIONSHIP OF THE MOLECULAR PARAMETERS OF PARTICLES

The four molecular parameters, namely the molecular weight, $M$, the sedimentation coefficient, s, the frictional ratio, $f/f_0$ and the partial specific volume, $\bar{v}$, are mutually inter-related as shown in Equation 2. If three of these are known, the fourth can be calculated by use of Equation 2. The sedimentation coefficient can be obtained directly from this formula, whereas the molecular weight and the frictional ratio can be obtained after slight rearrangements of Equation 2. The last parameter, the partial specific volume, cannot be obtained directly, but it can be computed by use of a bisectional procedure. A complete program for this purpose is given in the appendix, with the name PARAM1, and an example of its use is given below. The test parameters are those of normal human immunoglobulin G (IgG) of 7.2S having a molecular weight of 150 000, a frictional coefficient of 1.3 and a partial specific volume of 0.75 ml/g. Upon the RUN command the following text appears on the screen:

```
THE SEDIMENTATION COEFFICIENT, S (IN WATER AT 20 D.C.),
THE MOLECULAR WEIGHT, M, THE PARTIAL SPECIFIC VOLUME, N,
AND THE FRICTIONAL RATIO, F (F/FO) ARE INTERRELATED
PHYSICALLY CORRECTLY AS FOL.OWS

     S=M**0.67*(1.-N*1.)/(N**(1./3.)/K/F

WHERE K IS A NATURAL CONSTANT. THE PRESENT PROGRAM
CAN CALCULATE ANYONE OF THESE PARAMETRES, PROVIDED
THE REMAINING THREE VARIABLES ARE KNOWN.
INPUT PARAMETER TO BE COMPUTED (S, M, F OR N)
? s
INPUT M, F, N
? 150000,1.3,0.75
THE S-VALUE (SVEDBERG UNITS) IS    7.2
CONTINUE WITH SAME PARAMETRES INPUT 1, OTHER 2, STOP 3
? 2
INPUT PARAMETER TO BE COMPUTED (S, M, F OR N)
? m
INPUT S, F, N
? 7.2,1.3,0.75
THE MOLECULAR WEIGHT IS   150256
CONTINUE WITH SAME PARAMETRES INPUT 1, OTHER 2, STOP 3
? 2
INPUT PARAMETER TO BE COMPUTED (S, M, F OR N)
? f
INPUT S, M, N
? 7.2,150000,0.75
THE FRICTIONAL RATIO IS 1.299
CONTINUE WITH SAME PARAMETRES INPUT 1, OTHER 2, STOP 3
? 2
INPUT PARAMETER TO BE COMPUTED (S, M, F OR N)
? n
INPUT S, M, F
? 7.2,150000,1.3
THE PARTIAL SPECIFIC VOLUME IS    .750  ML/G
CONTINUE WITH SAME PARAMETRES INPUT 1, OTHER 2, STOP 3
? 3
```

It is worth pointing out that the equations used for developing this program are physically correct (6,7) and are not empirically derived as in other cases (17). The apparent, but slight inaccuracies, in the calculated data are due exclusively to rounding errors, and can be overcome by the use of more significant digits in the input data.

## 7. SIMULATION OF RATE-ZONAL GRADIENT CENTRIFUGATION

It is often possible to decide on the centrifugation conditions for rate-zonal separations by using similar gradients to those used by other workers with similar types of rotors. However, on occasions such duplications are not possible, for example, when using rotors of significantly different dimensions. In addition, it is sometimes not only inconvenient to follow another protocol but it may be possible to enhance the degree of separation obtained. Such investigations can be carried out empirically by separating samples on different types of gradient, but in practice it is possible to save both time and materials by using simulation techniques.

Gradient centrifugation can be simulated in different ways on computers (18,19). The approach presented here is fairly simple, and the example given assumes a rotor with the dimensions of a Kontron TST 41.14 swing-out rotor centrifuged at 40 000 r.p.m. The experiment to be simulated is defined by:

(i)   the total volume of the gradient;
(ii)   the sample volume;
(iii)   the rotor temperature;
(iv)   the particle density (in this case all particles are considered to have the same density);
(v)   the rotor speed;
(vi)   the run duration (the rotor is considered to accelerate with an acceleration of 5000 r.p.m./min;
(vii)   the weight fraction (w/w %) of sucrose at top of the gradient;
(viii)   the weight fraction of sucrose at the bottom of the gradient (then a linear gradient between these extremes will be used in the calculations).

The sample is characterised by the sedimentation coefficients of the individual particles and by the relative amounts of these particles in arbitrary units. Finally a

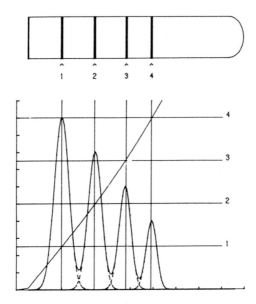

**Figure 6.** Simulation of sucrose gradient centrifugation. For details see the text.

band-width factor is required in the input.

The working principle of the program is as follows. The theoretical centrifuge tube is divided into a number of segments each containing 0.1 ml. On the basis of the input values, the sedimentation coefficients of all segments are calcuiated. Then the segments containing the particles of the sample are located, and the centre of the corresponding segments are taken as the mass centre of each zone. The individual zones are mathematically converted to Gaussian distributions with built-in standard parameters. The latter are controlled by the band-width factor. The effect of the standard parameters can be seen by setting the band-width factor to one.

The simulation program, SIMULATION, has been written in Tektronix BASIC, but the program has been listed using a CDC Cyber computer to achieve a readable listing. In this approach bell signals are executed during printing, and they are therefore not printed. Instead, the original location of these signals are shown as clusters of double apostrophes. In the Tektronix style, output appears on the screen and in this case has been copied manually from the screen picture. The plotter output, however, has been drawn by the computer. A tabular output (not shown) can be obtained by pressing key number 5. Key number 7 gives output on the plotter, otherwise it appears on the screen.

*Figure 6* shows an output example from the simulation program. The input data was:

1) ROTOR TYPE: TST 41.14 (Kontron)
2) TOTAL VOLUME (ML): 14.0
3) SAMPLE VOLUME (ML): 0.2
4) ROTOR TEMP (C): 8.0
5) PARTICLE DENSITY (G/ML): 1.35
6) ROTOR SPEED (RPM): 40000.
7) RUN DURATION (MIN): 960.
8) SUC. CONC. AT 1. SEGMENT: 0.1 (weight fraction)
9) SUC. CONC. AT LAST SEGMENT: 0.4
10) PARTICLE NUMBER 1. S-VAL.: 5.0. FACTOR 1.0.
11) PARTICLE NUMBER 2. S-VAL.: 10.0. FACTOR 0.8.
12) PARTICLE NUMBER 3. S-VAL.: 15.0. FACTOR 0.6.
13) PARTICLE NUMBER 4. S-VAL.: 20.0. FACTOR 0.4.
14) PARTICLE NUMBER 5. S-VAL.: 0.0 (This stop input here).
15) BAND WIDTH FACTOR: 1.5.

# 8. ACKNOWLEDGEMENTS

The authors wish to thank Dr. Bryan Young of the Beatson Institute (Glasgow) for permission to reproduce the listings of his SWINGOUT and VERT-ROTOR programs.

# 9. REFERENCES

1. Rickwood,D. (ed.) (1984) *Centrifugation: A Practical Approach,* 2nd edition, published by IRL Press, Oxford and Washington.
2. Eason,R. (1984) in *Centrifugation: A Practical Approach,* 2nd edition, Rickwood,D. (ed.), IRL Press, Oxford and Washington, p. 251.
3. Svedberg,T. and Pedersen,K.O. (1940) *The Ultracentrifuge,* published by Clarendon Press, Oxford.

4. Griffiths,O.M. (1979) *Techniques of Preparative, Zonal and Continuous Flow Ultracentrifugation,* published by Beckman Instruments, Palo Alto.
5. Graham,J. (1984) in *Centrifugation: A Practical Approach,* 2nd edition, Rickwood,D. (ed.), IRL Press, Oxford and Washington, p. 161.
6. Jacobsen,C. and Steensgaard,J. (1979) *Mol. Immunol.,* **16**, 571.
7. Tanford,C. (1961) *Physical Chemistry of Macromolecules,* published by John Wiley and Sons Inc., New York.
8. Martin,R.G. and Ames,B.N. (1961) *J. Biol. Chem.,* **236**, 1372.
9. Bishop,B.S. (1966) *Natl. Cancer Inst. Monogr.,* **21**, 175.
10. Steensgaard,J., Møller,N.P.H. and Funding,L. (1975) *Eur. J. Biochem.,* **51**, 483.
11. Fritsch,A. (1973) *Anal. Biochem.,* **55**, 57.
12. Rickwood,D. and Young,B.D. (1981) *J. Biochem. Biophys. Methods,* **4**, 163.
13. Sober,H.A. (1970) *Handbook of Biochemistry,* 2nd edition, published by CRC Press, Cleveland, Ohio.
14. Barber,E.J. (1966) *Natl. Cancer Inst. Monogr.,* **21**, 175.
15. Hames,B.D. (1984) in *Centrifugation: A Practical Approach,* 2nd edition, Rickwood,D. (ed.), IRL Press, Oxford and Washington, p. 45.
16. Young,B.D. and Rickwood,D. (1981) *J. Biochem. Biophys. Methods,* **5**, 95.
17. Young,B.D. (1984) in *Centrifugation: A Practical Approach,* 2nd edition, Rickwood,D. (ed.), IRL Press, Oxford and Washington, p. 127.
18. Steensgaard,J., Funding,L. and Meuwissen,J.A.T.P. (1973) *Eur. J. Biochem.,* **51**, 483.
19. Steensgaard,J., Møller,N.P.H. and Funding,L. (1978) in *Centrifugal Separations in Molecular and Cell Biology,* Birnie,G.D. and Rickwood,D. (eds.), Butterworths, London, p. 115.

# APPENDIX
## Program listings

1 **KFAC1**. This program evaluates the K and K* factors of rotors.

```
00100 REM 830810-JS. KFAC1. CDC-BASIC.
00110 REM THIS PROGRAM PROVIDES SOME COMMONLY USED FACTORS FOR
00120 REM COMPARISONS BETWEEN AND EVALUATIONS OF DIFFERENT
00130 REM ULTRACENTRIFUGE ROTORS.
00140 REM
00150 REM    MEANING OF SOME IMPORTANT VARIABLES :
00160 REM       R1=RMIN           R2=RMAX
00170 REM       M1=MAX RPM        G1=MAX RCF
00180 REM       G2=AVER. RCF      G3=MIN RCF
00190 REM       K1=K-FACTOR       K2=K*-FACTOR
00200 REM       T=ROTOR TEMPERATURE (5 D.C.)
00210 REM       S1=SUCROSE CONCENTRATION
00220 REM       P1=PARTICLE DENSITY (1.35 G/ML)
00230 REM       B=GRADIENT IMPACT ON SEDIMENTATION
00240 REM       O=OMEGA
00250 REM       P2=PI
00260 REM
00270 I1$="RMIN= ##.##   RMAX= ##.## (CM)"
00280 I2$="MAX RPM= #####"
00290 I3$="RCF MAX= ######, AV.= ######, MIN= ###### (XG)"
00300 I4$="K-VALUE= ####. (H)"
00310 I5$="K*-VALUE= #####. (H)"
00320 REM
00330 PRINT "INPUT ROTOR DESIGNATION"
00340 INPUT R$
00350 PRINT "INPUT RMIN, RMAX AND MAX RPM"
00360 INPUT R1,R2,M1
00370 REM
00380 REM CALCULATION OF RELATIVE CENTRIFUGAL FORCES.
00390 P2=4*ATN(1.)
00400 G1=(M1*P2/30)**2*R1/981
00410 G2=(M1*P2/30)**2*((R1+R2)/2)/981
00420 G3=(M1*P2/30)**2*R2/981
00430 REM
00440 REM CALCULATION OF NORMAL K-VALUE.
00450 O=M1/60*2*P2
00460 K1=(LOG(R2)-LOG(R1))*1.E13/O**2/3600
00470 REM
00480 REM CALCULATION OF K*-VALUES.
00490 R3=(R2-R1)/100.
00500 T=5.
00510 P1=1.35
00520 K2=0.
00530 O=M1/60*2*P2
```

```
00540 FOR R=R1+0.5*R3 TO R2-0.5*R3 STEP R3
00550 S1=5.+(R-R1)*(15/(R2-R1))
00560 C=S1/100.
00570 Y=(C/342.3)/(C/342.3+(1-C)/18.032)
00580 GOSUB 00700
00590 B=(1.002/V)*((P1-D)/(P1-1.000))
00600 K2=K2+R3/(R*0**2*B)
00610 NEXT R
00620 K2=K2*1.E13/3600
00630 PRINT R$
00640 PRINT USING I1$,R1,R2
00650 PRINT USING I2$,M1
00660 PRINT USING I3$,G3,G2,G1
00670 PRINT USING I4$,K1
00680 PRINT USING I5$,K2
00690 STOP
00700 REM
00710 REM DENSITY FOR 0<T<30 AND 0<C<.75
00720 D1=1.0003698+3.9680504E-5*T-5.8513271E-6*T**2
00730 D2=0.38982371-1.0578919E-3*T+1.2392833E-5*T**2
00740 D3=0.17097594+4.75300081E-4*T-8.9239737E-6*T**2
00750 D=D1+D2*C+D3*C**2
00760 REM
00770 REM VISCOSITY FOR 0<T<60 AND 0<C<.48
00780 G4=SQR(1.+(Y/0.070674842)**2)
00790 C2=146.06635-25.251728*G4
00800 A=-1.5018327+9.4112153*Y
00810 A=A-1.1435741E3*Y**2+1.0504137E5*Y**3
00820 A=A-4.6927102E6*Y**4+1.0323349E8*Y**5
00830 A=A-1.1028981E9*Y**6+4.5921911E9*Y**7
00840 B=2.1169907E2+1.6077073E3*Y
00850 B=B+1.6911611E5*Y**2-1.4184371E7*Y**3
00860 B=B+6.0654775E8*Y**4-1.2985834E10*Y**5
00870 B=B+1.3532907E11*Y**6-5.4970416E11*Y**7
00880 V=10**(A+B/(T+C2))
00890 RETURN
00900 REM
00910 END
```

2 **SUC1.** This program gives the physical properties of sucrose solutions.

```
00100 REM 830808-JS.SUC1. CDC-BASIC.
00110 REM PROPERTIES OF SUCROSE SOLUTIONS. COMPHRENSIVE PROGRAM.
00120 REM THIS PROGRAM PRODUCES A TABLE SHOWING W/W CONCENTRATIONS,
00130 REM W/V CONCENTRATIONS, MOLE FRACTION SUCROSE,DENSITY
00140 REM AND VISCOSITY OF SUCROSE SOLUTIONS FOR A GIVEN
00150 REM TEMPERATURE. POLYNOMIAL COEFFICIENTS ARE TAKEN
00160 REM FROM E.J.BARBER, NATL. CANC. INST. MONOGRAPH 21,
00170 REM 1966, 219-239.
00180 REM
00190 REM C=CONCENTRATION IN WEIGHT FRACTION (=W/W PC/100)
00200 REM C1=CONCENTRATION IN W/V PERCENT
00210 REM T=TEMPERATURE IN CENTIGRADES
00220 REM Y=MOLE FRACTION SUCROSE
00230 REM D=DENSITY (G/ML)
00240 REM V=VISCOSITY IN CENTIPOISES
00250 REM
00260 PRINT "SELECT TEMPERATURE"
00270 INPUT T
00280 IF 0>T OR T>60 THEN PRINT "TEMP. IS OUTSIDE PROPER RANGE"
00285 PRINT "  W/W PC   W/V PC   MOL.FR.   DENS.   VISC."
00288 PRINT " -------------------------------------------------"
00290 FOR C=0. TO .75 STEP .05
00300 Y=(C/342.3)/(C/342.3+(1-C)/18.032)
00310 IF T<=30. THEN GOSUB 1000 ELSE GOSUB 2000
00320 IF C<=.48 THEN GOSUB 3000 ELSE GOSUB 4000
00330 L$="  ##.   ###.##   #.####   #.###   ###.###"
00335 C1=D*C
00340 PRINT USING L$,C*100.,C1*100.,Y,D,V
00350 NEXT C
00450 STOP
00550 REM
01000 REM DENSITY FOR 0<T<30 AND 0<C<.75
01010 D1=1.0003698+3.9680504E-5*T-5.8513271E-6*T**2
01020 D2=0.38982371-1.0578919E-3*T+1.2392833E-5*T**2
01030 D3=0.17097594+4.75300081E-4*T-8.9239737E-6*T**2
01040 D=D1+D2*C+D3*C**2
01050 RETURN
01150 REM
02000 REM DENSITY FOR 30<T<60 AND 0<C<.75
02010 D1=Y*342.3+(1-Y)*18.032
02020 D2=(212.57059+0.13371672*T-2.9276449E-4*T**2)*Y
02030 D3=(1-Y)*(18.027525+4.8318329E-4*T+7.7830857E-5*T**2)
02040 D=D1/(D2+D3)
02050 RETURN
02150 REM
```

```
03000 REM VISCOSITY FOR 0<T<60 AND 0<C<.48
03010 G3=SQR(1.+(Y/0.070674842)**2)
03020 C2=146.06635-25.251728*G3
03030 A=-1.5018327+9.4112153*Y
03040 A=A-1.1435741E3*Y**2+1.0504137E5*Y**3
03050 A=A-4.6927102E6*Y**4+1.0323349E8*Y**5
03060 A=A-1.1028981E9*Y**6+4.5921911E9*Y**7
03070 B=2.1169907E2+1.6077073E3*Y
03080 B=B+1.6911611E5*Y**2-1.4184371E7*Y**3
03090 B=B+6.0654775E8*Y**4-1.2985834E10*Y**5
03100 B=B+1.3532907E11*Y**6-5.4970416E11*Y**7
03110 V=10**(A+B/(T+C2))
03120 RETURN
03220 REM
04000 REM VISCOSITY FOR 0<T<60 AND .48<C<.75
04010 G3=SQR(1.+(Y/0.070674842)**2)
04020 C2=146.06635-25.251728*G3
04030 A=-1.0803314-2.0003484E1*Y
04040 A=A+4.6066898E2*Y**2-5.9517023E3*Y**3
04050 A=A+3.5627216E4*Y**4-7.8542145E4*Y**5
04060 B=1.3975568E2+6.67473293E3*Y
04070 B=B-7.8716105E4*Y**2+9.0967578E5*Y**3
04080 B=B-5.5380830E6*Y**4+1.2451219E7*Y**5
04090 V=10**(A+B/(T+C2))
04100 RETURN
04150 REM
04200 END
```

3 **DENS1.** This program gives the relationships between percentages and density of sucrose solutions.

```
00100 REM 830805-JS.DENS1.
00110 DIM D(51,4),K(4)
00120 MAT READ D
00130 PRINT " "
00140 PRINT "   GRADIENT PROGRAMS.  DATA FROM M. BRAKKE. AT 25 DEGREES."
00150 PRINT "   ------------------------------------------------------"
00160 PRINT " "
00170 PRINT "THIS PROGRAM CAN CALCULATE:"
00180 PRINT "   1. DENSITY FROM CONCENTRATION  (W/W PERCENT)"
00190 PRINT "   2. DENSITY FROM CONCENTRATION  (W/V PERCENT)"
00200 PRINT "   3. W/W PERCENT FROM W/V PERCENT"
00210 PRINT "   4. W/V PERCENT FROM W/W PERCENT"
00220 PRINT " "
00230 PRINT "SELECT A PROGRAM BY ITS NUMBER"
00240 INPUT P1
00250 PRINT " "
00260 PRINT "SELECT GRADIENT MATERIAL:"
00270 PRINT " "
00280 PRINT "    LICL    1       CSSO4       8"
00290 PRINT "    LIBR    2       K-ACETATE   9"
00300 PRINT "    KBR     3       K-CITRATE   10"
00310 PRINT "    NABR    4       K-TARTRATE  11"
00320 PRINT "    RBBR    5       GLYCEROL    12"
00330 PRINT "    CSCL    6       SUCROSE     13"
00340 PRINT "    CSBR    7 "
00350 INPUT P2
00360 J=(P1-1)*13+P2-1.
00370 A$="SOMEBODY GOOFED"
00380 IF P1=1 THEN A$="DENS. G/ML : #.###"
00390 IF P1=2 THEN A$="DENS. G/ML : #.###"
00400 IF P1=3 THEN A$="CONC. W/W 0/0 : ##.##"
00410 IF P1=4 THEN A$="CONC. W/V 0/0 : ###.##"
00420 FOR I=0 TO 4
00430 K(I)=D(J,I)
00440 NEXT I
00450 PRINT "INPUT"
00460 INPUT X
00470 IF X<0 OR X>K(4) THEN 00550
00480 Y=((K(3)*X + K(2))*X + K(1))*X + K(0)
00490 PRINT USING A$,Y
00500 PRINT "CONTINUE: SAME MATERIAL INPUT 1, OTHER  2; STOP 3"
00510 INPUT P3
00520 IF P3=1 THEN 00450
00530 IF P3=2 THEN 00140
00540 STOP
00550 PRINT "INPUT MUST BE BETWEEN  0  AND",K(4)
00560 PRINT "TRY AGAIN"
00570 GOTO 00450
00580 STOP
00590 REM DATA FOR PROGRAM 1
00600 DATA 9.9724E-1,5.6E-3,2.0E-6,4.0E-7,41.
00610 DATA 9.96662E-1,7.60024E-3,5.02381E-6,1.13333E-6,61.
00620 DATA 9.97197E-1,6.9869E-3,4.62857E-5,3.16667E-7,41.
00630 DATA 9.97154E-1,7.59048E-3,4.55714E-5,5.66667E-7,41.
00640 DATA 9.97065E-1,7.83638E-3,3.09127E-5,9.25926E-7,51.
00650 DATA 9.96686E-1,8.03198E-3,2.02619E-5,1.07778E-6,61.
```

```
00660 DATA 9.97025E-1,7.99735E-3,3.52778E-5,1.0463E-6,51.
00670 DATA 9.972E-1,8.12E-3,7.6E-5,0,0,30.
00680 DATA 9.97376E-1,4.87762E-3,1.39254E-5,-3.33333E-8,61.
00690 DATA 9.972E-1,6.68E-3,1.7E-5,3.0E-7,31.
00700 DATA 9.97256E-1,6.67606E-3,1.60317E-5,2.31481E-7,51.
00710 DATA 9.97281E-1,2.28119E-3,6.69048E-6,-3.33333E-8,61.
00720 DATA 9.96752E-1,4.29794E-3,-1.12976E-5,3.86111E-7,61.
00730 REM DATA FOR PROGRAM 2
00740 DATA 9.97279E-1,5.52115E-3,-1.7383E-5,1.61294E-7,52.
00750 DATA 9.97437E-1,7.04834E-3,-2.87803E-6,2.15374E-8,106
00760 DATA 9.97194E-1,7.0067E-3,-2.27386E-6,-2.18629E-8,58.
00770 DATA 9.97158E-1,7.56612E-3,-5.19485E-6,1.46178E-8,59.
00780 DATA 9.97255E-1,7.61823E-3,-4.68709E-6,2.32478E-8,82.
00790 DATA 9.97202E-1,7.61567E-3,-3.82798E-6,1.30611E-8,110
00800 DATA 9.972E-1,7.77968E-3,-1.98696E-6,6.05895E-9,84.
00810 DATA 9.9720E-1,8.24054E-3,-5.8698E-6,0,0,40.
00820 DATA 9.9740E-1,4.88720E-3,-1.01961E-5,1.94922E-8,82.
00830 DATA 9.9720E-1,6.66497E-3,-2.16885E-5,1.78291E-7,38.
00840 DATA 9.97371E-1,6.57883E-3,-1.75249E-5,8.18248E-8,72.
00850 DATA 9.97268E-1,2.30119E-3,2.42196E-7,-1.92111E-8,71.
00860 DATA 9.96958E-1,4.10740E-3,-1.19190E-5,1.12705E-7,80.
00870 REM DATA FOR PROGRAM 3
00880 DATA 1.0445E-3,9.9709E-1,-4.80919E-3,1.73439E-5,52.
00890 DATA 5.18107E-2,9.76174E-1,-5.42544E-3,1.55491E-5,106
00900 DATA 2.84309E-3,9.96914E-1,-6.37452E-3,2.72752E-5,58.
00910 DATA 4.58095E-3,9.9449E-1,-6.67463E-3,2.86475E-5,59.
00920 DATA 2.13418E-2,9.84762E-1,-6.19252E-3,2.18951E-5,82.
00930 DATA 7.4468E-2,9.68674E-1,-5.59521E-3,1.65934E-5,110.
00940 DATA 2.353E-2,9.84183E-1,-6.34458E-3,2.25266E-5,84.
00950 DATA 3.53495E-13,9.88349E-1,-6.21902E-3,0,0,40.
00960 DATA 1.37372E-2,9.92294E-1,-4.12197E-3,1.36814E-5,82.
00970 DATA 2.22389E-2,9.99120E-1,-6.05728E-3,3.11224E-5,38.
00980 DATA 1.23788E-2,9.88288E-1,-5.28922E-3,1.96209E-5,72.
00990 DATA -7.87023E-4,1.00305,-2.33425E-3,5.65446E-6,71.
01000 DATA 2.24941E-2,9.90079E-1,-3.18835E-3,4.70931E-6,80.
01010 REM DATA FOR PROGRAM 4
01020 DATA -5.71429E-4,1.00238,4.85714E-3,3.33333E-5,41.
01030 DATA -7.04762E-2,1.05804,2.38214E-3,1.43056E-4,61.
01040 DATA -1.14286E-3,1.00176,6.36421E-3,7.16667E-5,41.
01050 DATA -2.85714E-3,1.00590,6.43571E-3,9.16667E-5,41.
01060 DATA -1.84127E-2,1.02468,4.92897E-3,1.24352E-4,51.
01070 DATA -6.95238E-2,1.05589,3.03214E-3,1.51944E-4,61.
01080 DATA -2.12698E-2,1.02844,4.7004E-3,1.41019E-4,51.
01090 DATA 2.96652E-13,9.820E-1,1.040E-2,0,0,30.
01100 DATA 4.76190E-3,9.94675E-1,5.07143E-3,9.44444E-6,61.
01110 DATA 2.85355E-12,9.990E-1,6.350E-3,3.50E-5,31.
01120 DATA -2.53968E-3,1.00322,6.00079E-3,3.87037E-5,51.
01130 DATA 2.85714E-3,9.95214E-1,2.44463E-3,2.500E-6,61.
01140 DATA -3.31429E-2,1.02071,2.38321E-3,3.7250E-5,61.
01150 REM DATA FOR EVALUATION OF THE POLYNOMIAL COEFFICIENTS
01160 REM IS TAKEN FROM MYRON BRAKKE AS QUOTED IN HANDBOOK OF
01170 REM BIOCHEMISTRY, CRC PRESS, 2ND ED.,PG J-298.
01180 END
```

**4 RI/DENSITY.** This program calculates the density of solutions from their refractive index.

```
READY.
 10 PRINT "LIST OF GRADIENT MEDIA"
 20 PRINT "1> SUCROSE"
 30 PRINT "2> FICOLL"
 40 PRINT "3> METRIZAMIDE"
 50 PRINT "4> NYCODENZ"
 60 PRINT "5> CSCL"
 70 PRINT "6> CSSO4"
 80 PRINT "7> NAI"
 90 PRINT "8> NONE OF THESE"
100 INPUT "WHICH MEDIUM (1-8)";I
110 IF I=1 GOTO 210
120 IF I=2 GOTO 310
130 IF I=3 GOTO 410
140 IF I=4 GOTO 510
150 IF I=5 GOTO 610
160 IF I=6 GOTO 710
170 IF I=7 GOTO 810
180 IF I=8 GOTO 910
210 PRINT "INSERT VALUE OF REFRACTIVE INDEX"
220 INPUT X
230 IF X=0 THEN 280
240 LET R=2.7329*X-2.6425
250 PRINT X,R
260 GOTO 210
280 END
310 PRINT "INSERT VALUE OF REFRACTIVE INDEX"
320 INPUT X
330 IF X=0 THEN 380
340 LET R=2.381*X-2.175
350 PRINT X,R
```

```
360 GOTO 310
380 END
410 PRINT "INSERT VALUE OF REFRACTIVE INDEX"
420 INPUT X
430 IF X=0 THEN 480
440 LET R=3.453*X-3.601
450 PRINT X,R
460 GOTO 410
480 END
510 PRINT "INSERT VALUE OF REFRACTIVE INDEX"
520 INPUT X
530 IF X=0 THEN 580
540 LET R=3.24225*X-3.32193
550 PRINT X,R
560 GOTO 510
580 END
610 PRINT "INSERT VALUE OF REFRACTIVE INDEX"
620 INPUT X
630 IF X=0 THEN 680
640 LET R=10.8601*X-13.4974
650 PRINT X,R
660 GOTO 610
680 END
710 PRINT "INSERT VALUE OF REFRACTIVE INDEX"
720 INPUT X
730 IF X=0 THEN 780
740 LET R=13.6986*X-17.323
750 PRINT X,R
760 GOTO 710
780 END
810 PRINT "INSERT VALUE OF REFRACTIVE INDEX"
820 INPUT X
830 IF X=0 THEN 880
840 LET R=5.333*X-6.118
850 PRINT X,R
860 GOTO 810
880 END
910 PRINT "REFRACTIVE INDEX(RI) AND DENSITY(D) ARE RELATED BY THE EQUATION"
920 PRINT "D=A*RI-B"
930 PRINT "ENTER VALUE OF A"
940 INPUT A
950 PRINT "ENTER VALUE OF B"
960 INPUT B
970 PRINT "INSERT VALUE OF REFRACTIVE INDEX"
980 INPUT X
990 IF X=0 THEN 1030
1000 LET R=A*X-B
1010 PRINT X,R
1020 GOTO 970
1030 END
```

**5 GRADIENT PROFILE.** Calculation of profiles of self-forming gradients and equilibration times of gradients and sample.

```
READY.

150 PRINTTAB(12)" CALCULATION OF "
160 PRINTTAB(11)"_____"
170 PRINTTAB(11)" GRADIENT PROFILE "
180 PRINTTAB(8)"DATA PROCESSING PROGRAM"
190 PRINTTAB(12)" NO.11111-9999 "
200 PRINT"":GOSUB 5000
210 PRINT""
230 PRINTTAB(6)" PLEASE INPUT THE FOLLOWING ":PRINT""
240 FORI=1TO19:PRINT"*":NEXT
250 PRINT"":PRINT""
260 GOSUB5100
270 INPUT"MAXIMUM RADIUS (CENTIMETRES)=";RX
280 GOSUB5100
290 INPUT"MINIMUM RADIUS (CENTIMETRES)=";RN
300 IFRX>RNGOTO360
310 PRINTTAB(3)"MINIMUM RADIUS MUST BE LESS THAN"
320 PRINTTAB(13)"MAXIMUM RADIUS"
330 FORI=1TO3000:NEXT
340 GOTO210
360 RC=SQR((RN↑2+RN*RX+RX↑2)/3)
370 GOSUB5100
380 PRINT"LESS THAN 1.8G/CC)"
390 INPUT"DENSIY OF MEDIUM (G/CC)      =";DO
400 IFDO<=1.8THENGOTO430
410 PRINTTAB(3)"DENSITY MUST BE LESS THAN 1.8G/CC"
420 GOTO330
430 GOSUB5100
440 INPUT"ROTOR SPEED (RPM)           =";RP
450 GOSUB5100
460 PRINT"ARE THE ABOVE CORRECT(YES/NO)?"
```

```
470 GETBB$:IFBB$=""GOTO470
480 IFBB$="N"GOTO210
490 W=2*RP*π/60
500 PRINT"◧"
510 GOTO4000
520 PRINT"◧TYPES OF MEDIA ARE AS FOLLOWS:                    CODE       MEDIUM"
530 PRINT"◧        120---CAESIUM CHLORIDE"
540 PRINT"        130---CAESIUM SULPHATE"
550 PRINT"        140---SODIUM IODIDE"
560 PRINT"        150---RHUBIDIUM CHLORIDE"
570 INPUT"◧ ENTER CODE FOR MEDIUM USED....";M
590 H=10*DO
600 IFM=120THEN B=CS(2,H):GOTO700
610 IFM=130THEN B=C4(3,H):GOTO700
620 IFM=140THEN B=NA(4,H):GOTO700
630 IFM=150THEN B=RB(5,H):GOTO700
640 GOTO570
700 BO=B*1E9
702 GOTO 2010
710 PRINT"◧THE ISOCONCENTRAION POINT (IE. WHERE THE"
720 PRINT"◧DENSITY =";DO;"G/CC)IS AT A RADIUS OF"
730 PRINTTAB(12)"◧"RC"◧CM"
740 PRINT"◧◧◧PLEASE INPUT THE RADIUS FOR WHICH A   DENSITY IS REQUIRED"
750 PRINT""
800 INPUT"RADIUS (CM).....";RI
810 IFRI<RNTHEN PRINT"◧VALUE SMALLER THAN MINIMUM RADIUS":GOTO750
820 IFRI>RXTHENPRINT"◧VALUE LARGER THAN MAXIMUM RADIUS":GOTO750
830 DI=DO+(W↑2/(2*BO))*(RI↑2-RC↑2)
840 PRINT"DENSITY AT "RI"CM ...."
845 PRINTTAB(24)"◧◧"DI
850 GOTO750
2010 PRINT"◧◧◧◧◧◧◧DO YOU WISH TO CALCULATE THE "
2020 PRINT"APPROXIMATE TIME REQUIRED FOR GRADIENT"
2030 PRINT"◧FORMATION AND SAMPLE EQUILIBRATION"
2040 PRINT"◧◧◧◧◧◧◧◧◧◧◧◧◧◧◧ YES/NO ◧◧◧◧◧◧◧?"
2045 GETGG$:IFGG$=""GOTO2045
2050 IFGG$="N"THEN GOTO 710
2060 IFGG$<>"Y"THENGOTO2010
2070 PRINT"◧◧◧◧◧◧◧◧◧◧◧◧USE AN ESTIMATE IF YOU DO NOT KNOW THE  CORRECT VALUE
2080 INPUT"◧◧◧◧◧◧◧PLEASE INPUT THE S20,W OF YOUR SAMPLE     S=.........";SW
2085 INPUT"◧....AND THE BUOYANT DENSITY           G/CC=......";BD
2100 PRINT"◧THE TIME TAKEN FOR THE GRADIENT TO FORM"
2105 TG=INT(5.6*((RX-RN)↑2)*100)/100
2110 PRINT"WILL BE APPROXIMATELY"
2115 PRINTTAB(10)".....";"◧"TG;"◧ HOURS"
2120 DT=DO+(W↑2/(2*BO))*(RN↑2-RC↑2)
2130 RQ=SQR(RN↑2+((2*BO)/W↑2)*(BD-DT))
2140 SQ=(9.83E13*BO*(BD-1))/(RP↑4*RQ↑2*SW)
2150 PRINT"◧◧THE TIME REQUIRED FOR THE SAMPLE TO"
2160 PRINT"REACH EQUILIBRIUM WILL BE APPROXIMATELY"
2170 PRINTTAB(10)".....";"◧"INT(SQ*100)/100;"◧ HOURS"
2180 PRINT"◧◧AT EQUILIBRIUM THE SAMPLE WILL BE AT "
2190 PRINT"AN APPROXIMATE RADIUS OF"
2200 PRINTTAB(10)".....";"◧"INT(RQ*100)/100;"◧CM"
2300 PRINT"◧◧THE ABOVE FIGURES ARE ONLY A GUIDE AND"
2330 PRINT"◧TO CALCULATE THE EXACT GRADIENT PROFILE"
2340 PRINT"          PRESS ANY KEY"
2350 GETZZ$:IFZZ$=""GOTO2350
2360 GOTO 710
3999 END
4000 DIMD(1,20),CS(2,20),C4(3,20),NA(4,20),RB(5,20)
4010 DATA0.00,2.04,1.55,1.33,1.22,1.17,1.14,1.12
4020 DATA0.00,1.06,0.76,0.64,0.66,0.69,0.74
4030 DATA5.10,3.19,2.82,0.00,0.00,0.00,0.00,0.00
4040 DATA0.00,3.42,2.76,2.25,0.00,0.00,0.00,0.00
4050 READCS(2,11),CS(2,12),CS(2,13),CS(2,14),CS(2,15),CS(2,16),CS(2,17)
4055 READCS(2,18)
4060 READC4(3,11),C4(3,12),C4(3,13),C4(3,14),C4(3,15),C4(3,16),C4(3,17)
4065 READC4(3,18)
4070 READNA(4,11),NA(4,12),NA(4,13),NA(4,14),NA(4,15),NA(4,16),NA(4,17)
4075 READNA(4,18)
4080 READRB(5,11),RB(5,12),RB(5,13),RB(5,14),RB(5,15),RB(5,16),RB(5,17)
4085 READRB(5,18)
4090 PRINTSPC(2)"DENSITY  GRADIENT  PROPORTIONALITY"
4100 PRINT"CONSTANTS  (BETA-VALUES)   FOR SOME"
4110 PRINT"COMMONLY USED DENSITY GRADIENT MEDIA"
4120 PRINT"◧DENSITY","◧◧◧BETA-VALUE *10E9"
4130 PRINT"◧◧AT"
4140 PRINT"◧25'C","◧◧◧◧CSCL":"◧◧◧◧CS2SO4":"◧◧◧◧NAI":"◧◧◧◧RBCL"
4150 FORI=1TO39:PRINTTAB(I)"◧⌐◧":NEXT
4160 DATA1.1,1.2,1.3,1.4,1.5,1.6,1.7,1.8
4165 READD(1,11),D(1,12),D(1,13),D(1,14),D(1,15),D(1,16),D(1,17),D(1,18)
4190 FORI=11TO18
4200 PRINT"◧"D(I,I):PRINT"◧◧◧◧◧◧"CS(2,I):PRINTTAB(14)"◧"C4(3,I)
4210 PRINTTAB(24)"◧"NA(4,I):PRINTTAB(33)"◧"RB(5,I):NEXT I
4220 FORI=1TO39:PRINTTAB(I)"◧⌐◧":NEXTI:GOTO 520
4999 END
5000 PRINTTAB(6)"PRESS ANY KEY TO CONTINUE"
5010 GETAA$:IFAA$=""GOTO5010
5020 RETURN
5100 PRINT"◧◆◆◆◆◆◆◆◆◆◆◆◆◆◆◆◆◆◆◆◆◆◆◆◆◆◆◆◆◆◆◆◆◆◆◆◆◆◆◆◆◆◆":RETURN
READY.
```

# Centrifugation

## 6 SWINGOUT. A program for calculating sedimentation coefficients in swing-out rotors.

```
10 REM      THIS PROGRAM CALCULATES SEDIMENTATION COEFFICIENTS
20 REM      FOR SUCROSE GRADIENTS IN SWING-OUT ROTORS.
30 REM
40 REM      IF FURTHER DETAILS OF THIS PROGRAM ARE REQUIRED
50 REM      CONTACT -  DR.BRYAN D.YOUNG
60 REM                 BEATSON INSTITUTE.GARSCUBE ESTATE.
70 REM                 BEARSDEN.GLASGOW.SCOTLAND.UK
80 REM
90 REM
100 DIM P(90).M(90)
110 DIM L(90).A$(10)
120 SELECT PRINT 005
130 PRINT HEX(03)
140 PRINT HEX(0A0A0A).TAB(10)."******** S-VALUE PROGRAM ********"
150 PRINT HEX(0A0A0A)
160 Z1=0
170 DATA 0.0529.0.4.0.0982.0.246
180 INPUT "IS SAMPLE DNA (Y/N)".C$
190 IF C$="N" THEN 250
200 INPUT "ALKALINE GRADIENT (Y/N)".C$
210 RESTORE
220 IF C$="Y" THEN 240
230 RESTORE 2
240 READ Z1.Z2
250 N0=10
260 REM      THE FOLLOWING DATA STATEMENTS CONTAIN THE
270 REM      BASIC INFORMATION FOR EACH ROTOR.i.e. distance
280 REM      FROM CENTRE OF ROTATION TO TUBE BOTTOM AND
290 REM      INTERNAL TUBE RADIUS(CM).
300 REM
310 DATA 12.92.1.08:A$(1)="MSE 3X25 ML"
320 DATA 10.27.0.6:A$(2)="MSE 3X6.5ML"
330 DATA 16.206.1.54:A$(3)="MSE 3X70 ML"
340 DATA 15.81.0.65:A$(4)="MSE 8X14 ML"
350 DATA 15.1.0.65:A$(5)="IEC 6X14 ML"
360 DATA 15.1.1.25:A$(6)="IEC 6X40 ML"
370 DATA 16.5.1.225:A$(7)="MSE 6X38 ML"
380 DATA 10.0.45:A$(8)="IEC 6X4.2 ML"
390 DATA 12.4.0.35:A$(9)="MSE 6X4.2 ML"
400 DATA 8.96.0.625:A$(10)="SW65 (Y5ML"
410 FOR N=1 TO N0:PRINT N.A$(N):NEXT N
420 PRINT
430 INPUT."WHICH ROTOR DO YOU REQUIRE".N1
440 IF N1>N0 THEN 430
450 RESTORE 2*N1 1+4
460 READ R1.R2
470 INPUT "TOTAL VOLUME (ML)".U1
480 INPUT "SAMPLE VOLUME".U2
490 INPUT "FRACTION VOLUME".U3
500 N3=U1/U3
510 PRINT
520 INPUT "ACCELERATION TIME(MINUTES)".T1
530 INPUT "RUN TIME (HOURS)".T4
540 T2=T4*60
550 INPUT "DECCELERATION TIME (MINUTES)".T3
560 INPUT "AVERAGE SPEED (RPM)".Q
570 INPUT "TEMPERATURE (DEG.C)".T5
580 INPUT "PARTICLE DENSITY".P5
590 I=15/((T2+(T1+T3)/2)*(#PI*Q)^2)
600 PRINTUSING 610.N3
610 %INPUT % SUCROSE OF THE ## FRACTIONS
620 FOR J=1 TO N3
630 PRINT J.
640 INPUT P(J)
650 NEXT J
660 INPUT "DATA OK".C$:IF C$="Y"THEN 690
670 INPUT "FRACTION NO".J:INPUT "% SUCROSE".P(J)
680 GOTO 660
690 J=1
700 L(J)=LOG(R1-R2+(J*U3-U1+2*#PI*(R2^3)/3)/(#PI*R2^2))
710 IF EXP(L(J)))R1-R2 THEN 740
720 J=J+1
730 GOTO 700
740 L(J)=0
750 J=J-1
760 M(1)=L(1)-LOG(R1-R2+(U2/2-U1+2*#PI*(R2^3)/3)/(#PI*R2^2))
770 FOR J1=2 TO J
780 M(J1)=L(J1)-L(J1-1)
790 NEXT J1
800 SELECT PRINT 215(120)
810 PRINT :PRINT :PRINT :PRINT :PRINT
820 PRINTUSING 830.A$(N1).Q.T4.T5.P5
830 %############AT ##### RPM FOR ## HOURS AT ## DEG.C /P.D.=#.#
840 PRINT
850 IF Z1=0 THEN 880
860 PRINT "FRACTION NO   % SUCROSE   S VALUE   MOL. WT."
```

266

```
870 GOTO 890
880 PRINT "FRACTION NO    % SUCROSE    S VALUE"
890 S0=0
900 FOR J1=1 TO J
910 GOSUB '2(T5,P(J1),P5)
920 S0=S0+H(J1)*E
930 IF Z1=0 THEN 970
940 PRINTUSING 950,J1,P(J1),S0*I*1E13,EXP((LOG(S0*I*1E13/Z1))/Z2
)
950 %      ##        ##.#      ###.#      #.#↑↑↑↑
960 GOTO 990
970 PRINTUSING 980,J1,P(J1),S0*I*1E13
980 %      ##        ##.#      ###.#
990 NEXT J1
1000 SELECT PRINT 005
1010 END
1020 DEFFN'1(T,P)
1030 REM SUBROUTINE TO CALCULATE DENSITY (D),VISCOSITY (V)
1040 REM FROM TEMPERATURE (T) AND SUCROSE PERCENTAGE (P)
1050 DATA 1.0003698,3.9680504E-5,-5.8513271E-6
1060 DATA 0.38982371,-1.0578919E-3,1.2392833E-5
1070 DATA 0.17097594,4.7530081E-4,-8.9239737E-6
1080 DATA 18.027525,4.8318329E-4,7.7830857E-5
1090 DATA 342.3,18.032
1100 DATA 212.57059,0.13371672,-2.9276449E-4
1110 DATA 146.06635,25.251728,0.070674842
1120 DATA -1.5018327,9.4112153,-1.1435741E3
1130 DATA 1.0504137E5,-4.6927102E6,1.0323349E8
1140 DATA -1.1028981E9,4.5921911E9,-1.0803214
1150 DATA -2.0003484E1,4.6066898E2,-5.9517023E3
1160 DATA 3.5627216E4,-7.8542145E4,0.0
1170 DATA 2.1169907E2,1.6077073E3,1.6911611E5
1180 DATA -1.4184371E7,6.0654775E8,-1.2995834E10
1190 DATA 1.3532907E11,-5.4970416E11,1.3975568E2
1200 DATA 6.6747329E3,-7.8716105E4,9.0967579E5
1210 DATA -5.5380830E6,1.2451219E7,0,0
1220 RESTORE 25
1230 READ B1,B2,B3,B4,B5,B6,B7,B8,B9
1240 READ A1,A2,A3,H1,H2,C1,C2,C3
1250 READ G1,G2,G3
1260 Y1=P/100
1270 Y=(Y1/M1)/(Y1/M1+(1-Y1)/M2)
1280 IF T>30 THEN 1310
1290 D=B1+B2*T+B3*T↑2+(B4+B5*T+B6*T↑2)*Y1+(B7+B8*T+B9*T↑2)*Y1↑2
1300 GOTO 1320
1310 D0=Y*M1+(1-Y)*M2
1320 D=D0/(Y*(C1+C2*T+C3*T↑2)+(1-Y)*(A1+A2*T+A3*T↑2))
1330 RESTORE 45
1340 IF P<=48 THEN 1360
1350 RESTORE 53
1360 READ D0,D1,D2,D3,D4,D5,D6,D7
1370 A=D0+D1*Y+D2*Y↑2+D3*Y↑2+D4*Y↑4+D5*Y↑5+D6*Y↑6+D7*Y↑7
1380 RESTORE 61
1390 IF P<=48 THEN 1410
1400 RESTORE 69
1410 READ D0,D1,D2,D3,D4,D5,D6,D7
1420 B=D0+D1*Y+D2*Y↑2+D3*Y↑3+D4*Y↑4+D5*Y↑5+D6*Y↑6+D7*Y↑7
1430 C=G1-G2*SQR(1+(Y/G3)↑2)
1440 V=10↑(A+B/(T+C))
1450 RETURN
1460 DEFFN'2(T1,P1,H1)
1470 REM SUBROUTINE TO CALCULATE SEDIM(E) FROM PARTICLE
1480 REM DENSITY(H1), TEMPERATURE (T1) AND % SUCROSE(P1)
1490 GOSUB '1(20,0)
1500 H2=D
1510 V2=V
1520 GOSUB '1(T1,P1)
1530 H3=D
1540 V3=V
1550 E=((H1-H2)/(H1-H3))*(V3/V2)
1560 RETURN
```

## Notes

1. The symbols used in the following listings are:

NO = Number of rotors
R1 = D cm (distance from centre of rotation to tube bottom)
R2 = r cm (internal radius of tube)
U1 = Total volume
U2 = Sample volume
U3 = Fraction volume
Q = Average speed
T1 = Acceleration time

T2 = Run time
T3 = Deceleration time
N1 = Number of rotor used
N3 = Number of fractions

2. Different rotors may be incorporated into the program by altering the statements 410 – 520. There is sufficient space for 10 different rotors.

3. The empirical formulae used to calculate density and viscosity from temperature and sucrose concentration are from Barber (14).

7 **SEDCOF**. A program for calculating sedimentation coefficients in zonal rotors.

```
00100 REM SEDCOF PROGRAM. 831001-JS. CDC-BASIC
00110 PRINT"        ****    SEDCOF PROGRAM    **** "
00120 PRINT" "
00130 PRINT"THIS PROGRAM MAKES IT POSSIBLE TO CALCULATE EQUIVALENT"
00140 PRINT"SEDIMENTATION COEFFICIENTS BY A PHYSICALLY CORRECT METHOD"
00150 PRINT"FROM SUCROSE DENSITY GRADIENT CENTRIFUGATION DATA."
00160 PRINT" "
00170 PRINT"THIS VERSION IS FOR USE WITH A B-14 (OR EQUIVALENT) ZONAL"
00180 PRINT"ROTOR. CHANGE RADIUS-VOLUME SUBROUTINE IF ANOTHER"
00190 PRINT"ROTOR IS USED."
00200 PRINT" "
00210 PRINT"TWO TYPES OF INPUTS ARE REQUIRED TO RUN THIS PROGRAM,"
00220 PRINT"NAMELY: A. GENERAL CENTRIFUGE DATA, AND"
00230 PRINT"        B. VOLUME AND SUCROSE CONC. OF EACH FRACTION."
00240 PRINT" "
00250 PRINT"INPUT OF PART A DATA:"
00260 PRINT"INPUT EXPERIMENT NO., AND DATE (DDMM.YY)"
00270 INPUT E1,E2
00280 PRINT"INPUT ROTOR SPEED (RPM), AND RUN DURATION (MINS)"
00290 INPUT R1,D1
00300 PRINT"INPUT PERIODS OF ACCELERATION AND DECELERATION (MINS)"
00310 INPUT D2,D3
00320 PRINT"INPUT SAMPLE VOLUME AND OVERLAY VOLUME (ML)"
00330 INPUT V1,V2
00340 PRINT"INPUT PARTICLE DENSITY (G/ML) AND ROTOR TEMP. (DC)"
00350 INPUT P1,T1
00360 PRINT"INPUT ROTOR DESIGNATION"
00370 INPUT A1$
00380 REM
00390 REM    ****    MEANING OF VARIABLES    ****
00400 REM    E1,E2   EXPERIMENT NUMBER,DATE
00410 REM    R1,D1   ROTOR SPEED, RUN DURATION
00420 REM    D2,D3   PERIODS OF ACCELERATION AND DECELERATION
00430 REM    V1,V2   SAMPLE AND OVERLAY VOLUMES
00440 REM    P1,T1   PARTICLE DENSITY, ROT. TEMPERATURE
00450 REM
00460 A2$="--------------------------------------------------------"
00470 A3$="EXPERIMENT NO. ####                      DATE ####.##"
00480 A4$="ROTOR SPEED: ##### RPM         RUN DURATION ##### MIN."
00490 A5$="ACCELERATION PERIOD ### MIN    DECELERATION PERIOD ### MIN"
00500 A6$="SAMPLE VOLUME ### ML           OVERLAY VOLUME ### ML"
00510 A7$="PARTICLE DENSITY #.### G/ML    ROTOR TEMPERATURE ##.# DEG."
00520
00530 PRINT"INPUT OF PART B DATA"
00540 PRINT"INPUT TOTAL NUMBER OF FRACTIONS"
00550 INPUT F1
00560 PRINT"INPUT NUMBER, VOLUME AND SUCROSE CONCENTRATION FOR EACH FRACTION"
00570 DIM F2(99), F3(99)
00580 FOR I=1 TO F1
00590 INPUT X9, F2(I), F3(I)
00600 REM HERE IS ROOM FOR TEST OF INPUT DATA
00610 NEXT I
00620 REM START OF CALCULATIONS
00630 REM    ****    MEANING OF VARIABLES    ****
00640 REM    F1      TOTAL NO. OF FRACTIONS
00650 REM    F2      VOLUME OF EACH FRACTION
00660 REM    F3      SUCROSE CONC. OF EACH FRACTION
00670 REM    C1      FORCE/TIME INTEGRAL
00680 REM    C2      BUOYANCY CONSTANT
00690 REM    M1,2,3  MDO VALUES
00700 REM    V0      ACCUMULATED FRACTION VOLUME
00710 REM    S0      OLD S-VALUE
00720 REM    V3      START OF SAMPLE MASS CENTRE
00730 REM    R2      OLD R-VALUE
00740 REM
00750 C1=((3.141593*R1)**2)*(D1+(D2+D3)/3)/15.
00760 C2=(P1-0.998)/1.005
00770 M0=(-5.8513271E-6*T1+3.9680504E-5)*T1+1.0003698
00780 M1=(1.2392833E-5*T1-1.0578919E-3)*T1+0.38982371
00790 M2=(-8.9239737E-6*T1+4.7530081E-4)*T1+0.17097594
```

```
00800 REM
00810 PRINT"    ****     ACTIVATE PRINTER AND INPUT SOMETHING    ****"
00820 INPUT Z9$
00830 REM
00840 PRINT " "
00850 PRINT " "
00860 PRINT A2$
00870 PRINT USING A3$,E1,E2
00880 PRINT USING A4$,R1,D1
00890 PRINT USING A5$,D2,D3
00900 PRINT USING A6$,V1,V2
00910 PRINT USING A7$,P1,T1
00920 PRINT A2$
00930 PRINT " "
00940 PRINT " NO     VOL     SUC     AVOL     RAD     DENS     VISCOS     S-VAL"
00950 PRINT " "
00960 REM
00970 V0=0.
00980 S0=0.
00990 V3=V1/2.+V2
01000 REM NEXT LINE DEFINES RADIUS-VOLUME RELATIONSSHIP
01010 DEF FNR(X)=0.5947+SQR(X*0.05495+1.394)
01020 REM START OF MAIN CALCULATIONS
01030 REM    ****     MEANING OF VARIABLES     ****
01040 REM    R3     ACTUAL ROTOR RADIUS
01050 REM    R4     DR/R
01060 REM    Y1,Y2     WEIGHT, MOLE FRACTION SUCROSE
01070 REM    D4     PRESENT DENSITY OF THE SUCROSE GRADIENT
01080 REM    A1,2,3     VISCOSITY CONSTANTS
01090 REM    V4     PRESENT VISCOSITY
01100 REM    S3     CALCULATED SEDIMENTATION COEFFICIENT
01110 REM
01120 R2=FNR(V3)
01130 FOR I=1 TO F1
01140 V0=V0+F2(I)
01150 IF V0 >641. THEN 01430
01160 IF V0>=V3   THEN 01200
01170 A8$="###   ##.#   ##.#"
01180 PRINT USING A8$, I, F2(I), F3(I)
01190 GOTO 01430
01200 R3=FNR(V0)
01210 R4=(R3-R2)/((R3+R2)/2.)
01220 R2=R3
01230 Y1=F3(I)/100.
01240 D4=(M2*Y1+M1)*Y1+M0
01250 Y1=Y1*100
01260 Y2=Y1/(Y1+(100.-Y1)*18.9924)
01270
01280 A1=-1.5018327+9.4112153*Y2-1.1435741E3*Y2**2
01290 A1=A1+1.0504137E5*Y2**3-4.6927102E6*Y2**4+1.0323349E8*Y2**5
01300 A1=A1-1.1028981E9*Y2**6+4.5921911E9*Y2**7
01310 A2=2.1169907E2+1.6077073E3*Y2+1.6911611E5*Y2**2
01320 A2=A2-1.4184371E7*Y2**3+6.0654775E8*Y2**4-1.2985834E10*Y2**5
01330 A2=A2+1.3532907E11*Y2**6-5.4970416E11*Y2**7
01340 A3=146.066635-25.251728*SQR(1+(Y2/0.070674842)**2)
01350 V4=10.**(A1+A2/(T1+A3))
01360 Z=R4*V4/(P1-D4)
01370 S1=Z*C2/C1
01380 S0=S0+S1
01390 S3=S0*1.E13
01400 A9$="###   ##.#   ##.#   ###.#   #.##   #.####   #.####   ###.#"
01410 PRINT USING A9$,I,F2(I),F3(I),V0,R3,D4,V4,S3
01420 J=I
01430 NEXT I
01440 FOR I=J TO F1
01450 PRINT USING A8$, I, F2(I), F3(I)
01460 NEXT I
01470 PRINT A2$
01480 PRINT A1$
01490 PRINT " "
01500 END
```

8 **VERT-ROTOR.** A program for calculating sedimentation coefficients in vertical rotors.

```
10 COM P(80),M(80),I,J,T5,P5,Z1,Z2
20 DIM L(80),A$(10)
30 SELECT PRINT 005
40 PRINT HEX(0C)
41 PRINT HEX(0A0A0A),TAB(10),"S VALUE PROGRAM FOR VERTICAL ROTOR
S"
42 PRINT HEX(0A0A0A)
50 Z1=0
60 DATA 0.0529,0.4,0.0992,0.246
70 INPUT "IS SAMPLE DNA (Y/N)",C$
80 IF C$="N" THEN 140
90 INPUT "ALKALINE GRADIENT (Y/N)",C$
```

```
100 RESTORE
110 IF C$="Y" THEN 130
120 RESTORE 3
130 READ Z1,Z2
140 N0=4
145 REM LIST OF ROTORS AND THEIR DIMENSIONS
150 DATA 7.217,1.232,7.4:A$(1)="MSE 8X25 ML"
160 DATA 4,0.57,7.95:A$(2)="BMAN 8X5 ML"
170 DATA 7.06,1.17,7.35:A$(3)="BMAN 8X38 ML"
180 DATA 7.1,22.7.2:A$(4)="SVALL 8X38 ML"
190 DATA 0,0,0,0,0:A$(5)="XXXXXXXXXXX"
200 DATA 0,0,0,0,0:A$(6)="XXXXXXXXXXX"
210 DATA 0,0,0,0,0:A$(7)="XXXXXXXXXXX"
220 DATA 0,0,0,0,0:A$(8)="XXXXXXXXXXXXX"
230 DATA 0,0,0,0,0:A$(9)="XXXXXXXXXXXX"
240 DATA 0,0,0,0,0:A$(10)="XXXXXXXXXXXXX"
250 FOR N=1 TO N0:PRINT N,A$(N):NEXT N
260 PRINT
270 INPUT "WHICH ROTOR DO YOU REQUIRE",N1
280 IF N1>N0 THEN 270
290 RESTORE (N1-1)*3+5
300 READ L,R1,R2
301 B0=1
302 INPUT "HEMISPHERICAL TOP",A$
304 IF A$="N" THEN 305:B0=B0+1
306 P=2:GOSUB 1000:PRINT "TOTAL VOL=",V:V9=V
320 INPUT "SAMPLE VOLUME",U2
330 INPUT "FRACTION VOLUME",U3
340 N2=V9/U3
350 PRINT
360 INPUT "ACCELERATION TIME(MINUTES)",T1
370 INPUT "RUN TIME (HOURS)",T4
380 T2=T4*60
390 INPUT "DECCELERATION TIME (MINUTES)",T3
400 INPUT "AVERAGE SPEED (RPM)",Q
410 INPUT "TEMPERATURE (DEG.C)",T5
420 INPUT "PARTICLE DENSITY",P5
430 I=15*((T2+(T1+T3)/3)*(#PI*Q)^2)
440 PRINTUSING 450,N2
450 %INPUT % SUCROSE OF THE ## FRACTIONS
460 FOR J=1 TO N2
461 PRINT J,
470 INPUT P(J)
480 NEXT J
490 J=1
495 V1=J*U3
496 IF V1>V9THEN 540
497 GOSUB 1200
500 L(J)=LOG(R2-R1+P*R1)
510 IF EXP(L(J))>R1+R2 THEN 540
520 J=J+1
530 GOTO 495
540 L(J)=0
550 J=J-1
552 V1=U2/2:GOSUB 1200
555 H(1)=L(1)-LOG(R2-R1+P*R1)
570 FOR J1=2 TO J
580 H(J1)=L(J1)-L(J1-1)
590 NEXT J1
600 SELECT PRINT 01D
610 PRINT :PRINT :PRINT :PRINT :PRINT
620 PRINTUSING 630,A$(N1),Q,T4,T5,P5
630%###############AT ##### RPM FOR ## HOURS AT ## DEG.C /P.D.=#.#
640 PRINT
650 IF Z1=0 THEN 680
660 PRINT "FRACTION NO    % SUCROSE    S VALUE    MOL. WT."
670 GOTO 690
680 PRINT "FRACTION NO    % SUCROSE    S VALUE"
690 GOTO 2000
998 REM SUBROUTINE TO CALCULATE VOLUME (V) FROM
999 REM RADIAL DISTANCE (P) ACROSS THE TUBE
1000V=ARCCOS(1-P)-(1-P)*SQR(2*P-P*P)
1010 V=V+B0*(#PI*P*P*(3-P)*R1)/(6*L)
1020 V=V*R1*R1*L
1030 RETURN
1198 REM SUBROUTINE TO CALCULATE RADIAL DISTANCE (P)
1199 REM ACROSS THE TUBE FROM VOLUME (V)
1200P=2*V1/V9
1210 GOSUB 1000:V2=V:IF ABS(V1-V2)/V1<0.001THEN 1250
1220 P=P*0.99:GOSUB 1000:D=(V2-V)/(0.01*P)
1230 P=P/0.99:P=P-(V2-V1)/D
1240 GOTO 1210
1250 RETURN
2000 S0=0
2010 FOR J1=1 TO J
2020 GOSUB '2(T5,P(J1),P5)
2030 S0=S0+H(J1)*E
2040 IF Z1=0 THEN 2090
2050 PRINTUSING 2060,J1,P(J1),S0*I*1E13,EXP((LOG(S0*I*1E13)/Z1))/
    Z2)
2060 %    ##          ##.#        ###.##    #.#####
```

270

```
2070 GOTO 2100
2080 PRINTUSING 2090.J1.P(J1).SO*I*1E12
2090 %   ##      ##.#     ###.##
2100 NEXT J1
2110 SELECT PRINT 005
2120 GOTO 10
2140 DEFFN'1(T.P)
2150 REM SUBROUTINE TO CALCULATE DENSITY (D),VISCOSITY (V)
2160 REM FROM TEMPERATURE (T) AND SUCROSE PERCENTAGE (P)
2170 DATA 1.0003698.2.9680504E-5.-5.9513271E-6
2180 DATA 0.38982371.-1.0578919E-3.1.2292823E-5
2190 DATA 0.17097594.4.7520091E-4.-8.9829737E-6
2200 DATA 18.027525.4.8219229E-4.7.7930957E-5
2210 DATA 242.2.18.032
2220 DATA 212.57059.0.13371672.-2.9276449E-4
2230 DATA 146.06605.25.251729.0.070674842
2240 DATA -1.5018327.9.4112153.-1.1435741E9
2250 DATA 1.0504137E5.-4.6927102E6.1.0232249E8
2260 DATA -1.1028981E9.4.5921911E9.-1.0803314
2270 DATA -2.0003494E1.4.5066899E2.-5.9517023E3
2280 DATA 3.5627216E4.-7.8542145E4.0.0
2290 DATA 2.1159907E2.1.6077073E3.1.6911611E5
2300 DATA -1.4184371E7.6.0654775E8.-1.2985834E10
2310 DATA 1.3532907E11.-5.4970416E11.1.3975568E2
2320 DATA 6.6747329E2.7.8716105E4.9.0967579E5
2330 DATA -5.5380820E6.1.2451219E7.0.0
2340 RESTORE 35
2350 READ B1.B2.B3.B4.B5.B6.B7.B8.B9
2360 READ A1.A2.A3.M1.M2.C1.C2.C3
2370 READ G1.G2.G3
2380 Y1=P/100
2390 Y=(Y1/M1)/(Y1/M1+(1-Y1)/M2)
2400 IF T>30 THEN 2430
2410 D=B1+B2*T+B3*T↑2+(B4+B5*T+B6*T↑2)*Y1+(B7+B8*T+B9*T↑2)*Y1↑2
2420 GOTO 2450
2430 D0=Y*M1+(1-Y)*M2
2440 D=D0/(Y*(C1+C2*T+C3*T↑2)+(1-Y)*(A1+A2*T+A3*T↑2))
2450 RESTORE 55
2460 IF P<=48 THEN 2480
2470 RESTORE 63
2480 READ D0.D1.D2.D3.D4.D5.D6.D7
2490 A=D0+D1*Y+D2*Y↑2+D3*Y↑3+D4*Y↑4+D5*Y↑5+D6*Y↑6+D7*Y↑7
2500 RESTORE 71
2510 IF P<=48 THEN 2530
2520 RESTORE 79
2530 READ D0.D1.D2.D3.D4.D5.D6.D7
2540 B=D0+D1*Y+D2*Y↑2+D3*Y↑3+D4*Y↑4+D5*Y↑5+D6*Y↑6+D7*Y↑7
2550 C=G1-G2*SQR(1+(Y/G3)↑2)
2560 V=10↑(A+B/(T+C))
2570 RETURN
2580 DEFFN'2(T1.P1.H1)
2590 REM SUBROUTINE TO CALCULATE SEDIM(E) FROM PARTICLE
2600 REM DENSITY(H1). TEMPERATURE (T1) % SUCROSE (P1)
2610 GOSUB '1(20.0)
2620 H2=D
2630 V2=V
2640 GOSUB '1(T1.P1)
2650 H3=D
2660 V3=V
2670 E=((H1-H2)/(H1-H3))*(V3/V2)
2680 RETURN
```

**Notes**

1.  The symbols used in the following listings are:

    NO = Number of rotors
    R1 = Internal tube radius (cm)
    R2 = Distance from axis of rotation to centre of tube (cm)
    L = Length of cylindrical part of tube (cm)
    V = Total volume
    U2 = Sample volume
    U3 = Fraction volume
    Q = Average speed
    T1 = Acceleration time
    T2 = Run time
    T3 = Deceleration time
    N1 = Number of rotor used
    N3 = Number of fractions

2.  Different rotors may be incorporated into the program by altering statements 150 – 240. There is sufficient space for 10 rotors.

271

# Centrifugation

**9 PARAM1.** This program calculates inter-relationships of molecular parameters.

```
00100 REM INTERRELATION OF MOLECULAR PARAMETRES. 830818-JS. PARAM1.
00110 PRINT "THE SEDIMENTATION COEFFICIENT, S (IN WATER AT 20 D.C.),"
00120 PRINT "THE MOLECULAR WEIGHT, M, THE PARTIAL SPECIFIC VOLUME, N,"
00130 PRINT "AND THE FRICTIONAL RATIO, F (F/FO) ARE INTERRELATED"
00140 PRINT "PHYSICALLY CORRECTLY AS FOLLOWS:"
00150 PRINT " "
00160 PRINT "      S=M**0.67*(1.-N**1.)/(N**(1./3.)/K/F"
00170 PRINT " "
00180 PRINT "WHERE K IS A NATURAL CONSTANT. THE PRESENT PROGRAM"
00190 PRINT "CAN CALCULATE ANYONE OF THESE PARAMETRES, PROVIDED"
00200 PRINT "THE REMAINING THREE VARIABLES ARE KNOWN."
00210 P1=4*ATN(1.)
00220 K=0.602E24*6*P1*0.01002*(0.75/(0.602E24*P1))**(1./3.)
00230 T1$="S"
00240 T2$="M"
00250 T3$="F"
00260 T4$="N"
00270 PRINT "INPUT PARAMETER TO BE COMPUTED (S, M, F OR N)"
00280 INPUT T$
00290 IF T$=T1$ THEN 1000
00300 IF T$=T2$ THEN 2000
00310 IF T$=T3$ THEN 3000
00320 IF T$=T4$ THEN 4000
00330 PRINT "TRY AGAIN. DO AS YOU ARE TOLD."
00340 GOTO 270
00350 STOP
01000 REM CALCULATION OF SEDIMENTATION COEFFICIENT
01010 PRINT "INPUT M, F, N"
01020 INPUT M,F,N
01030 S=M**(2./3.)*(1.-N*0.9982)/(N**(1./3.))*1.E13/K/F
01035 I1$="THE S-VALUE (SVEDBERG UNITS) IS ####.#"
01040 PRINT USING I1$,S
01050 PRINT "CONTINUE WITH SAME PARAMETRES INPUT 1, OTHER 2, STOP 3"
01060 INPUT X
01070 IF X=1 THEN 1010
01080 IF X=2 THEN 270
01090 IF X=3 THEN STOP
01100 PRINT "FOLLOW INSTRUCTIONS"
01110 GOTO 270
01120 STOP
02000 REM CALCULATION OF MOLECULAR WEIGHT
02010 PRINT "INPUT S, F, N"
02015 INPUT S,F,N
02020 M=(S*1.E-13*K*F/((1-N*0.9982)/(N**(1./3.))))**(3./2.)
02025 I2$="THE MOLECULAR WEIGHT IS #######"
02030 PRINT USING I2$,M
02040 PRINT "CONTINUE WITH SAME PARAMETRES INPUT 1, OTHER 2, STOP 3"
02050 INPUT X
02060 IF X=1 THEN 2010
02070 IF X=2 THEN 270
02080 IF X=3 THEN STOP
02090 PRINT "FOLLOW INSTRUCTIONS"
02100 GOTO 270
02110 STOP
03000 REM CALCULATION OF FRICTIONAL RATIO
03010 PRINT "INPUT S, M, N"
03020 INPUT S,M,N
03030 F=(M**(2./3.))*((1-N*0.9982)/(N**(1./3.)))/K/(S*1E-13)
03035 I3$="THE FRICTIONAL RATIO IS #.###"
03040 PRINT USING I3$,F
03050 PRINT "CONTINUE WITH SAME PARAMETRES INPUT 1, OTHER 2, STOP 3"
03060 INPUT X
03070 IF X=1 THEN 3010
03080 IF X=2 THEN 270
03090 IF X=3 THEN STOP
03100 PRINT "FOLLOW INSTRUCTIONS"
03110 GOTO 270
03120 STOP
04000 REM CALCULATION OF PARTIAL SPECIFIC VOLUME
04010 REM THIS IS DONE BY A BISECTIONAL METHOD
04011 PRINT "INPUT S, M, F"
04012 INPUT S,M,F
04013 N1=1.2
04014 N2=0.4
04015 N=0.8
04020 Q9=S*1.E-13*K*F/(M**(2./3.))
04030 Y=(1-N*0.9982)/(N**(1./3.))-Q9
04040 IF ABS(Y)<1.E-6 THEN 4090
04050 IF Y>0. THEN N2=N
04060 IF Y<0. THEN N1=N
04070 N=(N1+N2)/2.
04080 GOTO 4030
04090 I4$="THE PARTIAL SPECIFIC VOLUME IS #.###  ML/G"
04100 PRINT USING I4$,N
```

```
04110 PRINT "CONTINUE WITH SAME PARAMETRES INPUT 1, OTHER 2, STOP 3"
04120 INPUT X
04130 IF X=1 THEN 4020
04140 IF X=2 THEN 270
04150 IF X=3 THEN STOP
04160 PRINT "FOLLOW INSTRUCTIONS"
04170 GOTO 270
04180 END
```

10 **SIMULATION.** A program to simulate sedimentation in sucrose gradients.

```
1 GO TO 100
4 GO TO 2400
8 GO TO 2190
12 GO TO 1890
16 P1=32
17 PAGE
18 GO TO 2190
20 P1=41
21 GO TO 2190
24 RUN 2850
28 P2=1
29 GO TO 1890
100 INIT
110 P2=32
120 REM                     MEANING OF SOME IMPORTANT VARIABLES
130 REM
140 REM ••••••••••••••••••••••••••••••••••••••••••••••••••••••••••••••
150 REM • D1 IS THE DIAMETER OF THE TUBE AT TOP                       •
160 REM • D2 IS THE DIAMETER OF THE TUBE AT BOTTOM                    •
170 REM • V4 IS THE TOTAL VOLUME OF THE TUBE                          •
180 REM • V1 IS THE VOLUMEN INCREMENT                                 •
190 REM • R2 IS THE AMPUTED-CONE-PART'S LENGTH OF THE TUBE (WITHOUT   •
200 REM •        THE HALF-SPHERE)                                     •
210 REM • R1 IS THE MAXIMUM SWING OUT RADIUS                          •
220 REM • R0 IS THE MINIMUM SWING OUT RADIUS                          •
230 REM •        (COMPUTED FROM TUBE LENGHT)                          •
240 REM • V5 IS THE NUMBER OF SEGMENTS                                •
250 REM ••••••••••••••••••••••••••••••••••••••••••••••••••••••••••••••
260 REM
270 D1=1.34
280 D2=1.3
290 V1=0.1
300 R1=15.92
310 R0=R1-9.43
320 R2=R1-R0-D2/2
330 V4=PI•(R2•(D1•D1+D1•D2+D2•D2)+D2•D2•D2)/12
340 V5=INT(V4/V1+0.99999999)
350 DIM R(V5+1),W2(3,V5)
360 GOSUB 1970
370 PAGE
380 PRINT USING "30T,24A":"ZONAL SIMULATION PROGRAM"
390 PRINT USING "30T,24A":"------------------------"
400 PRINT USING "3""""":
410 PRINT USING "1""""":
420 PRINT "ROTOR TYPE: ,          ";
430 INPUT R$
440 PRINT USING "10""""":
450 PAGE
460 PRINT "TOTAL VOL (ml):          ";
470 INPUT O9
480 O9=V4-O9
490 PRINT "SAMPLE VOL (ml)          ";
500 INPUT S9
510 O9=O9-S9
520 IF S9>0 AND S9<100 THEN 550
530 PRINT "ERROR - RETYPE "
540 GO TO 490
550 PRINT "ROTOR TEMP (C)           ";
560 INPUT T9
570 IF T9>4 AND T9<40 THEN 600
580 PRINT "ERROR - RETYPE "
590 GO TO 550
600 PRINT "PARTICLE DENSITY (g/ml)  ";
610 INPUT P9
620 IF P9>1 AND P9<2 THEN 650
630 PRINT "ERROR - RETYPE "
640 GO TO 600
650 PRINT "ROTOR SPEED (rpm)        ";
660 INPUT R8
670 IF R8>2500 AND R8<49000 THEN 700
680 PRINT "ERROR - RETYPE "
690 GO TO 650
700 PRINT "RUN DURATION (min)       ";
710 INPUT R7
720 IF R7=>0 THEN 750
```

```
730 PRINT "ERROR - RETYPE "
740 GO TO 700
750 A9=R8/5000
760 REM ACCL. IS 5000 rpm/min/min
770 D9=0
780 REM DECCL IS 0
790 I9=0
800 PRINT "SUC. FRAC. AT 1.SEG.        ";
810 INPUT S1
820 PRINT "SUC. FRAC. AT LAST SEG.  ";
830 INPUT S2
840 DIM S3(20),S6(20)
850 N=0
860 PRINT "PARTICLE NUMBER ";N+1;" INPUT S-VALUE: ";
870 INPUT S5
880 IF S5<=0 THEN 940
890 PRINT "                                        FACTOR: ";
900 N=N+1
910 S3(N)=S5
920 INPUT S6(N)
930 GO TO 860
940 S5=S3(1)
950 FOR I=1 TO N
960 S5=S5 MAX S3(I)
970 NEXT I
972 PRINT "ENTER BAND WIDTH FACTOR: ";
974 INPUT B
980 PRINT USING "10""""":
990 PAGE
1000 PRINT "             ZONAL CENTRIFUGE SIMULATION PROGRAM"
1010 PRINT "             ---------------------------------"
1020 PRINT ""
1030 PRINT "                       of 15/12/80"
1040 PRINT "                          by"
1050 PRINT "             Jens Steensgaard and Jens Frich"
1060 PRINT "             Institute of Medical Biochemistry"
1070 PRINT "                   University of Aarhus"
1080 PRINT "                       Denmark"
1090 O5=0
1100 I9=(R8*PI)^2*(R7+(A9+D9)/3)/15
1110 R7=R7-A9
1120 REM COMPUTED INTEGRAL
1130 C3=(P9-0.9982)/1.005
1140 M0=(-5.8513271E-6*T9+3.9680504E-5)*T9+1.0003698
1150 M1=(1.2392833E-5*T9-0.0010578919)*T9+0.38982371
1160 M2=(-8.9239737E-6*T9+4.7530081E-4)*T9+0.17097594
1170 F=342.3/18.023
1180 A0=0
1190 A1=0
1200 Q=0
1210 REM A0 IS THE ACC. VOLUMEN AND A1 IS THE OLD ACC. VOL
1220 N5=0
1230 FOR L=1 TO V5
1240 REM LOOP TO COMPUTE SEDIM.COEF AND CORRECT ACTIVITIES
1250 W2(1,L)=(L-N5)*V1*(S2-S1)/(V4-09-S9/2)+S1
1260 REM
1270 REM SUCROSE IS STORED IN W2(1,..)
1280 Y=W2(1,L)
1290 REM Y IS THE SUCROSE FRACTION
1300 M4=Y/(Y+(1-Y)*F)
1310 M=(M2*Y+M1)*Y+M0
1320 REM M IS THE DENSITY
1330 A0=A0+V1
1340 REM UPDATE ACC. VOLUMEN
1350 W2(2,L)=(A0+A1)/2
1360 A1=A0
1370 IF A0<09+S9/2 THEN 1880
1380 IF Q THEN 1450
1390 S0=0
1400 Q=1
1410 V2=A0-09-S9/2
1420 N5=L
1430 W2(1,L)=(L-N5)*V1*(S2-S1)/(V4-09-S9/2)+S1
1440 GO TO 1470
1450 REM START OF SEDIM-COMPUTATIONS
1460 V2=V1
1470 IF A0>V4 THEN 1880
1480 REM W2(2,..) CONTAINS THE ACCUMULATED AND CORRIGATED VOLUME
1490 REM UPDATE OLD-VOLUME
1500 DATA 4.5921911E+9,-1.1028981E+9,1.0323349E+8,-4692710.2
1510 DATA 105041.37,-1143.5741,9.4112153,-1.5018327
1520 DATA -5.4970416E+11,1.3532907E+11,-1.2985834E+10,6.0654775E+8
1530 DATA -1.4184371E+7,169116.11,1607.7073,211.69907
1540 DATA -78542.145,35627.216,5951.7023,460.66898
1550 DATA -20.00348,-1.0803314
1560 DATA 1.2451219E+7,-5538083,909675.78,-78716.105
1570 DATA 6.6747329,139.75568
1580 IF Y>0.48 THEN 1620
1590 K=7
1600 RESTORE 1500
1610 GO TO 1640
```

```
1620 K=5
1630 RESTORE 1540
1640 READ X
1650 A2=X
1660 FOR I=1 TO K
1670 READ X
1680 A2=A2*M4+X
1690 NEXT I
1700 READ X
1710 B2=X
1720 FOR I=1 TO K
1730 READ X
1740 B2=B2*M4+X
1750 NEXT I
1760 REM END OF COMPUTING VISCOSITY-COEFFICIENTS
1770 C2=146.06635-25.251728*SQR(1+(M4/0.070674842)^2)
1780 V=10^(A2+B2/(T9+C2))
1790 REM V IS THE ACTUAL VISCOSITY
1800 Z=(R(L+1)-R(L))*V/(R(L)*(P9-M)) MAX 0
1810 IF Z>0 THEN 1830
1820 Z=S5*I9/C3
1830 S=Z*C3/I9
1840 S=S+S0
1850 W2(3,L)=S/1.0E-13
1860 O5=W2(3,L)
1870 S0=S
1880 NEXT L
1890 GOSUB 2400
1900 HOME
1910 P2=32
1920 PRINT "RUN TIME: ";R7+A9;"NEW RUN TIME: ";
1930 INPUT R7
1940 IF R7<=0 THEN 1960
1950 GO TO 1090
1960 END
1970 REM subroutine to compute radius as a function of volume
1980 REM with an approximative procedure (dr/dv - approx.)
1990 REM results are stored in the array r(.)
2000 REM
2010 R2=R1-R0-D2/2
2020 REM R2 is the lenght of the cone part of the tube
2030 REM computed from R1 (maximal swing-out radius), R0 (minimal or
2040 REM starting radius) and D2 (smallest cone diameter)
2050 REM D1 is the widest diameter of the cone
2060 R3=0
2070 REM start value of relative (to the top of the tube) radius
2080 FOR I=1 TO V5+1
2090 D3=D1-(D1-D2)*R3/R2
2100 REM D3 is the diameter of the tube at the relative radius R3
2110 REM R4 is the radius increment
2120 R4=4*V1/(D3*D3*PI)
2130 R3=R3+R4
2140 REM updatint relative radius
2150 R(I)=R3+R0-R4/2
2160 REM storing corrected radius of the i'th volume increment
2170 NEXT I
2180 RETURN
2190 PRINT @P1:"RESULTS FROM ZENTRIFUGATION SIMULATION"
2200 PRINT @P1:"-------------------------------------"
2210 PRINT @P1:""
2220 PRINT @P1:"PARTICLE DENSITY      : ";P9
2230 PRINT @P1:"ROTOR TEMPERATURE     : ";T9
2240 PRINT @P1:"SAMPLE VOLUME         : ";S9
2250 PRINT @P1:"ROTOR SPEED           : ";R8;" rpm"
2260 PRINT @P1:"RUN DURATION          : ";R7;" min"
2270 PRINT @P1:"ACCLERATION (comp.)   : ";A9;" min"
2280 PRINT @P1:"SUCROCE AT 1.SEG.     : ";S1*100;" %"
2290 PRINT @P1:"SUCROSE AT LAST SEG   : ";S2*100;" %"
2300 PRINT @P1:""
2310 PRINT @P1:"SEG. SUC.    VOL.    SED.     RAD."
2320 PRINT @P1:"-------------------------------------"
2330 FOR L=N5 TO V5-1
2340 PRINT @P1: USING 2380:L,W2(1,L),W2(2,L),W2(3,L),R(L)
2350 NEXT L
2360 PRINT @P1:"-------------------------------------"
2370 PRINT @P1:""
2380 IMAGE  4d,2d.4d,3d.3d,3e,4d.2d
2390 END
2400 REM SUBROUTINE USED TO DRAW TUBE
2410 REM
2420 PAGE
2430 VIEWPORT 30,130,0,100
2440 WINDOW 6,16,-9,1
2450 MOVE @P2:R0,-D1/2
2460 RDRAW @P2:0,D1
2470 RDRAW @P2:R2,-(D1-D2)/2
2480 SET DEGREES
2490 X1=D2*SIN(90)/2
2500 Y1=D2*COS(90)/2
2510 FOR I=90 TO -90 STEP -5
2520 X0=D2*SIN(I)/2
2530 Y0=D2*COS(I)/2
```

275

```
2540 RDRAW @P2:Y0-Y1,X0-X1
2550 X1=X0
2560 Y1=Y0
2570 NEXT I
2580 RDRAW @P2:-R2,-(D1-D2)/2
2590 D=(R(N5)-R0)/(R1-R0)*(D2-D1)/2+D1/2
2600 MOVE @P2:R(N5),-D
2610 DRAW @P2:R(N5),D
2620 FOR I=1 TO N
2630 FOR L=N5 TO V5-1
2640 IF S3(I)<=W2(3,L) THEN 2660
2650 NEXT L
2660 MOVE @P2:R(L-1)-0.03,-1
2670 PRINT @P2:"^"
2680 MOVE @P2:R(L-1)-0.03,-1.3
2690 A$=STR(I)
2700 A$=SEG(A$,2,2)
2710 PRINT @P2:A$
2720 FOR J=0 TO 5
2730 R5=J*(R(L)-R(L-1))/5+R(L-1)
2740 D=(R5-R0)/(R1-R0)*(D2-D1)/2+D1/2
2750 MOVE @P2:R5,-D
2760 DRAW @P2:R5,D
2770 NEXT J
2780 R5=(R(L)+R(L-1))/2
2790 MOVE @P2:R5,-2
2800 DRAW @P2:R5,-8
2810 NEXT I
2820 HOME
2830 GOSUB 2850
2840 RETURN
2850 VIEWPORT 30,130,10,70
2860 A=S5*1.1
2870 WINDOW 6,16,0,A
2880 AXIS @P2:1,A/11
2890 FOR I=N5 TO V5-1
2900 DRAW @P2:R(I),W2(3,I)
2910 NEXT I
2920 HOME @P2:
2930 FOR I=1 TO N
2940 MOVE @P2:6,S3(I)
2950 DRAW @P2:15,S3(I)
2960 PRINT @P2:I
2970 NEXT I
2980 HOME @P2:
2985 GOSUB 5000
2990 RETURN
5000 REM SUBROUTINE TO COMPUTE GAUSSIAN CURVES
5010 DEF FNS(S)=1/SQR(2*PI*B*B)*EXP(-(((S3(I)-S)/B)^2))
5020 REM *********************************
5030 REM
5040 DELETE W3
5050 DIM W3(N+1,V5)
5060 W3=0
5070 FOR L=N5 TO V5-1
5080 W=W2(3,L)
5090 FOR I=1 TO N
5100 IF W<S3(I)-3*B THEN 5130
5110 IF W>S3(I)+3*B THEN 5130
5120 W3(I,L)=FNS(W)*S6(I)
5130 NEXT I
5140 NEXT L
5150 W=0
5160 FOR L=N5 TO V5-1
5170 W1=0
5180 FOR I=1 TO N
5190 W1=W1+W3(I,L)
5200 NEXT I
5210 W=W1 MAX W
5220 W3(N+1,L)=W1
5230 NEXT L
5240 WINDOW 6,16,0,W*1.1
5250 FOR I=1 TO N
5260 MOVE @P2:R(N5),W3(I,N5)
5270 FOR L=N5+1 TO V5-1
5275 MOVE @P2:(R(L)+R(L-1))/2,(W3(I,L)+W3(I,L-1))/2
5280 DRAW @P2:R(L),W3(I,L)
5290 NEXT L
5300 NEXT I
5301 FOR L=N5 TO V5-1
5302 DRAW @P2:R(L),W3(N+1,L)
5303 NEXT L
5310 RETURN
```

# CHAPTER 10

# Microcomputers in Environmental Control

S.W. BURRAGE and M.J. VARLEY

## 1. INTRODUCTION

Control of environments has principally been carried out by analogue controllers providing on/off or proportional control. This allows individual environmental parameters to be controlled with a fair level of accuracy. However, as the number of environmental factors to be controlled increases this type of approach becomes increasingly difficult to construct and maintain. Integration between the various environmental components is often not possible and competition between the various control systems may occur resulting in hunting within the control operation. A microcomputer-based system can provide more dynamic and accurate control by integrating all control functions in a single unit.

Such a microcomputer-based system consists of sensors for measuring the various environmental parameters, interfacing electronics to allow the computer to read the sensors, the computer with appropriate software, and electronics to allow the computer to carry out active control functions. An example of such a system used for controlling the environment inside a glasshouse equipped with hydroponics is shown in *Figure 1*. The approach required for other environments is similar to that shown in *Figure 1*, although the sensors and control outputs might vary, and the software would be different.

In this chapter the various parts of a control system are described including details of sensors and interfaces, and techniques for writing control software are outlined. Constructional details for an appropriate 16-channel interface are presented. Practical details are based on our own experiences of constructing and programming control systems mainly using a Commodore PET computer. The interfacing electronics and programs are specific to the PET, but notes are given on using other computers. The construction of the electronics is well within the capabilities of an electronics workshop, or even of the individual with some appropriate experience.

## 2. SENSORS

The range of sensors used in a control system can vary considerably. For example, a glasshouse control system may include sensors for air temperature, air humidity, $CO_2$, radiation, wind speed, wind direction, surface wetness, solution temperature, solution conductivity and pH. Few of these sensors give outputs directly compatible with the input requirements of the analogue to digital A/D

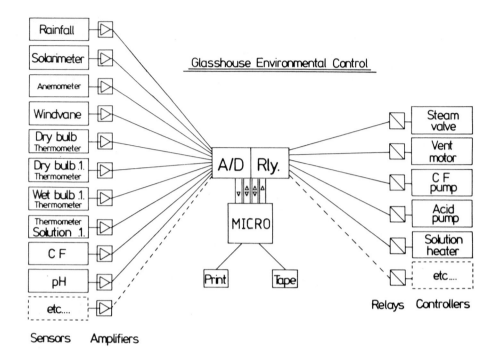

**Figure 1.** Glasshouse control system.

converter. They must therefore be adapted by amplification or attenuation to the correct voltage range. Amplification is generally achieved using an operational amplifier circuit, details of which are given in the relevant sections. Attenuation is usually via a potential divider.

The response time of the many sensors varies, for example, the fine thermocouple may sense changes in temperature over a fraction of a second, whereas a $CO_2$ analyser may take 30 sec for a single reading. The response time may be reduced by various means, for example, increasing the airflow over a large temperature sensor. For control purposes, however, it may be necessary to increase response time. This may be achieved physically (e.g., by fitting a metal tube on a fine thermocouple to increase its response time), or by software operations which result in frequent sampling but operations only being carried out on the mean value. The type of sensor used and its response should be carefully considered and will depend on the control required. The siting of the sensors within the controlled area will also play an important part in the efficiency of the control. For example, in a hydroponic system conductivity measurements should be made in the full flow if a fast response is required and areas of turbulence should be avoided because they will give inconsistent readings.

The accuracy of the control system depends on the accuracy of the sensor and the ability of the monitoring system to record changes in the sensors. The definition of the A/D converter is important in this respect. However, noise picked up on the transmission wires can greatly reduce definition and simply increasing the definition of the A/D converter may not lead to an overall increase in accuracy. This loss of definition can be reduced if individual channels are provided with screened twisted pair leads to the computer. Noise errors can often be further reduced by placing the amplifiers in close proximity to the sensors so that larger signals are used in the transmission cable and the level of noise is small in comparison with the overall signal.

In this section descriptions and some constructional details are given for some of the wide range of sensors used in environmental control. Circuit diagrams are provided of amplifiers necessary to increase sensor output to the levels required by the A/D converter (Section 3). It is recommended that these be constructed on printed circuit board, but 'Vero' board or wirewrap systems may be used. For further information on these techniques consult the manufacturer's leaflets.

## 2.1 Temperature

Temperature sensors commonly employed in environmental control are the thermocouple, the platinum resistance thermometer and the constant current silicon sensor. The type of sensor chosen depends on the type of measurement to be made.

The thermocouple can be made very small and is therefore useful for the measurement of surface temperatures in confined places, where a fast response time ($<0.1$ sec) is required. The thermocouple also has the advantage that when broken it can easily be repaired.

The platinum thermometer is generally larger and therefore has a slower response time (0.5 − 5 sec). It is more suited to the measurement of air and liquid temperatures. It is very accurate and is often used as the standard against which the other sensors are calibrated.

The constant current silicon chip is a low-cost sensor with a linear response to temperature. Mounted in a plastic case of poor thermal conductance, it has a slow response time (60 − 120 sec). It is useful in control functions where fast response times are not essential. Operated as a constant current source it has the attraction of being unaffected by lead length between sensor and amplifier.

All three sensors require amplification before connection to the input of the A/D converter. The thermocouple has an output of approximately 40 $\mu$V/$°$C and the platinum thermometer a resistance change of 0.38 $\Omega$/$°$C. The gain required on the amplifiers for these sensors is generally 1000 whereas the constant current silicon sensor which has an output of 10 mV/$°$C requires an amplifier gain of 30.

### 2.1.1 *Thermocouple*

This device is widely used and available in many forms. An electromotive force (e.m.f.) is produced (the Siebeck effect) when two dissimilar metals are joined together in the configuration shown in *Figure 2A*, and the temperature of the two junctions are different. In *Figure 2A* a voltage is generated between lead wires A and B when the junctions P and Q are at different temperatures. Several thermocouples may be joined in series to form a thermopile (*Figure 2B*), this is a useful technique where small temperature differences are to be detected, for ex-

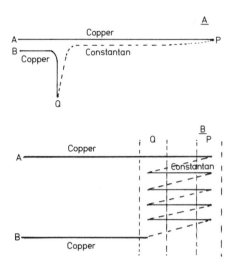

**Figure 2. (A)** Copper/constantan thermocouple. **(B)** Thermopile.

ample, in a solarimeter (Section 2.3). The e.m.f. will be positive or negative depending on whether the temperature at P is greater than Q or *vice versa*. The magnitude of the voltage depends on the temperature difference and the metals used for the wires. It is common practice to assume a linear relationship between e.m.f. and temperature (T) but this can lead to errors of $\pm 1°C$ (1). The relationship is more correctly described by the quadratic equation:

$$\text{e.m.f.} = a + bT + cT^2$$

Where $a$, $b$ and $c$ are $-0.09$, $38.7$ and $0.041$ respectively for a T-type (copper/constantan) thermocouple. The values for other combinations are given by Woodward and Sheehy (1).

When using the thermocouple it must be remembered that it measures temperature difference. If the temperature at some point, Q, is required (see *Figure 2*), the temperature of the thermocouple junction P and the standard output of the sensor must be known. The simplest way of achieving a constant value for junction P is to place it in an ice bath, output voltage is then directly referenced to 0°C. However, frequent replenishment of the ice bath is required and temperature stratification can occur in the bath which may cause errors of $1-2°C$. Electrically controlled ice baths, working on the Peltier effect, are available but are costly. An alternative is to use a constant temperature bath held above ambient temperature at 40°C for example.

An aluminium block may be used as the reference by monitoring its temperature with a platinum thermometer (Section 2.1.2) and then using this value to reference the thermocouple inputs through the computer software. This requires the use of an additional input channel on the A/D converter, but avoids the need for the construction of an electronic temperature controller.

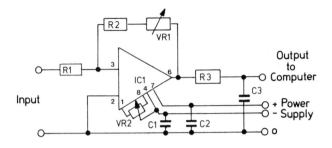

**Figure 3.** Thermocouple amplifier.

To increase the signal from a thermocouple to give a level of output compatible with the A/D converter described in Section 3, an amplifier similar to that shown in *Figure 3* should be used.

### 2.1.2 *Platinum Resistance*

The platinum resistance thermometer is available in various forms. The basic type is a ceramic tube with coils of platinum wire imbedded in it. Platinum film sensors are manufactured in a different way but operate similarly. Sensors are supplied unprotected or imbedded in a stainless steel tube; before use the unprotected units must be sealed in resin or other waterproof material. The Pt100 is the most common unit used; its basic resistance is 100 $\Omega$ at 0°C, increasing by 0.385 $\Omega$/°C to 138.5 $\Omega$ at 100°C. It is generally assumed that the response of a platinum thermometer is linear. Although this is not correct, errors arising from this assumption are very small over the range $-20$ to $+50$°C. The sensors vary in size from a few mm to 10 mm in diameter; the response time increasing with size.

For measurement purposes, the resistor units are mounted in a Wheatstone bridge. The current through the sensor is limited to reduce self-heating with a series resistor. The output from the bridge is amplified to give the range of voltage relevant to the particular study. The sensor should be mounted as close to the bridge as possible to avoid errors caused by changes in lead resistance and to avoid the pick up of noise on the lead wires.

### 2.1.3 *Constant Current Silicon Sensor*

Constant current silicon sensors are new low-cost integrated circuit temperature sensors in which an output of 10 mV/°C can be obtained. Accuracy levels of $\pm0.25$°C may be achieved over $-20$ to $+50$°C. The sensors are generally mounted in a conventional plastic package. Sensing is therefore limited to conditions where there is a slow rate of temperature change because of the large time constant of the plastic case.

## 2.2 Humidity

The most popular technique for measuring humidity in the atmosphere is the psychrometer. However, the psychrometer presents problems of replenishment of the water supply and replacement of the wick when used for long-term monitoring control. A number of sensors have been constructed that depend on the hygroscopic nature of various materials. These can yield an analogue signal which may be accessed by a microcomputer. Several of these sensors have poor response times, are easily contaminated and drift at high humidities. To overcome these difficulties some senors have been modified but this results in an increase in cost. The Valvo sensor from Philips is a new low-cost sensor with a high level of stability in the range $10-90\%$ RH. It consists of a perforated plastic case containing a membrane of non-conducting foil, coated on both sides with gold. The membrane and coating form the dielectric and electrodes respectively of a parallel plate capacitor whose capacitance depends upon the ambient relative humidity. The response is not linear and requires linearisation within the electronic circuitry (Mullard leaflet M80-0090).

## 2.3 Radiation

Radiation varies in quantity, quality and duration (1,2). Measurement reflects this and sensors are designed for specific purposes responding to specific wavelength distribution. The instruments can be divided into the specific function they determine (e.g., shortwave, photosynthetically active or net radiation) or according to the sensor used (e.g., thermopile, silicon or selenium cell). The number and type of sensors is wide and reviews of available instruments are given by Robinson (2) and Fritschen and Gay (3). Before considering the construction of any sensor a quality calibrated sensor relating to the measurement required must be acquired as a standard. For this reason, it may be more satisfactory to purchase a calibrated sensor and provide only the amplification necessary to enable the sensor to be linked to the monitoring system.

The most commonly used commercial radiometer in the UK is probably the Kipp and Zonen solarimeter used on weather stations and field experiments for the measurement of radiation in the wavelength $0.3-3.0$ $\mu$m. This is a thermopile device which detects the temperature difference between a blackened surface and air temperature, and converts the absorbed thermal energy into an electric signal. Robinson (2) described this in detail. Monteith (4) described the construction of a simple dome solarimeter to perform similar measurements.

A typical instrument has an output of approximately 0.5 mV per 100 $Wm^{-2}$. The type of amplifier required is that described for the thermocouple (*Figure 3, Table 1*) with a gain of approximately 500 (i.e., resistor $R_2$ = 500 K) to give a resolution of 1.0 $Wm^{-2}$ when linked to the microcomputer using the A/D converter described later in this chapter.

Silicon photodiodes are now used extensively for radiation measurement in biology. Given a known response of the diode to the radiation, spectrum filters may be introduced to adjust the spectral response to suite particular purposes, for example, photosynthetically active measurement (PAR). Biggs *et al.* (5) and Fitter *et al.* (6) describe specific instruments for the measurement of PAR.

It should be noted that non-linearity will arise if a photodiode is used in a photovoltaic mode because it is essentially a current-generating device. If we wish

**Table 1.** Component List for Thermocouple Amplifier shown in *Figure 3*.

| Component | Type | Description |
|---|---|---|
| IC1 | OP07 | Operational amplifier |
| $R_1$ | 1 K | Resistor metal film 0.25 W 1% |
| $R_2$ | 1 M | Resistor metal film 0.25 W 1% |
| VR1 | 100 K | Resistor variable 0.25 W |
| VR2 | 20 K | Resistor variable 0.25 W |
| $R_3$ | 1 K | Resistor metal film 0.25 W 5% |
| $C_1$, $C_2$ | 0.01 $\mu$F | Capacitor polystyrene |
| $C_3$ | 10 $\mu$F | Capacitor tantalum |

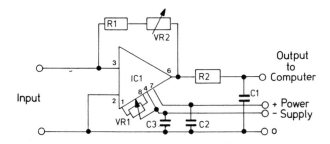

**Figure 4.** Amplifier used in current mode.

**Table 2.** Component List for $\mu$A Amplifier shown in *Figure 4*.

| Component | Type | Description |
|---|---|---|
| IC1 | OP07 | Operational amplifier |
| VR1 | 20 K | Multiturn potentiometer 0.25 W |
| VR2 | 5 K | Multiturn potentiometer 0.25 W |
| $R_1$ | 470 K | Resistor 0.25 W 2% |
| $R_2$ | 1 K | Resistor 0.25 W 5% |
| $C_1$ | 10 $\mu$F | Electrolytic capacitor |
| $C_2$, $C_3$ | 0.01 $\mu$F | Polystyrene capacitor |

to use the thermocouple amplifier to increase the signal from a photodiode to integrate with the A/D converter described in Section 3, a low value (e.g. 200 $\Omega$) resistor must be placed in parallel with the sensor. The typical gain required for such a sensor would be approximately 1000. Alternatively, the amplifier may be used in current mode as shown in *Figure 4*. This type of amplification is necessary for most commercially supplied sensors because they are generally supplied calibrated in the current mode.

## 2.4 **Windspeed and Direction**

### 2.4.1 *Anemometers*

A high level of technical skill is required to construct an anemometer, therefore they are generally purchased from a manufacturer. The output signal may be a pulse or varying analogue signal. Analogue signals can generally be fed directly into the A/D converter provided they lie within its input range. If they are too high they may require a series resistor attenuation. A capacitor, of approximately 10 $\mu$F in value, across the input to the A/D converter also reduces the rapid fluctuation in output one tends to get from an anemometer. The pulse type of output can be treated in a number of ways.

(i)   High frequency pulses can be smoothed using a simple resistor in series with a capacitor in parallel with the signal lines.
(ii)  The signals can be fed into a frequency to voltage circuit (see second stage of the opto-isolator for the pH probe; see Section 2.7).
(iii) The pulse signals can be fed directly into the counter module (see Section 3.1.3).

### 2.4.2 *Wind Vane*

The simplest form of wind direction indicator is a servo potentiometer connected directly onto the rotating shaft. Servo potentiometers, because they generally have no end stops will thus rotate freely and operate over almost the entire 360° rotation. It is preferable if the potentiometer does not go into open circuit when it passes the end stop. With a set voltage across the potentiometer, a signal varying from zero to maximum voltage across the potentiometer will be obtained for the different directions.

An alternative approach is to use reed switches in place of the potentiometer. These are arranged radially around a central spindle to which is attached a magnet. When the magnet comes close to the switch, its closure feeds a signal from the potentiometer set up on the periphery by fixed resistors and a voltage signal is sent to the computer system.

When using data from a wind vane, individual signals must be analysed; they cannot normally be averaged. This can easily be seen if we consider a wind vane moving close to the end stop so that the signal reads alternatively 0 V, 5 V, 0 V, 5 V. These two readings may indicate directional points 2° or 3° apart (e.g., northerly wind direction), however, if we average the signal we get 2.5 V which indicates a southerly wind. It is necessary therefore to process and then to indicate frequency distribution.

## 2.5 **Positional Indicators**

The position of shafts is often required for various control functions. The simplest approach is to use potentiometers in the same manner as the wind vane. The position of the shaft can therefore be directly related to the output voltage. Where a shaft is not available, simple mechanisms can be employed. For example, a pendulum device may be used to monitor the position of a ventilator; as the ventilator opens the pendulum swings, thereby rotating the shaft of the poten-tiometer and giving a signal relative to the position of the ventilator.

## 2.6 Solution Conductivity

Measuring the electrical conductivity of solutions is a useful way to determine their nutrient status. Water is a very poor conductor but the addition of a small quantity of electrolyte greatly increases its conductance.

The sensor for conductivity measurement consists of two electrodes across which an a.c. voltage is maintained. A.c. is used to prevent polarisation of the electrodes which results in a high level of drift in the readings and corrosion of the electrodes. The electrodes themselves may be made in a variety of materials such as graphite, platinum or stainless steel. A wide range of cells are available com-mercially from manufacturers such as Electronic Instruments Ltd., Chertsey; and LTH Electronics Ltd., Luton. Some of these are designed for use in static water, others in flowing systems.

The variation in conductivity with temperature is an increase in conductance of 2.5% per degree Celsius (7). This is large enough to necessitate the use of temperature compensation techniques either in the hardware or the software of the computer.

## 2.7 pH Measurement

pH or p ion can nowadays be measured relatively easily to $\pm 0.02$ pH unit using standard instruments and electrode systems. Measurements are made on an unknown solution by comparing the e.m.f. output of an electrode chemical cell (glass electrode/test solution/reference electrode) with the e.m.f. output of the same cell system containing a standard (buffer) solution of known or defined value. The glass electrode system exists in many forms and is generally purchased from commercial manufacturers. The simplest to use is the combination electrode which contains both test and reference electrodes and is simply immersed in the solution to be monitored. A potential difference is generated between the two electrodes when immersed in the solution under test. The voltage developed is quite small and requires amplification before it can be used in the data-logging system. The very high impedance of the electrode membrane ( $>40$ M$\Omega$) requires that a high input impedance amplifier be used to process the voltage signal (see R.S. Supplies leaflet 4737).

A similar type of circuitry may be used to monitor selective ion electrode out-put, but this type of sensor may have even higher internal probe impedances and a circuit with a higher input impedance may be required. An important point when using these electrodes is that the leads should be screened to a point as close as possible to the amplifer and all connections to the central electrode should be isolated from the printed circuit board with a PTFE isolated terminal pin.

The very high impedance of the pH electrode presents a problem of earth loops when connecting into the data-logging system. The result is interference with other readings from sensors present in the solution being sampled (e.g., conduct-ivity measurements). To overcome this, the pH circuitry should be electrically

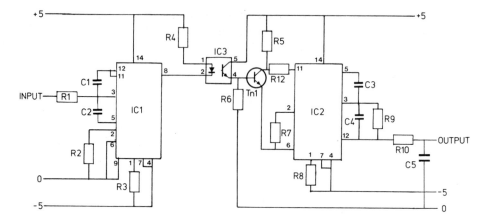

**Figure 5.** Opto-isolation of pH signal.

**Table 3.** Components List for pH Opto-Isolator Circuit.

| Component | Type | Description |
|---|---|---|
| IC1, IC2 | 9400 | V to F – F to V convertor |
| IC3 | H11A1 | Opto-isolator |
| Tr1 | BC107 | Transistor |
| $R_1$, $R_9$, $R_{12}$ | 1 M | Resistor 0.25 W 5% |
| $R_2$, $R_5$ | 10 K | Resistor 0.25 W 5% |
| $R_3$, $R_8$ | 100 K | Resistor 0.25 W 5% |
| $R_4$, $R_7$ | 22 K | Resistor 0.25 W 5% |
| $R_6$ | 12 K | Resistor 0.25 W 5% |
| $R_{10}$ | 1 K | Resistor 0.25 W 5% |
| $C_1$ | 600 pF | Capacitor polystyrene |
| $C_2$ | 150 pF | Capacitor polystyrene |
| $C_3$ | 100 pF | Capacitor polystyrene |
| $C_4$ | 1000 pF | Capacitor polystyrene |
| $C_5$ | 10 $\mu$F | Electrolytic |

isolated from the other circuitry. This is best achieved by optically isolating the pH circuitry from the other electronics; a suitable circuit is given in *Figure 5*.

## 2.8 Carbon Dioxide

The most commonly used method of determining $CO_2$ levels in the atmosphere is the infra-red gas analyser (IRGA). For the control of a single area the IRGA is ideal because it is precise and reliable. If several sites are to be controlled, the electronic sophistication and high cost generally preclude the purchase of in-dividual units for each area, so a solenoid valve switching system is required to enable gas samples to be fed through the IRGA in sequence. These can be controlled by an electronic timer or by the computer system. The latter is preferable because relating the reading to source of the gas in the microcomputer is difficult if an independent system is used. The IRGA provides a simple analogue output that may be readily fed to an A/D converter and accessed by a microcomputer system.

A less costly alternative to the IRGA technique has been developed by Bowman (8) and involves bubbling the sample gas through a cell containing de-ionised water. The $CO_2$ dissolves in the water creating a weak acid. This causes a change in conductivity which may be detected as previously described in Section 2.6. Alternatively, the $CO_2$ content of the solution may be monitored using a $CO_2$ electrode.

## 3. INTERFACES FOR ENVIRONMENTAL CONTROL SYSTEMS

Communication between equipment (sensors and controllers) and the microcomputer is obviously of primary importance in any control system. In this section communication is discussed as it concerns environmental control. The construction of an appropriate interface is described.

### 3.1 Types of Inputs and Outputs used in Control Systems

#### 3.1.1 *Digital Inputs*

The simplest form of input that the computer can be expected to read is the digital input. This is a single line that carries either a voltage or no voltage. Depending on what the line is connected to, the signal on it could be translated as on or off, open or closed (for a switch), high or low, binary 1 or 0, and yes or no. This type of input is mainly of use when the information to be read has only two possible states. Several digital inputs can be read together to represent a larger binary number. Only simple interfacing is necessary to ensure the voltage of the input line is compatible with the computer circuitry, and that the input is accessible to the program.

#### 3.1.2 *Analogue Inputs*

Interfacing analogue voltages to the digital computer is more complex. The voltage must be represented to the computer as a digital (binary) number. This is achieved by an A/D converter. These devices are available with a number of voltage ranges and with a variety of resolutions. The resolution of the A/D converter is governed by how many binary digits (bits) it uses to represent the input voltage. Eight bits will give 256 divisions (2↑8) over the full voltage range, 12 bits will give 4096 divisions (2↑12). With an 8-bit device working over a full range of 5 V, the definition of the signal will be 5/256 (approximately 20 mV). One A/D converter can provide many analogue input channels if the inputs are multiplexed. A/D converters usually work at voltages compatible with the computer circuitry, but interfacing must include electronics to control the A/D converter and enable channel selection in multichannel devices. These types of interface are discussed in more detail in Chapter 2.

Analogue inputs are the most widely used type of input for environmental control, catering for sensors measuring infinitely varying parameters such as temperature, humidity, radiation, wind speed, pH and conductivity.

### 3.1.3 *Pulse Counting Inputs*

Pulse counting inputs are similar to digital inputs in as much as the state of a single line is observed. However, pulse counters must count the number of low-to-high or high-to-low transitions on a line and present the total in a form accessible to the computer. With suitable programming a digital input can be used to perform this function, but as the input is asynchronous (i.e., a pulse can occur at any time) the computer is tied up considerably by having to watch for these transitions.

Pulse counting inputs can be used to total the number of transitions and present them in binary form to the computer. The width of the binary number determines the number of counts the input will detect before re-setting. For example, a 12-bit counter will record up to 4096 counts, a 16-bit counter will record 65535 counts. Counter inputs can usually be re-set to zero when required.

Uses for pulse counters include frequency counting, rotation measurement, and tipping bucket or syphon-type volume measurement.

### 3.1.4 *Digital Outputs*

These outputs present either a high or low state on a single line. As with digital inputs, the meaning of the output depends on what it is connected to. A combination of digital outputs can be used to transfer larger binary numbers to external devices. Interfacing may be required to confer upon the output the appropriate voltage and current levels for the type of device connected and to make operation by the program possible.

### 3.1.5 *Switch Outputs*

These are basically digital outputs which have been further modified so that switches are closed and opened by the output line. Usually the switches are latched in position until a further command is received. The switches can vary from low power reed relays to high current handling conventional or solid state relays, depending on their usage.

### 3.1.6 *Analogue Outputs*

Analogue voltage outputs are a reversal of analogue inputs. A binary number generated by the computer is converted into a voltage. This complex function is carried out by a D/A converter. It requires similar interfacing to an A/D converter, but less complex control circuitry because it usually operates continuously and new binary numbers are latched into the device. D/A converters can be multiplexed to provide more than one output per device by using a 'sample and hold' amplifier for each output.

288

### 3.2 **Commercial Input/Output Units**

There are many commercially available interfaces that allow microcomputers to connect to sensors and actuators, and are thus the basis of a control system. They range in complexity from a single channel of analogue input to a self-contained microprocessor based process controller with integral disc drive. A few are described here, but a review of features is beyond the scope of this book, and the notes are only intended to indicate the type of device available at the time of going to press.

CIL Microsystems of Worthing, Sussex, produce a range of data aquisition and control interfaces, mostly based on the IEEE 488 communication bus. Their PCI range includes A/D converters, D/A converters, and relay switching units, either as separate units or within one case and controlled by a microprocessor. CIL also make the PCI 6380 series controller, which is microprocessor controlled and can perform many functions such as data acquisition and output waveform generation on its own, thus cutting down the time spent by the controlling computer in operating the interface. A serial (RS232C) interface is available for this unit.

3D Digital Design and Development of Warren Street, London, also produce a range of IEEE 488 compatible units. Their range includes 8-bit and 12-bit A/D converters, relay switching units and D/A converters. Their INLAB system is modular, allowing choice of input and output functions to suit the application, and there is a serial (RS232C) interface available as an option. This company will also undertake design and installation of large or small control systems.

ICI have produced the REXAGAN system of interfaces for microcomputers. This is a modular system, with A/D converters, D/A converters, digital input and output, relay switching, and pulse counting modules available. For larger applications the SUPER REXAGAN can handle power switching. Either interface can be included in a complete control package called the REXAGAN Integrated Control System, put together by Parkway Computer Consultants of Welwyn Garden City. This includes a Commodore 64 microcomputer, and the interface and VDU in an industrial enclosure.

Measurement Systems Ltd. of Newbury, Berkshire, produce a number of different control systems and interfaces. The Trojan is a computer with card slots for various input/output modules to be plugged in. It has an integral disc drive, with an option for large drives to be added. The Monolog is also modular, using the same modules as the Trojan, but is meant to be controlled by a separate computer, *via* either an IEEE 488 or RS232 link. It can also be used as a stand alone controller, using the Trojan as a development system.

Kemitron of Hoole, Chester, produce the K3000 microcomputer which has a card slot system for input/output modules, and integral disc drives. It supports the popular CP/M operating system which can be programmed in several languages. There is also a special Control and Monitoring BASIC available. The K2000e is a lower cost system with a similar modular I/O arrangement.

Sintrom Electronics of Reading, Berkshire, produce the LAB 36 data aquisition and control system. It is based on the Hewlett Packard 9920 computer, combined with the DI-AN microsystems DMS 550 interface. The interface is also available separately.

Most of these companies will help in the development of applications, but most users will wish to write their own programs to suit the particular needs of their system.

### 3.3 Constructing a Versatile Interface

Although commercially made interfaces are available for most types of input and output it is often expensive to obtain the configuration required for each control application. The use of a modular design of interface may prove more economical. Construction details are presented for a modular control interface, which should give enough flexibility for most applications. It is relatively cheap to build. The interface as described is designed to work with the Commodore PET, but notes will be given in a later section on modifying it to work with other computers that use the 6502 and 6510 microprocessors.

Construction of electronic equipment of this complexity is not recommended for someone with no previous experience of the techniques involved (e.g., soldering, wire wrap, fault finding). An electronics workshop should be able to construct the interface with little difficulty. Only circuit diagrams and constructional hints are given. Ideally the circuits would be translated onto printed circuit boards. Wire wrap construction is the only other recommended technique. Power supply designs are not given and should be carefully chosen, especially the power supply to the A/D converter circuitry, which should have a high stability. Connections of the inputs and outputs are not described as they can vary considerably depending on the application, but guidelines are given in a later section.

#### 3.3.1 *Overview of the Interface*

The microprocessor address and data signals from the computer, along with associated timing signals, are carried *via* a backplane to a number of card slots. Cards containing the relevant electronics for any of the input or output functions can be slotted into the unit at any of the slots, giving complete configurational versatility to the interface.

The cards are standard 114 mm x 203 mm (RS part 434-021 is suitable for wire wrap, 434-150 for making PCBs) with 43 way edge plugs. These slot into 43 way edge connectors (RS 466-999 or 467-043). The edge connectors are best mounted into a standard 19 inch racking system. Each card carries decoding electronics for the address signals, and control electronics for the function of the card. The decoding is switch selectable to allow any card to occupy any slot without interfering with any other card present in the rack.

#### 3.3.2 *Construction of the Backplane and Boards*

*The backplane and card slot assembly.* It is up to the individual user how many card slots the racking unit contains. The maximum number that can be used at any one time is 16, although physical size may limit this number, especially if wire wrap cards are used.

**Table 4.** Address, Data and Timing Signals on the Memory Expansion Port of the Commodore PET Microcomputer.

| Function | Connector | Pin |
|---|---|---|
| Address 0 | J9 | A2 |
| Address 1 | J9 | A3 |
| Address 2 | J9 | A4 |
| Address 3 | J9 | A5 |
| Address 7 | J9 | A9 |
| Address 8 | J9 | A10 |
| Address 9 | J9 | A11 |
| Address 10 | J9 | A12 |
| Address 11 | J9 | A13 |
| Phase 2 clock | J9 | A21 |
| R/W | J9 | A22 |
| Data 0 | J4 | A2 |
| Data 1 | J4 | A3 |
| Data 2 | J4 | A4 |
| Data 3 | J4 | A5 |
| Data 4 | J4 | A6 |
| Data 5 | J4 | A7 |
| Data 6 | J4 | A8 |
| Data 7 | J4 | A9 |
| Select Block 8 | J4 | A16 |
| Reset | J4 | A22 |
| Ground | J4, J9 | B1 − B25 |

The signals carried by the backplane are derived from the Memory Expansion Port (connectors J4 and J9) within the Commodore PET. These connectors are situated along the right-hand side of the main computer circuit board inside the PET, J4 being nearest the front of the computer. Both are male 25 by 2 pin connectors, the pins being on a 0.1 inch matrix. Suitable female connectors for these would be RS part 469-926, which is an insulation displacement type connector for use with ribbon cables. Not all the signals present on J4 and J9 are required. *Table 4* contains a list of those used on the backplane and their position on J4 or J9. *Figure 6* shows a plan (top view) of the position of J4 and J9 within the PET and the type of connector used for J4 and J9. *Table 5* shows the card slot connections on the backplane. Note that every card slot carries the same signals and power supplies. The power supplies are not derived from the PET but must be provided externally.

The cards are designed to appear as various memory locations to the microprocessor of the PET. These memory locations are between $8800 and $8fff (hexadecimal) which is 34816 to 36863 decimal. Each card has address decoding circuitry that divides this area into 16 sections. The section occupied by a card is

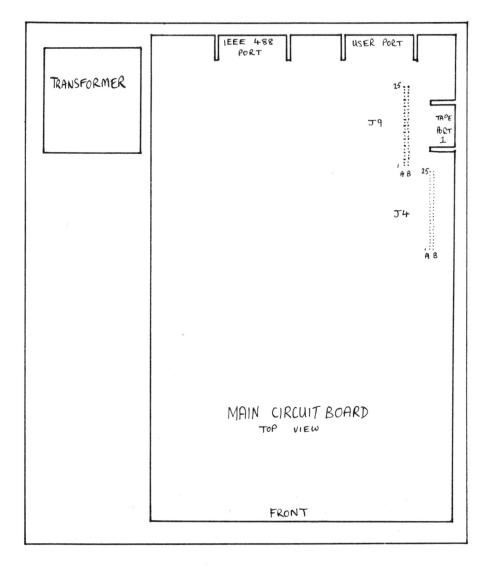

**Figure 6.** Internal view of PET (12 in screen) showing position of J4 and J9 connectors and pin layout.

set with a 16 position switch. All cards must be placed in different sections of memory or they will interfere with each other. This may be achieved by numbering all the card slots and setting the area select switch on each board to the number of the slot it is occupying. The switch positions and related memory area are shown in *Table 6*.

*The analogue input board.* The circuit diagram for the analogue input board is shown in *Figure 7*. The board gives 16 channels of single-sided analogue input over a range of −5 to +5 V. The resolution is 2.44 mV. The parts list for the board is given in *Table 7*.

**Table 5.** Backplane Signals and Card Slot Connections.

| Function | Card slot pin |
|---|---|
| + 5 V | 1 |
| Address 0 | 2 |
| Address 1 | 3 |
| Address 2 | 4 |
| Address 3 | 5 |
| Address 7 | 6 |
| Address 8 | 7 |
| Address 9 | 8 |
| Address 10 | 9 |
| Address 11 | 10 |
| Select Block 8 | 11 |
| Data 0 | 20 |
| Data 1 | 21 |
| Data 2 | 22 |
| Data 3 | 23 |
| Data 4 | 24 |
| Data 5 | 25 |
| Data 6 | 26 |
| Data 7 | 27 |
| Phase 2 clock | 30 |
| R/W | 31 |
| Reset | 32 |
| + 15 V | 35 |
| Analogue ground | 36 |
| − 15 V | 38 |
| Digital ground | 43 |

N.B. Digital and analogue grounds should be kept separate right back to the power supply.

The board consists of an address select section, a control section, an A/D converter, a multiplexer and input buffer amplifiers. In order to obtain maximum stability and resolution from the A/D converter, the following construction points should be noted.

(i) The separate analogue and digital grounds must only be joined directly under the A/D converter.

(ii) The bipolar offset and reference voltage input adjustment potentiometers should be located as near as possible to the A/D converter.

(iii) The OP-07 amplifier should be of the metal can type.

(iv) If using PCB construction, a large area of ground plane should be placed under the A/D converter.

**Table 6.** Memory Select Switch Positions and Related Memory Locations.

| Switch position (decimal) | Memory locations (Hex) | Memory locations |
|---|---|---|
| 0 | $8800 – $887f | 34816 – 34943 |
| 1 | $8880 – $88ff | 34944 – 35071 |
| 2 | $8900 – $897f | 35072 – 35199 |
| 3 | $8980 – $89ff | 35200 – 35327 |
| 4 | $8a00 – $8a7f | 35328 – 35455 |
| 5 | $8a80 – $8aff | 35456 – 35583 |
| 6 | $8b00 – $8b7f | 35584 – 35711 |
| 7 | $8b80 – $8bff | 35712 – 35839 |
| 8 | $8c00 – $8c7f | 35840 – 35967 |
| 9 | $8c80 – $8cff | 35968 – 36095 |
| A | $8d00 – $8d7f | 36096 – 36223 |
| B | $8d80 – $8dff | 36224 – 36351 |
| C | $8e00 – $8e7f | 36352 – 36479 |
| D | $8e80 – $8eff | 36480 – 36607 |
| E | $8f00 – $8f7f | 36608 – 36735 |
| F | $8f80 – $8fff | 36736 – 36863 |

The A/D converter is controlled by a 6522 Versatile Interface Adapter (VIA) which consists of two 8-bit data ports and four control lines. Internally it appears as 16 memory locations, each location corresponding to one of the VIAs registers. Port A is used to receive the digital information from the A/D converter, port B is used to select the multiplexer channel, and the control lines CA1, CA2 and CB2 are used to initiate A/D conversion, sense 'data valid' signals, and switch between high and low bytes of the 12-bit digital number presented by the A/D converter.

The A/D converter (AD 574), is a 12-bit device with either unipolar or bipolar operation. The voltage input range is $0-10$ V (or $\pm 5$ V) or $0-20$ V (or $\pm 10$ V) unipolar. The configuration used on the board is for 5 V bipolar operation. Being a 12-bit device, its voltage range is split into 4096 divisions. Over a 10 V range each division corresponds to 2.44 mV, so each change in input voltage of 2.44 mV results in a 1-bit change in the digital number presented on the A/D converter output port.

The operation of the A/D converter is controlled by the VIA control lines. A negative going pulse on CA2 starts the conversion, and the end of conversion is signalled by a high-to-low transition on CA1. The data can then be read by port A, with CB2 high for bits $0-3$, and low for bits $4-11$. The 16 input amplifiers (LM 324) and the buffer amplifier (OP-07) between the multiplexer (MUX-16) and the A/D converter are used to provide the required source and output impedances for the multiplexer, and are used as unity gain voltage followers. The 1 M$\Omega$ resistors to ground on the inputs are used to stop the open circuit inputs

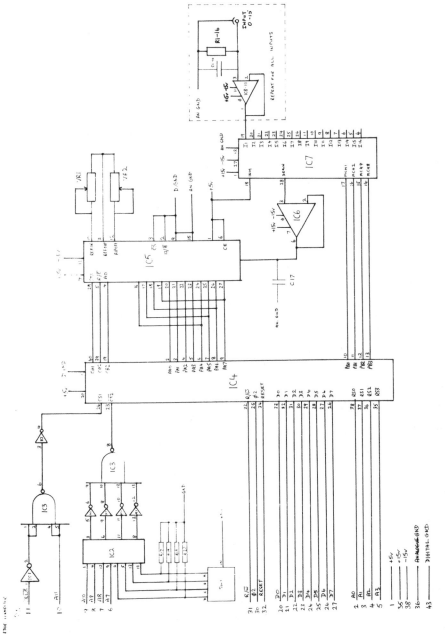

**Figure 7.** Circuit diagram for 16 channel analogue input board.

**Table 7.** Parts Lists for A/D Converter Board.

| Component | Type | Description |
|---|---|---|
| IC1 | 74LS04 | Hex inverter |
| IC2 | 74LS86 | Quad 2-input XOR gate |
| IC3 | 74LS20 | Dual 4-input NAND gate |
| IC4 | 6522 | Versatile interface adapter |
| IC5 | AD574J | 12-bit ADC |
| IC6 | OP-07 | Operational amplifier |
| IC7 | MUX-16 | 16 channel analogue multiplexer |
| IC8 − 11 | LM324N | Quad CMOS operational amplifiers |
| R1 − 16 | 1 M | Resistor 0.25 W 5% |
| R17 − 20 | 1.0 k | Resistor 0.25 W 5% |
| VR1 − 2 | 100 R | Cermet preset potentiometer |
| C1 − 16 | 0.1 $\mu$F | Capacitor (non-polar) |
| C17 | 0.01 $\mu$F | Capacitor (non-polar) |
| SW1 | 16 Position PCB mounting DIL switch with BCD output | |

producing a 15 V output. Setting up and fault finding is dealt with in Section 3.3.3.

*The pulse counter input board.* The circuit diagram of the pulse counter input board is shown in *Figure 8*, and the parts list in *Table 8*. The board contains four separate 16-bit pulse counters, each of which is read directly by the microprocessor as two memory locations. The counters can display between 0 and 65535 counts. If an overflow occurs the counters restart counting at zero. The counters can be individually re-set to zero.

The circuit operates by first conditioning the input pulse (which should be square wave form) and applying it to a monostable (555 timer). The monostable produces a uniform output pulse at TTL level (compatible with the rest of the circuitry) of a length determined by C13 − 16. During the time of this output pulse all further inputs are ignored, thus multiple counts due to 'bouncing' of contacts and other noise sources can be avoided. The duration of this output pulse limits the maximum input pulse frequency. *Table 9* shows C13 − 16 values against maximum input frequencies.

The monostable output is fed to a series of cascaded 4-bit counters (74LS393) which produce a binary result at their outputs. These outputs are fed to tri-state buffers (74LS244) which are individually enabled by address decoding circuitry to allow the microprocessor to read them as memory locations. Other address decoding circuitry produces individual re-sets for each counter if certain memory locations are accessed.

*Digital input and output board.* The board providing digital input and output is shown as a circuit diagram in *Figure 9*. It consists of a 6522 VIA, and address decoding circuitry. The parts list is given in *Table 10*.

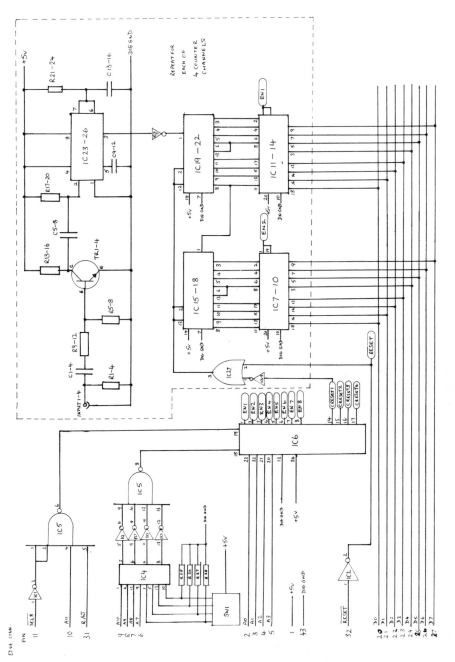

**Figure 8.** Circuit diagram for 4 channel pulse counter board.

**Table 8.** Parts List for Pulse Counter Board.

| Component | Type | Description |
|---|---|---|
| IC1 – 3 | 74LS04 | Hex inverter |
| IC4 | 74LS86 | Quad 2-input XOR gate |
| IC5 | 74LS20 | Dual 4-input NAND gate |
| IC6 | 74LS154 | 4 to 16 line decoder |
| IC7 – 14 | 74LS244 | Tri-state octal buffer |
| IC15 – 22 | 74LS393 | Dual 4-bit counters |
| IC23 – 26 | NE555 | Timer |
| IC27 | 74LS32 | Quad 2-input OR gate |
| TR1 – 4 | BC107 | NPN general purpose transistor |
| R1 – 4,21 – 24 | 100 k | Resistor 0.25 W 5% |
| R5 – 12 | 10 k | Resistor 0.25 W 5% |
| R13 – 20 | 2.2 k | Resistor 0.25 W 5% |
| R25 – 28 | 1.0 k | Resistor 0.25 W 5% |
| C1 – 4 | 1 $\mu$F | Capacitor (not polar) |
| C5 – 12 | 0.01 $\mu$F | Capacitor |
| C13 – 16 | See *Table 9* | |
| SW1 | | 16 position PCB mounting DIL switch with BCD output |

**Table 9.** Maximum Input Pulse Frequencies for Values of C13 – 16.

| C13 – 16 ($\mu$F) | Maximum input frequency (Hz) |
|---|---|
| 10 | 0.83 |
| 1 | 8.3 |
| 0.1 | 83 |
| 0.01 | 830 |
| 0.001 | 8300 |

This device can provide up to 16 digital inputs or outputs, or any combination of inputs and outputs, up to a total of 16. Additional inputs and outputs are provided by the control lines, which can be arranged in a variety of ways, even providing automatic handshaking of data into or out of the data ports of the 6522. A full treatment of 6522 operation is beyond the scope of this book, but can be found in several references (9,10).

*The switch output board.* The circuit diagram for the switch output board is shown in *Figure 10*, and the parts list in *Table 11*. The board consists of two 8-bit latches, drivers, reed relays and address decoding. The latches each appear in memory as one byte. When this byte is written to, the data lines D1 – D3 address a single latch, while DO is the required state of the latch. Data line D4 selects which of the two latches is enabled. Hence, even numbers written to the location will set an output low, and odd numbers will set an output high. The outputs

298

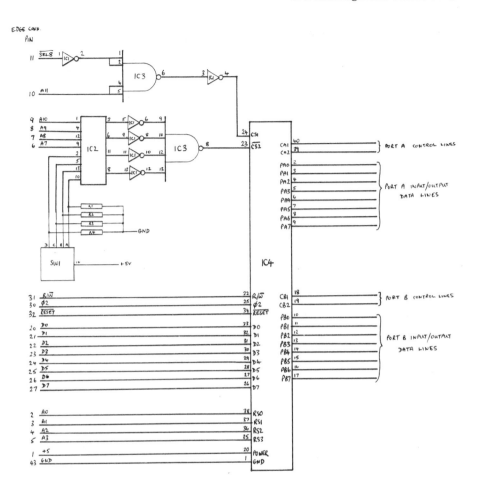

**Figure 9.** Circuit diagram for digital input and output board.

**Table 10.** Parts List for the Digital Input/Ouput Board.

| Component | Type | Description |
|-----------|------|-------------|
| IC1 | 74LS04 | Hex inverter |
| IC2 | 74LS86 | Quad 2-input XOR gate |
| IC3 | 74LS20 | Dual 4-input NAND gate |
| IC4 | 6522 | Versatile interface adapter (VIA) |
| R1−4 | 1.0 k | Resistor 0.25 W 5% |
| SW1 | 16 position PCB mounting DIL switch with BCD output | |

from the latches are driven by 7417 buffers to work reed relays.

The reed relays have a contact current rating of 0.5 A at 240 V AC. This is not a very large current handling capacity, and if higher currents have to be handled

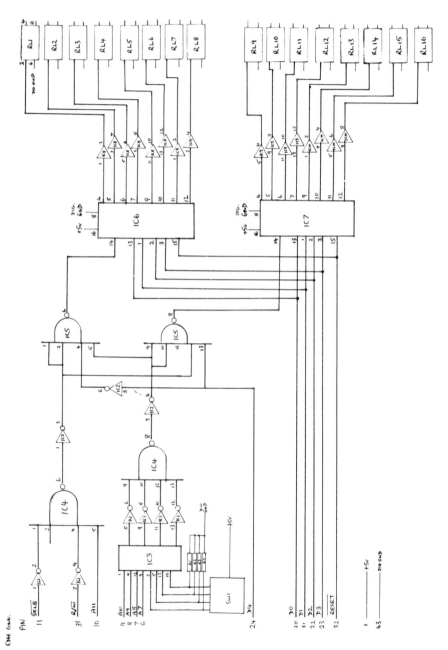

**Figure 10.** Circuit diagram for 16 channel switch output board.

**Table 11.** Parts List for Switch Output Board.

| Component | Type | Description |
|---|---|---|
| IC1 − 2 | 74LS04 | Hex inverter |
| IC3 | 74LS86 | Quad 2-input XOR gate |
| IC4 − 5 | 74LS20 | Dual 4-input NAND gate |
| IC6 − 7 | 74LS259 | Octal latch |
| IC8 − 10 | 7417 | Hex buffer/driver |
| R1 − 4 | 1.0 k | Resistor 0.25 W 5% |
| RL1 − 16 | RS 349-383 | DIL reed relay Type A (5 V) |
| SW1 | 16 position PCB mounting DIL switch with BCD output | |

the reed relays can be used to switch power to larger relays or solid state relays. Alternatively, the larger relays or solid state relays can be directly substituted for the reed relays, providing the current demand is no more than the 7417 buffers can supply.

*The analogue output board.* The circuit diagram for the analogue output board appears in *Figure 11*. The board provides eight analogue outputs with a range of ±5 V and a resolution of 39.1 mV. Each output is buffered. The parts list for the board is given in *Table 12*.

Each D/A converter (ZN 428E) is treated as a single memory location by the microprocessor. A write to the location will latch the written value into the D/A converter and produce a voltage on the output corresponding to 39.1 times the written value mV, − 5 V. It is not possible to read a value from a D/A converter with a read from the relevant location. The output from the D/A converter is fed to a buffer amplifier (741) which is set up to produce the ±5 V output over the range of the D/A converter. Other output ranges could be provided and circuits for ±10 V bipolar and unipolar outputs appear in RS Data Sheet 4642 for the ZN 428E D/A converter. Note that only one D/A converter section of the board is shown in *Figure 11*. This should be repeated eight times to obtain an 8 output board.

Analogue outputs may be useful in driving servo systems or comparator operated switches. Variable speed electric motors could also be operated but careful attention should be paid to the current demand of such devices.

*Connecting the inputs and outputs.* No mention has yet been made of the method of connecting the various inputs and outputs of the interface to the sensors and controllers. It is very difficult to give definitive directions as every application is likely to be different in its needs.

The usual method is to take all the inputs and outputs to a single panel carrying the chosen method of connection. This is best achieved by using insulation displacement type connectors and ribbon cable from the boards to the panel. As the boards are intended to be removable, a plug and socket type of connection on the board is preferable to solder. A suitable combination would be a male header on each board, and a female plug and ribbon cable assembly to take the inputs or

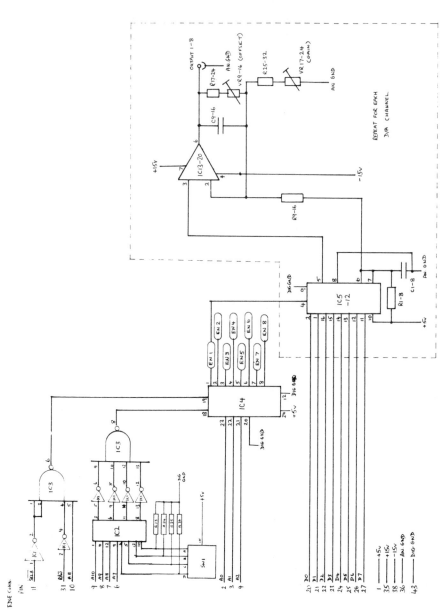

**Figure 11.** Circuit diagram for 8 channel analogue output board.

**Table 12.** Parts List for D/A Converter Board.

| Component | Type | Description |
|---|---|---|
| IC1 | 74LS04 | Hex inverter |
| IC2 | 74LS86 | Quad 2-input XOR gate |
| IC3 | 74LS20 | Dual 4-input NAND gate |
| IC4 | 74LS154 | 4 to 16 line decoder |
| IC5 − 12 | ZN428E | 8-bit DAC with latched inputs |
| IC13 − 20 | 741 | Operational amplifier |
| R1 − 8 | 390R | Resistor 0.25 W 5% |
| R9 − 16 | 7.5 k | Resistor 0.25 W 5% |
| R17 − 32 | 13 k | Resistor 0.25 W 5% |
| R33 − 36 | 1.0 k | Resistor 0.25 W 5% |
| VR9 − 24 | 5 k | Preset linear potentiometer |
| C1 − 8 | 1 μF | Capacitor |
| C9 − 16 | 33 pF | Capacitor |
| SW1 | 16 position PCB mounting DIL rotary switch with BCD output | |

outputs to the panel. The connections on the panel can be (for example) terminal strips, 2 mm sockets, BNC type sockets, or DIN sockets. It is worth being careful in the choice of connection, as bad connections can seriously affect the performance of the interface.

*Using the interface with computers other than the Commodore PET.* Any computer using the 6502 and 6510 as its main microprocessor should be able to operate the interface, providing it has a memory expansion port from which to derive the address and data bus lines and the timing lines. A suitable connecting cable must be made. The block select line can be derived from A12 to A15 by feeding these lines into a 4 − 16 line decoder (such as the 74LS154) if such a line is not present. The block select line positions the interface in a portion of the computer memory map that is not needed for any other function. 6502A processors working at 2 MHz will not be able to control the interface without considerable extra electronics to slow the processor when accessing the interface, which is designed to use a 1 MHz clock frequency.

Microcomputers using any other microprocessor will not be able to use the interface directly, except possibly the 6809, because timing signals (clock, write enable) are usually not compatible with the 6502 timing signals. It is possible to derive the correct timing signals in some cases but an explanation of how to do this is beyond the scope of this book. It should be possible to control the interface with Apple, Aim 65, BBC, Acorn, Tangerine, Kim and Commodore computers.

### 3.3.3 *Using the Interface*

The interface alone is not capable of performing any operation; it must be controlled by the computer which is running a suitable program. It is therefore only possible to test the unit by connecting it to the computer and trying to make it operate. Before this is done the unit should be thoroughly checked for power supply faults on all the boards and slots, because such faults can damage the computer.

Some of the functions of the board are simple to program, being merely the reading of the correct memory location or the writing of specific values to a memory location. These functions are easily programmed in BASIC. More complex functions such as controlling the analogue input boards are more difficult and time consuming in BASIC, and machine code routines can be used to good effect. Programs for testing and operating the interface are given in this section.

*The backplane and card slots.* To check this assembly:

(i)   make sure all power is turned off to both computer and interface;
(ii)  plug interface into computer (connectors J4 and J9);
(iii) turn on power to interface;
(iv) turn on power to computer.

If the computer does not follow its usual turn-on procedure, turn off power to both computer and interface immediately. Check for short circuits between the address and data lines and timing lines on the backplane. Correct any faults before repeating the turn-on test.

If the computer responds normally, and if the equipment is available, check with a logic probe or data analyser that the Phase 2 clock, R/W, and address and data lines on the card slots are present and behaving normally. Also check that the power supplies to the card slots are correct. If all is correct, procedures to test the boards can be undertaken.

*The boards.* To test any of the boards, the turn-on sequence given for the backplane assembly should be followed. The board to be tested should have its address select switch set to postion 0. It should be plugged into the backplane while all power is off, and only one card should be present on the backplane. If upon switching on, the computer does not function normally, immediately turn off the power and check the board for short circuits or incorrect wiring. Make sure all devices are correctly oriented in their sockets.

If the computer behaves normally the board can be tested:

(i)  load the relevant test program (these are listed below);
(ii) run the test program.

The computer will ask into which memory section the board has been placed, this being the position set on the address select switch $(0-15)$.

The A/D converter board is the most complicated, and some notes on testing it follow. Load and run the A/D converter test program. If the board is working properly, the sixteen channels will be shown on the screen as both input voltages and the digital number that is being returned for the channel by the A/D converter. A typical line would read:

0                       .01220725                          2052

which shows Channel 0 reading 12 mV, the digital code for that voltage being 2052. The digital code for $-5$ V and $+5$ V would be 0 and 4095, respectively.

The channels will not read 0 V if they are open circuit. Connect Channel 0 to the analogue ground line with a jumper lead. The A/D converter can now be calibrated using the following procedure.

(i) Turn the BIPOLAR OFFSET adjustment potentiometer until a reading of 0 V (number 2047) appears on Channel 0.

(ii) Disconnect the Channel 0 input from the analogue ground and connect instead an accurated voltage source of between 1 and 5 V. Connect the ground of the voltage source to the analogue ground.

(iii) Turn the REFERENCE INPUT potentiometer until the reading on the screen matches the voltage source. The A/D converter is now calibrated.

(iv) Reverse the ground and input leads to Channel 0 and make sure the correct negative voltage is shown.

(v) Test all the channels to ensure correct functioning of the multiplexer.

The A/D converter need only be calibrated once. Instead of displaying all 16 channels on the screen during calibration, you may find it quicker and easier to display the channel that is being calibrated. To do this change line 220 of the test program to loop on the required channel number. For example, to inspect only Channel 7, the line would be modified to:

```
220      FOR I = 7 TO 7
```

Remember the channel numbers start at 0 not 1.

**Program for calibrating A/D converter**

```
 50 INPUT''BOARD SELECT SWITCH POSITION'';BD
100 SL=34816+(BD*128):REM CALCULATES START LOCATION OF BOARD
110 DA=SL+1: REM LOCATION OF PORT A DATA REGISTER
120 DB=SL+0: REM LOCATION OF PORT B DATA REGISTER
130 RA=SL+3: REM DIRECTION REGISTER FOR PORT A
140 RB=SL+2: REM DIRECTION REGISTER FOR PORT B
150 PC=SL+12: REM PERIPHERAL CONTROL REGISTER
160 IR=SL+13: REM INTERUPT FLAG REGISTER
200 POKE RA,O:POKE RB,255: REM PORT A INPUT – PORT B OUTPUT
210 POKE PC,206:REM FLAG ON CA1 H-L TRANSITION – CA2 HIGH – CB2 LOW
215 PRINT CHR$(147):REM CLEAR SCREEN
220 FOR I = 0 TO 15
230 POKE DB,I: REM SELECT CHANNEL ON MULTIPLEXER
240 POKE PC, PEEK(PC) AND 253
250 POKE PC, PEEK(PC) OR 2: REM PULSE CA2 LOW
260 IF PEEK(IR) AND 2 < > 2 THEN 260: REM WAIT FOR VALID DATA
270 A=PEEK(DA): REM GET BITS 4–11
280 POKE PC, PEEK(PC) OR 32: REM CB2 HIGH
290 B=PEEK(DA): REM GET BITS 0–3
300 X=A*16+B/16: REM CALCULATE 12BIT BINARY NUMBER AS DECIMAL
310 V=X/409.6 – 5: REM CALCULATE VOLTS
320 PRINT I, V, X: REM DISPLAY RESULTS
330 NEXT I: REM NEXT CHANNEL
340 GOTO 200: REM REPEAT
```

Environmental Control

If the board does not behave in the way described, there is either a wiring or construction error, or possibly a faulty component on the board. Fault finding is difficult without specialised equipment such as a data analyser or at least a storage oscilloscope. Work outwards from the computer, first checking that the address select section is operating correctly. Then check the operation of the 6522 VIA by examining its internal registers (a program is given below) and making sure it sends the correct control pulses to the A/D converter device. Continue until the fault is diagnosed.

**6522 VIA Register display program**

```
10 DIM LL$(16)
50 INPUT''BOARD SELECT SWITCH POSITION'';BD
100 SL = 34816 + (BD*128):REM CALCULATES START LOCATION OF BOARD
110 FOR I = 0 TO 15:READ LL$(I):NEXT
120 PRINT CHR$(147): REM CLEAR SCREEN
130 PRINT CHR$(19): REM HOME CURSOR TO SCREEN TOP LEFT
140 FOR I = 0 TO 15:CL = SL + I
150 PRINT CL, LL$(I),PEEK(CL)
160 NEXT I
170 GOTO130
180 DATA ORB,ORA1,DDRB,DDRA,T1L,T1H,T1L,T1H,T2L,T2H,SSR,
    ACR,PCR,IFR,IER,ORA2
```

The D/A converter board also needs setting up. This procedure should be carried out for each channel.
(i)   Write 0 to the D/A converter.
(ii)  Adjust the OFFSET potentiometer until the output reads − 5.0000 V.
(iii) Write 255 to the D/A converter.
(iv)  Adjust the GAIN potentiometer until the output reads + 4.9609 V.
(v)   Repeat for each D/A converter channel.

This assumes a 5 V bipolar output is desired. A program to aid setting up of the D/A converter board appears below.

**Program for setting up D/A converter board**

```
50 INPUT''BOARD SELECT SWITCH POSITION'';BD
100 SL = 34816 + (BD*128): REM CALCULATES START LOCATION OF BOARD
110 INPUT''CHANNEL TO BE SET UP (0−7)'';DA
120 DL = SL + DA: REM LOCATION OF DEVICE
130 GOSUB 1000: REM PRESS RETURN TO CONTINUE
180 POKE DL,O: REM WRITE ZERO TO DAC DEVICE − FULL SCALE NEGATIVE OUTPUT
190 PRINT''ADJUST OFFSET POT. UNTIL OUTPUT IS − 5.0000 VOLTS''
200 GOSUB 1000
210 POKE DL,255: REM WRITE 255 TO DAC DEVICE − FULL SCALE POSITIVE OUTPUT
220 PRINT''ADJUST GAIN POT. UNTIL OUTPUT IS 4.9609 VOLTS''
230 GOSUB 1000
```

```
240 PRINT''DAC DEVICE''DA'' NOW CALIBRATED – CONTINUE FOR OUTPUT TEST''
250 GOSUB 1000
260 INPUT''REQUIRED VOLTAGE ON THIS DEVICE'';V
270 BN = INT(V*25.6 + 128): REM CALCULATE NUMBER TO PRODUCE VOLTAGE
280 PRINT''NEAREST VOLTAGE IS ''(BN-128)/25.6'' VOLTS''
290 POKE DL, BN: REM WRITE TO DAC
300 PRINT''DEVICE''DA'' NOW OUTPUTTING''(BN-128)/25.6 ''VOLTS''
310 GOSUB 1000
320 GOTO 260: REM SELECT ANOTHER VOLTAGE
1000 PRINT''PRESS RETURN TO CONTINUE''

1010 GETA$:IFA$ < >CHR$(13)THEN 1010
1020 RETURN
```

The pulse counter input board does not need setting up. When turning on all the counter channels are re-set to zero by the computer re-set line. The counters appear as 8 consecutive memory locations, two for each counter, with the low order bits $(0-7)$ appearing as the first location of a pair. To obtain the total count for any counter it is necessary to use the equation:

$$(\text{LOCATION 2 COUNT} * 256) + \text{LOCATION 1 COUNT}$$

which will produce a number between 0 and 65535. The counters can be individually re-set to zero by reading certain locations. The relevant location is found by the equation:

$$\text{START LOCATION OF BOARD} + 13 + (\text{COUNTER NUMBER} - 1)$$

A demonstration program for reading and re-setting the counter appears below. To test the counters, feed into each input in turn a known frequency square wave pulse train, and observe the diplayed count rate. If the maximum frequency of the monostable is exceeded, the count will appear much lower than the input frequency (see *Table 8)*.

**Program for testing counter boards**

```
50 INPUT''BOARD SELECT SWITCH POSITION'';BD
100 SL = 34816 + (BD*128):REM CALCULATES START LOCATION OF BOARD
110 REM TO READ A COUNTER CHANNEL
120 REM CN = CHANNEL NUMBER (0 – 3)
130 A = PEEK(SL + 2*CN): REM LOW BITS 0 – 7
140 B = PEEK(SL + 2*CN + 1): REM HIGH BITS 8 – 15
150 X = B*256 + A: REM READING 0-65535
160 END
170 REM TO RESET A COUNTER CHANNEL
180 REM CN = CHANNEL NUMBER
190 X = PEEK(SL + 12 + CN): REM RESETS COUNTER CHANNEL CN – X IS DUMMY VALUE
200 END
210 REM SIMPLE FREQUENCY COUNTER
220 INPUT''COUNTER CHANNEL FOR FREQUENCY COUNT'';CN
```

```
230 PRINT CHR$(147): REM CLEAR SCREEN
240 T = TI: REM ACCESS INTERNAL REAL TIME CLOCK AND RECORD TIME
250 IF TI-T <60 THEN 250: REM WAIT FOR 60 CLOCK INCREMENTS (1 SECOND)
260 X = (PEEK(SL + 2*CN + 1)*256 + PEEK(SL + 2*CN): REM GET COUNTER READING
270 PRINT CHR$(147): REM CLEAR SCREEN
280 PRINT''FREQUENCY = ''X'' Hz''
290 A = PEEK(SL + 12 + CN): REM RESET COUNTER CHANNEL TO ZERO
300 GOTO 240: REM REPEAT
```

Other boards should be simpler to test and fault find. The digital input/output board is identical to the first stage of the A/D converter board. Make sure you check the test program as well as the electronics, because one typing error can cause it to malfunction.

### Program for switch board operation

```
50 INPUT''BOARD SELECT SWITCH POSITION'';BD
100 SL + 34816 + (BD*128)   :REM CALCULATES START LOCATION OF BOARD
110 REM SWITCHES ARE NUMBERED 0 TO 15
120 REM SWITCH OPERATIONS ARE NUMBERED 0 TO 31
130 REM EVEN NUMBERED OPERATIONS SWITCH OFF (OPEN CONTACTS)
140 REM ODD NUMBERED OPERATIONS SWITCH ON (CLOSE CONTACTS)
150 REM EG. OPERATION 1 – TURNS ON SWITCH 0 – OPERATION 0 TURNS OFF
    SWITCH 0
160 REM TO TURN ON SWITCH
170 INPUT''SWITCH NUMBER'';SN
180 SO = SN*2 + 1: REM CALCULATE SWITCH OPERATION
190 POKE SL,SO: REM WRITE SWITCH OPERATION TO LATCH
200 REM TO TURN OFF SWITCH
210 SO = SN*2
220 POKE SL,SO: REM WRITE TO LATCH
230 END
```

These test programs contain the BASIC routines that can be used to operate the interface. They are best treated as subroutines within a control program and called when an interface function is required.

## 4. WRITING PROGRAMS FOR ENVIRONMENTAL CONTROL

### 4.1 Languages for Control

Until recently BASIC was the only language available to microcomputer users. The advent of machines capable of running other languages, and the demand for other languages by users, has meant that versions of many of the main frame languages have been produced for use on various microcomputers. There has even been a microcomputer produced that is based on FORTH, the Jupiter Ace, and many of the latest microcomputers allow BASIC to be switched out and other languages loaded.

The language used to write the control program influences the performance and appearance of the control system. Speed of operation is the greatest limiting factor, especially when the environment being controlled is relatively unstable and the control functions have to be operated rapidly. Mathematical computing power is also important because it is a major factor limiting the operating speed. The ability to handle such items as floating point arithmetic and trigonometric functions is also important. Ease of alteration and de-bugging (fault finding and correction of programs) is vital for developing control systems, or if an existing system is likely to be modified frequently to suit short-term projects.

BASIC is perhaps the most widely used language on microcomputers. It is relatively easy to learn, and is easy to edit and de-bug. It is a very powerful language on many microcomputers, particularly since some manufacturers have extended the standard language to facilitate operation of printers, discs, modems, displays and even sound modules. However, BASIC has drawbacks for control programming. It is relatively slow in operation, especially with interpreted versions (as opposed to compiled versions) and there is little opportunity to expand it unless you are an experienced systems programmer (and have a lot of time to spare). Its critics correctly accuse it of being 'unstructured', however, programs may be produced which are as good as those produced with structured languages such as PASCAL if attention is paid to good programming rules.

PASCAL is a structured language and therefore has many advantages. However, it is not widely available for microcomputers in its full form, and the user may have to make do with a 'tiny' or condensed version of the language. FORTH is now available for many of the more flexible microcomputers and is considered by some to be an ideal language for control because it is very fast in operation and it is very easy to program machine level functions (for example working input/output ports). Some versions will not handle decimal mathematics but only integers, which renders the language unsuitable for some applications.

Machine code is the lowest level of programming. It is a series of numbers that are interpreted by the microprocessor as either instructions or data, depending on the preceding numbers. There are no composite commands, and every action of the microprocessor must be programmed. Assemblers are programs which aid machine code programming by allowing the programmer to use a set of standard mnemonics instead of numbers, and then converting them to the final machine code. Machine code programs operate quickly, but are very difficult to alter, and take a comparatively long time to develop. Anyone contemplating using machine code should acquire the appropriate assembler and monitor (a program that allows inspection and alteration of memory at a machine code level) for the microprocessor in question, and possibly also a disassembler (a program that decodes machine code into the standard mnemonics). Some microcomputers have some or all of these facilities as standard, and some allow machine code programming with a BASIC program.

Hybrid programs containing sections of machine code within a high level language program can be created, the machine code being accessed by a CALL, SYS, or USR command (in BASIC). This approach is very suitable for control programs. The communication between interface and computer is written in machine code for speed, and the control algorithms are written in BASIC for easy editing and and mathematical handling. Further discussion of microcomputer languages, including the use of machine code, appears in Chapter 1.

## 4.2 **Environmental Control Program**

The rules of good programming apply just as strictly to environmental control programs as they do to other programs. Control programs vary in complexity, from simple on/off control to multifunctional control with data recording and display. The general structure is similar for all control programs. There are five sections:

(i)   Initialisation − this sets up all the control limits, alarm limits, sensor calibrations and graphic displays.

(ii)  Clock loop − this generates the timing of the control cycle and is generally based on a real-time clock.

(iii) Main control loop − the sensors are scanned and the results compared with the control and the alarm limits set in (i). If action is required the relevant control subroutines are called.

(iv)  Control subroutines − these contain the calculations and communication with the control interface for all parameters under control.

(v)   Housekeeping subroutines − including updating the real-time clock, handling graphic displays and keyboard inputs, and recording data.

### 4.2.1 *Initialisation*

This section should include any array dimensioning, function definitions and the allocation of constant values. BASIC programs generally run faster if all constants, both numerical and strings, are placed in variables. For example:

```
100 PI = 3.142
200 FOR I = 1 TO 100
300 A = R(I) * R(I) * PI
400 NEXT
```

will run faster than

```
100 FOR I = 1 TO 100
200 A = R(I) * R(I) * 3.142
300 NEXT
```

Further, placing frequently used strings in variables considerably reduces the size of a program.

If any section of memory is to be set aside for use as a data store or location of machine code routines, this should be done at the very beginning of the program to avoid overwriting with strings or variables that are created during the initialisation.

It is good practice at this stage to check that any peripheral used by the computer is connected and operating properly. This is not always possible as some computers consider any attempt to access a peripheral that does not respond as a fatal error and jump out of program mode. This is especially so in operations involving the IEEE 488 bus. This type of operation results in a DEVICE NOT PRESENT ERROR. This can only be overcome by using machine code techniques. Computers with error trapping facilities do not suffer from this problem.

With any fairly sophisticated control program written in BASIC, program size is likely to be a problem. It is helpful to know that numbers stored as integer arrays are very space efficient, and this type of data storage should be used wherever possible.

### 4.2.2 *Clock Loops*

The simplest control program will have no clock loop, but will simply cycle through its control loop continuously. This can result in very precise control, but usually at the expense of much greater use of the control equipment (e.g., switches, valves, motors). Usually it is better to set a time interval between control cycles. The length of the intervals will be selected to suit the response times of the various systems under control.

The timing of control cycles is best achieved in a BASIC program by a clock loop. This synchronises the control cycles with a finite time period, and the program is thus said to operate in real time. To measure real time, one needs a real-time clock. Some microcomputers have real-time clocks as part of their operating systems. For example, the Commodore PET has a 24 h real-time clock that can be accessed directly from BASIC as a string variable (TI$) containing hours, minutes and seconds. The clock can be set to any time by writing to the string variable TI$. Other computers have real-time clocks which also contain calendar functions. Real-time clocks can be bought as add-on modules for most microcomputers. The accuracy of a clock varies depending on the method of time measurement. Most add-on modules, and some built-in clocks, use quartz crystals to generate their time increments. This type of clock is generally very accurate if it has been set up properly.

Other real-time clocks can be software generated. This is the case in the PET, where the clock is incremented by a software routine called by an interupt which is generated every time the flyback (i.e., the return of the spot to the left-hand corner of the screen) occurs on the video circuitry. This is either 50 or 60 times a second, depending on the size of the screen. However, under certain circumstances, these interupts can be ignored by the microprocessor, and inaccuracies occur. These inaccuracies can be corrected if they are constant, merely by adding or subtracting time from the clock at regular intervals, but experience has shown that the errors are not constant. The PET clock is disabled completely if the stop key is disabled, which may be desirable for a control program.

A simple clock loop using the internal PET clock is given below:

```
100 TS = VAL ( RIGHT$ (TI$,2) /  60 : REM CALCULATES SECONDS
110 TM = VAL ( MID$ (TI$,3,2) ) : REM CALCULATES MINUTES
120 TH = VAL ( LEFT$ (TI$,2) ) * 60 : REM CALCULATES HOURS
130 TD = TH + TM + TS : REM TD IS DECIMALISED TIME IN MINUTES
140 T3 = TD / T1 : REM T1 IS CONTROL CYCLE REQUIRED (IN MINUTES)
150 T4 = INT ( TD/T1 )
160 IF T3 < > T4 THEN 100 : REM IF INTERVAL DOESN'T DIVIDE INTO TIME EXACTLY
       CONTINUE TO LOOP
170 REM CONTROL LOOP ETC
```

This decimalises the time in minutes, then inspects whether the required time interval in minutes can be divided exactly into the result. If so, the loop is exited, if not the loop is continued. By altering the calculations in lines 100 – 120 the loop could be made to operate at second intervals. Care must be taken that the loop is not re-entered within one second, or the control cycle will be repeated. This is only likely if the control loop is small and no control operations are required.

An even simpler clock loop is used in the program demonstrating the use of the counter board as a frequency meter. This uses the variable TI which is incremented every 60th of a second. The value of TI is read initially, and then read until it is 60 more than the initial value, which produces a one second timing period. Using this method control cycles can be less than a second, although to achieve this speed the control would have to be very simple. Machine code programs can access the counter that makes up the value of TI, in which case much more sophisticated control could be attempted within short control cycles.

If a hardware real-time clock is used, it can be programmed to produce a pulse at set intervals, for example once a second or once a minue. This pulse can be used to trigger the control cycle, in which case the clock loop is merely a scanning loop for the detection of the pulse. It is a good idea to position any keyboard scanning routines within the clock loop. This allows, for example, the calling of interactive input routines for the changing of setpoints, control cycle intervals, sensor calibration factors and examination of graphical data displays. This means that such variables are always changed between control cycles, and never during them. Bear in mind that while such keyboard activity is going on the clock loop is not operating, and the control cycles will not be carried out.

### 4.2.3 *Main Control Loop*

This section includes the sensor scanning operation, which is essentially the same as for data-logging programs. The various sensors are read and the readings converted to the relevant engineering units. At this stage the readings can be checked for validity and combined to produce other readings, for example, humidity derived from wet and dry bulb thermometers. Once the sensor readings and composite readings have been calculated, they are compared against the pre-set control limits. In their simplest form, these limits are single setpoints, and action is initiated if the reading is above or below the setpoint, depending on the parameter. This can be programmed as:

IF READING > SETPOINT THEN GOSUB ACTION

or

IF READING < SETPOINT THEN GOSUB ACTION

In this case ACTION is a subroutine which can be a simple ON or OFF command for a switch, or a complicated position calculation and associated interface communication to activate the required control system. Using a list of conditional statements which call action subroutines is an efficient way of organising the control loop.

More sophisticated control can be obtained by calculating the SETPOINT value from the pre-set value and other contributing factors. For example, a heating setpoint can be calculated from the required temperature, plus factors representing the cooling effect experienced by the environment. The greater the cooling effect, the earlier the heating system is turned on. This technique allows correction for slow response times within control systems. As well as comparing actual values with setpoints, they can be compared with alarm limits if alarms are required. The reaction to an alarm condition can range from display on screen or printer, to activation of automatic telephone paging equipment. The speed of response to an alarm by the operator must be gauged to the particular application. The sophistication of the alarm system usually depends on the value of the material being grown or kept in the controlled environment.

Once a control loop has been completed, it is often necessary that some housekeeping be undertaken within the program, such as updating data stores and visual displays. The sequence for these operations must be decided by the programmer. Again, subroutines should be used and called by conditional or non-conditional statements. The program can now re-enter the clock loop to await the next control cycle.

### 4.2.4 *Control Subroutines*

The control subroutines are likely to be unique for every application, as they depend on the parameter being controlled, the method of control used, and the facility of the control interface to operate the control system. The subroutines are also likely to vary considerably in sophistication depending on the needs of each application. For these reasons it is not possible to give definitive algorithms that can be used within control programs, but some general principles can be outlined.

As a practical example, the flow diagram of a control subroutine for operating the ridge ventilator of a glasshouse is shown in *Figure 12*. The routine can be broken down into the following sections.

(i)    Check for the operation of manual overrides that would affect vent operation (e.g., vent closed).

(ii)   Cancel opposing actions (in this case make sure heating system is turned off).

(iii)  Calculate the vent opening required, with correction applied for factors affecting vent efficiency (e.g., non-linearity of vent position/vent efficiency relationship, outside temperature and wind speed).

(iv)   Check for pre-set maximum and minimum values.

(v)    Check required movement is at least 5% (to avoid excessive fine adjustment).

(vi)   Decide direction of movement required.

(vii)  Cancel opposing movement if necessary, and allow delay for motor to come to complete halt.

(viii) Operate vent motor in direction required.

(ix)   Set correct flag to indicate motor is operating and cancel unwanted flags.

(x)    Repeat for windward side if necessary.

(xi)   Return to main program.

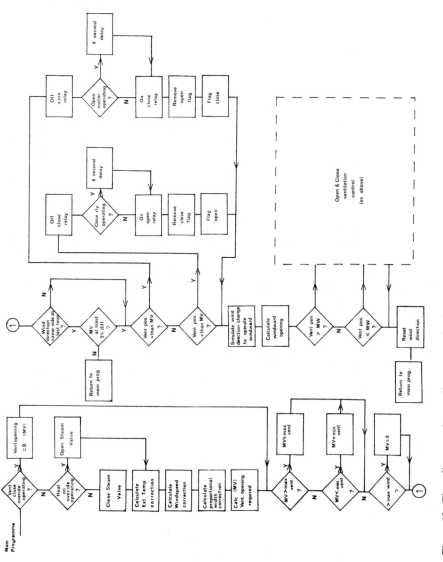

**Figure 12.** Flow digaram of a ventilator control subroutine.

Although this is a long and complicated subroutine, it contains many of the features that will be common to most control subroutines.

Checking for manual overrides and pre-set maximum and minimum values is very important to avoid excessive operation of the control equipment. The priority of these checks is important, as it is not worthwhile staying in the subroutine if its operation is already negated by an overriding condition. Attention to this can save a lot of time during the control loop. Cancellation of opposing actions is also important, for example to avoid fuel wastage if both ventilation and heating are operating, and to avoid physical damage if a motor is called to operate in both directions at the same time.

For operations with a relatively long response time, it would be inefficient to remain within the control subroutine until the required result was obtained. In the above example, a glasshouse vent can take several minutes to open to the required position, and constant observation would mean that the rest of the control cycle would be delayed. To overcome this, 'flags' are used. These are variables that are set to a certain value to indicate if an operation is taking place. The flags can be periodically checked and comparison of actual value with required value made. This is repeated until the vent reaches the required position, when the motor can be turned off and the flag re-set accordingly.

The above example is an instance of closed-loop control, where actions are monitored by means of a feedback sensor. An example of open-loop control would be the operation of blackout blinds at a given time, relying on micro-switches to turn off the blind motors when they had reached the correct position.

Timing control can be an important part of an environmental control program. Lighting control, blackout screens, thermal screens and feeding cycles are all examples of time-based control functions. The usual method of implementing timing in a control algorithm is to refer to the real-time clock within the system. Another method is to count control cycles. For example, addition of acid to a hydroponic nutrient solution can be limited by only allowing operation of the acid dispenser for a specified number of the control cycles occurring within a specified time period.

## 4.3 Example of an Environmental Control Program

The following short program is designed to control temperature and humidity in a simple enclosure such as a growth cabinet. It is written in PET BASIC and is designed to control via an A/D converter and a relay switch unit. The examples given are for the 3D Digital Design and Development units, a 16 channel A/D converter unit with 8-bit resolution, and a 16 switch relay unit. These are IEEE 488 bus units with (in this example) device numbers of 13 and 11 respectively. For use with other interfaces the subroutines at 1070 − 1140 and 1170 − 1210 would need changing.

The sensors used are a temperature module with a linear output of 0 − 2.5 V over a 0 − 50°C temperature range, and a humidity module with a linear output of $0-1$ V over a $0-100\%$ relative humidity range. The channel allocation for the A/D converter is:

(i)   channel 0 — temperature input;
(ii)  channel 1 — humidity input;

and for the switch unit:

(i)    switch 0 — heater on/off;
(ii)   switch 1 — cooler on/off;
(iii)  switch 2 — humidifier on/off;
(iv)   switch 3 — dehumidifier on/off;

assuming that a switch closure turns a device on and switch opening turns the device off.

The program consists of an initialisation section, where the clock is set, the setpoints and alarm limits are read, and various constants initialised. The next section is the clock loop, which governs the time interval between control cycles using the variable TI. This loop also contains a check for any keypresses, which are dealt with if they are function keys or ignored if they are not. When it is time for a control cycle, the two sensors are read via the A/D converter unit, and the control section entered. Temperature and humidity values are compared with the setpoints and the appropriate action is taken by calling the control subroutines. The values are then checked against the alarm limits, and any alarm condition flagged by the variable AL. Finally, the main display is updated, with the current data being displayed and any control devices that are active shown. If an alarm condition arises this is also indicated.

The program is an extremely simple demonstration of environmental control, but the main ideas are included. The control algorithms are simple 'stat' type comparisons, and the lack of a deadband between turning off one device and turning on the opposing function would lead to continual hunting of the temperature and humidity around their setpoints. The displays could be made much more readable, for example by using diagramatical representation of the data, and more than one environment could be controlled at the same time. The alarm flag could be made to close a switch and activate a warning device such as a bell, light or telephone paging system.

## 5. REFERENCES

1. Woodward,F.I. and Sheehy,J.E. (1983) *Principles and Measurements in Environmental Biology*, published by Butterworth, London.
2. Robinson,N. (1966) *Solar Radiation*, published by Elsevier, Amsterdam, p. 227.
3. Fritschen,L.J. and Gay,L.W. (1979) *Environmental Instrumentation*, published by Springer-Verlag, New York.
4. Monteith,J.L. (1959) *J. Sci. Instruments,* **32**, 341.
5. Biggs,W.W., Edison,A.R., Eastin,J.D., Brown,K.W., Maranville,J.W. and Clegg,M.D. (1971) *Ecology,* **52**, 125.
6. Fitter,D.J., Knapp,P.H. and Warren Wilson,J. (1983) *J. Appl. Ecol.,* **17**, 183.
7. Rosenthal,R. (1950) *Instruments,* **23**, 774.
8. Bowman,G.E. (1968) in *The Measurement of Environmental Factors in Terrestrial Ecology*, Wadsworth,R.M. *et al.* (eds.), published by Blackwell Scientific Publications, Oxford, p. 131.
9. Osborne,A. and Kane,J. (1978) *An Introduction to Microcomputers*, published by Osborne/McGraw Hill, Berkeley, California, Vol. 2, p. 1034.
10. Zaks,R. (1979) *6502 Applications Book*, published by Sybex Inc., Berkeley, California, p. 31.

# APPENDIX

## Growth cabinet environment control program

```
100 REM *** GROWTH CABINET CONTROL ***
110 REM  INITIALISATION SECTION
120 :
130 REM SET TIME
140 PRINT"[]TIME SET ROUTINE": REM CLEAR SCREEN AND PRINT TITLE
150 PRINT"[]ENTER TIME AS SIX DIGIT NUMBER BETWEEN 000000 AND 235959"
160 REM "[]" STANDS FOR CURSOR DOWN ONE LINE
170 PRINT"[][][]"
180 INPUT T$
190 IF LEN (T$) <>6 THEN PRINT "SIX DIGITS PLEASE":GOTO 180
200 IF VAL (T$) <0 OR VAL (T$) > 235959 THEN PRINT "OUT OF LIMITS":GOTO 180
210 TI$=T$ : REM SETS REAL-TIME CLOCK
220 :
230 :
240 REM INTIALISE CONTROL SETPOINTS ; ALARM LIMITS
250 S1=18  :REM TEMP SETPOINT
260 S2=65  :REM HUMIDITY SETPOINT
270 A1=25  :REM HIGH TEMP ALARM LIMIT
280 A2=12  :REM LOW TEMP ALARM LIMIT
290 A3=80  :REM HIGH HUMIDITY ALARM LIMIT
300 A4=50  :REM LOW HUMIDITY ALARM LIMIT
310 :
320 T1=1  :REM 1 MINUTE CONTROL CYCLE
330 K(0)=.05:K(1)=.01  :REM CONSTANTS FOR TEMP AND RH SENSORS - SEE TEXT
340 :
350 REM CLOCK LOOP
360 TS=VAL(RIGHT$(TI$,2))/60
370 TM=VAL(MID$(TI$,3,2))
380 TH=VAL(LEFT$(TI$,2))*60
390 TD=TH+TM+TS
400 T3=TD/T1
410 T4=INT(TD/T1)
420 :
430 GET A$: IF A$ <>"" THEN 1250 : REM CHECK FOR KEYPRESS EACH LOOP
440 :
450 IF T3 <> T4 THEN 350  :REM CONTINUE IF NOT TIME FOR CONTROL CYCLE
460 :
470 :
480 REM TAKE READINGS FROM SENSORS
490 C=0
500 GOSUB 1070  :REM READ CHANNEL 0 ON THE A/D INTERFACE
510 TP=X  : REM PUT TEMP INTO VARIABLE TP
520 C=1
530 GOSUB 1070  :REM READ CHANNEL 1
540 HD=X  :REM PUT HUMIDITY INTO VARIABLE HD
550 :
560 REM CONTROL SECTION
570 REM TEMPERATURE CONTROL
580 IF TP < S1 THEN GOSUB 870  :REM CALL HEATING ON SUBROUTINE IF TEMP LOW
590 IF TP > S1 THEN GOSUB 920  :REM CALL COOLING ON SUBROUTINE IF TEMP HIGH
600 :
610 REM HUMIDITY CONTROL
620 IF HD < S2 THEN GOSUB 970  :REM CALL HUMIDIFIER ROUTINE IF RH LOW
630 IF HD > S2 THEN GOSUB 1020  :REM CALL DEHUMIDIFIER ROUTINE IF RH HIGH
640 :
650 REM ALARM CHECK
660 IF TP > A1 OR TP < A2 OR HD > A3 OR HD < A4 THEN AL=1
670 REM AL IS ALARM FLAG - AL=1 IS ALARM CONDITION  AL=0 IS OK
680 :
690 :
700 REM MAIN DISPLAY
710 PRINT"[]GROWTH CABINET CONTROL - MAIN DISPLAY":REM CLEAR SCREEN + TITLE
720 PRINT"[]PRESS:- (*)TO ALTER SETPOINTS"
730 PRINT"          (+)TO ALTER ALARM LIMITS"
740 PRINT"          (=)TO RESET ALARM"
750 PRINT"[][]":REM CURSOR DOWN TWO LINES
760 PRINT"TEMPERATURE ="TP
770 PRINT"HUMIDITY ="HD
780 PRINT"[][]"
790 IF AL=1 THEN PRINT "WARNING - ALARM CONDITION EXISTS"
800 IF HO=1 THEN PRINT "HEATER ON"
810 IF CO=1 THEN PRINT "COOLER ON"
820 IF HU=1 THEN PRINT "HUMIDIFIER ON"
830 IF DH=1 THEN PRINT "DEHUMIDIFIER ON"
840 FORI=1TO2000:NEXT:GOTO350 :REM BRIEF DELAY THEN RETURN TO CLOCK LOOP
850 :
860 :
870 REM HEATING ON SUBROUTINE
880 SW=2:GOSUB 1170 :REM TURN OFF COOLER
890 SW=1:GOSUB 1170 :REM TURN ON HEATER
900 HO=1:CO=0:RETURN :SET FLAGS
910 :
```

```
920 REM COOLER ON ROUTINE
930 SW=0:GOSUB 1170 :REM TURN OFF HEATER
940 SW=3:GOSUB 1170 :REM TURN ON COOLER
950 CO=1:HO=0:RETURN
960 :
970 REM HUMIDIFIER ON ROUTINE
980 SW=6:GOSUB 1170 :REM DEHUMIDIFIER OFF
990 SW=5:GOSUB 1170 :REM HUMIDIFIER ON
1000 HU=1:DH=0: RETURN
1010 :
1020 REM DEHUMIDIFIER ON ROUTINE
1030 SW=4: GOSUB 1170 :REM HUMIDIFIER OFF
1040 SW=7: GOSUB 1170 :REM DEHUMIDIFIER ON
1050 DH=1:HU=0: RETURN
1060 :
1070 REM READ A/D CHANNEL HELD IN C
1080 OPEN 1, 13, C :REM CAUSE A/D UNIT TO READ CHANNEL C
1090 GET#1,A$ :IF ST=2 THEN 1090 :REM GET CHARACTER OVER IEEE BUS FROM A/D
1100 CLOSE1
1110 VA$=A$+CHR$(0) :REM ALLOW FOR NULL CHARACTER RETURN
1120 V=ASC(VA$)/100 :REM CONVERT CHARACTER TO VOLTAGE READING
1130 X=V/K(C) :REM CONVERT TO ENGINEERING UNITS
1140 RETURN
1150 :
1160 :
1170 REM OPERATE SWITCH UNIT
1180 OPEN 1, 11, SW
1190 PRINT#1
1200 CLOSE1
1210 RETURN
1220 :
1230 :
1240 REM CHECK FOR FUNCTION KEYPRESS - IF FOUND CALL RELEVANT SUBROUTINE
1250 IF A$ = "+" THEN GOSUB 1290
1260 IF A$ = "+" THEN GOSUB 1420
1270 IF A$ = "=" THEN GOSUB 1590
1280 GOTO700 :REM REPLACE MAIN DISPLAY
1290 REM ALTER SETPOINTS
1300 PRINT"⊐SETPOINT ALTERATION" :REM CLEAR SCREEN AND PRINT TITLE
1310 PRINT"⊠CURRENT SETPOINTS"
1320 PRINT"⊠"
1330 PRINT"TEMPERATURE ="S1
1340 PRINT"HUMIDITY    ="S2
1350 PRINT"⊠ENTER NEW SETPOINTS BELOW"
1360 INPUT"⊠TEMPERATURE";S1
1370 INPUT"⊠HUMIDITY    ";S2
1380 PRINT"⊠PRESS <RETURN> TO CONTINUE"
1390 GETA$:IFA$<>CHR$(13)THEN1390
1400 GOTO700
1410 :
1420 REM ALTER ALARM LIMITS
1430 PRINT"⊐ALARM LIMIT ALTERATION" :REM CLEAR SCREEN AND PRINT TITLE
1440 PRINT"⊠CURRENT ALARM LIMITS
1450 PRINT"⊠"
1460 PRINT"HIGH TEMPERATURE ="A1
1470 PRINT"LOW TEMPERATURE  ="A2
1480 PRINT"HIGH HUMIDITY ="A3
1490 PRINT"LOW HUMIDITY  ="A4
1500 PRINT"⊠ENTER NEW SETPOINTS BELOW"
1510 INPUT"⊠HIGH TEMP";A1
1520 INPUT"⊠LOW TEMP  ";A2
1530 INPUT"⊠HIGH HUMID";A3
1540 INPUT"⊠LOW HUMID ";A4
1550 PRINT"⊠PRESS <RETURN> TO CONTINUE"
1560 GETA$:IFA$<>CHR$(13)THEN1560
1570 GOTO700
1580 :
1590 REM ALARM RESET
1600 AL=0
1610 RETURN
1620 :
READY.
```

Published in the Practical Approach series

# Spectrophotometry and spectrofluorimetry
## a practical approach

Edited by D A Harris, *University of Oxford,* and C L Bashford, *St George's Hospital Medical School, London*

Spectrophotometry & spectrofluorimetry

a practical approach

Edited by
D A Harris & C L Bashford

*February 1987; 192pp;*
hardbound:
*0 947946 69 1*
softbound:
*0 947946 46 2*

Using this book biochemists can determine how spectrophotometry can contribute to laboratory analyses – what is required in the experimental set up and how the information obtainable should be optimized. Researchers and clinicians will find the detailed protocols and thorough introduction to the use of fluorimeters and spectrophotometers invaluable, particularly if they are using them for the first time or with only a rudimentary knowledge. Technicians carrying out routine analyses will also benefit from such a laboratory handbook.

**Contents**

An introduction to spectrophotometry and fluorescence spectrometry *C L Bashford*
● Spectra *R K Poole and C L Bashford*
● Spectrophotometric assays *D A Harris*
● Measurement of ligand binding to proteins *C R Bagshaw and D A Harris*
● Spectrophotometry and fluorimetry of cellular compartments *C L Bashford* ● Stopped-flow spectrophotometric techniques *J F Eccleston*
● The determination of photochemical action spectra *D Lloyd and R I Scott*

For details of price and ordering consult our current catalogue or contact:

**IRL Press Ltd,**
PO Box 1, Eynsham,
Oxford OX8 1JJ, UK
**IRL Press Inc,**
PO Box Q,
McLean, VA 22101-0850,
USA

## ◇ IRL PRESS

Oxford · Washington DC